Mrs. Ambrose Birdsall

~~Pauline P. Craig~~

WHAT I LIKE IN POETRY

WILLIAM LYON PHELPS

CHARLES SCRIBNER'S SONS

NEW YORK　　　　　　　　LONDON

MCMXXXIV

PREFACE

The cordial reception enjoyed by my recent anthology of prose, called *What I Like*, has emboldened me to add a companion-volume of verse.

The same method—or rather the absence of method—exhibited in the book of prose is once more employed. There is no significance—chronological or logical—in the order in which the selections are printed; there is no attempt to indicate the development of English poetry or to classify the poets in various groups or schools or fashions. And I have made no attempt to place together poems that either in subject-matter or in mood might be considered kindred, such as poems on love, on nature, on religion, and so on.

Those who do not like this haphazard method have the privilege of disliking it; and to those who do not like the name of the volume, I will merely reply in the words of Orlando: there was no thought of pleasing them when it was christened.

I have consulted no one in order to find out whether or not certain poems should be included. All the poems that are included are here because I like them. There is no other reason for their inclusion. And, as in my prose book, I include living authors.

I have decided to omit translations; and for two reasons. Poetry is more difficult to translate than prose, unless one translates it into prose; and as there are more great poems written in the English language than in any other, ancient or modern, we have God's plenty in the native tongue. As the Austrian artist, the late Paul Cohen-Portheim, remarked, in English poetry it is always summer.

For it is one of the innumerable mysteries that add so much to the wonder and excitement of life, that the English, the most practical people since the Romans, the best self-governors and the best colonizers, who in the ordinary affairs of daily intercourse are so reserved, who seem so sensible as to appear insensible, who hate above all things a display of sentiment and expansive emotion; it is the stolid, unresponsive, immovable English, who have written the most glorious, the most beautiful, the most sublime romantic poetry that the world has ever known.

How astounding it is, on a parcel of land no bigger than the State of Michigan, that Chaucer, Shakespeare, Spenser, Milton, Donne, Herrick, Gray, Wordsworth, Byron, Shelley, Keats, Tennyson, Browning, Arnold, Rossetti, Swinburne, Thompson, should have found sufficient space for a take-off for a flight into the empyrean!

Strange and striking is the contrast between the English and the French. The French, excitable in political affairs, have as a nation exalted in their literature the qualities of soberness, restraint, regularity and reserve; above all things they love intelligence; whereas the English, who regard political excesses either with disgust or with humour, have always loved melodrama in the theatre and romance in poetry. Shakespeare may be the universal poet, but he is as English as a village green; whereas only native Frenchmen can really appreciate Racine. Did you ever read a good translation of Racine?

A real problem was what to do with long poems—should I include selections from Shakespeare's plays, from Milton's *Paradise Lost*, from Browning's *The Ring and the Book*? I have finally decided to omit all poems of great length; not because I don't like them, but because I love them too well to mutilate them. I have made an exception in the cases of *The Ancient Mariner, Saul, The Eve of St. Agnes, Christabel*; these are too long to include as wholes, and too beautiful to leave out. This garden will have only flowers, not the branches of trees.

[vi]

PREFACE

Poetry is not a means to an end; it is an end in itself. I am not at all sure that it is a criticism of life. It is rather an illumination of life. The poets are the soothsayers, the clairvoyants; they see beyond the vision of the ordinary man, and they tell us what they see.

This book is filled with poems written for our delight; it is my hope that the reader, opening almost anywhere at random, may find that delight which should always be found in a union of truth and beauty.

WILLIAM LYON PHELPS.

BRANFORD COLLEGE,
YALE UNIVERSITY,
Tuesday, May Day, 1934.

ACKNOWLEDGMENTS

For permission to use poems in this book we are indebted to the following: The Bobbs Merrill Company for poems by James Whitcomb Riley, "Little Orphant Annie" and "A Life Lesson" from *Rhymes of Childhood*, copyright 1890 and 1918, and "When the Frost Is on the Punkin" from *Neighborly Poems*, copyright 1891 and 1919, used by special permission of the publishers; Brandt and Brandt for "When the Year Grows Old" and "Afternoon on a Hill," by Edna St. Vincent Millay from *Renascence and Other Poems*, published by Harper & Brothers, copyright, 1914, by Edna St. Vincent Millay; Constable & Company and the author for "The Sweet o' the Year," by Charles G. D. Roberts; Dodd, Mead and Company for "The Old Vicarage" by Rupert Brooke, "A Christmas Carol" by G. K. Chesterton, and "Gladstone" by Stephen Phillips; Doubleday, Doran and Company for "Trees" from *Trees and Other Poems* by Joyce Kilmer, copyrighted, 1914, and "The Fairies Have Never a Penny to Spend" from *Fairies and Chimneys* by Rose Fyleman, copyrighted, 1920; Doubleday, Doran and Company, A. P. Watt & Son, and the author for "Mandalay" and "Danny Deever" from *Barrack Room Ballads*, "The Song of the Banjo" from *The Seven Seas*, and "Recessional" from *The Five Nations* by Rudyard Kipling; Arthur Davison Ficke for his "I Am Weary of Being Bitter"; John W. Garvin for "The Rose" by Isabella Valancy Crawford; Harcourt, Brace and Company for "Prayer" from *Challenge* by Louis Untermeyer; Pamela Hinkson for "Sheep and Lambs" by Katharine Tyson reprinted from *Innocencies* (Sidgwick & Jackson) and from *Collected Poems* (Macmillan); Henry Holt and Company for "A Saint's Hours" from *Portraits and Protests* by Sarah Cleghorn, "The Listeners," "Winter Dusk," and "Old Susan" from *The Listeners and Other Poems* by Walter De La Mare, "Birches" from *Mountain Interval*, "After Apple-Picking," "Mending Wall," and "Good Hours" from *North of Boston* by Robert Frost, "Fog" and "Nocturne in a Deserted Brickyard" from *Chicago Poems* by Carl Sandburg, "Nunc Dimittis" by Henry A. Beers from *The Ways of Yale ;* Houghton Mifflin Company for "Patterns" by Amy Lowell, "Her Words" and "The Silence of the Poets" by Anna Hempstead Branch, "Memorial Rain" by Archibald MacLeish, and "Gloucester Moors" by William Vaughn Moody, and by special permission, selections from Emerson, Holmes, Lowell, Longfellow, and Whittier; Alfred A. Knopf for "Ancestry," "The Violets," and "The Wayfarer" by Stephen Crane and "Velvet Shoes" from *Collected Poems of Elinor Wylie ;* Little Brown and Company for "I Never Saw a Moor," "The Railway Train," and "Autumn," from the Centenary Edition of *The Poems of Emily Dickinson ;* McClelland & Stewart for "Off Rivière du Loup" by Duncan Campbell Scott; Macmillan Company for "An Old Woman of the Roads" from *Poems* by Padraic Colum, "The Orphans" and "The Lonely Tree" from *Collected Poems* by Wilfrid Wilson Gibson and "Northumberland" from *The Golden Room and Other Poems* by Wilfrid Wilson Gibson, "The Darkling Thrush," "The Oxen," "Afterwards" from *Collected Poems* by Thomas Hardy, "The Mystery," "The Bells of Heaven," "Stupidity Street," and "After" from *Poems* by Ralph Hodgson, "General William Booth Enters into Heaven" and "Columbus" from *Collected Poems* by Vachel Lindsay, "Sea-Fever," "Beauty," and "Cargoes" from *Collected Poems* by John Masefield, "The Nightingale Near the House" from *Real Property* by Harold Monro, "Childhood" and "By the Margin of the Great Deep" from *Collected Poems* by George William Russell (A. E.), "Righteous Anger" from *Reincarnations* by James Stephens, "Barter" from *Love Songs* and "Pity" from *Rivers to the Sea* by Sara Teasdale, "September, 1913," "The Lake Isle of Innisfree," "Into the Twilight," "The White Birds," from *Collected Poems* by William Butler Yeats; Edgar Lee Masters for his "Bert Kessler"; Dr. Eugene E. Murphey for his "Lines to Accompany a Flagon of Georgia's Famous Product on its Way to California," "Bobolinks," "Brown-headed Nuthatch," and "The Barn Owl"; John Murray for "London to Paris by Air" by Lord Gorell; Jonathan Cape, Ltd., for "The Two Flocks" from *The Poems of W. H. Davies* (1934); Dr. Duncan Campbell Scott for "January Morning" by Archibald Lampman; Martin Secker for "The Old Ships" and "Tenebris Interlucentem" by James Elroy Flecker; Frederick A. Stokes Company for "The Full Heart" from *Ardours and Endurances* by Robert Nichols, and "The Barrel-Organ," and "The Highwayman" from *Collected Poems* by Alfred Noyes; Edward Synge for "The Curse" by J. M. Synge; Sir William Watson for his "How Weary Is Our Heart," "Wordsworth's Grave," and three selections from "Epigrams of Art, Life, and Nature"; C. D. Woodberry for "The Rose of Stars" by G. E. Woodberry; Yale University Press for "A Comparison" by John Farrar from *Songs for Parents*, and "Overtones" by William Alexander Percy from *In April Once ;* Yale University Press and the author for "Ghosts" by Brian Hooker; Charles Scribner's Sons for "A Pitcher of Mignonette" by H. C. Bunner, "Little Boy Blue" by Eugene Field, "Over the Hills and Far Away," "Invictus" and "Romance" by W. E. Henley, "Old Age" and "The Shadow" by Bernice Kenyon, "A Ballad of Trees and the Master" and "The Mocking Bird" by Sidney Lanier, "Credo," "L'Envoi," "For a Dead Lady," "The Dead Village," "The Garden," and "The House on the Hill" by E. A. Robinson, "A Wall, a Wall," "O World," and "On a Volume of Scholastic Philosophy" by George Santayana, "A Lad That Is Gone," "Bed in Summer," "Christmas at Sea," "Happy Thought," "My Shadow," "Requiem," and "Whole Duty of Children" by Robert Louis Stevenson, "The Hound of Heaven," "The Kingdom of God," "Lilium Regis," and "The Veteran of Heaven" by Francis Thompson, "Reliance" by Henry van Dyke, and "The Letter," "Noon: Amagansett Beach," and "The Fish-Hawk" by John Hall Wheelock.

CONTENTS

CONTENTS

[x]

CONTENTS

CONTENTS

[xii]

CONTENTS

[xiii]

CONTENTS

[xiv]

CONTENTS

CONTENTS

[xvi]

CONTENTS

CONTENTS

[xviii]

CONTENTS

[xix]

CONTENTS

WHAT I LIKE IN POETRY

WHAT I LIKE IN POETRY

Henley died in 1903. "It is always summer in English poetry," said the late Paul Cohen-Portheim; meaning there is no renaissance in English verse, because there is no hibernation. Since the year 1564 there has always been living at least one great English poet.

Although Henley was a cripple, he was one hundred per cent masculine; he delighted in virility and his heroes were like Victor Hugo's Burgraves.

> A fig for Satan, burgraves!
> Burgraves, a fig for God!

Thus, it was this Englishman, who, filled with admiration for the Confederate soldiers when faced with certain defeat, wrote the best of all poems written in their honour. It is natural that his defiant

> *Out of the night that covers me*

should be the most popular of his poems; but there was even a higher side to Henley's genius than defiance: his imagination. He took the old refrain "Over the hills and far away" and transfigured it with poignant beauty. This is the greatest of his poems.

OVER THE HILLS AND FAR AWAY

WHERE forlorn sunsets flare and fade
  On desolate sea and lonely sand,
Out of the silence and the shade
  What is the voice of strange command
Calling you still, as friend calls friend
  With love that cannot brook delay,
To rise and follow the ways that wend
  Over the hills and far away?

Hark in the city, street on street
  A roaring reach of death and life,
Of vortices that clash and fleet
  And ruin in appointed strife,
Hark to it calling, calling clear,
  Calling until you cannot stay
From dearer things than your own most dear
  Over the hills and far away.

Out of the sound of ebb and flow,
  Out of the sight of lamp and star,
It calls you where the good winds blow,
  And the unchanging meadows are:
From faded hopes and hopes agleam,
  It calls you, calls you night and day
Beyond the dark into the dream
  Over the hills and far away.

WILLIAM ERNEST HENLEY

It took the world a long time to discover that the most resplendent genius of the Three Weird Sisters was Emily. The popularity of *Jane Eyre* eclipsed the fame of *Wuthering Heights*. Then the fame of that revelation of the perversities of a damned soul eclipsed the blaze of its author's poems. But after the lapse of nearly a century, we know now that Emily wrote one of the greatest love-poems in literature. It makes absolutely no difference whether this poem is the expression of her own love or not; I do not care at all. We learn for the first time in 1934 that she originally wrote it March 3, 1845, as part of the imaginary "Gondal" cycle. Yet it is the authentic expression of her wild, turbulent, passionate heart. And no one can read the sixth stanza without immense respect for the unconquerable integrity of her mind. Strange that such terrific passion should be accompanied by such austerity of intellect, such splendid supremacy of will. Great as was her genius, she was even greater as a woman.

(This poem appeared in a small volume called *Poems by Currer, Ellis, and Acton Bell,* in May, 1846. The complete sale was two copies.)

Remembrance

Cold in the earth—and the deep snow piled above thee,
    Far, far removed, cold in the dreary grave!
Have I forgot, my only Love, to love thee,
    Severed at last by Time's all-severing wave?

Now, when alone, do my thoughts no longer hover
    Over the mountains on that northern shore,
Resting their wings where heath and fern-leaves cover
    Thy noble heart for ever, evermore?

Cold in the earth—and fifteen wild Decembers
    From those brown hills have melted into spring:
Faithful, indeed, is the spirit that remembers
    After such years of change and suffering.

Sweet Love of youth, forgive, if I forget thee,
  While the world's tide is bearing me along,
Other desires and other hopes beset me,
  Hopes which obscure, but cannot do thee wrong.

No later light has lightened up my heaven,
  No second morn has ever shone for me;
All my life's bliss from thy dear life was given,
  All my life's bliss is in the grave with thee.

But when the days of golden dreams had perished,
  And even Despair was powerless to destroy,
Then did I learn how existence could be cherished,
  Strengthened and fed, without the aid of joy.

Then did I check the tears of useless passion,
  Weaned my young soul from yearning after thine;
Sternly denied its burning wish to hasten
Down to that tomb already more than mine.

And even yet I dare not let it languish,
  Dare not indulge in memory's rapturous pain;
Once drinking deep of that divinest anguish,
  How could I seek the empty world again?

EMILY BRONTË

Diverted occasionally from the true path of his genius by
theatrical and political enterprises, Yeats always returned
to the Muse—the Muse which knows no country and no age.

THE LAKE ISLE OF INNISFREE

I WILL arise and go now, and go to Innisfree,
  And a small cabin build there, of clay and wattles made;
Nine bean rows will I have there, a hive for the honey bee,
  And live alone in the bee-loud glade.

And I shall have some peace there, for peace comes dropping
    slow,
  Dropping from the veils of the morning to where the
    cricket sings;
There midnight's all a glimmer, and noon a purple glow,
  And evening full of the linnet's wings.

I will arise and go now, for always night and day
  I hear lake water lapping with low sounds by the shore;
While I stand on the roadway, or on the pavements grey,
  I hear it in the deep heart's core.

WILLIAM BUTLER YEATS

INTO THE TWILIGHT

OUT-WORN heart, in a time out-worn,
Come clear of the nets of wrong and right;
Laugh, heart, again in the grey twilight,
Sigh, heart, again in the dew of the morn.

Your mother Eire is always young,
Dew ever shining and twilight grey;
Though hopes fall from you and love decay,
Burning in fires of a slanderous tongue.

Come, heart, where hill is heaped upon hill:
For there the mystical brotherhood
Of sun and moon and hollow and wood
And river and stream work out their will;

And God stands winding his lonely horn,
And time and the world are ever in flight;
And love is less kind than the grey twilight,
And hope is less dear than the dew of the morn.

WILLIAM BUTLER YEATS

THE WHITE BIRDS

I WOULD that we were, my beloved, white birds on the foam
of the sea!
We tire of the flame of the meteor, before it can fade and
flee;
And the flame of the blue star of twilight, hung low on the
rim of the sky,
Has awaked in our hearts, my beloved, a sadness that may
not die.

A weariness comes from those dreamers, dew-dabbled, the
lily and rose;
Ah, dream not of them, my beloved, the flame of the meteor
that goes,
Or the flame of the blue star that lingers hung low in the
fall of the dew:
For I would we were changed to white birds on the wandering foam: I and you!

I am haunted by numberless islands, and many a Danaan
shore,
Where Time would surely forget us, and Sorrow come near
us no more;
Soon far from the rose and the lily, and fret of the flames
would we be,
Were we only white birds, my beloved, buoyed out on the
foam of the sea!

WILLIAM BUTLER YEATS

I like these two songs by Waller, and think they are both
superior to the overpraised Girdle poem. Remember the
word *noise* simply meant *sound*.

SONG

WHILE I listen to thy voice,
    Chloris! I feel my life decay;
  That powerful noise
  Calls my fleeting soul away.
Oh! suppress that magic sound,
Which destroys without a wound!

Peace, Chloris, peace! or singing die;
    That together you and I
  To Heaven may go:
  For all we know
Of what the Blessed do above
Is, that they sing, and that they love.

EDMUND WALLER

SONG

  Go, lovely rose!
Tell her that wastes her time and me,
  That now she knows,
When I resemble her to thee,
How sweet and fair she seems to be.

  Tell her that's young,
And shuns to have her graces spied,
  That hadst thou sprung
In deserts where no men abide,
Thou must have uncommended died.

  Small is the worth
Of beauty from the light retired;
  Bid her come forth,
Suffer herself to be desired,
And not blush so to be admired.

[7]

Then die, that she
The common fate of all things rare
May read in thee:
How small a part of time they share
That are so wondrous sweet and fair!

EDMUND WALLER

This is the only poem Mellen wrote that is remembered (1825), and it is the last line that has kept it alive. It was written to celebrate the battle of Bunker Hill.

THE LONELY BUGLE GRIEVES

THE trump hath blown,
And now upon that reeking hill
Slaughter rides screaming on the vengeful ball;
While with terrific signal shrill,
The vultures, from their bloody eyries flown,
Hang o'er them like a pall.
Now deeper roll the maddening drums,
And the mingling host like ocean heaves:
While from the midst a horrid wailing comes,
And high above the fight the lonely bugle grieves!

GRENVILLE MELLEN

Professor Beers admired Mellen's poem and said so in admirable verse.

THE SINGER OF ONE SONG

HE sang one song and died—no more but that:
A single song and carelessly complete.
He would not bind and thresh his chance-grown wheat,
Nor bring his wild fruit to the common vat,
To store the acid rinsings, thin and flat,
Squeezed from the press or trodden under feet.
A few slow beads, blood-red and honey-sweet,

[8]

Oozed from the grape, which burst and spilled its fat.
But Time, who soonest drops the heaviest things
That weight his pack, will carry diamonds long.
So through the poets' orchestra, which weaves
One music from a thousand stops and strings,
Pierces the note of that immortal song:
"High over all the lonely bugle grieves."

HENRY A. BEERS

SOME CHRISTMAS CAROLS

The best poem on Christmas I have ever read is by Christina Rossetti; it begins with divinity and reaches a tremendous climax in humanity. Chesterton's *Christmas Carol* is buoyantly characteristic. Thomas Hardy's *The Oxen* has the sincere sceptic's sincere wish for sincere faith; the last line has a poignant agony.

A CHRISTMAS CAROL

In the bleak mid-winter
  Frosty wind made moan,
Earth stood hard as iron,
  Water like stone;
Snow had fallen, snow on snow,
  Snow on snow,
In the bleak mid-winter
  Long ago.

Our God, Heaven cannot hold Him
  Nor earth sustain;
Heaven and earth shall flee away
  When He comes to reign:
In the bleak mid-winter
  A stable-place sufficed
The Lord God Almighty
  Jesus Christ.

Enough for Him whom cherubim
  Worship night and day,
A breastful of milk
  And a manger full of hay;
Enough for Him whom angels
  Fall down before,
The ox and ass and camel
  Which adore.

Angels and archangels
  May have gathered there,
Cherubim and seraphim
  Throng'd the air;
But only His mother
  In her maiden bliss
Worshiped her Beloved
  With a kiss.

What can I give Him,
  Poor as I am?
If I were a shepherd
  I would bring a lamb,
If I were a wise man
  I would do my part,—
Yet what can I give Him,
  Give my heart.

CHRISTINA ROSSETTI

A CHRISTMAS CAROL

THE Christ-child lay on Mary's lap,
  His hair was like a light.
(O weary, weary were the world,
  But here is all aright.)

The Christ-child lay on Mary's breast,
His hair was like a star.
(O stern and cunning are the kings,
But here the true hearts are.)

The Christ-child lay on Mary's heart,
His hair was like a fire,
(O weary, weary is the world,
But here the world's desire.)

The Christ-child stood at Mary's knee,
His hair was like a crown,
And all the flowers looked up at Him,
And all the stars looked down.

GILBERT K. CHESTERTON

THE OXEN

CHRISTMAS EVE, and twelve of the clock.
"Now they are all on their knees,"
An elder said as we sat in a flock
By the embers in hearthside ease.

We pictured the meek mild creatures where
They dwelt in their strawy pen,
Nor did it occur to one of us there
To doubt they were kneeling then.

So fair a fancy few could weave
In these years! Yet, I feel,
If someone said on Christmas Eve,
"Come; see the oxen kneel

"In the lonely barton by yonder coomb
Our childhood used to know,"
I should go with him in the gloom,
Hoping it might be so.

THOMAS HARDY

If I had to name my favourite among the poems of Poe, I should choose Ulalume. It has more sustained beauty than any other of his lyrical pieces, and the climax in the penultimate stanza is almost unbearable.

ULALUME

THE skies they were ashen and sober;
　　The leaves they were crispèd and sere—
　　The leaves they were withering and sere;
It was night, in the lonesome October
　　Of my most immemorial year:
It was hard by the dim lake of Auber,
　　In the misty mid region of Weir—
It was down by the dank tarn of Auber,
　　In the ghoul-haunted woodland of Weir.

Here once, through an alley Titanic,
　　Of cypress, I roamed with my Soul—
　　Of cypress, with Psyche, my Soul.
These were days when my heart was volcanic
　　As the scoriac rivers that roll—
　　As the lavas that restlessly roll
Their sulphurous currents down Yaanek
　　In the ultimate climes of the Pole—
That groan as they roll down Mount Yaanek
　　In the realms of the Boreal Pole.

Our talk had been serious and sober,
　　But our thoughts they were palsied and sere—
　　Our memories were treacherous and sere—
For we knew not the month was October,
　　And we marked not the night of the year—
　　(Ah, night of all nights in the year!)—

We noted not the dim lake of Auber—
　　(Though once we had journeyed down here)—
Remembered not the dank tarn of Auber,
　　Nor the ghoul-haunted woodland of Weir.

And now, as the night was senescent
　　And star-dials pointed to morn—
　　As the star-dials hinted of morn—
At the end of our path a liquescent
　　And nebulous lustre was born,
Out of which a miraculous crescent
　　Arose with a duplicate horn—
Astarte's bediamonded crescent
　　Distinct with its duplicate horn.

And I said—"She is warmer than Dian:
　　She rolls through an ether of sighs—
　　She revels in a region of sighs:
She has seen that the tears are not dry on
　　These cheeks, where the worm never dies,
And has come past the stars of the Lion
　　To point us the path to the skies—
　　To the Lethean peace of the skies—
Come up, in despite of the Lion,
　　To shine on us with her bright eyes—
Come up through the lair of the Lion,
　　With love in her luminous eyes."

But Psyche, uplifting her finger,
　　Said—"Sadly this star I mistrust—
　　Her pallor I strangely mistrust:
Oh, hasten!—oh, let us not linger!
　　Oh, fly!—let us fly!—for we must."
In terror she spoke, letting sink her
　　Wings till they trailed in the dust—

In agony sobbed, letting sink her
  Plumes till they trailed in the dust—
  Till they sorrowfully trailed in the dust.

I replied—"This is nothing but dreaming:
  Let us on by this tremulous light!
  Let us bathe in this crystalline light!
Its Sibyllic splendour is beaming
  With Hope and in Beauty tonight:—
  See!—it flickers up the sky through the night!
Ah, we safely may trust to its gleaming,
  And be sure it will lead us aright—
We safely may trust to a gleaming
  That cannot but guide us aright,
  Since it flickers up to Heaven through the night."

Thus I pacified Psyche and kissed her,
  And tempted her out of her gloom—
  And conquered her scruples and gloom;
And we passed to the end of the vista,
  But were stopped by the door of a tomb—
  By the door of a legended tomb;
And I said—"What is written, sweet sister,
  On the door of this legended tomb?"
  She replied—"Ulalume—Ulalume—
  'Tis the vault of thy lost Ulalume!"

Then my heart it grew ashen and sober
  As the leaves that were crispèd and sere,
  As the leaves that were withering and sere,
And I cried—"It was surely October
  On *this* very night of last year
  That I journeyed—I journeyed down here—
  That I brought a dread burden down here—
  On this night of all nights in the year,
  Ah, what demon has tempted me here?

[14]

Well I know, now, this dim lake of Auber—
This misty mid region of Weir—
Well I know, now, this dank tarn of Auber,
This ghoul-haunted woodland of Weir."

EDGAR ALLAN POE

This early poem by Robinson was a revelation of his extraordinary power of concision and of his skill in outline drawing rather than in painting.

RICHARD CORY

WHENEVER Richard Cory went down town,
We people on the pavement looked at him:
He was a gentleman from sole to crown,
Clean favoured, and imperially slim.

And he was always quietly arrayed,
And he was always human when he talked;
But still he fluttered pulses when he said,
"Good-morning," and he glittered when he walked.

And he was rich,—yes, richer than a king,—
And admirably schooled in every grace:
In fine, we thought that he was everything
To make us wish that we were in his place.

So on we worked, and waited for the light,
And went without the meat, and cursed the bread;
And Richard Cory, one calm summer night,
Went home and put a bullet through his head.

EDWIN ARLINGTON ROBINSON

HUMOROUS VERSE

This graduate of Harvard University wrote a masterpiece which millions of ambitious men wish they had written. For *Casey* is absolute perfection. The psychology of the hero and the psychology of the crowd leave nothing to be desired. There is more knowledge of human nature displayed in this poem than in many of the works of the psychiatrists. Furthermore, it is a tragedy of Destiny. There is nothing so stupid as Destiny. It is a centrifugal tragedy, by which our minds are turned from the fate of Casey to the universal. For this is the curse that hangs over humanity —our ability to accomplish any feat is in inverse ratio to the intensity of our desire. The declamatory art of De Wolf Hopper gave to this tragedy supreme unction.

CASEY AT THE BAT

THE outlook wasn't brilliant for the Mudville nine that day:
The score stood four to two, with but one inning more to
  play,
And then when Cooney died at first, and Barrows did the
  same,
A pall-like silence fell upon the patrons of the game.

A straggling few got up to go in deep despair. The rest
Clung to that hope which springs eternal in the human
  breast;
They thought, "If only Casey could but get a whack at
  that—
We'd put up even money now, with Casey at the bat."

But Flynn preceded Casey, as did also Jimmy Blake,
And the former was a hoodoo, while the latter was a fake;
So upon that stricken multitude grim melancholy sat,
For there seemed but little chance of Casey getting to the
  bat.

But Flynn let drive a single, to the wonderment of all,
And Blake, the much despised, tore the cover off the ball;
And when the dust had lifted, and men saw what had oc-
    curred,
There was Jimmy safe at second and Flynn a-hugging third.

Then from five thousand throats and more there rose a lusty
    yell;
It rumbled through the valley, it rattled in the dell;
It pounded on the mountain and recoiled upon the flat,
For Casey, mighty Casey, was advancing to the bat.

There was ease in Casey's manner as he stepped into his
    place;
There was pride in Casey's bearing and a smile lit Casey's
    face.
And when, responding to the cheers, he lightly doffed his
    hat,
No stranger in the crowd could doubt 'twas Casey at the bat.

Ten thousand eyes were on him as he rubbed his hands with
    dirt;
Five thousand tongues applauded when he wiped them on
    his shirt;
Then while the writhing pitcher ground the ball into his
    hip,
Defiance flashed in Casey's eye, a sneer curled Casey's lip.

And now the leather-covered sphere came hurtling through
    the air,
And Casey stood a-watching it in haughty grandeur there.
Close by the sturdy batsman the ball unheeded sped—
"That ain't my style," said Casey. "Strike one!" the umpire
    said.

From the benches, black with people, there went up a muffled
 roar,
Like the beating of the storm-waves on a stern and distant
 shore;
"Kill him! Kill the umpire!" shouted some one on the stand;
And it's likely they'd have killed him had not Casey raised
 his hand.

With a smile of Christian charity great Casey's visage
 shone;
He stilled the rising tumult; he bade the game go on;
He signalled to the pitcher, and once more the dun sphere
 flew;
But Casey still ignored it, and the umpire said, "Strike
 two!"

"Fraud!" cried the maddened thousands, and echo answered
 "Fraud!"
But one scornful look from Casey and the audience was
 awed.
They saw his face grow stern and cold, they saw his muscles
 strain,
And they knew that Casey wouldn't let that ball go by again.

The sneer has fled from Casey's lip, his teeth are clenched in
 hate;
He pounds with cruel violence his bat upon the plate.
And now the pitcher holds the ball, and now he lets it go,
And now the air is shattered by the force of Casey's blow.

Oh, somewhere in this favoured land the sun is shining bright;
The band is playing somewhere, and somewhere hearts are
 light,
And somewhere men are laughing, and little children shout;
But there is no joy in Mudville—great Casey has struck out.

                                    ERNEST L. THAYER

THE GREAT AUK'S GHOST

THE Great Auk's ghost rose on one leg,
    Sighed thrice and three times winkt,
And turned and poached a phantom egg,
    And muttered, "I'm extinct."

RALPH HODGSON

Mr. Beers wrote many charming nonsense verses, of which this is one of the best.

A FISH STORY

A WHALE of high porosity,
And low specific gravity,
Dived down with much velocity
Beneath the sea's concavity.

But soon the weight of water
Squeezed in his fat immensity,
Which varied—as it ought to—
Inversely as his density.

It would have moved to pity
An Ogre or a Hessian,
To see poor Spermaceti
Thus suffering compression.

The while he lay a-roaring
In agonies gigantic,
The lamp-oil out came pouring
And greased the wide Atlantic.

(Would we'd been in the Navy,
And cruising there! Imagine us
All in a sea of gravy,
With billows oleaginous!)

At length old million-pounder
Low on a bed of coral,
Gave his last dying flounder,
Whereto I pen this moral.

Moral

O let this tale dramatic
Anent this whale Norwegian,
And pressures hydrostatic
Warn you, my young collegian,
That down-compelling forces
Increase as you get deeper;
The lower down your course is,
The upward path's the steeper.

HENRY A. BEERS

Studied attentively, this poem shows why it is so difficult to persuade city people to leave the slums and work on a farm.

UP AT A VILLA—DOWN IN THE CITY

(As Distinguished by an Italian Person of Quality)

HAD I but plenty of money, money enough and to spare,
The house for me, no doubt, were a house in the city-square;
Ah, such a life, such a life, as one leads at the window there!

Something to see, by Bacchus, something to hear, at least!
There, the whole day long, one's life is a perfect feast;
While up at a villa one lives, I maintain it, no more than a
    beast.

Well now, look at our villa! stuck like the horn of a bull
Just on a mountain-edge as bare as the creature's skull,
Save a mere shag of a bush with hardly a leaf to pull!
—I scratch my own, sometimes, to see if the hair's turned
    wool.

But the city, oh the city—the square with the houses! Why?
They are stone-faced, white as a curd, there's something to
    take the eye!
Houses in four straight lines, not a single front awry;
You watch who crosses and gossips, who saunters, who hur-
    ries by;
Green blinds, as a matter of course, to draw when the sun
    gets high;
And the shops with fanciful signs which are painted prop-
    erly.

What of a villa? Though winter be over in March by rights,
'Tis May perhaps ere the snow shall have withered well off
    the heights:
You've the brown ploughed land before, where the oxen
    steam and wheeze,
And the hills over-smoked behind by the faint gray olive-
    trees.

Is it better in May, I ask you? You've summer all at once;
In a day he leaps complete with a few strong April suns.
'Mid the sharp short emerald wheat, scarce risen three fin-
    gers well,

The wild tulip, at end of its tube, blows out its great red bell
Like a thin clear bubble of blood, for the children to pick
and sell.

Is it ever hot in the square? There's a fountain to spout
and splash!
In the shade it sings and springs: in the shine such foam-
bows flash
On the horses with curling fish-tails, that prance and paddle
and pash
Round the lady atop in her conch—fifty gazers do not
abash,
Though all that she wears is some weeds round her waist in
a sort of sash.

All the year long at the villa, nothing to see though you
linger,
Except yon cypress that points like death's lean lifted fore-
finger.
Some think fireflies pretty, when they mix i' the corn and
mingle,
Or thrid the stinking hemp till the stalks of it seem a-tingle.
Late August or early September, the stunning cicala is
shrill,
And the bees keep their tiresome whine round the resinous
firs on the hill.
Enough of the seasons,—I spare you the months of the
fever and chill.

Ere you open your eyes in the city, the blessed church-bells
begin:
No sooner the bells leave off than the diligence rattles in:
You get the pick of the news, and it costs you never a pin.
By-and-by there's the travelling doctor gives pills, lets blood,
draws teeth;

Or the Pulcinello-trumpet breaks up the market beneath.

At the post-office such a scene-picture—the new play, pip-
    ing hot!

And a notice how, only this morning, three liberal thieves
    were shot.

Above it, behold the Archbishop's most fatherly of rebukes,

And beneath, with his crown and his lion, some little new
    law of the Duke's!

Or a sonnet with flowery marge, to the Reverend Don So-
    and-so,

Who is Dante, Boccaccio, Petrarcà, Saint Jerome, and Ci-
    cero,

"And moreover" (the sonnet goes rhyming), "the skirts of
    Saint Paul has reached,

Having preached us those six Lent-lectures more unctuous
    than ever he preached."

Noon strikes,—here sweeps the procession! our Lady borne
    smiling and smart

With a pink gauze gown all spangles, and seven swords
    stuck in her heart!

Bang-whang-whang goes the drum, *tootle-te-tootle* the fife;

No keeping one's haunches still: it's the greatest pleasure
    in life.

But bless you, it's dear—it's dear! fowls, wine, at double
    the rate.

They have clapped a new tax upon salt, and what oil pays
    passing the gate

It's a horror to think of. And so, the villa for me, not the
    city!

Beggars can scarcely be choosers: but still—ah, the pity,
    the pity!

Look, two and two go the priests, then the monks with cowls
    and sandals,

And the penitents dressed in white shirts, a-holding the yel-
 low candles;
One, he carries a flag up straight, and another a cross with
 handles,
And the Duke's guard brings up the rear, for the better
 prevention of scandals:
Bang-whang-whang goes the drum, *tootle-te-tootle* the fife.
Oh, a day in the city-square, there is no such pleasure in life!

ROBERT BROWNING

Sir William Watson is the most underrated of living
poets. Not only has he written a masterpiece—*Wordsworth's
Grave*—but his skill in terseness and pith is shown in the
following epigrams.

From EPIGRAMS OF ART, LIFE, AND NATURE

(1)

KING LEAR

HERE Love the slain with Love the slayer lies:
 Deep drown'd are both in the same sunless pool.
Up from its depths that mirror thundering skies
 Bubbles the wan mirth of the mirthless Fool.

(2)

HIS friends he loved. His direst earthly foes—
 Cats—I believe he did but feign to hate.
My hand will miss the insinuated nose,
 Mine eyes the tail that wagg'd contempt at fate.

[24]

(3)

Your Marlowe's page I close, my Shakespeare's ope.
　How welcome—after gong and cymbal's din—
The continuity, the long slow slope
　And vast curves of the gradual violin!

WILLIAM WATSON

Longfellow was one of the great sonneteers. The simile in the following poem has always seemed to me beautiful.

NATURE

As a fond mother, when the day is o'er,
Leads by the hand her little child to bed,
Half willing, half reluctant to be led,
And leave his broken playthings on the floor,
Still gazing at them through the open door,
Nor wholly reassured and comforted
By promises of others in their stead,
Which, though more splendid, may not please him more;
So Nature deals with us, and takes away
Our playthings one by one, and by the hand
Leads us to rest so gently, that we go
Scarce knowing if we wish to go or stay,
Being too full of sleep to understand
How far the unknown transcends the what we know.

HENRY WADSWORTH LONGFELLOW

In the closing years of the eighteenth century, two enthusiastic young Englishmen took long walks together over the Quantock Hills. Out of their animated conversation came in 1798 the epoch-making book *Lyrical Ballads*, which contained *The Rime of the Ancient Mariner* and *Tintern Abbey*. There was not room here for the whole of Coleridge's poem, but I could not leave it out; so it appears with certain omissions.

THE RIME OF THE ANCIENT MARINER

PART I

It is an ancient Mariner,
And he stoppeth one of three,
"By thy long grey beard and glittering eye,
Now wherefore stopp'st thou me?

The Bridegroom's doors are opened wide,
And I am next of kin;
The guests are met, the feast is set:
May'st hear the merry din."

He holds him with his skinny hand,
"There was a ship," quoth he.
"Hold off! unhand me, grey-beard loon!"
Eftsoons his hand dropt he.

He holds him with his glittering eye—
The wedding-guest stood still,
And listens like a three years' child:
The Mariner hath his will.

The wedding-guest sat on a stone:
He cannot choose but hear;
And thus spake on that ancient man,
The bright-eyed Mariner.

"The ship was cheered, the harbour cleared,
Merrily did we drop
Below the kirk, below the hill,
Below the lighthouse top.

The sun came up upon the left,
Out of the sea came he!
And he shone bright, and on the right
Went down into the sea.

Higher and higher every day,
Till over the mast at noon—"
The wedding-guest here beat his breast,
For he heard the loud bassoon.

The bride hath paced into the hall,
Red as a rose is she;
Nodding their heads before her goes
The merry minstrelsy.

The wedding-guest he beat his breast,
Yet he cannot choose but hear;
And thus spake on that ancient man,
The bright-eyed Mariner.

"And now the storm-blast came, and he
Was tyrannous and strong:
He struck with his o'ertaking wings,
And chased us south along.

With sloping masts and dipping prow,
As who pursued with yell and blow
Still treads the shadow of his foe,
And forward bends his head,
The ship drove fast, loud roared the blast,
And southward aye we fled.

And now there came both mist and snow,
And it grew wondrous cold;
And ice, mast-high, came floating by,
As green as emerald;

And through the drifts the snowy clifts
Did send a dismal sheen:
Nor shapes of men nor beasts we ken—
The ice was all between.

The ice was here, the ice was there,
The ice was all around:
It cracked and growled, and roared and howled,
Like noises in a swound!

At length did cross an Albatross:
Thorough the fog it came:
As if it had been a Christian soul,
We hailed it in God's name.

It ate the food it ne'er had eat,
And round and round it flew.
The ice did split with a thunder-fit;
The helmsman steered us through!

And a good south wind sprung up behind;
The Albatross did follow,
And every day, for food or play,
Came to the mariners' hollo!

In mist or cloud, on mast or shroud,
It perched for vespers nine;
Whiles all the night, through fog-smoke white,
Glimmered the white moon-shine."

"God save thee, ancient Mariner!
From the fiends, that plague thee thus!—
Why look'st thou so?"—"With my crossbow
I shot the Albatross!

PART II

The sun now rose upon the right:
Out of the sea came he,
Still hid in mist, and on the left
Went down into the sea.

And the good south wind still blew behind,
But no sweet bird did follow,
Nor any day, for food or play,
Came to the mariners' hollo!

And I had done a hellish thing,
And it would work 'em woe;
For all averred, I had killed the bird
That made the breeze to blow.
Ah wretch! said they, the bird to slay
That made the breeze to blow!

Nor dim nor red, like God's own head,
The glorious sun uprist:
Then all averred, I had killed the bird
That brought the fog and mist.
'Twas right, said they, such birds to slay,
That bring the fog and mist.

The fair breeze blew, the white foam flew,
The furrow followed free:
We were the first that ever burst
Into that silent sea.

[29]

Down dropt the breeze, the sails dropt down
'Twas sad as sad could be;
And we did speak only to break
The silence of the sea!

All in a hot and copper sky,
The bloody sun, at noon,
Right up above the mast did stand,
No bigger than the Moon.

Day after day, day after day,
We stuck, nor breath nor motion;
As idle as a painted ship
Upon a painted ocean.

Water, water, every where,
And all the boards did shrink;
Water, water, every where,
Nor any drop to drink.

The very deep did rot: O Christ!
That ever this should be!
Yea, slimy things did crawl with legs
Upon the slimy sea.

About, about, in reel and rout,
The death-fires danced at night;
The water, like a witch's oils,
Burnt green, and blue and white.

And some in dreams assured were
Of the Spirit that plagued us so:
Nine fathom deep he had followed us,
From the land of mist and snow.

And every tongue, through utter drought,
Was withered at the root;
We could not speak, no more than if
We had been choked with soot.

Ah, well-a-day! what evil looks
Had I from old and young!
Instead of the cross, the Albatross
About my neck was hung.

PART III

There passed a weary time. Each throat
Was parched, and glazed each eye.
A weary time! A weary time!
How glazed each weary eye!
When looking westward I beheld
A something in the sky.

At first it seemed a little speck,
And then it seemed a mist;
It moved and moved, and took at last
A certain shape, I wist.

A speck, a mist, a shape, I wist!
And still it neared and neared:
As if it dodged a water-sprite,
It plunged and tacked and veered.

With throats unslaked, with black lips baked,
We could nor laugh nor wail;
Through utter drought all dumb we stood!
I bit my arm, I sucked the blood,
And cried, A sail! a sail!

PART V

Oh sleep, it is a gentle thing,
Beloved from pole to pole!
To Mary Queen the praise be given!
She sent the gentle sleep from Heaven,
That slid into my soul.

The silly buckets on the deck,
That had so long remained,
I dreamt that they were filled with dew;
And when I awoke, it rained.

My lips were wet, my throat was cold,
My garments all were dank;
Sure I had drunken in my dreams,
And still my body drank.

I moved, and could not feel my limbs:
I was so light—almost
I thought that I had died in sleep,
And was a blessèd ghost.

And soon I heard a roaring wind:
It did not come anear;
But with its sound it shook the sails,
That were so thin and sere.

The upper air burst into life!
And a hundred fire-flag sheen,
To and fro they were hurried about;
And to and fro, and in and out,
The wan stars danced between.

And the coming wind did roar more loud,
And the sails did sigh like sedge;
And the rain poured down from one black cloud;
The Moon was at its edge.

The thick black cloud was cleft, and still
The Moon was at its side:
Like waters shot from some high crag,
The lightning fell with never a jag,
A river steep and wide.

The loud wind never reached the ship,
Yet now the ship moved on!
Beneath the lightning and the Moon
The dead men gave a groan.

They groaned, they stirred, they all uprose,
Nor spake, nor moved their eyes;
It had been strange, even in a dream,
To have seen those dead men rise.

The helmsman steered, the ship moved on;
Yet never a breeze up-blew;
The mariners all 'gan work the ropes,
Where they were wont to do;
They raised their limbs like lifeless tools—
We were a ghastly crew.

The body of my brother's son
Stood by me, knee to knee:
The body and I pulled at one rope,
But he said naught to me."

"I fear thee, ancient Mariner!"
"Be calm, thou Wedding-Guest!
'Twas not those souls that fled in pain,
Which to their corses came again,
But a troop of spirits blest:

For when it dawned—they dropped their arms,
And clustered round the mast;
Sweet sounds rose slowly through their mouths,
And from their bodies passed.

Around, around, flew each sweet sound,
Then darted to the Sun;
Slowly the sounds came back again,
Now mixed, now one by one.

Sometimes a-dropping from the sky
I heard the sky-lark sing;
Sometimes all little birds that are,
How they seemed to fill the sea and air
With their sweet jargoning!

And now 'twas like all instruments,
Now like a lonely flute;
And now it is an angel's song,
That makes the Heavens be mute.

It ceased; yet still the sails made on
A pleasant noise till noon,
A noise like of a hidden brook
In the leafy month of June,
That to the sleeping woods all night
Singeth a quiet tune.

.　.　.　.　.　.　.　.　.

PART VI

Swiftly, swiftly flew the ship,
Yet she sailed softly too:
Sweetly, sweetly blew the breeze—
On me alone it blew.

Oh! dream of joy; is this indeed
The light-house top I see
Is this the hill? is this the kirk?
Is this mine own countree?

We drifted o'er the harbour-bar,
And I with sobs did pray—
O let me be awake, my God!
Or let me sleep alway.

The harbour-bay was clear as glass
So smoothly it was strewn!
And on the bay the moonlight lay
And the shadow of the Moon.

The rock shone bright, the kirk no less
That stands above the rock:
The moonlight steeped in silentness
The steady weathercock.

And the bay was white with silent light,
Till rising from the same,
Full many shapes, that shadows were,
In crimson colors came.

A little distance from the prow
Those crimson shadows were:
I turned my eyes upon the deck—
Oh, Christ! what saw I there!

Each corse lay flat, lifeless and flat,
And, by the holy rood!
A man all light, a seraph-man,
On every corse there stood.

This seraph-band, each waved his hand:
It was a heavenly sight!
They stood as signals to the land,
Each one a lovely light:

This seraph-band, each waved his hand,
No voice did they impart—
No voice; but oh! the silence sank
Like music on my heart.

But soon I heard the dash of oars,
I heard the Pilot's cheer;
My head was turned perforce away,
And I saw a boat appear.

The Pilot, and the Pilot's boy,
I heard them coming fast:
Dear Lord in Heaven! it was a joy
The dead men could not blast.

I saw a third—I heard his voice:
It is the Hermit good!
He singeth loud his godly hymns
That he makes in the wood.
He'll shrieve my soul, he'll wash away
The Albatross's blood.

PART VII

This Hermit good lives in that wood
Which slopes down to the sea.
How loudly his sweet voice he rears!
He loves to talk with marineres
That come from a far countree.

He kneels at morn, and noon, and eve—
He hath a cushion plump:
It is the moss that wholly hides
The rotted old oak-stump.

The skiff-boat neared: I heard them talk,
'Why, this is strange, I trow!
Where are those lights so many and fair,
That signal made but now?'

'Strange, by my faith!' the Hermit said—
'And they answered not our cheer!
The planks look warped! and see those sails,
How thin they are and sere!
I never saw aught like to them,
Unless perchance it were

Brown skeletons of leaves that lag
My forest-brook along;
When the ivy-tod is heavy with snow,
And the owlet whoops to the wolf below
That eats the she-wolf's young.'

'Dear Lord! it hath a fiendish look'
(The Pilot made reply)
'I am a-feared'—'Push on, push on!'
Said the Hermit cheerily.

[37]

The boat came closer to the ship,
But I nor spake nor stirred;
The boat came close beneath the ship,
And straight a sound was heard.

Under the water it rumbled on,
Still louder and more dread:
It reached the ship, it split the bay;
The ship went down like lead.

Stunned by that loud and dreadful sound,
Which sky and ocean smote,
Like one that hath been seven day drowned,
My body lay afloat;
But swift as dreams, myself I found
Within the Pilot's boat

Upon the whirl, where sank the ship,
The boat spun round and round;
And all was still, save that the hill
Was telling of the sound.

I moved my lips—the Pilot shrieked
And fell down in a fit;
The holy Hermit raised his eyes
And prayed where he did sit.

I took the oars: the Pilot's boy,
Who now doth crazy go,
Laughed loud and long, and all the while
His eyes went to and fro.
'Ha! ha!' quoth he, 'full plain I see,
The Devil knows how to row.'

And now, all in my own countree,
I stood on the firm land!
The Hermit stepped forth from the boat,
And scarcely he could stand.

'O shrieve me, shrieve me, holy man!'
The Hermit crossed his brow.
'Say quick,' quoth he, 'I bid thee say—
What manner of man art thou?'

Forthwith this frame of mine was wrenched
With a woeful agony,
Which forced me to begin my tale;
And then it left me free.

Since then at an uncertain hour,
That agony returns;
And till my ghastly tale is told,
This heart within me burns.

I pass, like night, from land to land:
I have strange power of speech;
That moment that his face I see,
I know the man that must hear me:
To him my tale I teach.

What loud uproar bursts from that door!
The wedding-guests are there;
But in the garden-bower the bride
And bride-maids singing are:
And hark the little vesper bell,
Which biddeth me to prayer!

O Wedding-Guest! this soul hath been
Alone on a wide wide sea:
So lonely 'twas, that God himself
Scarce seemed there to be.

O sweeter than the marriage-feast,
'Tis sweeter far to me,
To walk together to the kirk
With a goodly company!—

To walk together to the kirk,
And all together pray,
While each to his great Father bends,
Old men, and babes, and loving friends,
And youths and maidens gay!

Farewell, farewell! but this I tell
To thee, thou Wedding-Guest!
He prayeth well, who loveth well
Both man and bird and beast.

He prayeth best, who loveth best
All things both great and small;
For the dear God who loveth us,
He made and loveth all."

The Mariner, whose eye is bright,
Whose beard with age is hoar,
Is gone; and now the Wedding-Guest
Turned from the bridegroom's door.

He went like one that hath been stunned,
And is of sense forlorn:
A sadder and a wiser man
He rose the morrow morn.

SAMUEL TAYLOR COLERIDGE

When Thomas Hardy was on his deathbed, he asked his wife to read aloud to him *The Listeners*, which is surely the most imaginative of its author's poems. It is a good illustration of the highest kind of poetry because it cannot be translated into prose, nor can its meaning be definitely described. Its significance, however, needs no explanation.

THE LISTENERS

"Is there anybody there?" said the Traveller,
  Knocking on the moonlit door;
And his horse in the silence champed the grasses
  Of the forest's ferny floor;
And a bird flew up out of the turret,
  Above the Traveller's head;
And he smote upon the door again a second time;
  "Is there anybody there?" he said.
But no one descended to the Traveller;
  No head from the leaf-fringed sill
Leaned over and looked into his grey eyes,
  Where he stood perplexed and still.
But only a host of phantom listeners
  That dwelt in the lone house then
Stood listening in the quiet of the moonlight
  To that voice from the world of men:
Stood thronging the faint moonbeams on the dark stair,
  That goes down to the empty hall,
Hearkening in an air stirred and shaken
  By the lonely Traveller's call.
And he felt in his heart their strangeness,
  Their stillness answering his cry,
While his horse moved, cropping the dark turf,
  'Neath the starred and leafy sky;
For he suddenly smote on the door, even
  Louder, and lifted his head:—

"Tell them I came, and no one answered;
  That I kept my word," he said.
Never the least stir made the listeners,
  Though every word he spake
Fell echoing through the shadowiness of the still house
  From the one man left awake:
Ay, they heard his foot upon the stirrup,
  And the sound of iron on stone,
And how the silence surged softly backward,
  When the plunging hoofs were gone.

                              WALTER DE LA MARE

Ralph Hodgson does not allow his delight in beauty to
be destroyed by philosophy.

THE MYSTERY

He came and took me by the hand
  Up to a red rose tree,
He kept His meaning to Himself
  But gave a rose to me.

I did not pray Him to lay bare
  The mystery to me,
Enough the rose was Heaven to smell,
  And His own face to see.

                              RALPH HODGSON

Browning printed this in a magazine when he was twenty-four; he originally called this and a companion-piece *Madhouse Cells*, and as he grew older, wisely removed the description. What does the last line mean?

PORPHYRIA'S LOVER

THE rain set early in tonight,
   The sullen wind was soon awake,
It tore the elm-tops down for spite,
   And did its worst to vex the lake:
I listened with heart fit to break.
When glided in Porphyria; straight
   She shut the cold out and the storm,
And kneeled and made the cheerless grate
   Blaze up, and all the cottage warm;
Which done, she rose, and from her form
Withdrew the dripping cloak and shawl,
   And laid her soiled gloves by, untied
Her hat and let the damp hair fall,
   And, last, she sat down by my side
And called me. When no voice replied,
She put my arm about her waist,
   And made her smooth white shoulder bare,
And all her yellow hair displaced,
   And, stooping, made my cheek lie there,
And spread, o'er all, her yellow hair,
Murmuring how she loved me—she
   Too weak, for all her heart's endeavour,
To set its struggling passion free
   From pride, and vainer ties dissever,
And give herself to me forever.
But passion sometimes would prevail,
   Nor could tonight's gay feast restrain

A sudden thought of one so pale
  For love of her, and all in vain:
So, she was come through wind and rain.
Be sure I looked up at her eyes
  Happy and proud; at last I knew
Porphyria worshipped me; surprise
  Made my heart swell, and still it grew
While I debated what to do.
That moment she was mine, mine, fair,
  Perfectly pure and good: I found
A thing to do, and all her hair
  In one long yellow string I wound
Three times her little throat around,
And strangled her. No pain felt she;
  I am quite sure she felt no pain.
As a shut bud that holds a bee,
  I warily oped her lids: again
Laughed the blue eyes without a stain.
And I untightened next the tress
  About her neck; her cheek once more
Blushed bright beneath my burning kiss:
  I propped her head up as before,
Only, this time my shoulder bore
Her head, which droops upon it still:
  The smiling rosy little head,
So glad it has its utmost will,
  That all it scorned at once is fled,
And I, its love, am gained instead!
Porphyria's love: she guessed not how
  Her darling one wish would be heard.
And thus we sit together now,
  And all night long we have not stirred,
And yet God has not said a word!

ROBERT BROWNING

The philosophy of acquiescence. Observe it is not the
busyness of the bee, which improves each shining hour, that
Emerson praises; it is the bee's lovely laziness; his ability to
"relax."

THE HUMBLE-BEE

BURLY, dozing humble-bee,
Where thou art is clime for me.
Let them sail for Porto Rique,
Far-off heats through seas to seek;
I will follow thee alone,
Thou animated torrid-zone!
Zigzag steerer, desert cheerer,
Let me chase thy waving lines;
Keep me nearer, me thy hearer,
Singing over shrubs and vines.

Insect lover of the sun,
Joy of thy dominion!
Sailor of the atmosphere;
Swimmer through the waves of air;
Voyager of light and noon;
Epicurean of June;
Wait, I prithee, till I come
Within earshot of thy hum,—
All without is martyrdom.

When the south wind, in May days,
With a net of shining haze
Silvers the horizon wall,
And with softness touching all,
Tints the human countenance
With a color of romance,
And infusing subtle heats,

Turns the sod to violets,
Thou, in sunny solitudes,
Rover of the underwoods,
The green silence dost displace
With thy mellow, breezy bass.

Hot midsummer's petted crone,
Sweet to me thy drowsy tone
Tells of countless sunny hours,
Long days, and solid banks of flowers;
Of gulfs of sweetness without bound
In Indian wildernesses found;
Of Syrian peace, immortal leisure,
Firmest cheer, and bird-like pleasure.

Aught unsavory or unclean
Hath my insect never seen;
But violets and bilberry bells,
Maple-sap and daffodels,
Grass with green flag half-mast high,
Succory to match the sky,
Columbine with horn of honey,
Scented fern, and agrimony,
Clover, catchfly, adder's-tongue
And brier-roses, dwelt among;
All beside was unknown waste,
All was picture as he passed.

Wiser far than human seer,
Yellow-breeched philosopher!
Seeing only what is fair,
Sipping only what is sweet,
Thou dost mock at fate and care,
Leave the chaff, and take the wheat.

When the fierce northwestern blast
Cools sea and land so far and fast,
Thou already slumberest deep;
Woe and want thou canst outsleep;
Want and woe, which torture us,
Thy sleep makes ridiculous.

RALPH WALDO EMERSON

═══

THE NIGHTINGALE

The most famous song-bird in literature. Many persons
wonder why, with all the variety of climate we have in
America, this bird cannot live in the United States. Some
say it is because of the diet; nonsense. The reason should be
obvious.

To the Nightingale

O Nightingale that on yon bloomy spray
　Warblest at eve, when all the woods are still,
　Thou with fresh hope the lover's heart dost fill,
While the jolly hours lead on propitious May.
Thy liquid notes that close the eye of day,
　First heard before the shallow cuckoo's bill,
　Portend success in love. O, if Jove's will
Have linked that amorous power to thy soft lay,
　Now timely sing, ere the rude bird of hate
Foretell my hopeless doom, in some grove nigh;
　As thou from year to year hast sung too late
For my relief, yet hadst no reason why.
　Whether the Muse or Love call thee his mate,
Both them I serve, and of their train am I.

JOHN MILTON

[47]

O NIGHTINGALE!

O NIGHTINGALE! thou surely art
A creature of a "fiery heart":—
These notes of thine—they pierce and pierce;
Tumultuous harmony and fierce!
Thou sing'st as if the God of wine
Had helped thee to a Valentine;
A song in mockery and despite
Of shades, and dews, and silent night;
And steady bliss, and all the loves
Now sleeping in these peaceful groves.

I heard a Stock-dove sing or say
His homely tale, this very day;
His voice was buried among trees,
Yet to be come-at by the breeze:
He did not cease; but cooed—and cooed;
And somewhat pensively he wooed:
He sang of love, with quiet blending,
Slow to begin, and never ending;
Of serious faith, and inward glee;
That was the song—the song for me!

WILLIAM WORDSWORTH

ODE TO A NIGHTINGALE

I

MY heart aches, and a drowsy numbness pains
My sense, as though of hemlock I had drunk,
Or emptied some dull opiate to the drains
One minute past, and Lethe-wards had sunk:

[48]

'T is not through envy of thy happy lot,
But being too happy in thine happiness,—
That thou, light-wingèd Dryad of the trees,
In some melodious plot
Of beechen green, and shadows numberless,
Singest of summer in full-throated ease.

II

O, for a draught of vintage, that hath been
Cooled a long age in the deep-delvèd earth,
Tasting of Flora and the country green,
Dance, and Provençal song, and sunburnt mirth!
O for a beaker full of the warm South,
Full of the true, the blushful Hippocrene,
With beaded bubbles winking at the brim,
And purple-stainèd mouth;
That I might drink, and leave the world unseen,
And with thee fade away into the forest dim:

III

Fade far away, dissolve, and quite forget
What thou among the leaves hast never known,
The weariness, the fever, and the fret
Here, where men sit and hear each other groan;
Where palsy shakes a few, sad, last grey hairs,
Where youth grows pale, and spectre-thin, and dies;
Where but to think is to be full of sorrow
And leaden-eyed despairs,
Where Beauty cannot keep her lustrous eyes,
Or new Love pine at them beyond to-morrow.

IV

Away! away! for I will fly to thee,
Not charioted by Bacchus and his pards,

[49]

But on the viewless wings of Poesy,
　Though the dull brain perplexes and retards:
Already with thee! tender is the night,
　And haply the Queen-Moon is on her throne,
　　Clustered around by all her starry Fays;
　　　But here there is no light,
Save what from heaven is with the breezes blown
　Through verdurous glooms and winding mossy ways.

V

I cannot see what flowers are at my feet,
　Nor what soft incense hangs upon the boughs,
But, in embalmèd darkness, guess each sweet
　Wherewith the seasonable month endows
The grass, the thicket, and the fruit-tree wild;
　White hawthorn, and the pastoral eglantine;
　　Fast fading violets covered up in leaves;
　　　And mid-May's eldest child,
　The coming musk-rose, full of dewy wine,
　　The murmurous haunt of flies on summer eves.

VI

Darkling I listen; and, for many a time
　I have been half in love with easeful Death,
Called him soft names in many a musèd rhyme,
　To take into the air my quiet breath;
Now more than ever seems it rich to die,
　To cease upon the midnight with no pain,
　　While thou art pouring forth thy soul abroad
　　　In such an ecstasy!
　Still wouldst thou sing, and I have ears in vain—
　　To thy high requiem become a sod.

VII

Thou wast not born for death, immortal Bird!
No hungry generations tread thee down;
The voice I hear this passing night was heard
In ancient days by emperor and clown:
Perhaps the self-same song that found a path
Through the sad heart of Ruth, when, sick for home,
She stood in tears amid the alien corn;
The same that oft-times hath
Charmed magic casements, opening on the foam
Of perilous seas, in faery lands forlorn.

VIII

Forlorn! the very word is like a bell
To toll me back from thee to my sole self!
Adieu! the fancy cannot cheat so well
As she is famed to do, deceiving elf.
Adieu! adieu! thy plaintive anthem fades
Past the near meadows, over the still stream,
Up the hill-side; and now 'tis buried deep
In the next valley-glades:
Was it a vision, or a waking dream?
Fled is that music:—do I wake or sleep?

JOHN KEATS

PHILOMELA

HARK, ah, the nightingale—
The tawny-throated!
Hark, from that moonlit cedar what a burst!
What triumph! hark!—what pain!

O Wanderer from a Grecian shore,
Still, after many years, in distant lands,
Still nourishing in thy bewilder'd brain
That wild, unquench'd, deep-sunken, old-world pain—
Say, will it never heal?
And can this fragrant lawn
With its cool trees, and night,
And the sweet, tranquil Thames,
And moonshine, and the dew,
To thy rack'd heart and brain
Afford no balm?

Dost thou to-night behold,
Here, through the moonlight on this English grass,
The unfriendly palace in the Thracian wild?
Dost thou again peruse
With hot cheeks and sear'd eyes
The too clear web, and thy dumb sister's shame?
Dost thou once more assay
Thy flight, and feel come over thee,
Poor fugitive, the feathery change
Once more, and once more seem to make resound
With love and hate, triumph and agony,
Lone Daulis, and the high Cephissian vale?
Listen, Eugenia—
How thick the bursts come crowding through the leaves!
Again—thou hearest?
Eternal passion!
Eternal pain!

MATTHEW ARNOLD

The most recent and the best editions of Donne's Complete Poems begin with this question; and the reader knows he is in the presence of genius.

Donne had more influence on the lyric poetry of the seventeenth century than any other man. Ben Jonson told Drummond that Donne, for not keeping of accent, deserved hanging; that Donne, for not being understood, would perish; that Donne was "the first poet in the world for some things." He is; and today the reputation of Donne is greater than at any time since his death.

The Good-Morrow

I WONDER by my troth, what thou, and I
Did, till we lov'd? were we not wean'd till then?
But suck'd on country pleasures, childishly?
Or snorted we in the seven sleepers den?
'Twas so; but this, all pleasures fancies be.
If ever any beauty I did see,
Which I desir'd, and got, 'twas but a dream of thee.

And now good morrow to our waking souls,
Which watch not one another out of fear;
For love, all love of other sights controls,
And makes one little room, an every where.
Let sea-discoverers to new worlds have gone,
Let Maps to other, worlds on worlds have shown,
Let us possess one world, each hath one, and is one.

My face in thine eye, thine in mine appears,
And true plain hearts do in the faces rest.
Where can we find two better hemispheres
Without sharp North, without declining West?
What ever dies, was not mixt equally;
If our two loves be one, or, thou and I
Love so alike, that none do slacken, none can die.

JOHN DONNE

[53]

Henry Vaughan the Silurist, physician, poet, mystic, living in the beautiful Welsh countryside along the banks of the Usk, wrote many perfect lines and two great poems. Had he been able to write a dozen poems equal in expression to *They Are All Gone*, he would be one of the major poets of English literature. This poem was not the result of serious thought or of painstaking effort; it was sheer inspiration.

THEY ARE ALL GONE

THEY are all gone into the world of light!
  And I alone sit lingering here;
Their very memory is fair and bright,
  And my sad thoughts doth clear.

It glows and glitters in my cloudy breast
  Like stars upon some gloomy grove,
Or those faint beams in which this hill is drest
  After the sun's remove.

I see them walking in an air of glory,
  Whose light doth trample on my days;
My days, which are at best but dull and hoary,
  Mere glimmerings and decays.

O holy hope! and high humility!
  High as the heavens above;
These are your walks, and you have showed them me,
  To kindle my cold love.

Dear, beauteous death! the jewel of the just,
  Shining nowhere but in the dark,
What mysteries do lie beyond thy dust,
  Could man outlook that mark!

He that hath found some fledged bird's nest may know
  At first sight if the bird be flown;
But what fair well or grove he sings in now,
  That is to him unknown.

And yet, as angels in some brighter dreams
  Call to the soul when man doth sleep,
So some strange thoughts transcend our wonted themes,
  And into glory peep.

If a star were confined into a tomb,
  Her captive flames must needs burn there;
But when the hand that locked her up gives room,
  She'll shine through all the sphere.

O Father of eternal life, and all
  Created glories under Thee,
Resume Thy spirit from this world of thrall
  Into true liberty!

Either disperse these mists, which blot and fill
  My perspective still as they pass,
Or else remove me hence unto that hill
  Where I shall need no glass.

HENRY VAUGHAN

Hardy regarded man as morally superior to God and the animals as superior to man. This poem shows that combination of wonder and tenderness that often filled Hardy's mind when he contemplated the harmless and resentless nature of birds.

THE DARKLING THRUSH

I LEANT upon a coppice gate
　　When Frost was spectre-grey,
And Winter's dregs made desolate
　　The weakening eye of day.
The tangled bine-stems scored the sky
　　Like strings from broken lyres,
And all mankind that haunted nigh
　　Had sought their household fires.

The land's sharp features seemed to be
　　The Century's corpse outleant,
His crypt the cloudy canopy,
　　The wind his death-lament.
The ancient pulse of germ and birth
　　Was shrunken hard and dry,
And every spirit upon earth
　　Seemed fervourless as I.

At once a voice outburst among
　　The bleak twigs overhead
In a full-hearted evensong
　　Of joy illimited;
An aged thrush, frail, gaunt, and small,
　　In blast-beruffled plume,
Had chosen thus to fling his soul
　　Upon the growing gloom.

So little cause for carollings
  Of such ecstatic sound
Was written on terrestrial things
  Afar or nigh around,
That I could think there trembled through
  His happy good-night air
Some blessed Hope, whereof he knew
  And I was unaware.

THOMAS HARDY

Amy Lowell's tireless industry produced a monumental *Life of Keats* and many volumes of verse; but it was only occasionally that her violence of emotion found adequate poetic diction. Of all her poems, *Patterns* is the best; it was a memorable experience to hear her read it.

PATTERNS

I WALK down the garden paths,
And all the daffodils
Are blowing, and the bright blue squills.
I walk down the patterned garden paths
In my stiff, brocaded gown.
With my powdered hair and jewelled fan,
I too am a rare
Pattern. As I wander down
The garden paths.

My dress is richly figured,
And the train
Makes a pink and silver stain
On the gravel, and the thrift
Of the borders.
Just a plate of current fashion,
Tripping by in high-heeled, ribboned shoes.

Not a softness anywhere about me,
Only whalebone and brocade.
And I sink on a seat in the shade
Of a lime tree. For my passion
Wars against the stiff brocade.
The daffodils and squills
Flutter in the breeze
As they please.
And I weep;
For the lime tree is in blossom
And one small flower has dropped upon my bosom.

And the plashing of waterdrops
In the marble fountain
Comes down the garden paths.
The dripping never stops.
Underneath my stiffened gown
Is the softness of a woman bathing in a marble basin,
A basin in the midst of hedges grown
So thick, she cannot see her lover hiding,
But she guesses he is near,
And the sliding of the water
Seems the stroking of a dear
Hand upon her.
What is Summer in a fine brocaded gown!
I should like to see it lying in a heap upon the ground.
All the pink and silver crumpled up on the ground.

I would be the pink and silver as I ran along the paths,
And he would stumble after,
Bewildered by my laughter.
I should see the sun flashing from his sword-hilt and the
    buckles on his shoes.
I would choose
To lead him in a maze along the patterned paths,

A bright and laughing maze for my heavy-booted lover,
Till he caught me in the shade,
And the buttons of his waistcoat bruised my body as he
    clasped me,
Aching, melting, unafraid.
With the shadows of the leaves and the sundrops,
And the plopping of the waterdrops,
All about us in the open afternoon—
I am very like to swoon
With the weight of this brocade,
For the sun sifts through the shade.

Underneath the fallen blossom
In my bosom,
Is a letter I have hid.
It was brought to me this morning by a rider from the
    Duke.
"Madam, we regret to inform you that Lord Hartwell
Died in action Thursday se'nnight."
As I read it in the white, morning sunlight,
The letters squirmed like snakes.
"Any answer, Madam" said my footman.
"No," I told him.
"See that the messenger takes some refreshment.
No, no answer."
And I walked into the garden,
Up and down the patterned paths,
In my stiff, correct brocade.
The blue and yellow flowers stood up proudly in the sun,
Each one.
I stood upright too,
Held rigid to the pattern
By the stiffness of my gown.
Up and down I walked,
Up and down.

In a month he would have been my husband.
In a month, here, underneath this lime,
We would have broke the pattern;
He for me, and I for him,
He as Colonel, I as Lady,
On this shady seat.
He had a whim
That sunlight carried blessing.
And I answered, "It shall be as you have said."
Now he is dead.

In Summer and in Winter I shall walk
Up and down
The patterned garden paths
In my stiff, brocaded gown.
The squills and daffodils
Will give place to pillared roses, and to asters, and to snow.
I shall go
Up and down,
In my gown.
Gorgeously arrayed,
Boned and stayed.
And the softness of my body will be guarded from embrace
By each button, hook, and lace.
For the man who should loose me is dead,
Fighting with the Duke of Flanders
In a pattern called a war.
Christ! What are patterns for?

AMY LOWELL

Robert Nichols has written many long and short poems; but this particular lyric expresses with perfection the emotions aroused by the starry firmament in the hungry heart.

THE FULL HEART

ALONE on the shore in the pause of the nighttime
I stand and I hear the long wind blow light;
I view the constellations quietly, quietly burning;
I hear the wave fall in the hush of the night.

Long after I am dead, ended this bitter journey,
Many another whose heart holds no light
Shall your solemn sweetness hush, awe, and comfort,
O my companions, Wind, Waters, Stars, and Night.

ROBERT NICHOLS

POEMS ON BOOKS

The poets have paid royally, like King Solomon, out of their royal bounty, the debt they owe to the books that have pleased or inspired them. Keats's sonnet on Chapman's Homer is worthy of both the great Elizabethan and the great Greek. That it was Balboa and not Cortez makes no difference poetically. Genius is sometimes shown in revisions: Keats originally wrote "Yet could I never tell what men could mean" instead of the splendid line "Yet did I never breathe its pure serene."

Longfellow's sonnet on his books is the lament of the old warrior who can no longer wield his weapons. Ralph Hodgson's *My Books* is the intimate, affectionate conversation with friends so familiar that formality is annihilated. Arthur Colton's lines on Chaucer's *Troilus and Criseyde* are beautifully expressive of the spirit of that romance.

ON FIRST LOOKING INTO CHAPMAN'S HOMER

MUCH have I travelled in the realms of gold,
  And many goodly states and kingdoms seen;
  Round many western islands have I been
Which bards in fealty to Apollo hold.
Oft of one wide expanse had I been told
  That deep-browed Homer ruled as his demesne:
  Yet did I never breathe its pure serene
Till I heard Chapman speak out loud and bold:
Then felt I like some watcher of the skies
  When a new planet swims into his ken;
Or like stout Cortez, when with eagle eyes
  He stared at the Pacific—and all his men
Looked at each other with a wild surmise—
Silent, upon a peak in Darien.

JOHN KEATS

MY BOOKS

SADLY as some old mediæval knight
Gazed at the arms he could no longer wield,
The sword two-handed and the shining shield
Suspended in the hall, and full in sight,
While secret longings for the lost delight
Of tourney or adventure in the field
Came over him, and tears but half concealed
Trembled and fell upon his beard of white,
So I behold these books upon their shelf,
My ornaments and arms of other days;
Not wholly useless, though no longer used,
For they remind me of my other self,
Younger and stronger, and the pleasant ways
In which I walked, now clouded and confused.

HENRY WADSWORTH LONGFELLOW

My Books

When the folks have gone to bed,
   And the lamp is burning low,
And the fire burns not so red
   As it burned an hour ago,

Then I turn about my chair
   So that I can dimly see
Into the dark corners where
   Lies my modest library.

Volumes gay and volumes grave,
   Many volumes have I got;
Many volumes though I have,
   Many volumes have I not.

I have not the rare Lucasta,
   London, 1649;
I'm a lean-pursed poetaster,
   Or the book had long been mine. . . .

Near the "Wit's Interpreter"
   (Like an antique Whitaker,
Full of strange etcetera),
   "Areopagitica,"

And the muse of Lycidas,
   Lost in meditation deep,
Give the cut to Hudibras,
   Unaware the knave's asleep. . . .

There lies Coleridge, bound in green,
   Sleepily still wond'ring what
He meant Kubla Khan to mean;
   In that early Wordsworth, Mat.

Arnold knows a faithful prop,—
Still to subject-matter leans,
Murmurs of the loved hill-top,
Fyfield tree and Cumnor scenes.

RALPH HODGSON

TROILUS AND CRISEYDE

A SMILE, of flowers, and fresh May, across
The dreamy, drifting face of old Romance;
The same reiterate tale of love and loss
And joy that trembles in the hands of chance;
And midst his rippling lines old Geoffrey stands,
Saying, "Pray for me when the tale is done,
Who see no more the flowers, nor the sun."

ARTHUR COLTON

Longfellow's *Sonnets* written to accompany his translation of *Divina Commedia* are the most beautiful of all English poetic tributes to Dante. The comparison of the vast poem to a Gothic cathedral is splendidly conceived and successful in its detailed execution.

DIVINA COMMEDIA

I

OFT have I seen at some cathedral door
A labourer, pausing in the dust and heat,
Lay down his burden, and with reverent feet
Enter, and cross himself, and on the floor
Kneel to repeat his paternoster o'er;
Far off the noises of the world retreat;

[64]

The loud vociferations of the street
Become an undistinguishable roar.
So, as I enter here from day to day,
And leave my burden at this minster gate,
Kneeling in prayer, and not ashamed to pray,
The tumult of the time disconsolate
To inarticulate murmurs dies away,
While the eternal ages watch and wait.

II

How strange the sculptures that adorn these towers!
  This crowd of statues, in whose folded sleeves
  Birds build their nests; while canopied with leaves
  Parvis and portal bloom like trellised bowers.
And the vast minster seems a cross of flowers!
  But fiends and dragons on the gargoyled eaves
  Watch the dead Christ between the living thieves,
  And, underneath, the traitor Judas lowers!
Ah! from what agonies of heart and brain,
  What exultation trampling on despair,
  What tenderness, what tears, what hate of wrong,
What passionate outcry of a soul in pain,
  Uprose this poem of the earth and air,
  This mediæval miracle of song!

III

I enter, and I see thee in the gloom
  Of the long aisles, O poet saturnine!
  And strive to make my steps keep pace with thine.
  The air is filled with some unknown perfume;
The congregation of the dead make room
  For thee to pass; the votive tapers shine;

Like rooks that haunt Ravenna's groves of pine
The hovering echoes fly from tomb to tomb.
From the confessionals I hear arise
Rehearsals of forgotten tragedies,
And lamentations from the crypts below:
And then a voice celestial that begins
With the pathetic words, "Although your sins
As scarlet be," and ends with "as the snow."

IV

With snow-white veil and garments as of flame,
She stands before thee, who so long ago
Filled thy young heart with passion and the woe
From which thy song and all its splendours came;
And while with stern rebukes she speaks thy name,
The ice about thy heart melts as the snow
On mountain heights, and in swift overflow
Comes gushing from thy lips in sobs of shame.
Thou makest full confession; and the gleam
As of the dawn on some dark forest cast,
Seems on thy lifted forehead to increase;
Lethe and Eunoë—the remembered dream
And the forgotten sorrow—bring at last
That perfect pardon which is perfect peace.

V

I lift mine eyes, and all the windows blaze
With forms of Saints and holy men who died,
Here martyred and hereafter glorified;
And the great Rose upon its leaves displays
Christ's Triumph, and the angelic roundelays,
With splendour upon splendour multiplied;

And Beatrice again at Dante's side
No more rebukes, but smiles her words of praise.
And then the organ sounds, and unseen choirs
Sing the old Latin hymns of peace and love
And benedictions of the Holy Ghost;
And the melodious bells among the spires
O'er all the house-tops and through heaven above
Proclaim the elevation of the Host!

VI

O star of morning and of liberty!
O bringer of the light, whose splendour shines
Above the darkness of the Apennines,
Forerunner of the day that is to be!
The voices of the city and the sea,
The voices of the mountains and the pines,
Repeat thy song, till the familiar lines
Are footpaths for the thought of Italy!
Thy flame is blown abroad from all the heights,
Through all the nations, and a sound is heard,
As of a mighty wind, and men devout,
Strangers of Rome, and the new proselytes,
In their own language hear thy wondrous word,
And many are amazed and many doubt.

HENRY WADSWORTH LONGFELLOW

The Reverend George Herbert, pastor of the little church at Bemerton in 1633, belonged to an aristocratic and wealthy family, and gave up social ambitions for religion. His struggle was neither with the flesh nor with the Devil; his struggle was with the world.

THE COLLAR

I STRUCK the board, and cried, "No more!
    I will abroad!
What! shall I ever sigh and pine?
My lines and life are free, free as the road,
    Loose as the wind, as large as store.
      Shall I be still in suit?
Have I no harvest but a thorn
To let me blood, and not restore
What I have lost with cordial fruit?
      Sure there was wine
Before my sighs did dry it; there was corn
    Before my tears did drown it.
Is the year only lost to me?
    Have I no bays to crown it?
No flowers, no garlands gay? All blasted?
      All wasted?
Not so, my heart! but there is fruit,
    And thou hast hands.
Recover all thy sigh-blown age
On double pleasures. Leave thy cold dispute
Of what is fit and not. Forsake thy cage,
    Thy rope of sands,
Which petty thoughts have made, and made to thee
    Good cable, to enforce and draw,
      And be thy law,

While thou didst wink and wouldst not see.
    Away! Take heed!
    I will abroad.
Call in thy death's head there! Tie up thy fears!
    He that forbears
        To suit and serve his need
        Deserves his load."
But as I raved, and grew more fierce and wild
    At every word,
    Methought I heard One calling, "Child,"
        And I replied, "My Lord."

GEORGE HERBERT

Best of all I like the first two lines of the last stanza.

SAY NOT THE STRUGGLE NOUGHT AVAILETH

SAY not the struggle nought availeth,
    The labour and the wounds are vain,
The enemy faints not, nor faileth,
    And as things have been they remain.

If hopes were dupes, fears may be liars;
    It may be, in yon smoke concealed,
Your comrades chase e'en now the fliers,
    And, but for you, possess the field.

For while the tired waves, vainly breaking,
    Seem here no painful inch to gain,
Far back, through creeks and inlets making,
    Comes silent, flooding in, the main.

And not by eastern windows only,
When daylight comes, comes in the light,
In front, the sun climbs slow, how slowly,
But westward, look, the land is bright.

ARTHUR HUGH CLOUGH

=====

LOVE AMONG THE RUINS

WHERE the quiet-coloured end of evening smiles
Miles and miles
On the solitary pastures where our sheep
Half-asleep
Tinkle homeward through the twilight, stray or stop
As they crop—
Was the site once of a city great and gay,
(So they say)
Of our country's very capital, its prince
Ages since
Held his court in, gathered councils, wielding far
Peace or war.

Now,—the country does not even boast a tree,
As you see,
To distinguish slopes of verdure, certain rills
From the hills
Intersect and give a name to, (else they run
Into one)
Where the domed and daring palace shot its spires
Up like fires
O'er the hundred-gated circuit of a wall
Bounding all,
Made of marble, men might march on nor be pressed,
Twelve abreast.

[70]

And such plenty and perfection, see, of grass
        Never was!
Such a carpet as, this summer-time, o'erspreads
        And embeds
Every vestige of the city, guessed alone,
        Stock or stone—
Where a multitude of men breathed joy and woe
        Long ago;
Lust of glory pricked their hearts up, dread of shame
        Struck them tame;
And that glory and that shame alike, the gold
        Bought and sold.

Now,—the single little turret that remains
        On the plains,
By the caper overrooted, by the gourd
        Overscored,
While the patching houseleek's head of blossom winks
        Through the chinks—
Marks the basement whence a tower in ancient time
        Sprang sublime,
And a burning ring, all round, the chariots traced
        As they raced,
And the monarch and his minions and his dames
        Viewed the games.

And I know, while thus the quiet-coloured eve
        Smiles to leave
To their folding, all our many-tinkling fleece
        In such peace,
And the slopes and rills in undistinguished grey
        Melt away—
That a girl with eager eyes and yellow hair
        Waits me there

In the turret whence the charioteers caught soul
      For the goal,
When the king looked, where she looks now, breathless, dumb
      Till I come.

But he looked upon the city, every side,
      Far and wide,
All the mountains topped with temples, all the glades'
      Colonnades,
All the causeys, bridges, aqueducts,—and then,
      All the men!
When I do come, she will speak not, she will stand,
      Either hand
On my shoulder, give her eyes the first embrace
      Of my face,
Ere we rush, ere we extinguish sight and speech
      Each on each.

In one year they sent a million fighters forth
      South and North,
And they built their gods a brazen pillar high
      As the sky,
Yet reserved a thousand chariots in full force—
      Gold, of course.
Oh heart! oh blood that freezes, blood that burns!
      Earth's returns
For whole centuries of folly, noise and sin!
      Shut them in,
With their triumphs and their glories and the rest!
      Love is best.

ROBERT BROWNING

Keats, in the letter accompanying the manuscript of the poem he sent to his brother George, had some amusement in advance over the number of kisses, which he knew critics would pounce on. He wrote, "I was obliged to choose an even number that both eyes might have fair play. . . . Suppose I had said seven there would have been three and a half a piece."

LA BELLE DAME SANS MERCI

O WHAT can ail thee, knight-at-arms,
    Alone and palely loitering!
The sedge has wither'd from the lake,
    And no birds sing.

O what can ail thee, knight-at-arms!
    So haggard and so woe-begone?
The squirrel's granary is full,
    And the harvest's done.

I see a lily on thy brow
    With anguish moist and fever dew,
And on thy cheeks a fading rose
    Fast withereth too.

I met a lady in the meads,
    Full beautiful—a faery's child,
Her hair was long, her foot was light,
    And her eyes were wild.

I made a garland for her head,
    And bracelets too, and fragrant zone;
She look'd at me as she did love,
    And made sweet moan.

I set her on my pacing steed,
  And nothing else saw all day long.
For sidelong would she bend, and sing
  A faery's song.

She found me roots of relish sweet,
  And honey wild, and manna dew,
And sure in language strange she said—
  "I love thee true."

She took me to her elfin grot,
  And there she wept, and sigh'd full sore,
And there I shut her wild wild eyes
  With kisses four.

And there she lulled me asleep,
  And there I dream'd—Ah! woe betide!
The latest dream I ever dream'd
  On the cold hill's side.

I saw pale kings and princes too,
  Pale warriors, death-pale were they all;
They cried—"La Belle Dame sans Merci
  Hath thee in thrall!"

I saw their starv'd lips in the gloam,
  With horrid warning gaped wide,
And I awoke and found me here,
  On the cold hill's side.

And this is why I sojourn here,
  Alone and palely loitering,
Though the sedge is wither'd from the lake
  And no birds sing.

JOHN KEATS

Wordsworth wrote the five *Lucy Poems* while trav
in Germany in 1799. They illustrate his theory that th
language of poetry should be that of simple, ordinary life;
only a very great poet could have successfully illustrated
such a theory, and he only occasionally.

LUCY POEMS

STRANGE FITS OF PASSION HAVE I KNOWN

STRANGE fits of passion have I known:
And I will dare to tell,
But in the Lover's ear alone,
What once to me befell.

When she I loved looked every day
Fresh as a rose in June,
I to her cottage bent my way,
Beneath an evening-moon.

Upon the moon I fixed my eye,
All over the wide lea;
With quickening pace my horse drew nigh
Those paths so dear to me.

And now we reached the orchard-plot;
And, as we climbed the hill,
The sinking moon to Lucy's cot
Came near, and nearer still.

In one of those sweet dreams I slept,
Kind Nature's gentlest boon!
And all the while my eyes I kept
On the descending moon.

My horse moved on; hoof after hoof
He raised, and never stopped:
When down behind the cottage roof,
At once, the bright moon dropped.

What fond and wayward thoughts will slide
Into a Lover's head!
"O mercy!" to myself I cried,
"If Lucy should be dead!"

SHE DWELT AMONG THE UNTRODDEN WAYS

SHE dwelt among the untrodden ways
   Beside the springs of Dove,
A Maid whom there were none to praise
   And very few to love.

A violet by a mossy stone
   Half hidden from the eye!
—Fair as a star, when only one
   Is shining in the sky.

She lived unknown, and few could know
   When Lucy ceased to be;
But she is in her grave, and, oh,
   The difference to me!

I TRAVELLED AMONG UNKNOWN MEN

I TRAVELLED among unknown men,
   In lands beyond the sea;
Nor, England! did I know till then
   What love I bore to thee.

'Tis past, that melancholy dream!
　　Nor will I quit thy shore
A second time; for still I seem
　　To love thee more and more.

Among thy mountains did I feel
　　The joy of my desire;
And she I cherished turned her wheel
　　Beside an English fire.

Thy mornings showed, thy nights concealed
The bowers where Lucy played;
And thine too is the last green field
　　That Lucy's eyes surveyed.

Three Years She Grew

THREE years she grew in sun and shower;
Then Nature said, "A lovelier flower
On earth was never sown;
This Child I to myself will take;
She shall be mine, and I will make
A Lady of my own.

"Myself will to my darling be
Both law and impulse: and with me
The Girl, in rock and plain,
In earth and heaven, in glade and bower,
Shall feel an overseeing power
To kindle or restrain.

"She shall be sportive as the fawn
That wild with glee across the lawn

Or up the mountain springs;
And hers shall be the breathing balm,
And hers the silence and the calm
Of mute insensate things.

"The floating clouds their state shall lend
To her; for her the willow bend;
Nor shall she fail to see
Even in the motions of the Storm
Grace that shall mould the Maiden's form
By silent sympathy.

"The stars of midnight shall be dear
To her; and she shall lean her ear
In many a secret place
Where rivulets dance their wayward round,
And beauty born of murmuring sound
Shall pass into her face.

"And vital feelings of delight
Shall rear her form to stately height,
Her virgin bosom swell;
Such thoughts to Lucy I will give
While she and I together live
Here in this happy dell."

Thus Nature spake—The work was done—
How soon my Lucy's race was run!
She died, and left to me
This heath, this calm, and quiet scene;
The memory of what has been,
And never more will be.

A Slumber Did My Spirit Seal

A SLUMBER did my spirit seal;
  I had no human fears:
She seemed a thing that could not feel
  The touch of earthly years.

No motion has she now, no force;
  She neither hears nor sees;
Rolled round in earth's diurnal course,
  With rocks, and stones, and trees.

WILLIAM WORDSWORTH

===

Addison wrote two hymns which are in all well-arranged hymn books; this one, and *When all thy mercies*. This splendid astronomical hymn is regularly sung to the music by Haydn—a good combination of eighteenth-century genius.

The Spacious Firmament

THE spacious firmament on high,
With all the blue ethereal sky,
And spangled heavens, a shining frame,
Their great Original proclaim.
Th' unwearied sun from day to day
Does his Creator's power display;
And publishes to every land
The work of an almighty hand.

[79]

Soon as the evening shades prevail,
The moon takes up the wondrous tale;
And nightly to the listening earth
Repeats the story of her birth;
Whilst all the stars that round her burn,
And all the planets in their turn,
Confirm the tidings as they roll,
And spread the truth from pole to pole.

What though in solemn silence all
Move round the dark terrestrial ball;
What though no real voice nor sound
Amidst their radiant orbs be found?
In reason's ear they all rejoice,
And utter forth a glorious voice:
Forever singing as they shine,
"The hand that made us is divine."

JOSEPH ADDISON

Doctor Johnson was as sententious in verse as he was in prose; only his verse, owing perhaps to space-limitation, was more simple in style. The anfractuosities were forced into the strait-jacket.

PROLOGUE

SPOKEN BY MR. GARRICK AT THE OPENING OF THE
THEATRE-ROYAL, DRURY-LANE, 1747

WHEN Learning's triumph o'er her barbarous foes
First rear'd the stage, immortal Shakespeare rose;
Each change of many-colour'd life he drew,
Exhausted worlds, and then imagin'd new:
Existence saw him spurn her bounded reign,
And panting Time toil'd after him in vain.

[80]

His powerful strokes presiding truth impress'd,
And unresisted passion storm'd the breast.
    Then Jonson came, instructed from the school,
To please in method, and invent by rule;
His studious patience and laborious art,
By regular approach, essay'd the heart;
Cold approbation gave the lingering bays;
For those who durst not censure, scarce could praise.
A mortal born, he met the gen'ral doom,
But left, like Egypt's king, a lasting tomb.
    The wits of Charles found easier ways to fame,
Nor wish'd for Jonson's art, or Shakespeare's flame;
Themselves they studied; as they felt, they writ;
Intrigue was plot, obscenity was wit.
Vice always found a sympathetic friend;
They pleas'd their age, and did not aim to mend.
Yet bards like these aspir'd to lasting praise,
And proudly hop'd to pimp in future days.
Their cause was gen'ral, their supports were strong;
Their slaves were willing, and their reign was long:
Till shame regain'd the post that sense betray'd,
And virtue call'd oblivion to her aid.
    Then crush'd by rules, and waken'd as refin'd,
For years the pow'r of Tragedy declin'd;
From bard to bard the frigid caution crept,
Till declamation roar'd whilst passion slept;
Yet still did virtue deign the stage to tread;
Philosophy remain'd tho' nature fled.
But forc'd, at length, her ancient reign to quit,
She saw great Faustus lay the ghost of wit;
Exulting folly hail'd the joyous day,
And pantomime and song confirm'd her sway.
    But who the coming changes can presage,
And mark the future periods of the stage?
Perhaps if skill could distant times explore,

New Behns, new Durfeys, yet remain in store;
Perhaps where Lear has rav'd, and Hamlet died,
On flying cars new sorcerers may ride;
Perhaps (for who can guess th' effects of chance)
Here Hunt may box, or Mahomet may dance.
    Hard is his lot that here by fortune plac'd,
Must watch the wild vicissitudes of taste;
With every meteor of caprice must play,
And chase the new-blown bubbles of the day.
Ah! let not censure term our fate our choice,
The stage but echoes back the public voice;
The drama's laws, the drama's patrons give,
For we that live to please, must please to live.
    Then prompt no more the follies you decry,
As tyrants doom their tools of guilt to die.
'Tis yours, this night, to bid the reign commence
Of rescu'd nature and reviving sense;
To chase the charms of sound, the pomp of show,
For useful mirth and salutary woe;
Bid scenic virtue form the rising age,
And truth diffuse her radiance from the stage.

SAMUEL JOHNSON

In addition to his graceful and affectionate poems about
birds and flowers, Herrick was a great love-poet, showing
passion with reverential delicacy.

The Night Piece, to Julia

HER eyes the glowworm lend thee;
The shooting stars attend thee;
    And the elves also,
    Whose little eyes grow
Like the sparks of fire, befriend thee.

No will-o'-the-wisp mislight thee;
Nor snake or slowworm bite thee;
 But on, on thy way,
 Not making a stay,
Since ghost there's none to affright thee.

Let not the dark thee cumber;
What though the moon does slumber?
 The stars of the night
 Will lend thee their light,
Like tapers clear without number.

Then, Julia, let me woo thee,
Thus, thus to come unto me;
 And when I shall meet
 Thy silvery feet,
My soul I'll pour into thee.
     ROBERT HERRICK

Upon Julia's Clothes

Whenas in silks my Julia goes,
Then, then, methinks, how sweetly flows
The liquefaction of her clothes.

Next, when I cast mine eyes, and see
That brave vibration, each way free,
O, how that glittering taketh me!
     ROBERT HERRICK

From 1832 to 1892 Tennyson was writing about the Knights of the Round Table. The Lady of Shalott in the later version became the lily maid of Astolat. But I like this gorgeous tapestry better than the long, detailed narrative; and although purposely remote, it deals with a situation common enough today, and asks a question no one can answer.

THE LADY OF SHALOTT

PART I

ON either side the river lie
Long fields of barley and of rye,
That clothe the world and meet the sky;
And thro' the field the road runs by
    To many-tower'd Camelot;
And up and down the people go,
Gazing where the lilies blow
Round an island there below,
    The island of Shalott.

Willows whiten, aspens quiver,
Little breezes dusk and shiver
Thro' the wave that runs forever
By the island in the river
    Flowing down to Camelot.
Four gray walls, and four gray towers,
Overlook a space of flowers,
And the silent isle imbowers
    The Lady of Shalott.

By the margin, willow-veil'd,
Slide the heavy barges trail'd
By slow horses; and unhail'd

The shallop flitteth silken-sail'd
    Skimming down to Camelot:
But who hath seen her wave her hand?
Or at the casement seen her stand?
Or is she known in all the land,
    The Lady of Shalott?

Only reapers, reaping early
In among the bearded barley,
Hear a song that echoes cheerly
From the river winding clearly,
    Down to tower'd Camelot:
And by moon the reaper weary,
Piling sheaves in uplands airy,
Listening, whispers, " 'Tis the fairy
    Lady of Shalott."

PART II

There she weaves by night and day
A magic web with colours gay.
She has heard a whisper say,
A curse is on her if she stay
    To look down to Camelot.
She knows not what the curse may be,
And so she weaveth steadily,
And little other care hath she,
    The Lady of Shalott.

And moving thro' a mirror clear
That hangs before her all the year,
Shadows of the world appear.
There she sees the highway near
    Winding down to Camelot:
There the river eddy whirls,

And there the surly village-churls,
And the red cloaks of market girls,
    Pass onward from Shalott.

Sometimes a troop of damsels glad,
An abbot on an ambling pad,
Sometimes a curly shepherd-lad,
Or long-hair'd page in crimson clad,
    Goes by to tower'd Camelot;
And sometimes thro' the mirror blue
The knights come riding two and two:
She hath no loyal knight and true,
    The Lady of Shalott.

But in her web she still delights
To weave the mirror's magic sights,
For often thro' the silent nights
A funeral, with plumes and lights
    And music, went to Camelot:
Or when the moon was overhead,
Came two young lovers lately wed;
"I am half sick of shadows," said
    The Lady of Shalott.

PART III

A bow-shot from her bower-eaves,
He rode between the barley-sheaves,
The sun came dazzling thro' the leaves,
And flamed upon the brazen greaves
    Of bold Sir Lancelot.
A red-cross knight for ever kneel'd
To a lady in his shield,
That sparkled on the yellow field,
    Beside remote Shalott.

The gemmy bridle glitter'd free,
Like to some branch of stars we see
Hung in the golden Galaxy.
The bridle bells rang merrily
    As he rode down to Camelot:
And from his blazon'd baldric slung
A mighty silver bugle hung,
And as he rode his armour rung,
    Beside remote Shalott.

All in the blue unclouded weather
Thick-jewell'd shone the saddle-leather,
The helmet and the helmet-feather
Burn'd like one burning flame together,
    As he rode down to Camelot.
As often thro' the purple night,
Below the starry clusters bright,
Some bearded meteor, trailing light,
    Moves over still Shalott.

His broad clear brow in sunlight glow'd;
On burnish'd hooves his war-horse trode;
From underneath his helmet flow'd
His coal-black curls as on he rode,
    As he rode down to Camelot.
From the bank and from the river
He flash'd into the crystal mirror,
"Tirra lirra," by the river
    Sang Sir Lancelot.

She left the web, she left the loom,
She made three paces thro' the room,
She saw the water-lily bloom,
She saw the helmet and the plume,

She look'd down to Camelot.
Out flew the web and floated wide;
The mirror crack'd from side to side;
"The curse is come upon me," cried
    The Lady of Shalott.

PART IV

In the stormy east-wind straining,
The pale yellow woods were waning,
The broad stream in his banks complaining,
Heavily the low sky raining
    Over tower'd Camelot;
Down she came and found a boat
Beneath a willow left afloat,
And round about the prow she wrote
    The Lady of Shalott.

And down the river's dim expanse
Like some bold seër in a trance,
Seeing all his own mischance—
With a glassy countenance
    Did she look to Camelot.
And at the closing of the day
She loosed the chain, and down she lay;
The broad stream bore her far away,
    The Lady of Shalott.

Lying, robed in snowy white,
That loosely flew to left and right—
The leaves upon her falling light—
Thro' the noises of the night
    She floated down to Camelot:
And as the boat-head wound along

The willowy hills and fields among,
They heard her singing her last song,
    The Lady of Shalott.

Heard a carol, mournful, holy,
Chanted loudly, chanted lowly,
Till her blood was frozen slowly,
And her eyes were darken'd wholly,
    Turn'd to tower'd Camelot.
For ere she reach'd upon the tide
The first house by the water-side,
Singing in her song she died,
    The Lady of Shalott.

Under tower and balcony,
By garden-wall and gallery,
A gleaming shape she floated by,
Dead-pale between the houses high,
    Silent into Camelot.
Out upon the wharfs they came,
Knight and burgher, lord and dame,
And round the prow they read her name,
    The Lady of Shalott.

Who is this? and what is here?
And in the lighted palace near
Died the sound of royal cheer;
And they cross'd themselves for fear,
    All the knights at Camelot:
But Lancelot mused a little space;
He said, "She has a lovely face;
God in his mercy lend her grace,
    The Lady of Shalott."

                    ALFRED TENNYSON

Henry Vaughan wrote two great poems; this is the other one; seldom has nostalgia for childhood been more poignantly expressed. Its relation to a greater poem on the same theme must be settled for himself by the individual reader.

THE RETREAT

HAPPY those early days, when I
Shined in my angel-infancy!
Before I understood this place
Appointed for my second race,
Or taught my soul to fancy aught
But a white, celestial thought;
When yet I had not walked above
A mile or two from my first love,
And looking back, at that short space,
Could see a glimpse of His bright face;
When on some gilded cloud or flower
My gazing soul would dwell an hour,
And in those weaker glories spy
Some shadows of eternity;
Before I taught my tongue to wound
My conscience with a sinful sound,
Or had the black art to dispense
A several sin to every sense,
But felt through all this fleshly dress
Bright shoots of everlastingness.
　O how I long to travel back
And tread again that ancient track!
That I might once more reach that plain
Where first I left my glorious train;
From whence the enlightened spirit sees
That shady city of palm trees,
But ah, my soul with too much stay

Is drunk, and staggers in the way!
Some men a forward motion love,
But I by backward steps would move,
And, when this dust falls to the urn,
In that state I came, return.

HENRY VAUGHAN

Between the writing of the first four stanzas of the Ode and the remaining part, two years elapsed. There is no doubt that the poem was partly inspired by Vaughan; though I believe Wordsworth never said so. In his library was a well-thumbed copy of Vaughan. I cannot agree with Matthew Arnold's slightly disparaging remark that Wordsworth's Ode is declamatory. Its sublimity is verifiable in human experience. Every thoughtful person has had the visions that Wordsworth speaks of "in a season of calm weather."

ODE ON INTIMATIONS OF IMMORTALITY FROM RECOLLECTIONS OF EARLY CHILDHOOD

THERE was a time when meadow, grove, and stream,
The earth, and every common sight,
        To me did seem
        Apparelled in celestial light,
The glory and the freshness of a dream.
It is not now as it hath been of yore;—
        Turn whereso'er I may,
        By night or day,
The things which I have seen I now can see no more.

        The Rainbow comes and goes,
        And lovely is the Rose,

[91]

The Moon doth with delight
Look round her when the heavens are bare;
Waters on a starry night
Are beautiful and fair;
The sunshine is a glorious birth;
But yet I know, where'er I go,
That there hath past away a glory from the earth.

Now, while the birds thus sing a joyous song,
And while the young lambs bound
As to the tabor's sound,
To me alone there came a thought of grief;
A timely utterance gave that thought relief,
And I again am strong:
The cataracts blow their trumpets from the steep;
No more shall grief of mine the season wrong;
I hear the Echoes through the mountains throng,
The Winds come to me from the fields of sleep,
And all the earth is gay;
Land and sea
Give themselves up to jollity,
And with the heart of May
Doth every Beast keep holiday;—
Thou Child of Joy,
Shout round me, let me hear thy shouts,
Thou happy Shepherd-boy!

Ye blessèd Creatures, I have heard the call
Ye to each other make; I see
The heavens laugh with you in your jubilee;
My heart is at your festival,
My head hath its coronal,
The fulness of your bliss, I feel—I feel it all.
O evil day! if I were sullen

While Earth herself is adorning,
    This sweet May-morning,
And the Children are culling
    On every side,
In a thousand valleys far and wide,
Fresh flowers; while the sun shines warm,
And the Babe leaps up on his Mother's arm:—
    I hear, I hear, with joy I hear!
    —But there's a Tree, of many, one,
A single Field which I have looked upon,
Both of them speak of something that is gone:
    The Pansy at my feet
    Doth the same tale repeat:
Whither is fled the visionary gleam?
Where is it now, the glory and the dream?

Our birth is but a sleep and a forgetting:
The Soul that rises with us, our life's Star,
    Hath had elsewhere its setting,
        And cometh from afar:
    Not in entire forgetfulness,
    And not in utter nakedness,
But trailing clouds of glory do we come
    From God, who is our home:
Heaven lies about us in our infancy!
Shades of the prison-house begin to close
    Upon the growing Boy,
But he beholds the light, and whence it flows,
    He sees it in his joy;
The Youth, who daily farther from the east
    Must travel, still is Nature's Priest,
    And by the vision splendid
    Is on his way attended;
At length the Man perceives it die away,
And fade into the light of common day.

Earth fills her lap with pleasures of her own;
Yearnings she hath in her own natural kind,
And, even with something of a Mother's mind,
    And no unworthy aim,
    The homely Nurse doth all she can
To make her Foster-child, her Inmate Man,
    Forget the glories he hath known,
And that imperial palace whence he came.

Behold the Child among his new-born blisses,
A six years' Darling of a pigmy size!
See, where 'mid work of his own hand he lies,
Fretted by sallies of his mother's kisses,
With light upon him from his father's eyes!
See, at his feet, some little plan or chart,
Some fragment from his dream of human life,
Shaped by himself with newly-learnèd art;
    A wedding or a festival,
    A mourning or a funeral;
    And this hath now his heart,
    And unto this he frames his song:
    Then will he fit his tongue
To dialogues of business, love, or strife;
    But it will not be long
    Ere this be thrown aside,
    And with new joy and pride
The little Actor cons another part;
Filling from time to time his "humorous stage"
With all the Persons, down to palsied Age,
That Life brings with her in her equipage;
    As if his whole vocation
    Were endless imitation.

Thou, whose exterior semblance doth belie
    Thy Soul's immensity;

Thou best Philosopher, who yet dost keep
Thy heritage, thou Eye among the blind,
That, deaf and silent, read'st the eternal deep,
Haunted for ever by the eternal mind,—
    Mighty Prophet! Seer blest!
On whom those truths do rest,
Which we are toiling all our lives to find,
In darkness lost, the darkness of the grave;
Thou, over whom thy Immortality
Broods like the Day, a Master o'er a Slave,
A Presence which is not to be put by;
Thou little Child, yet glorious in the might
Of heaven-born freedom on thy being's height,
Why with such earnest pains dost thou provoke
The years to bring the inevitable yoke,
Thus blindly with thy blessedness at strife?
Full soon thy Soul shall have her earthly freight,
And custom lie upon thee like a weight,
Heavy as frost, and deep almost as life!

    O joy! that in our embers
    Is something that doth live,
    That nature yet remembers
    What was so fugitive!
The thought of our past years in me doth breed
Perpetual benediction: not indeed
For that which is most worthy to be blest—
Delight and liberty, the simple creed
Of Childhood, whether busy or at rest,
With new-fledged hope still fluttering in his breast:—
    Not for these I raise
    The song of thanks and praise;
    But for those obstinate questionings
    Of sense and outward things,
    Fallings from us, vanishings;

Blank misgivings of a Creature
Moving about in worlds not realised,
High instincts before which our mortal Nature
Did tremble like a guilty Thing surprised:
    But for those first affections,
        Those shadowy recollections,
  Which, be they what they may,
Are yet the fountain light of all our day,
Are yet a master light of all our seeing;
  Uphold us, cherish, and have power to make
Our noisy years seem moments in the being
Of the eternal Silence: truths that wake,
    To perish never;
Which neither listlessness, nor mad endeavour,
    Nor Man nor Boy,
Nor all that is at enmity with joy,
Can utterly abolish or destroy!
    Hence in a season of calm weather
    Though inland far we be,
Our Souls have sight of that immortal sea
    Which brought us hither,
    Can in a moment travel thither,
And see the Children sport upon the shore,
And hear the mighty waters rolling evermore.

Then sing, ye Birds, sing, sing a joyous song!
    And let the young Lambs bound
    As to the tabor's sound!
We in thought will join your throng,
    Ye that pipe, ye that play,
    Ye that through your hearts today
    Feel the gladness of the May!
What though the radiance which was once so bright
Be now forever taken from my sight,
    Though nothing can bring back the hour

Of splendour in the grass, of glory in the flower;
    We will grieve not, rather find
    Strength in what remains behind;
    In the primal sympathy
    Which having been must ever be;
    In the soothing thoughts that spring
    Out of human suffering;
    In the faith that looks through death,
In years that bring the philosophic mind.

And O ye Fountains, Meadows, Hills, and Groves,
Forebode not any severing of our loves!
Yet in my heart of hearts I feel your might;
I only have relinquished one delight
To live beneath your more habitual sway.
I love the Brooks which down their channels fret,
Even more than when I tripped lightly as they;
The innocent brightness of a new-born Day
        Is lovely yet;
The Clouds that gather round the setting sun
Do take a sober colouring from an eye
That hath kept watch o'er man's mortality;
Another race hath been, and other palms are won.
Thanks to the human heart by which we live,
Thanks to its tenderness, its joys, and fears,
To me the meanest flower that blows can give
Thoughts that do often lie too deep for tears.

                  WILLIAM WORDSWORTH

———

The famous Elizabethan, Michael Drayton, made a vast
poem out of the geography of England, called *Polyolbion;*
he also wrote a magnificent battle-poem on Agincourt, beginning *Fair stood the wind for France,* the metre of

which Tennyson used two centuries later for *The Charge of the Light Brigade*. But best of all his works I like this Sonnet—I like it for its intimacy, its intense feeling, its simple and sincere language.

Since There's No Help

Since there's no help, come, let us kiss and part!
Nay, I have done; you get no more of me!
And I am glad, yea, glad, with all my heart,
That thus so cleanly I myself can free.
Shake hands for ever, cancel all our vows,
And when we meet at any time again,
Be it not seen in either of our brows,
That we one jot of former love retain!
Now at the last gasp of Love's latest breath,
When, his pulse failing, Passion speechless lies;
When Faith is kneeling by his bed of death,
And Innocence is closing up his eyes,—
Now, if thou wouldst, when all have given him over,
From death to life thou might'st him yet recover!

MICHAEL DRAYTON

This has the spontaneous charm of Elizabethan song.

There Is a Garden in Her Face

There is a garden in her face,
Where roses and white lilies grow;
A heavenly paradise is that place,
Wherein all pleasant fruits do flow.
There cherries grow, which none may buy
Till 'Cherry ripe' themselves do cry.

[98]

Those cherries fairly do enclose
Of orient pearl a double row;
Which when her lovely laughter shows,
They look like rosebuds filled with snow.
Yet them nor peer nor prince can buy
Till 'Cherry ripe' themselves do cry.

Her eyes like angels watch them still;
Her brows like bended bows do stand,
Threatening with piercing frowns to kill
All that attempt with eye or hand
Those sacred cherries to come nigh,
Till 'Cherry ripe' themselves do cry.

THOMAS CAMPION

Burns is the most passionate poet, the greatest song-
writer, the most ardent democrat in the history of Scotland.
He could make any theme musical, and his music seemed to
be as spontaneous as an Aeolian harp. His mind seemed
to be an instrument by which thought and feeling were
transmuted into melody.

My Luve Is Like a Red, Red Rose

O, my luve is like a red, red rose,
    That's newly sprung in June.
O, my luve is like the melodie
    That's sweetly play'd in tune.
As fair art thou, my bonie lass,
    So deep in luve am I,
And I will luve thee still, my dear,
    Till a' the seas gang dry.

Till a' the seas gang dry, my dear,
And the rocks melt wi' the sun!
I will luve thee still, my dear,
While the sands o' life shall run.

And fare thee weel, my only luve,
And fare thee weel awhile!
And I will come again, my luve,
Tho' it were ten thousand mile.

ROBERT BURNS

O, Wert Thou in the Cauld Blast

O, WERT thou in the cauld blast,
On yonder lea, on yonder lea,
My plaidie to the angry airt,
I'd shelter thee, I'd shelter thee;
Or did misfortune's bitter storms
Around thee blaw, around thee blaw,
Thy bield should be my bosom,
To share it a', to share it a'.

Or were I in the wildest waste,
Sae black and bare, sae black and bare,
The desert were a paradise
If thou wert there, if thou wert there!
Or were I monarch of the globe,
Wi' thee to reign, wi' thee to reign,
The brightest jewel in my crown
Wad be my queen, wad be my queen.

ROBERT BURNS

Auld Lang Syne

Should auld acquaintance be forgot,
  And never brought to min'?
Should auld acquaintance be forgot,
  And auld lang syne?

    Cho.—For auld lang syne, my dear,
        For auld lang syne,
          We'll tak a cup o' kindness yet
          For auld lang syne

And surely ye'll be your pint-stowp,
  And surely I'll be mine!
And we'll tak a cup o' kindness yet
  For auld lang syne.

We twa hae run about the braes,
  And pu'd the gowans fine;
But we've wandered monie a weary fit
  Sin' auld lang syne.

We twa hae paidled i' the burn,
  From mornin' sun till dine;
But seas between us braid hae roared
  Sin' auld lang syne.

And there's a hand, my trusty fiere,
  And gie's a hand o' thine;
And we'll tak a right guid-willie waught
  For auld lang syne.
                              ROBERT BURNS

[101]

HIGHLAND MARY

YE banks, and braes, and streams around
    The castle o' Mongomery,
Green be your woods and fair your flowers,
    Your waters never drumlie!
There simmer first unfald her robes,
    And there the langest tarry;
For there I took the last fareweel,
    O' my sweet Highland Mary.

How sweetly bloomed the gay green birk,
    How rich the hawthorn's blossom,
As underneath their fragrant shade
    I clasped her to my bosom!
The golden hours on angel wings
    Flew o'er me and my dearie;
For dear to me as light and life,
    Was my sweet Highland Mary.

Wi' monie a vow and locked embrace
    Our parting was fu' tender;
And, pledging aft to meet again,
    We tore oursels asunder;
But O! fell death's untimely frost,
    That nipt my flower sae early!
Now green's the sod, and cauld's the clay
    That wraps my Highland Mary!

O pale, pale now, those rosy lips,
    I aft hae kissed sae fondly!
And closed for ay the sparkling glance,
    That dwalt on me sae kindly!
And mouldering now in silent dust,

That heart that lo'ed me dearly!
But still within my bosom's core
Shall live my Highland Mary.

ROBERT BURNS

My Heart's in the Highlands

My heart's in the Highlands, my heart is not here,
My heart's in the Highlands a-chasing the deer,
A-chasing the wild deer and following the roe—
My heart's in the Highlands, wherever I go!

Farewell to the Highlands, farewell to the North,
The birthplace of valour, the country of worth!
Wherever I wander, wherever I rove,
The hills of the Highlands for ever I love.

Farewell to the mountains high covered with snow,
Farewell to the straths and green valleys below,
Farewell to the forests and wild-hanging woods,
Farewell to the torrents and loud pouring floods!

My heart's in the Highlands, my heart is not here,
My heart's in the Highlands a-chasing the deer,
A-chasing the wild deer and following the roe—
My heart's in the Highlands, wherever I go!

ROBERT BURNS

To Mary in Heaven

Thou ling'ring star, with less'ning ray,
    That lov'st to greet the early morn,
Again thou usher'st in the day
    My Mary from my soul was torn.

[103]

O Mary! dear departed shade!
   Where is thy place of blissful rest?
See'st thou thy lover lowly laid?
   Hear'st thou the groans that rend his breast?

That sacred hour can I forget,
   Can I forget the hallowed grove,
Where by the winding Ayr we met
   To live one day of parting love?
Eternity will not efface
   Those records dear of transports past,
Thy image at our last embrace—
   Ah! little thought we 't was our last!

Ayr, gurgling, kiss'd his pebbl'd shore,
   O'erhung with wild woods, thick'ning green;
The fragrant birch and hawthorn hoar
   Twin'd amorous round the raptur'd scene:
The flow'rs sprang wanton to be prest,
   The birds sang love on every spray,
Till too, too soon the glowing west
   Proclaim'd the speed of winged day.

Still o'er these scenes my mem'ry wakes,
   And fondly broods with miser care!
Time but th' impression stronger makes
   As streams their channels deeper wear.
My Mary, dear departed shade!
   Where is thy place of blissful rest?
See'st thou thy lover lowly laid?
   Hear'st thou the groans that rend his breast?

ROBERT BURNS

LINES

Written on the window of the Globe tavern, Dumfries

THE graybeard, Old Wisdom, may boast of his treasures,
  Give me with gay Folly to live:
I grant him his calm-blooded, time-settled pleasures,
  But Folly has raptures to give.

ROBERT BURNS

When Edward King, a Cambridge student, was drowned
during the Long Vacation of 1637, some of his friends got
together and printed a little collection of verses in his honour
which is now one of the rarest of English books. Most of
these poems are without value; but the last one in the collection is *Lycidas*. It was characteristic of Milton to do his
best.

Edith Wharton, in her autobiography called *A Backward
Glance* (1934), says that when she was fifteen or sixteen,
she tried to write as essay on English verse rhythms, which
began: "No one who cannot feel the enchantment of

'Yet once more, O ye laurels, and once more,'

without knowing even the next line, or having any idea whatever of the context of the poem, has begun to understand the
beauty of English poetry."

Years ago in the short-lived British periodical *Literature*,
I read a dialogue supposed to take place in the Elysian fields
between Edward King and Arthur Henry Hallam. They
congratulated themselves on the fact, that although they had

both died too young to make any name for themselves on earth, each had had the good fortune to have a great poet as a friend, who had given him immortality. And then followed a keen debate as to the respective merits of *In Memoriam* and *Lycidas*. It is of course difficult to compare them; *In Memoriam* has a much wider range and touches humanity at more points; but the austere beauty of *Lycidas* reaches a height quite beyond the powers of Tennyson. One poem might be called horizontal; the other, vertical.

The last line of *Lycidas* is usually misquoted.

LYCIDAS

YET once more, O ye laurels, and once more,
Ye myrtles brown, with ivy never sere,
I come to pluck your berries harsh and crude,
And with forced fingers rude
Shatter your leaves before the mellowing year.
Bitter constraint, and sad occasion dear,
Compels me to disturb your season due;
For Lycidas is dead, dead ere his prime,
Young Lycidas, and hath not left his peer.
Who would not sing for Lycidas? he knew
Himself to sing, and build the lofty rhyme.
He must not float upon his watery bier
Unwept, and welter to the parching wind,
Without the meed of some melodious tear.
Begin, then, Sisters of the sacred well
That from beneath the seat of Jove doth spring;
Begin, and somewhat loudly sweep the string;
Hence with denial vain and coy excuse:
So may some gentle Muse
With lucky words favour my destined urn,
And, as he passes, turn
And bid fair peace be to my sable shroud!
For we were nursed upon the selfsame hill,

Fed the same flock, by fountain, shade, and rill;
Together both, ere the high lawns appeared
Under the opening eyelids of the morn,
We drove a-field, and both together heard
What time the grey-fly winds her sultry horn,
Battening our flocks with the fresh dews of night,
Oft till the star that rose at evening bright
Toward heaven's descent had sloped his westering
    wheel.
Meanwhile the rural ditties were not mute,
Tempered to the oaten flute:
Rough satyrs danced, and fauns with cloven heel
From the glad sound would not be absent long,
And old Damœtas loved to hear our song.

   But O the heavy change, now thou art gone,
Now thou art gone, and never must return!
Thee, shepherd, thee the woods and desert caves,
With wild thyme and the gadding vine o'ergrown,
And all their echoes, mourn.
The willows and the hazel copses green
Shall now no more be seen
Fanning their joyous leaves to thy soft lays.
As killing as the canker to the rose,
Or taint-worm to the weanling herds that graze,
Or frost to flowers that their gay wardrobe wear
When first the white-thorn blows,
Such, Lycidas, thy loss to shepherd's ear.

   Where were ye, nymphs, when the remorseless deep
Closed o'er the head of your loved Lycidas?
For neither were ye playing on the steep
Where your old bards, the famous druids, lie,
Nor on the shaggy top of Mona high,
Nor yet where Deva spreads her wizard stream.
Ay me, I fondly dream!
Had ye been there—for what could that have done?

What could the Muse herself that Orpheus bore,
The Muse herself, for her enchanting son,
Whom universal nature did lament,
When by the rout that made the hideous roar
His gory visage down the stream was sent,
Down the swift Hebrus to the Lesbian shore?
    Alas! what boots it with uncessant care
To tend the homely, slighted shepherd's trade,
And strictly meditate the thankless Muse?
Were it not better done, as others use,
To sport with Amaryllis in the shade,
Or with the tangles of Neæra's hair?
Fame is the spur that the clear spirit doth raise
(That last infirmity of noble mind)
To scorn delights and live laborious days;
But the fair guerdon when we hope to find,
And think to burst out into sudden blaze,
Comes the blind Fury with the abhorrèd shears
And slits the thin-spun life. "But not the praise,"
Phœbus replied, and touched my trembling ears:
"Fame is no plant that grows on mortal soil,
Nor in the glistering foil
Set off to the world, nor in broad rumour lies,
But lives and spreads aloft by those pure eyes
And perfect witness of all-judging Jove;
As He pronounces lastly on each deed,
Of so much fame in heaven expect thy meed."
    O fountain Arethuse, and thou honoured flood,
Smooth-sliding Mincius, crowned with vocal reeds,
That strain I heard was of a higher mood;
But now my oat proceeds,
And listens to the Herald of the Sea,
That came in Neptune's plea.
He asked the waves, and asked the felon winds,
"What hard mishap hath doomed this gentle swain?"

And questioned every gust of rugged wings
That blows from off each beakèd promontory.
They knew not of his story;
And sage Hippotades their answer brings,
That not a blast was from his dungeon strayed;
The air was calm, and on the level brine
Sleek Panope, with all her sisters, played.
It was that fatal and perfidious bark,
Built in the eclipse, and rigged with curses dark,
That sunk so low that sacred head of thine.

Next, Camus, reverend sire, went footing slow,
His mantle hairy and his bonnet sedge,
Inwrought with figures dim, and on the edge
Like to that sanguine flower inscribed with woe.
"Ah, who hath reft," quoth he, "my dearest pledge?"
Last came, and last did go,
The Pilot of the Galilean Lake;
Two massy keys he bore of metals twain
(The golden opes, the iron shuts amain).
He shook his mitred locks and stern bespake:
"How well could I have spared for thee, young swain,
Enow of such as, for their bellies' sake,
Creep, and intrude, and climb into the fold!
Of other care they little reckoning make
Than how to scramble at the shearers' feast,
And shove away the worthy bidden guest.
Blind mouths! that scarce themselves know how to
    hold
A sheep-hook, or have learnt aught else the least
That to the faithful herdsman's art belongs!
What recks it them? What need they? They are
    sped;
And when they list, their lean and flashy songs
Grate on their scrannel pipes of wretched straw:
The hungry sheep look up, and are not fed,

But, swoln with wind and the rank mist they draw,
Rot inwardly, and foul contagion spread;
Besides what the grim wolf with privy paw
Daily devours apace, and nothing said.
But that two-handed engine at the door
Stands ready to smite once, and smite no more."
　　Return, Alpheus, the dread voice is past
That shrunk thy streams; return, Sicilian Muse,
And call the vales, and bid them hither cast
Their bells and flowrets of a thousand hues.
Ye valleys low, where the mild whispers use
Of shades and wanton winds and gushing brooks,
On whose fresh lap the swart star sparely looks,
Throw hither all your quaint enamelled eyes,
That on the green turf suck the honeyed showers,
And purple all the ground with vernal flowers:
Bring the rathe primrose that forsaken dies,
The tufted crow-toe, and pale jessamine,
The white pink, and the pansy freaked with jet,
The glowing violet,
The musk-rose, and the well-attired woodbine,
With cowslips wan that hang the pensive head,
And every flower that sad embroidery wears;
Bid amaranthus all his beauty shed,
And daffodillies fill their cups with tears,
To strew the laureate hearse where Lycid lies.
For so, to interpose a little ease,
Let our frail thoughts dally with false surmise;
Ay me! whilst thee the shores and sounding seas
Wash far away, where'er thy bones are hurled:
Whether beyond the stormy Hebrides,
Where thou, perhaps, under the whelming tide
Visit'st the bottom of the monstrous world;
Or whether thou, to our moist vows denied,
Sleep'st by the fable of Bellerus old,

Where the great vision of the guarded mount
Looks toward Namancos and Bayona's hold.
Look homeward, angel, now, and melt with ruth;
And, O ye dolphins, waft the hapless youth.

Weep no more, woeful shepherds, weep no more;
For Lycidas, your sorrow, is not dead,
Sunk though he be beneath the watery floor.
So sinks the day-star in the ocean bed,
And yet anon repairs his drooping head,
And tricks his beams, and with new-spangled ore
Flames in the forehead of the morning sky:
So Lycidas sunk low, but mounted high,
Through the dear might of Him that walked the waves,
Where, other groves and other streams along,
With nectar pure his oozy locks he laves,
And hears the unexpressive nuptial song,
In the blest kingdoms meek of joy and love.
There entertain him all the saints above,
In solemn troops and sweet societies,
That sing, and singing in their glory move,
And wipe the tears forever from his eyes.
Now, Lycidas, the shepherds weep no more;
Henceforth thou art the genius of the shore,
In thy large recompense, and shalt be good
To all that wander in that perilous flood.

Thus sang the uncouth swain to the oaks and rills,
While the still morn went out with sandals grey;
He touched the tender stops of various quills,
With eager thought warbling his Doric lay.
And now the sun had stretched out all the hills,
And now was dropt into the western bay;
At last he rose and twitched his mantle blue:
Tomorrow to fresh woods and pastures new.

JOHN MILTON

The life of Walter Raleigh was a greater poem than anything he wrote in verse; but in the few lines quoted below, we feel that majesty of thought and expression that was natural in the age of great Elizabeth.

THE CONCLUSION

EVEN such is time, that takes in trust
   Our youth, our joys, our all we have,
And pays us but with earth and dust;
   Who, in the dark and silent grave,
When we have wandered all our ways,
Shuts up the story of our days;
   But from this earth, this grave, this dust,
My God shall raise me up, I trust!

SIR WALTER RALEIGH

The great and thundering speech of Tamburlaine is softened to the strains of love. He who blows through bronze may breathe through silver. No lyric of the Elizabethan age was more popular than this, as is shown by the numerous imitations and parodies. All the music of Elizabethan times is collected into one line: *Melodious birds sing madrigals.*

THE PASSIONATE SHEPHERD

COME live with me, and be my love;
And we will all the pleasures prove
That hills and valleys, dales and fields,
Woods, or steepy mountain yields.

And we will sit upon the rocks,
Seeing the shepherds feed their flocks
By shallow rivers, to whose falls
Melodious birds sing madrigals.

And I will make thee beds of roses,
And a thousand fragrant posies;
A cap of flowers, and a kirtle
Embroidered all with leaves of myrtle;

A gown made of the finest wool
Which from our pretty lambs we pull;
Fair-linèd slippers for the cold,
With buckles of the purest gold;

A belt of straw and ivy-buds,
With coral clasps and amber studs:
And, if these pleasures may thee move,
Come live with me, and be my love.

The shepherd-swains shall dance and sing
For thy delight each May-morning:
If these delights thy mind may move,
Then live with me, and be my love.

CHRISTOPHER MARLOWE

One of the greatest love-poems. The rejected lover blesses the name of the girl in pride and thankfulness: proud to love her without hope of union, thankful that he has met and known such a woman. No lover in life or in art was ever a greater gentleman.

The Last Ride Together

I SAID—Then, dearest, since 't is so,
Since now at length my fate I know,
Since nothing all my love avails,
Since all my life seemed meant for, fails,
    Since this was written and needs must be—
My whole heart rises up to bless
Your name in pride and thankfulness!
Take back the hope you gave,—I claim
Only a memory of the same,
—And this beside, if you will not blame,
    Your leave for one more last ride with me.

My mistress bent that brow of hers;
Those deep dark eyes where pride demurs
When pity would be softening through,
Fixed me a breathing-while or two
    With life or death in the balance: right!
The blood replenished me again;
My last thought was at least not vain:
I and my mistress, side by side
Shall be together, breathe and ride,
So, one day more am I deified.
    Who knows but the world may end tonight?

Hush! if you saw some western cloud
All billowy-bosomed, over-bowed
By many benedictions—sun's
And moon's and evening-star's at once—
    And so, you, looking and loving best,
Conscious grew, your passion drew
Cloud, sunset, moonrise, star-shine too,
Down on you, near and yet more near,
Till flesh must fade for heaven was here!—
Thus leant she and lingered—joy and fear!
    Thus lay she a moment on my breast.

Then we began to ride. My soul
Smoothed itself out, a long-cramped scroll
Freshening and fluttering in the wind.
Past hopes already lay behind.
    What need to strive with a life awry?
Had I said that, had I done this,
So might I gain, so might I miss.
Might she have loved me? just as well
She might have hated, who can tell!
Where had I been now if the worst befell?
    And here we are riding, she and I.

Fail I alone, in words and deeds?
Why, all men strive, and who succeeds?
We rode; it seemed my spirit flew,
Saw other regions, cities new,
    As the world rushed by on either side.
I thought,—All labour, yet no less
Bear up beneath their unsuccess.
Look at the end of work, contrast
The petty done, the undone vast,
This present of theirs with the hopeful past!
    I hoped she would love me; here we ride.

What hand and brain went ever paired?
What heart alike conceived and dared?
What act proved all its thought had been?
What will but felt the fleshly screen?
   We ride and I see her bosom heave.
There's many a crown for who can reach.
Ten lines, a statesman's life in each!
The flag stuck on a heap of bones,
A soldier's doing! what atones?
They scratch his name on the Abbey-stones.
   My riding is better, by their leave.

What does it all mean, poet? Well,
Your brains beat into rhythm, you tell
What we felt only; you expressed
You hold things beautiful the best,
   And place them in rhyme so, side by side.
'T is something, nay 't is much: but then,
Have you yourself what's best for men?
Are you—poor, sick, old ere your time—
Nearer one whit your own sublime
Than we who never have turned a rhyme?
   Sing, riding's a joy! For me, I ride.

And you, great sculptor—so, you gave
A score of years to Art, her slave,
And that's your Venus, whence we turn
To yonder girl that fords the burn!
You acquiesce, and shall I repine?
What, man of music, you grown grey
With notes and nothing else to say,
Is this your sole praise from a friend,
"Greatly his opera's strains intend,
But in music we know how fashions end!"
   I gave my youth; but we ride, in fine.

Who knows what's fit for us? Had fate
Proposed bliss here should sublimate
My being—had I signed the bond—
Still one must lead some life beyond,
   Have a bliss to die with, dim-descried.
This foot once planted on the goal,
This glory-garland round my soul,
Could I descry such? Try and test!
I sink back shuddering from the quest.
Earth being so good, would heaven seem best?
   Now, heaven and she are beyond this ride.

And yet—she has not spoke so long!
What if heaven be that, fair and strong
At life's best, with our eyes upturned
Whither life's flower is first discerned,
   We, fixed so, ever should so abide?
What if we still ride on, we two,
With life forever old yet new,
Changed not in kind but in degree,
The instant made eternity,—
And heaven just prove that I and she
   Ride, ride together, forever ride?

ROBERT BROWNING

THE POET CONSIDERS HIS OWN DEATH

A favourite subject with poets; their mental vitality is so vigorous that its extinction appeals to them dramatically, by way of contrast. I am sorry that there is not room for Swift's verses on the death of Doctor Swift; but there is a large plenty from which to choose. Landor's four lines are deservedly familiar; though the beginning is ludicrously inaccurate. Hardy's *Afterwards* is in the characteristic minor key. (He lived ten years after its publication.) Whitman's *Goodbye My Fancy* is a valediction forbidding mourning. Tennyson's is nobly acquiescent; the lines came into his head as he stood on a ferry-boat. He was eighty years old. Browning's *Epilogue*, written the last year of his life, is inspiringly aggressive. *Venienti Occurrite Morbo!*

On His Seventy-fifth Birthday

I strove with none; for none was worth my strife.
  Nature I loved, and next to Nature, Art;
I warmed both hands before the fire of life,
  It sinks, and I am ready to depart.

WALTER SAVAGE LANDOR

Afterwards

When the Present has latched its postern behind my
    tremulous stay,
  And the May month flaps its glad green leaves like wings,
Delicate-filmed as new-spun silk, will the neighbours say,
  "He was a man who used to notice such things"?

If it be in the dusk when, like an eyelid's soundless blink,
  The dewfall-hawk comes crossing the shades to alight
Upon the wind-warped upland thorn, a gazer may think,
  "To him this must have been a familiar sight."

If I pass during some nocturnal blackness, mothy and warm,
  When the hedgehog travels furtively over the lawn,
One may say, "He strove that such innocent creatures
    should come to no harm,
  But he could do little for them; and now he is gone."

If, when hearing that I have been stilled at last, they stand
    at the door,
  Watching the full-starred heavens that winter sees,
Will this thought rise on those who will meet my face no
    more,
  "He was one who had an eye for such mysteries"?

And will any say when my bell of quittance is heard in the
    gloom,
  And a crossing breeze cuts a pause in its outrollings,
Till they rise again, as they were a new bell's boom,
  "He hears it not now, but used to notice such things"?

THOMAS HARDY

Crossing the Bar

Sunset and evening star,
  And one clear call for me!
And may there be no moaning of the bar,
  When I put out to sea,

But such a tide as moving seems asleep,
  Too full for sound and foam,
When that which drew from out the boundless deep
  Turns again home.

[119]

Twilight and evening bell,
 And after that the dark!
And may there be no sadness of farewell,
 When I embark;

For tho' from out our bourne of Time and Place
 The flood may bear me far,
I hope to see my Pilot face to face
When I have crossed the bar.

ALFRED TENNYSON

The third stanza is an accurate description of Browning's attitude through life.

EPILOGUE TO ASOLANDO

AT the midnight in the silence of the sleep-time,
 When you set your fancies free,
Will they pass to where—by death, fools think, im-
  prisoned—
Low he lies who once so loved you, whom you loved so,
  —Pity me?

Oh to love so, be so loved, yet so mistaken!
 What had I on earth to do
With the slothful, with the mawkish, the unmanly?
Like the aimless, helpless, hopeless, did I drivel
  —Being—who?

One who never turned his back but marched breast forward,
 Never doubted clouds would break,
Never dreamed, though right were worsted, wrong would
  triumph,
Held we fall to rise, are baffled to fight better,
 Sleep to wake.

No, at noonday in the bustle of man's work-time
    Greet the unseen with a cheer!
Bid him forward, breast and back as either should be,
"Strive and thrive!" cry "Speed,—fight on, fare ever
        There as here!"

ROBERT BROWNING

"From sudden death, good Lord deliver us." This poem, written nearly thirty years before Browning died, is the most audacious challenge to death of which we have any record; he wished to be fully conscious during his last moments on earth. He was.

PROSPICE

FEAR death?—to feel the fog in my throat,
    The mist in my face,
When the snows begin, and the blasts denote
    I am nearing the place,
The power of the night, the press of the storm,
    The post of the foe;
Where he stands, the Arch Fear in a visible form,
    Yet the strong man must go:
For the journey is done and the summit attained,
    And the barriers fall,
Though a battle's to fight ere the guerdon be gained,
    The reward of it all.
I was ever a fighter, so—one fight more,
    The best and the last!
I would hate that death bandaged my eyes, and forbore,
    And bade me creep past.
No! let me taste the whole of it, fare like my peers
    The heroes of old,

[121]

Bear the brunt, in a minute pay glad life's arrears
  Of pain, darkness and cold.
For sudden the worst turns the best to the brave,
  The black minute's at end,
And the elements' rage, the fiend-voices that rave,
  Shall dwindle, shall blend,
Shall change, shall become first a peace out of pain,
  Then a light, then thy breast,
O thou soul of my soul! I shall clasp thee again,
  And with God be the rest!

ROBERT BROWNING

Song

When I am dead, my dearest,
  Sing no sad songs for me;
Plant thou no roses at my head,
  Nor shady cypress-tree:
Be the green grass above me
  With showers and dewdrops wet;
And if thou wilt, remember,
  And if thou wilt, forget.

I shall not see the shadows,
  I shall not feel the rain;
I shall not hear the nightingale
  Sing on, as if in pain:
And dreaming through the twilight
  That doth not rise nor set,
Haply I may remember,
  And haply may forget.

CHRISTINA ROSSETTI

[122]

WHEN THE LAMP IS SHATTERED

REQUIEM

UNDER the wide and starry sky,
Dig the grave and let me lie.
Glad did I live and gladly die,
  And I laid me down with a will.

This be the verse you grave for me:
Here he lies where he longed to be;
Home is the sailor, home from sea,
  And the hunter home from the hill.

ROBERT LOUIS STEVENSON

WHEN THE LAMP IS SHATTERED

WHEN the lamp is shattered
The light in the dust lies dead—
  When the cloud is scattered
The rainbow's glory is shed.
  When the lute is broken,
Sweet tones are remembered not;
  When the lips have spoken,
Love accents are soon forgot.

  As music and splendour
Survive not the lamp and the lute,
  The heart's echoes render
No song when the spirit is mute:—
  No song but sad dirges,
Like the wind through a ruined cell,
  Or the mournful surges
That ring the dead seaman's knell.

[123]

When hearts have once mingled
Love first leaves the well-built nest,
The weak one is singled
To endure what it once possessed.
O Love! who bewailest
The frailty of all things here,
Why choose you the frailest
For your cradle, your home, and your bier?

Its passions will rock thee
As the storms rock the ravens on high:
Bright reason will mock thee,
Like the sun from a wintry sky.
From thy nest every rafter
Will rot, and thine eagle home
Leave thee naked to laughter,
When leaves fall and cold winds come.

PERCY BYSSHE SHELLEY

William Butler Yeats has done more for English poetry than any other Irishman, for he is the greatest poet in the English language that Ireland has ever produced. He is a notable figure in contemporary literature, having made additions to verse, prose and stage-plays. He has by no means obliterated Clarence Mangan, but he has surpassed him.

SEPTEMBER, 1913

WHAT need you, being come to sense,
But fumble in a greasy till
And add the halfpence to the pence
And prayer to shivering prayer, until

You have dried the marrow from the bone;
For men were born to pray and save,
Romantic Ireland's dead and gone,
It's with O'Leary in the grave.

Yet they were of a different kind
The names that stilled your childish play;
They have gone about the world like wind,
But little time had they to pray
For whom the hangman's rope was spun,
And what, God help us, could they save;
Romantic Ireland's dead and gone,
It's with O'Leary in the grave.

Was it for this the wild geese spread
The grey wing upon every tide;
For this that all that blood was shed,
For this Edward Fitzgerald died,
And Robert Emmet and Wolfe Tone,
All that delirium of the brave;
Romantic Ireland's dead and gone,
It's with O'Leary in the grave.

Yet could we turn the years again,
And call those exiles as they were,
In all their loneliness and pain
You'd cry "Some woman's yellow hair
Has maddened every mother's son:"
They weighed so lightly what they gave,
But let them be, they're dead and gone,
They're with O'Leary in the grave.

WILLIAM BUTLER YEATS

Francis Thompson died in 1907. He saw the World War coming with the eclipse but not the destruction of the Church.

LILIUM REGIS

O LILY of the King! low lies thy silver wing,
And long has been the hour of thine unqueening;
And thy scent of Paradise on the night-wind spills its sighs,
Nor any take the secrets of its meaning.
O Lily of the King! I speak a heavy thing,
O patience, most sorrowful of daughters!
Lo, the hour is at hand for the troubling of the land,
And red shall be the breaking of the waters.

Sit fast upon thy stalk, when the blast shall with thee talk,
With the mercies of the king for thine awning;
And the just understand that thine hour is at hand,
Thine hour at hand with power in the dawning.
When the nations lie in blood, and their kings a broken
    brood,
Look up, O most sorrowful of daughters!
Lift up thy head and hark what sounds are in the dark,
For His feet are coming to thee on the waters!

O Lily of the King! I shall not see, that sing,
I shall not see the hour of thy queening!
But my song shall see, and wake, like a flower that dawn-
    winds shake,
And sigh with joy the odours of its meaning.
O Lily of the King, remember then the thing
That this dead mouth sang; and thy daughters,
As they dance before His way, sing there on the Day,
What I sang when the Night was on the waters!

FRANCIS THOMPSON

If these words were meaningless, they would still be poetry.

MAID OF ATHENS, ERE WE PART

MAID OF ATHENS, ere we part,
Give, oh, give me back my heart!
Or, since that has left my breast,
Keep it now, and take the rest!
Hear my vow before I go,
Ζώη μοῦ, σάς ἀγαπῶ.

By those tresses unconfined,
Woo'd by each Ægean wind;
By those lids whose jetty fringe
Kiss thy soft cheeks' blooming tinge;
By those wild eyes like the roe,
Ζώη μοῦ, σάς ἀγαπῶ.

By that lip I long to taste;
By that zone-encircled waist;
By all the token-flowers that tell
What words can never speak so well;
By love's alternate joy and woe,
Ζώη μοῦ, σάς ἀγαπῶ.

Maid of Athens! I am gone:
Think of me, sweet! when alone.
Though I fly to Istambol,
Athens holds my heart and soul;
Can I cease to love thee? No!
Ζώη μοῦ, σάς ἀγαπῶ.

LORD BYRON

The Canadian poet, Wilson MacDonald, is a booklover and an athlete.

I LOVE OLD THINGS

I LOVE old things:
Streets of old cities
Crowded with ghosts
And banked with oranges,
Gay scarfs and shawls
That flow like red water.

I love old abbeys
With high, carved portals
And dim, cool corners
Where tired hearts pray:
I join them in the silence
And repair my soul.

I love old inns
Where floors creak eerily
And doors blow open
On windless nights,
Where heavy curtains
Dance a slow waltz.

I love old trees
That lift up their voices
High above the grasses.
They do not sing
At the light wind's bidding:
They chant alone to storms.

I love old china,
Knowing well the flavour
Of great, strong men
And fair, sweet women
Lurks at the rim
Of each deep brown bowl.

I love old books
Frayed from the searching
Of truth-hungry fingers:
Their warm, soft vellum
Leads me up through sorrow
Like a dear friend's hand.

I love old men
And old, dear women
Who keep red cheeks
As the snows of winter
Keep the round red berry
Of the winter-green.

(This verse to be chanted)

I love old things:
Weather-beaten, worn things,
Cracked, broken, torn things,
The old sun, the old moon,
The old earth's face,
Old wine in dim flagons,
Old ships and old wagons—
OLD SHIPS AND OLD WAGONS—(*This line softly*)
Old coin and old lace,
Rare old lace.

WILSON MACDONALD

[129]

THE SONG OF THE SKI

NORSE am I when the first snow falls;
  Norse am I till the ice departs.
The fare for which my spirit calls
  Is blood from a hundred viking-hearts.
The curved wind wraps me like a cloak;
The pines blow out their ghostly smoke.
I'm high on the hill and ready to go—
A wingless bird in a world of snow:
      Yet I'll ride the air
      With a dauntless dare
That only a child of the North can know.

The bravest ski has a cautious heart
And moves like a tortoise at the start,
But when it tastes the tang of the air
It leaps away like a frightened hare.
The day is gloomy, the curtains half-drawn,
The light is stunted as at the dawn:
But my foot is sure and my arm is brawn.

I poise on the hill and I wave adieu
(My curving skis are firm and true):
The slim wood quickens, the air takes fire
And sings to me like a gipsy's lyre.
Swifter and swifter grows my flight:
The dark pines ease the unending white.
The lean, cold birches, as I go by,
Are like blurred etchings against the sky.

One am I for a moment's joy
  With the falling star and the plunging bird.
The world is swift as an Arab boy;

The world is sweet as a woman's word.
Never came such a pure delight
To a bacchanal or a sybarite:
Swifter and swifter grows my flight,
And glad am I as I near the leap,
That the snow is fresh and the banks are deep.

Swifter and swifter on I fare,
And soon I'll float with the birds on air.
The speed is blinding; I'm over the ridge,
Spanning space on a phantom bridge.
The drift awaits me; I float, I fall:
    The world leaps up like a plunging carp.
I land erect and the tired winds drawl
    A lazy rune on a broken harp.

Child of the roofless world am I;
    Not of those hibernating drones
Who fear the grey of a winter sky
    And the shrieking wind's ironic tones,
Who shuffle cards in a cloud of smoke
    Or crawl like frozen flies at chess,
Or gossip all day with meddling folk
    In collar of starch and a choking dress.

Come, ye maids of the vanity-box,
    Come, ye men of the stifling air:
The white wind waits at your door and knocks.
    The white snow calls you everywhere.
Come, ye lads of the lounge and chair,
    And gird your feet with the valiant skis
And mount the steed of the winter air
    And hold the reins of the winter breeze.

Lord of the mountains dark with pine!
  Lord of the fields of the smoking snow!
Grant to this vagrant heart of mine
  A path of wood where my feet may go,
And a roofless world to my journeys' end,
  And a cask of wind for my cup of wine,
And yellow gold of the sun to spend,
  And at night the stars in endless line,
And, after it all, the hand of a friend—
  The hand of a trusted friend in mine.

                                   WILSON MACDONALD

Flecker wrote two versions of this poem. I give them both
and let readers choose between them.

"TENEBRIS INTERLUCENTEM"

ONCE a poor song-bird that had lost her way
Sang down in Hell upon a blackened bough,
Till all the lazy ghosts remembered how
The forest trees stood up against the day.

Then suddenly they knew that they had died,
Hearing this music mock their shadow-land;
And some one there stole forth a timid hand
To draw a phantom brother to his side.

.   .   .   .

A LINNET *who had lost her way*
Sang on a blackened bough in Hell,
Till all the ghosts remembered well
The trees, the wind, the golden day.

[132]

At last they knew that they had died
When they heard music in that land,
And some one there stole forth a hand
To draw a brother to his side.

JAMES ELROY FLECKER

A healthy, cheerful, virile, open-air man, with a gift for singing.

THE TWO FLOCKS

WHERE are you going to now, white sheep,
　　Walking the green hill-side;
To join that whiter flock on top,
　　And share their pride?

Stay where you are, you silly sheep:
　　When you arrive up there,
You'll find that whiter flock on top
　　Clouds in the air!

Death can but play one game with me—
　　If I do live alone;
He cannot strike me a foul blow
　　Through a belovèd one.

Today he takes my neighbour's wife,
　　And leaves a little child
To lie upon his breast and cry
　　Like the Night-wind, so wild.

And every hour its voice is heard—
　　Tell me where she is gone!
Death cannot play that game with me—
　　If I do live alone.

W. H. DAVIES

Here's a Health to King Charles

From WOODSTOCK, CHAPTER XX

Bring the bowl which you boast,
　Fill it up to the brim;
'Tis to him we love most,
　And to all who love him.
Brave gallants, stand up,
　And avaunt, ye base carles!
Were there death in the cup,
　Here's a health to King Charles!

Though he wanders through dangers,
　Unaided, unknown,
Dependent on strangers,
　Estranged from his own;
Though 'tis under our breath,
　Amidst forfeits and perils,
Here's to honour and faith,
　And a health to King Charles!

Let such honours abound
　As the time can afford,
The knee on the ground,
　And the hand on the sword:
But the time shall come round,
　When, 'mid Lords, Dukes, and Earls,
The loud trumpets shall sound
　Here's a health to King Charles!

WALTER SCOTT

If by some miracle, Whitman could have spoken this poem over the radio, the effect and the response could not have been more immediate.

O Captain! My Captain!

O Captain! my Captain! our fearful trip is done:
The ship has weather'd every rack, the prize we sought is
     won;
The port is near, the bells I hear, the people all exulting,
While follow eyes the steady keel, the vessel grim and daring:
          But O heart! heart! heart!
          O the bleeding drops of red,
        Where on the deck my Captain lies,
          Fallen cold and dead.

O Captain! my Captain! rise up and hear the bells;
Rise up—for you the flag is flung—for you the bugle trills;
For you bouquets and ribbon'd wreaths—for you the shores
     a-crowding,
For you they call, the swaying mass, their eager faces
     turning;
          Here, Captain, dear father!
          This arm beneath your head;
        It is some dream that on the deck,
          You've fallen cold and dead.

My Captain does not answer, his lips are pale and still;
My father does not feel my arm, he has no pulse nor will;
The ship is anchor'd safe and sound, its voyage closed and
     done;
From fearful trip the victor ship comes in with object won:
          Exult, O shores, and ring, O bells!
          But I, with mournful tread,
        Walk the deck my Captain lies,
          Fallen cold and dead.

WALT WHITMAN

[135]

The transitory nature of all beauty is a theme running through all Herrick's compositions, grave and gay. The matter gives weight to his lightest pieces and the manner enlivens the tragic idea.

To the Virgins, to Make Much of Time

GATHER ye rosebuds while ye may:
　　Old Time is still a-flying;
And this same flower that smiles to-day,
　　To-morrow will be dying.

The glorious lamp of heaven, the sun,
　　The higher he's a-getting,
The sooner will his race be run,
　　And nearer he's to setting.

That age is best which is the first,
　　When youth and blood are warmer;
But being spent, the worse, and worst
　　Times still succeed the former.

Then be not coy, but use your time,
　　And while ye may, go marry;
For having lost but once your prime,
　　You may forever tarry.

ROBERT HERRICK

The Mad Maid's Song

GOOD morrow to the day so fair;
　　Good morning, sir, to you;
Good morrow to mine own torn hair,
　　Bedabbled with the dew.

Good morning to this primrose too;
  Good morrow to each maid
That will with flowers the tomb bestrew
  Wherein my love is laid.

Ah, woe, woe, woe, woe, woe is me,
  Alack, and well-a-day!
For pity, sir, find out that bee
  Which bore my love away.

I'll seek him in your bonnet brave;
  I'll seek him in your eyes;
Nay, now I think they've made his grave
  I' the bed of strawberries.

I'll seek him there; I know, ere this,
  The cold, cold earth doth shake him;
But I will go, or send a kiss
  By you, sir, to awake him.

Pray hurt him not; though he be dead,
  He knows well who do love him,
And who with green turfs rear his head,
  And who do rudely move him.

He's soft and tender; pray take heed;
  With bands of cowslips bind him,
And bring him home;—but 'tis decreed
  That I shall never find him.

                                    ROBERT HERRICK

Some of Brian Hooker's best poetry has been written for music. This poem also shows his imagination.

GHOSTS

THE dead return to us continually;
    Not at the void of night, as fables feign,
    In some lone spot where murdered bones have lain
Wailing for vengeance to the passer-by;
But in the merry clamour and full cry
    Of the brave noon, our dead whom we have slain
    And in forgotten graves hidden in vain,
Rise up and stand beside us terribly.

Sick with the beauty of their dear decay
    We conjure them with laughter onerous
    And drunkenness of labour; yet not thus
May we absolve ourselves of yesterday—
We cannot put those clinging arms away,
    Nor those glad faces yearning over us.

                   BRIAN HOOKER

Of all the poems written by living men, none has a fairer prospect for immortality than these two.

MANDALAY

By the old Moulmein Pagoda, lookin' eastward to the sea,
There's a Burma girl a-settin', and I know she thinks o' me;
For the wind is in the palm-trees, and the temple-bells they
    say:
"Come you back, you British soldier; come you back to
    Mandalay!"

Come you back to Mandalay,
Where the old Flotilla lay:
Can't you 'ear their paddles chunkin' from Rangoon
    to Mandalay?
On the road to Mandalay,
Where the flyin'-fishes play,
An' the dawn comes up like thunder outer China 'crost
    the Bay!

'Er petticoat was yaller an' 'er little cap was green,
An' 'er name was Supi-yaw-lat—jes' the same as Theebaw's
    Queen,
An' I seed her first a-smokin' of a whackin' white cheroot,
An' a-wastin' Christian kisses on an 'eathen idol's foot:
    Bloomin' idol made o' mud—
    Wot they called the Great Gawd Budd—
    Plucky lot she cared for idols when I kissed 'er where
        she stud!
    On the road to Mandalay . . .

When the mist was on the rice-fields an' the sun was droppin'
    slow,
She'd git 'er little banjo an' she'd sing *"Kulla-lo-lo!"*
With 'er arm upon my shoulder an' 'er cheek agin my cheek
We useter watch the steamers an' the *hathis* pilin' teak.
    Elephints a-pilin' teak
    In the sludgy, squdgy creek,
    Where the silence 'ung that 'eavy you was 'arf afraid
        to speak!
    On the road to Mandalay . . .

But that's all shove be'ind me—long ago an' fur away,
An' there ain't no 'buses runnin' from the Bank to Man-
    dalay;
An' I'm learnin' 'ere in London what the ten-year soldier
    tells:

"If you've 'eard the East a-callin', you won't never 'eed
    naught else."
    No! you won't 'eed nothin' else
    But them spicy garlic smells,
    An' the sunshine an' the palm-trees an' the tinkly
        temple-bells;
    On the road to Mandalay . . .

I am sick o' wastin' leather on these gritty pavin'-stones,
An' the blasted Henglish drizzle wakes the fever in my
    bones;
'Tho' I walks with fifty 'ousemaids outer Chelsea to the
    Strand,
An' they talks a lot o' lovin', but wot do they understand?
    Beefy face an' grubby 'and—
    Law! wot do they understand?
    I've a neater, sweeter maiden in a cleaner, greener land!
    On the road to Mandalay . . .

Ship me somewheres east of Suez, where the best is like the
    worst,
Where there aren't no Ten Commandments an' a man can
    raise a thirst;
For the temple-bells are callin', an' it's there that I would
    be—
By the old Moulmein Pagoda, looking lazy at the sea;
    On the road to Mandalay,
    Where the old Flotilla lay,
    With our sick beneath the awnings when we went to
        Mandalay!
    Oh, the road to Mandalay,
    Where the flyin'-fishes play,
    An' the dawn comes up like thunder outer China 'crost
        the Bay!

RUDYARD KIPLING

Danny Deever

"What are the bugles blowin' for?" said Files-on-Parade.
"To turn you out, to turn you out," the Colour-Sergeant
said.
"What makes you look so white, so white?" said Files-on-
Parade.
"I'm dreadin' what I've got to watch," the Colour-Sergeant
said.
> For they're hangin' Danny Deever, you can 'ear the
> Dead March play,
> The regiment's in 'ollow square—they're hangin' him
> to-day;
> They've taken of his buttons off an' cut his stripes
> away,
> An' they're hangin' Danny Deever in the mornin'.

"What makes the rear-rank breathe so 'ard?" said Files-
on-Parade.
"It's bitter cold, it's bitter cold," the Colour-Sergeant said.
"What makes that front-rank man fall down?" says Files-
on-Parade.
"A touch of sun, a touch of sun," the Colour-Sergeant said.
> They are hangin' Danny Deever, they are marchin' of
> 'im round.
> They 'ave 'alted Danny Deever by 'is coffin on the
> ground:
> An' 'e'll swing in 'arf a minute for a sneakin' shootin'
> hound—
> O they're hangin' Danny Deever in the mornin'!

" 'Is cot was right-'and cot to mine," said Files-on-Parade.
" 'E's sleepin' out an' far tonight," the Colour-Sergeant
said.

"I've drunk 'is beer a score o' times," said Files-on-Parade.
" 'E's drinkin' bitter beer alone," the Colour-Sergeant said.
> They are hangin' Danny Deever, you must mark 'im
> to 'is place,
> For 'e shot a comrade sleepin'—you must look 'im in
> the face;
> Nine 'undred of 'is county an' the regiment's disgrace,
> While they're hangin' Danny Deever in the mornin'.

"What's that so black against the sun?" said Files-on-Parade.
"It's Danny fightin' 'ard for life," the Colour-Sergeant said.
"What's that that whimpers over'ead?" said Files-on-Parade.
"It's Danny's soul that's passin' now," the Colour-Sergeant said.
> For they're done with Danny Deever, you can 'ear the
> quickstep play,
> The regiment's in column, an' they're marchin' us
> away;
> Ho! the young recruits are shakin', and they'll want
> their beer today,
> After hangin' Danny Deever in the mornin'.

RUDYARD KIPLING

Vachel Lindsay made poetry out of a calliope and Alfred Noyes out of a barrel-organ. The street hand-organ has never seemed to me either commonplace or interruptive, since I first read this poem.

THE BARREL-ORGAN

THERE'S a barrel-organ caroling across a golden street
In the City as the sun sinks low;

And the music's not immortal; but the world has made it
   sweet
  And fulfilled it with the sunset glow;
And it pulses through the pleasures of the City and the pain
  That surround the singing organ like a large eternal
     light;
And they've given it a glory and a part to play again
  In the Symphony that rules the day and night.
And now it's marching onward through the realms of old
   romance,
  And trolling out a fond familiar tune,
And now it's roaring cannon down to fight the King of
   France,
  And now it's prattling softly to the moon.
And all around the organ there's a sea without a shore
  Of human joys and wonders and regrets;
To remember and to recompense the music evermore
  For what the cold machinery forgets . . .

     Yes; as the music changes,
       Like a prismatic glass,
     It takes the light and ranges
       Through all the moods that pass:
     Dissects the common carnival
       Of passions and regrets,
     And gives the world a glimpse of all
       The colour it forgets.

     And there *La Traviata* sighs
       Another sadder song;
     And there *Il Trovatore* cries
       A tale of deeper wrong;
     And bolder knights to battle go
       With sword and shield and lance,
     Than ever here on earth below
       Have whirled into—a dance!—

Go down to Kew in lilac-time, in lilac-time, in lilac-time;
  Go down to Kew in lilac-time (it isn't far from London!)
And you shall wander hand in hand with love in summer's
    wonderland;
  Go down to Kew in lilac-time (it isn't far from London!)

The cherry-trees are seas of bloom and soft perfume and
    sweet perfume,
  The cherry-trees are seas of bloom (and oh, so near to
    London!)
And there they say, when dawn is high and all the world's
    a blaze of sky
  The cuckoo, though he's very shy, will sing a song for
    London.

The nightingale is rather rare and yet they say you'll hear
    him there
  At Kew, at Kew in lilac-time (and oh, so near to London!)
The linnet and the throstle, too, and after dark the long
    halloo
  And golden-eyed *tu-whit, tu-whoo* of owls that ogle
    London.

For Noah hardly knew a bird of any kind that isn't heard
  At Kew, at Kew in lilac-time (and oh, so near to London!)
And when the rose begins to pout and all the chestnut spires
    are out
  You'll hear the rest without a doubt, all chorusing for
    London:—

Come down to Kew in lilac-time, in lilac-time, in lilac-time;
  Come down to Kew in lilac-time (it isn't far from
    London!)
And you shall wander hand in hand with love in summer's
    wonderland;

*Come down to Kew in lilac-time (it isn't far from
   London!)*

And then the troubadour begins to thrill the golden street,
   In the City as the sun sinks low;
And in all the gaudy buses there are scores of weary feet
Marking time, sweet time, with a dull mechanic beat,
And a thousand hearts are plunging to a love they'll never
      meet,
Through the meadows of the sunset, through the poppies
      and the wheat,
   In the land where the dead dreams go.

Verdi, Verdi, when you wrote *Il Trovatore* did you dream
   Of the City when the sun sinks low,
Of the organ and the monkey and the many-coloured stream
On the Piccadilly pavement, of the myriad eyes that seem
To be litten for a moment with a wild Italian gleam
As *A che la morte* parodies the world's eternal theme
   And pulses with the sunset-glow?

There's a thief, perhaps, that listens with a face of frozen
      stone
   In the City as the sun sinks low;
There's a portly man of business with a balance of his own,
There's a clerk and there's a butcher of a soft reposeful tone,
And they're all of them returning to the heavens they have
      known:
They are crammed and jammed in buses and—they're each
      of them alone
   In the land where the dead dreams go.

There's a labourer that listens to the voices of the dead
   In the City as the sun sinks low;
And his hand begins to tremble and his face is rather red

As he sees a loafer watching him and—there he turns his
    head
And stares into the sunset where his April love is fled,
For he hears her softly singing and his lonely soul is led
    Through the land where the dead dreams go . . .

There's a barrel-organ caroling across a golden street
    In the City as the sun sinks low;
Though the music's only Verdi there's a world to make it
    sweet
Just as yonder yellow sunset where the earth and heaven
    meet
Mellows all the sooty City! Hark, a hundred thousand feet
Are marching on to glory through the poppies and the wheat
    In the land where the dead dreams go.

      So it's Jeremiah, Jeremiah,
        What have you to say
      When you meet the garland girls
        Tripping on their way?
      All around my gala hat
        I wear a wreath of roses
      (A long and lonely year it is
        I've waited for the May!)
      If anyone should ask you,
        The reason why I wear it is—
      My own love, my true love, is coming home today.

And it's buy a bunch of violets for the lady
    (It's lilac-time in London; it's lilac-time in London!)
Buy a bunch of violets for the lady;
    While the sky turns blue above:
On the other side the street you'll find it shady,
    (It's lilac-time in London; it's lilac-time in London!)
But buy a bunch of violets for the lady,
    And tell her she's your own true love.

There's a barrel-organ caroling across a golden street
  In the City as the sun sinks glittering and slow;
And the music's not immortal; but the world has made it
    sweet
And enriched it with the harmonies that make a song
    complete
In the deeper heavens of music where the night and morning
    meet,
  As it dies into the sunset glow;
And it pulses through the pleasures of the City and the
    pain
  That surround the singing organ like a large eternal
    light,
And they've given it a glory and a part to play again
  In the Symphony that rules the day and night.

      And there, as the music changes,
        The song runs round again;
      Once more it turns and ranges
        Through all its joy and pain:
      Dissects the common carnival
        Of passions and regrets;
      And the wheeling world remembers all
        The wheeling song forgets.

      Once more *La Traviata* sighs
        Another sadder song:
      Once more *Il Trovatore* cries
        A tale of deeper wrong;
      Once more the knights to battle go
        With sword and shield and lance
      Till once, once more, the shattered foe
        Has whirled into—a dance!

Come down to Kew in lilac-time, in lilac-time, in lilac-time;
  Come down to Kew in lilac-time (it isn't far from
    London!)
And you shall wander hand in hand with Love in summer's
    wonderland,
  Come down to Kew in lilac-time (it isn't far from
    London!)

ALFRED NOYES

Even a fog and a steam-tug can be transfigured by a poet.

FOG

DESOLATE and lone
All night long on the lake
Where fog trails and mist creeps,
The whistle of a boat
Calls and cries unendingly,
Like some lost child
In tears and trouble
Hunting the harbour's breast
And the harbour's eyes.

CARL SANDBURG

As Schubert's is the greatest serenade in music, so I think
Shelley's is in words.

THE INDIAN SERENADE

I ARISE from dreams of thee
In the first sweet sleep of night,
When the winds are breathing low,
And the stars are shining bright:
I arise from dreams of thee,
And a spirit in my feet
Hath led me—who knows how?
To thy chamber window, Sweet!

[148]

The wandering airs they faint
On the dark, the silent stream—
And the Champak odours fail
Like sweet thoughts in a dream;
The nightingale's complaint,
It dies upon her heart;—
As I must die on thine,
Belovèd as thou art!

Oh lift me from the grass!
I die! I faint! I fail!
Let thy love in kisses rain
On my lips and eyelids pale.
My cheek is cold and white, alas!
My heart beats loud and fast;—
Oh! press it close to thine again,
Where it will break at last.

PERCY BYSSHE SHELLEY

Innumerable undergraduate Glee Clubs have sung Serenade from "The Spanish Student."

Serenade from "The Spanish Student"

Stars of the summer night!
Far in yon azure deeps,
Hide, hide your golden light!
She sleeps!
My lady sleeps!
Sleeps!

Moon of the summer night!
Far down yon western steeps,
Sink, sink in silver light!
She sleeps!
My lady sleeps!
Sleeps!

[149]

Wind of the summer night!
　　Where yonder woodbine creeps,
Fold, fold thy pinions light!
　　She sleeps!
My lady sleeps!
　　Sleeps!

Dreams of the summer night!
　　Tell her, her lover keeps
Watch! while in slumbers light
　　She sleeps!
My lady sleeps!
　　Sleeps!

HENRY WADSWORTH LONGFELLOW

At a large dinner-party Lord Houghton asked Carlyle if he might present young Swinburne. "Not before you tell him what I think of him and his writings!" "And that is?" "He is sitting in a cesspool and adding to it." So they did not meet, or did, I've forgotten which.

THE GARDEN OF PROSERPINE

HERE, where the world is quiet;
　　Here, where all trouble seems
Dead winds' and spent waves' riot
　　In doubtful dreams of dreams;
I watch the green field growing
For reaping folk and sowing,
For harvest-time and mowing,
　　A sleepy world of streams.

[150]

I am tired of tears and laughter,
  And men that laugh and weep;
Of what may come hereafter
  For men that sow to reap:
I am weary of days and hours,
Blown buds of barren flowers,
Desires and dreams and powers
  And everything but sleep.

Here life has death for neighbour,
  And far from eye or ear
Wan waves and wet winds labour,
  Weak ships and spirits steer;
They drive adrift, and whither
They wot not who make thither;
But no such winds blow hither,
  And no such things grow here.

No growth of moor or coppice,
  No heather-flower or vine,
But bloomless buds of poppies,
  Green grapes of Proserpine,
Pale beds of blowing rushes
Where no leaf blooms or blushes
Save this whereout she crushes
  For dead men deadly wine.

Pale, without name or number,
  In fruitless fields of corn,
They bow themselves and slumber
  All night till light is born;
And like a soul belated,
In hell and heaven unmated,
By cloud and mist abated
  Comes out of darkness morn.

Though one were strong as seven,
  He too with death shall dwell,
Nor wake with wings in heaven,
  Nor weep for pains in hell;
Though one were fair as roses,
His beauty clouds and closes;
And well though love reposes,
  In the end it is not well.

Pale, beyond porch and portal,
  Crowned with calm leaves, she stands
Who gathers all things mortal
  With cold immortal hands;
Her languid lips are sweeter
Than love's who fears to greet her
To men that mix and meet her
  From many times and lands.

She waits for each and other,
  She waits for all men born;
Forgets the earth her mother,
  The life of fruits and corn;
And spring and seed and swallow
Take wing for her and follow
Where summer song rings hollow
  And flowers are put to scorn.

There go the loves that wither,
  The old loves with wearier wings;
And all dead years draw thither,
  And all disastrous things;
Dead dreams of days forsaken,
Blind buds that snows have shaken,
Wild leaves that winds have taken,
  Red strays of ruined springs.

We are not sure of sorrow,
  And joy was never sure;
Today will die tomorrow;
  Time stoops to no man's lure;
And love, grown faint and fretful,
With lips but half regretful
Sighs, and with eyes forgetful
  Weeps that no loves endure.

From too much love of living,
  From hope and fear set free,
We thank with brief thanksgiving
  Whatever gods may be
That no life lives for ever;
That dead men rise up never;
That even the weariest river
  Winds somewhere safe to sea.

Then star nor sun shall waken,
  Nor any change of light:
Nor sound of waters shaken,
  Nor any sound or sight:
Nor wintry leaves nor vernal,
Nor days nor things diurnal;
Only the sleep eternal
  In an eternal night.

ALGERNON CHARLES SWINBURNE

It is possible to be a preacher and a poet.

RELIANCE

NOT to the swift, the race:
Not to the strong, the fight:
Not to the righteous, perfect grace:
Not to the wise, the light.

But often faltering feet
Come surest to the goal;
And they who walk in darkness meet
The sunrise of the soul.

A thousand times by night
The Syrian hosts have died;
A thousand times the vanquished right
Hath risen, glorified.

The truth by wise men sought
Was spoken by a child;
The alabaster box was brought
In trembling hands defiled.

Not from the torch, the gleam,
But from the stars above:
Not from my heart, life's crystal stream,
But from the depths of love.

HENRY VAN DYKE

But the mighty heart will never stop beating again until the end of civilization.

COMPOSED UPON WESTMINSTER BRIDGE, SEPTEMBER 3, 1802

EARTH has not anything to show more fair;
Dull would he be of soul who could pass by
A sight so touching in its majesty:
This City now doth, like a garment, wear
The beauty of the morning; silent, bare,
Ships, towers, domes, theatres, and temples lie
Open unto the fields, and to the sky;
All bright and glittering in the smokeless air.
Never did sun more beautifully steep
In his first splendour, valley, rock, or hill;
Ne'er saw I, never felt, a calm so deep!
The river glideth at his own sweet will:
Dear God! the very houses seem asleep;
And all that mighty heart is lying still!

WILLIAM WORDSWORTH

This poet found tranquillity both in city and seaside, for he had it always in his heart.

IT IS A BEAUTEOUS EVENING

IT is a beauteous evening, calm and free:
The holy time is quiet as a Nun
Breathless with adoration; the broad sun
Is sinking down in its tranquillity;
The gentleness of heaven broods o'er the Sea:

Listen! the mighty Being is awake,
And doth with his eternal motion make
A sound like thunder—everlastingly.
Dear Child; dear Girl! that walkest with me here,
If thou appear untouched by solemn thought,
Thy nature is not therefore less divine:
Thou liest in Abraham's bosom all the year;
And worship'st at the Temple's inner shrine,
God being with thee when we know it not

WILLIAM WORDSWORTH

====

The death of Keats is the greatest loss English literature or any other literature ever sustained; he is the only English poet whose language had the felicity of Shakespeare's.

This poem is as flawless as the work of art that inspired it; the idea for once found the perfect form in words. The poem does not sound as if it had been written, but as if it had been created as a complete whole, in one divine moment.

ODE ON A GRECIAN URN

I

THOU still unravished bride of quietness,
   Thou foster-child of silence and slow time,
Sylvan historian, who canst thus express
   A flowery tale more sweetly than our rhyme:
What leaf-fringed legend haunts about thy shape
   Of deities or mortals, or of both,
      In Tempe or the dales of Arcady?
What men or gods are these? What maidens loth?
What mad pursuit? What struggle to escape?
      What pipes and timbrels? What wild ecstasy?

II

Heard melodies are sweet, but those unheard
  Are sweeter; therefore, ye soft pipes, play on;
Not to the sensual ear, but, more endeared,
  Pipe to the spirit ditties of no tone:
Fair youth, beneath the trees, thou canst not leave
  Thy song, nor ever can those trees be bare;
    Bold Lover, never, never canst thou kiss,
Though winning near the goal—yet, do not grieve;
  She cannot fade, though thou hast not thy bliss,
    For ever wilt thou love, and she be fair!

III

Ah, happy, happy boughs! that cannot shed
  Your leaves, nor ever bid the Spring adieu;
And, happy melodist, unwearied,
  For ever piping songs for ever new;
More happy love! more happy, happy love!
  For ever warm and still to be enjoyed,
    For ever panting, and for ever young;
All breathing human passion far above,
  That leaves a heart high-sorrowful and cloyed,
    A burning forehead, and a parching tongue.

IV

Who are these coming to the sacrifice?
  To what green altar, O mysterious priest,
Lead'st thou that heifer lowing at the skies,
  And all her silken flanks with garlands drest?
What little town by river or sea shore,
  Or mountain-built with peaceful citadel,

Is emptied of this folk, this pious morn?
And, little town, thy streets for evermore
Will silent be; and not a soul to tell
Why thou art desolate, can e'er return.

V

O attic shape! Fair attitude! with brede
Of marble men and maidens overwrought,
With forest branches and the trodden weed;
    Thou, silent form, dost tease us out of thought
As doth eternity: Cold Pastoral!
    When old age shall this generation waste,
    Thou shalt remain, in midst of other woe
Than ours, a friend to man, to whom thou say'st,
    "Beauty is truth, truth beauty,"—that is all
Ye know on earth, and all ye need to know.

JOHN KEATS

To Autumn

I

SEASON of mists and mellow fruitfulness!
    Close bosom-friend of the maturing sun;
Conspiring with him how to load and bless
    With fruit the vines that round the thatch-eves run;
To bend with apples the mossed cottage-trees,
    And fill all fruit with ripeness to the core;
        To swell the gourd, and plump the hazel shells
With a sweet kernel; to set budding more,
And still more, later flowers for the bees,
Until they think warm days will never cease,
        For Summer has o'er-brimmed their clammy cells.

II

Who hath not seen thee oft amid thy store?
  Sometimes whoever seeks abroad may find
Thee sitting careless on a granary floor,
  Thy hair soft-lifted by the winnowing wind;
Or on a half-reaped furrow sound asleep,
  Drowsed with the fume of poppies, while thy hook
    Spares the next swath and all its twinèd flowers:
And sometimes like a gleaner thou dost keep
  Steady thy laden head across a brook;
  Or by a cider-press, with patient look,
    Thou watchest the last oozings hours by hours.

III

Where are the songs of Spring? Ay, where are they?
  Think not of them, thou hast thy music too,—
While barrèd clouds bloom the soft-dying day,
  And touch the stubble-plains with rosy hue;
Then in a wailful choir the small gnats mourn
  Among the river sallows, borne aloft
    Or sinking as the light wind lives or dies;
And full-grown lambs loud bleat from hilly bourn;
  Hedge-crickets sing; and now with treble soft
  The red-breast whistles from a garden-croft;
    And gathering swallows twitter in the skies.

JOHN KEATS

Lowell addressed this poem to those who attempted to give consolation instead of sympathy.

AFTER THE BURIAL

YES, faith is a goodly anchor;
 When skies are sweet as a psalm,
At the bows it lolls so stalwart,
 In its bluff, broad-shouldered calm.

And when over breakers to leeward
 The tattered surges are hurled,
It may keep our head to the tempest,
 With its grip on the base of the world.

But, after the shipwreck, tell me
 What help in its iron thews,
Still true to the broken hawser,
 Deep down among sea-weed and ooze?

In the breaking gulfs of sorrow,
 When the helpless feet stretch out
And find in the deeps of darkness
 No footing so solid as doubt,

Then better one spar of Memory,
 One broken plank of the Past,
That our human heart may cling to,
 Though hopeless of shore at last!

To the spirit its splendid conjectures,
 To the flesh its sweet despair,
Its tears o'er the thin-worn locket
 With its anguish of deathless hair!

Immortal? I feel it and know it,
  Who doubts it of such as she?
But that is the pang's very secret,—
  Immortal away from me.

There's a narrow ridge in the graveyard
  Would scarce stay a child in his race,
But to me and my thought it is wider
  Than the star-sown vague of Space.

Your logic, my friend, is perfect,
  Your moral most drearily true;
But, since the earth clashed on *her* coffin,
  I keep hearing that, and not you.

Console if you will, I can bear it;
  'Tis a well-meant alms of breath;
But not all the preaching since Adam
  Has made Death other than Death.

It is pagan; but wait till you feel it,—
  That jar of our earth, that dull shock
When the ploughshare of deeper passion
  Tears down to our primitive rock.

Communion in spirit! Forgive me,
  But I, who am earthly and weak,
Would give all my incomes from dreamland
  For a touch of her hand on my cheek.

That little shoe in the corner,
  So worn and wrinkled and brown,
With its emptiness confutes you,
  And argues your wisdom down.

                    JAMES RUSSELL LOWELL

This is not only one of Milton's greatest sonnets; it has more intense personal feeling than he usually was willing to express. It is the quintessence of the agony of separation.

ON HIS DECEASED WIFE

METHOUGHT I saw my late espousèd saint
Brought to me like Alcestis from the grave,
Whom Jove's great son to her glad husband gave,
Rescued from Death by force, though pale and faint.
Mine, as whom washed from spot of child-bed taint
Purification in the Old Law did save,
And such as yet once more I trust to have
Full sight of her in heaven without restraint,
Came vested all in white, pure as her mind.
Her face was veiled; yet to my fancied sight
Love, sweetness, goodness in her person shined
So clear as in no face with more delight.
But O, as to embrace me she inclined,
I waked, she fled, and day brought back my night.

JOHN MILTON

The recognition of obstacles does not necessarily mean despair.

CREDO

I CANNOT find my way: there is no star
In all the shrouded heavens anywhere;
And there is not a whisper in the air
Of any living voice but one so far
That I can hear it only as a bar
Of lost, imperial music, played when fair
And angel fingers wove, and unaware,

Dead leaves to garlands where no roses are.
No, there is not a glimmer, nor a call,
For one that welcomes, welcomes when he fears,
The black and awful chaos of the night;
For through it all—above, beyond it all—
I know the far-sent message of the years,
I feel the coming glory of the Light.

EDWIN ARLINGTON ROBINSON

It has been said that the last part of the sonnet is not so good as the first part; those who say that have never been in love or have forgotten.

BRIGHT STAR

BRIGHT star, would I were steadfast as thou art—
Not in lone splendour hung aloft the night
And watching, with eternal lids apart,
Like nature's patient, sleepless Eremite,
The moving waters at their priestlike task
Of pure ablution round earth's human shores,
Or gazing on the new soft-fallen mask
Of snow upon the mountains and the moors—
No—yet still steadfast, still unchangeable,
Pillowed upon my fair love's ripening breast,
To feel for ever its soft fall and swell,
Awake for ever in a sweet unrest,
Still, still to hear her tender-taken breath,
And so live ever—or else swoon to death.

JOHN KEATS

Rupert Brooke wrote sonnets, lyrics, humorous poems; in *Grantchester* all his various gifts found expression. It is lyrical, its love of both country and the country is passionate, it has the undying spirit of youth and the nostalgia for Home. Perhaps no one has ever more clearly shown in verse the difference between the German love of order and regularity, and the English informality.

Rupert Brooke enjoyed every moment of his youth; he rejoiced in his youth and was more conscious of his youth than most young people are; for many do not realize what it means to be young until youth is past. Brooke could not endure old men and women; to him all old persons were Struldbrugs. He lived with tremendous gusto; he said that the mere sight of steam coming out of a locomotive excited him.

THE OLD VICARAGE, GRANTCHESTER

(*Café des Westens, Berlin, May, 1912*)

JUST now the lilac is in bloom,
All before my little room;
And in my flower-beds, I think,
Smile the carnation and the pink;
And down the borders, well I know,
The poppy and the pansy blow. . . .
Oh! there the chestnuts, summer through,
Beside the river make for you
A tunnel of green gloom, and sleep
Deeply above; and green and deep
The stream mysterious glides beneath,
Green as a dream and deep as death.

—Oh, damn! I know it! and I know
How the May fields all golden show,
And when the day is young and sweet,
Glide gloriously the bare feet
That run to bathe . . .
                    Du lieber Gott!
Here am I, sweating, sick, and hot,
And there the shadowed waters fresh
Lean up to embrace the naked flesh.
Temperamentvoll German Jews
Drink beer around; and *there* the dews
Are soft beneath a morn of gold.
Here tulips bloom as they are told;
Unkempt about those hedges blows
An English unofficial rose;
And there the unregulated sun
Slopes down to rest when day is done,
And wakes a vague unpunctual star,
A slippered Hesper; and there are
Meads towards Haslingfield and Coton
Where *das Betreten's* not *verboten.*

εἴθε γενοίμην . . . . would I were
In Grantchester, in Grantchester!—
Some, it may be, can get in touch
With Nature there, or Earth, or such.
And clever modern men have seen
A Faun a-peeping through the green,
And felt the classics were not dead,
To glimpse a Naiad's reedy head,
Or hear the Goat-foot piping low; . . .
But these are things I do not know.
I only know that you may lie
Day long and watch the Cambridge sky,
And, flower-lulled in sleepy grass,

Hear the cool lapse of hours pass,
Until the centuries blend and blur
In Grantchester, in Grantchester. . . .
Still in the dawnlit waters cool
His ghostly Lordship swims his pool,
And tries the strokes, essays the tricks,
Long learnt on Hellespont, or Styx.
Dan Chaucer hears his river still
Chatter beneath a phantom mill.
Tennyson notes, with studious eye,
How Cambridge waters hurry by. . . .
And in that garden, black and white,
Creep whispers through the grass all night;
And spectral dance, before the dawn
A hundred vicars down the lawn;
Curates, long dust, will come and go
On lissom, clerical, printless toe;
And oft between the boughs is seen
The sly shade of a Rural Dean . . .
Till, at a shiver in the skies,
Vanishing with Satanic cries,
The prim ecclesiastic rout
Leaves but a startled sleeper-out,
Grey heavens, the first bird's drowsy calls
The falling house that never falls.

God! I will pack, and take a train,
And get me to England once again!
For England's the one land, I know,
Where men with Splendid Hearts may go;
And Cambridgeshire, of all England,
The shire for Men who Understand;
And of *that* district I prefer
The lovely hamlet Grantchester.
For Cambridge people rarely smile,

Being urban, squat, and packed with guile;
And Royston men in the far South
Are black and fierce and strange of mouth;
At Over they fling oaths at one,
And worse than oaths at Trumpington,
And Ditton girls are mean and dirty,
And there's none in Harston under thirty,
And folks in Shelford and those parts
Have twisted lips and twisted hearts,
And Barton men make Cockney rhymes,
And Coton's full of nameless crimes,
And things are done you'd not believe
At Madingley on Christmas Eve.
Strong men have run for miles and miles,
When one from Cherry Hinton smiles;
Strong men have blanched, and shot their wives,
Rather than send them to St. Ives;
Strong men have cried like babes, bydam,
To hear what happened in Babraham.
But Grantchester! ah, Grantchester!
There's peace and holy quiet there,
Great clouds along pacific skies,
And men and women with straight eyes,
Lithe children lovelier than a dream,
A bosky wood, a slumb'rous stream,
And little kindly winds that creep
Round twilight corners, half asleep.
In Grantchester their skins are white;
They bathe by day, they bathe by night;
The women there do all they ought;
The men observe the Rules of Thought;
They love the Good; they worship Truth;
They laugh uproariously in youth;
(And when they get to feeling old,
They up and shoot themselves, I'm told) . . .

Ah God! to see the branches stir
Across the moon at Grantchester!
To smell the thrilling-sweet and rotten
Unforgettable, unforgotten
River-smell, and hear the breeze
Sobbing in the little trees.
Say, do the elm-clumps greatly stand
Still guardians of that holy land?
The chestnuts shade, in reverend dream,
The yet unacademic stream?
Is dawn a secret shy and cold
Anadyomene, silver-gold?
And sunset still a golden sea
From Haslingfield to Madingley?
And after, ere the night is born,
Do hares come out about the corn?
Oh, is the water sweet and cool,
Gentle and brown, above the pool?
And laughs the immortal river still
Under the mill, under the mill?
Say, is there Beauty yet to find?
And Certainty? And Quiet kind?
Deep meadows yet, for to forget
The lies, and truths, and pain? . . . oh! yet
Stands the Church clock at ten to three?
And is there honey still for tea?

RUPERT BROOKE

Henry Beers studied law and lived in New York awhile; but his happiness in exchanging New York for quiet New Haven is expressed with whimsical humour and tenderness. This is the literature of escape.

NUNC DIMITTIS

HIGHLANDS of Navesink,
By the blue ocean's brink,
Let your grey bases drink
   Deep of the sea.
Tide that comes flooding up,
Fill me a stirrup cup,
Pledge me a parting sup,
   Now I go free.

Wall of the Palisades,
I know where greener glades,
Deeper glens, darker shades,
   Hemlock and pine,
Far toward the morning lie
Under a bluer sky,
Lifted by cliffs as high,
   Haunts that are mine.

Marshes of Hackensack,
See, I am going back
Where the Quinnipiac
   Winds to the bay.
Down its long meadow track,
Piled in the myriad stack,
Where in wide bivouac
   Camps the salt hay.

Spire of old Trinity,
Never again to be
Seamark and goal to me
   As I walk down;
Chimes on the upper air,
Calling in vain to prayer,
Squandering your music where
   Roars the black town:

Bless me once ere I ride
Off to God's countryside,
Where in the treetops hide
   Belfry and bell;
Tongues of the steeple towers
Telling the slow-paced hours—
Hail, thou still town of ours—
   Bedlam, farewell!

                    HENRY A. BEERS

Among the works of Charles Lamb, this poem is lonesome
in every sense of the word. It will outlast, however, the Complete Works of the majority of writers. The proverb out of
sight, out of mind, is not always true; with some persons
Memory strengthens visibility. Did you know that the first
time that "out of sight" phrase appears in literature is in
The Imitation of Christ by Thomas à Kempis (1380–
1471)?

THE OLD FAMILIAR FACES

I HAVE had playmates, I have had companions,
In my days of childhood, in my joyful school-days—
All, all are gone, the old familiar faces.

[170]

I have been laughing, I have been carousing,
Drinking late, sitting late, with my bosom cronies—
All, all are gone, the old familiar faces.

I loved a love once, fairest among women;
Closed are her doors on me, I must not see her—
All, all are gone, the old familiar faces.

I have a friend, a kinder friend has no man;
Like an ingrate, I left my friend abruptly;
Left him, to muse on the old familiar faces.

Ghost-like I paced round the haunts of my childhood;
Earth seemed a desert I was bound to traverse,
Seeking to find the old familiar faces.

Friend of my bosom, thou more than a brother,
Why wert not thou born in my father's dwelling?
So might we talk of the old familiar faces—

How some they have died, and some they have left me,
And some are taken from me; all are departed;
All, all are gone, the old familiar faces.

CHARLES LAMB

No poet has a higher percentage of gold than A. E. Housman. His two small volumes contain indestructible metal: and mettle.

INTO MY HEART AN AIR THAT KILLS

Into my heart an air that kills
From yon far country blows:
What are those blue remembered hills,
What spires, what farms are those?

That is the land of lost content,
I see it shining plain,
The happy highways where I went
And cannot come again.

A. E. HOUSMAN

REVEILLE

WAKE: the silver dusk returning
Up the beach of darkness brims,
And the ship of sunrise burning
Strands upon the eastern rims.

Wake: the vaulted shadow shatters,
Trampled to the floor it spanned,
And the tent of night in tatters
Straws the sky-pavilioned land.

Up, lad, up, 'tis late for lying:
Hear the drums of morning play;
Hark, the empty highways crying
"Who'll beyond the hills away?"

Towns and countries woo together,
Forelands beacon, belfries call;
Never lad that trod on leather
Lived to feast his heart with all.

Up, lad: thews that lie and cumber
Sunlit pallets never thrive;
Morns abed and daylight slumber
Were not meant for man alive.

Clay lies still, but blood's a rover:
Breath's a ware that will not keep;
Up, lad: when the journey's over
There'll be time enough to sleep.

A. E. HOUSMAN

To an Athlete Dying Young

THE time you won your town the race
We chaired you through the market-place;
Man and boy stood cheering by,
And home we brought you shoulder-high.

Today, the road all runners come,
Shoulder-high we bring you home,
And set you at your threshold down,
Townsman of a stiller town.

Smart lad, to slip betimes away
From fields where glory does not stay
And early though the laurel grows
It withers quicker than the rose.

Eyes the shady night has shut
Cannot see the record cut,
And silence sounds no worse than cheers
After earth has stopped the ears:

Now you will not swell the rout
Of lads that wore their honours out,
Runners whom renown outran
And the name died before the man.

[173]

So set, before its echoes fade,
The fleet foot on the sill of shade,
And hold to the low lintel up
The still-defended challenge-cup.

And round that early-laurelled head
Will flock to gaze the strengthless dead,
And find unwithered on its curls
The garland briefer than a girl's.

A. E. HOUSMAN

If Truth in Hearts That Perish

If truth in hearts that perish
Could move the powers on high,
I think the love I bear you
Should make you not to die.

Sure, sure, if stedfast meaning,
If single thought could save,
The world might end tomorrow,
You should not see the grave.

This long and sure-set liking,
This boundless will to please,
—Oh, you should live forever
If there were help in these.

But now, since all is idle,
To this lost heart be kind,
Ere to a town you journey
Where friends are ill to find.

A. E. HOUSMAN

White in the Moon the Long Road Lies

White in the moon the long road lies,
    The moon stands blank above;
White in the moon the long road lies
    That leads me from my love.

Still hangs the hedge without a gust,
    Still, still the shadows stay:
My feet upon the moonlit dust
    Pursue the ceaseless way.

The world is round, so travellers tell,
    And straight though reach the track,
Trudge on, trudge on, 'twill all be well,
    The way will guide one back.

But ere the circle homeward hies
    Far, far must it remove:
White in the moon the long road lies
    That leads me from my love.

A. E. HOUSMAN

Say, Lad, Have You Things to Do?

Say, lad, have you things to do?
    Quick then, while your day's at prime.
Quick, and if 'tis work for two,
    Here am I, man: now's your time.

Send me now, and I shall go;
    Call me, I shall hear you call;
Use me ere they lay me low
    Where a man's no use at all;

Ere the wholesome flesh decay,
  And the willing nerve be numb,
And the lips lack breath to say,
  "No, my lad, I cannot come."

A. E. HOUSMAN

WHEN I WAS ONE-AND-TWENTY

WHEN I was one-and-twenty
  I heard a wise man say,
"Give crowns and pounds and guineas
  But not your heart away;
Give pearls away and rubies
  But keep your fancy free."
But I was one-and-twenty,
  No use to talk to me.

When I was one-and-twenty
  I heard him say again,
"The heart out of the bosom
  Was never given in vain;
'Tis paid with sighs a plenty
  And sold for endless rue."
And I am two-and-twenty,
  And oh, 'tis true, 'tis true.

A. E. HOUSMAN

FAR IN A WESTERN BROOKLAND

FAR in a western brookland
  That bred me long ago
The poplars stand and tremble
  By pools I used to know.

There, in the windless night-time,
    The wanderer, marvelling why,
Halts on the bridge to hearken
    How soft the poplars sigh.

He hears: no more remembered
    In fields where I was known,
Here I lie down in London
    And turn to rest alone.

There, by the starlit fences,
    The wanderer halts and hears
My soul that lingers sighing
    About the glimmering weirs.

A. E. HOUSMAN

Browning wrote this poem on 3 January 1852, in his apartments on the Champs Elysées at Paris, where he and his wife were spending the winter. It must have been a memorable day in his life, but so far as I know, he never alluded to it. To the accompaniment of street omnibuses and all the noises of traffic, he wrote these lines of pure imagination, seeing appalling visions and hearing the horn in the horrible sunset.

In *King Lear*, at the close of the fourth scene of the third act, Edgar sings

Childe Rowland to the dark tower came,
His word was still, Fie, foh, and fum,
I smell the blood of a British man.

These lines are probably the fragment of an old ballad familiar to Elizabethan audiences. Out of the first line Browning created his poem. Innumerable attempts have been made at allegorical interpretation; the poem has survived these attempts.

"CHILDE ROLAND TO THE DARK TOWER CAME"

My first thought was, he lied in every word,
  That hoary cripple, with malicious eye
  Askance to watch the working of his lie
On mine, and mouth scarce able to afford
Suppression of the glee that pursed and scored
  Its edge at one more victim gained thereby.

What else should he be set for, with his staff?
  What, save to waylay with his lies, ensnare
  All travellers that might find him posted there,
And ask the road? I guessed what skull-like laugh
Would break, what crutch 'gin write my epitaph
  For pastime in the dusty thoroughfare,

If at his counsel I should turn aside
  Into that ominous tract which, all agree,
  Hides the Dark Tower. Yet acquiescingly
I did turn as he pointed; neither pride
Nor hope rekindling at the end descried,
  So much as gladness that some end might be.

For, what with my whole world-wide wandering,
  What with my search drawn out through years, my hope
  Dwindled into a ghost not fit to cope
With that obstreperous joy success would bring,—
I hardly tried now to rebuke the spring
  My heart made, finding failure in its scope.

As when a sick man very near to death
  Seems dead indeed, and feels begin and end
  The tears and takes the farewell of each friend,
And hears one bid the other go, draw breath
Freelier outside, ("since all is o'er," he saith,
  "And the blow fallen no grieving can amend;")

While some discuss if near the other graves
  Be room enough for this, and when a day
  Suits best for carrying the corpse away,
With care about the banners, scarves and staves,—
And still the man hears all, and only craves
  He may not shame such tender love and stay.

Thus, I had so long suffered in this quest,
  Heard failure prophesied so oft, been writ
  So many times among "The Band"—to wit,
The knights who to the Dark Tower's search addressed
Their steps—that just to fail as they, seemed best,
  And all the doubt was now—should I be fit?

So, quiet as despair, I turned from him,
  That hateful cripple, out of his highway
  Into the path he pointed. All the day
Had been a dreary one at best, and dim
Was settling to its close, yet shot one grim
  Red leer to see the plain catch its estray.

For mark! no sooner was I fairly found
  Pledged to the plain, after a pace or two,
  Than, pausing to throw backward a last view
O'er the safe road, 'twas gone; grey plain all round:
Nothing but plain to the horizon's bound.
  I might go on; nought else remained to do.

So, on I went. I think I never saw
  Such starved ignoble nature; nothing throve;
  For flowers—as well expect a cedar grove!
But cockle, spurge, according to their law
Might propagate their kind, with none to awe,
  You'd think; a burr had been a treasure-trove.

No! penury, inertness and grimace,
　In some strange sort, were the land's portion. "See
　Or shut your eyes," said Nature peevishly,
"It nothing skills: I cannot help my case:
'Tis the Last Judgment's fire must cure this place,
　Calcine its clods and set my prisoners free."

If there pushed any ragged thistle-stalk
　Above its mates, the head was chopped—the bents
　Were jealous else. What made those holes and rents
In the dock's harsh swarth leaves—bruised as to baulk
All hope of greenness? 'tis a brute must walk
　Pashing their life out, with a brute's intents.

As for the grass, it grew as scant as hair
　In leprosy; thin dry blades pricked the mud
　Which underneath looked kneaded up with blood.
One stiff blind horse, his every bone a-stare,
Stood stupefied, however he came there:
　Thrust out past service from the devil's stud!

Alive? he might be dead for aught I know,
　With that red, gaunt and colloped neck a-strain,
　And shut eyes underneath the rusty mane;
Seldom went such grotesqueness with such woe;
I never saw a brute I hated so;
　He must be wicked to deserve such pain.

I shut my eyes and turned them on my heart.
　As a man calls for wine before he fights,
　I asked one draught of earlier, happier sights,
Ere fitly I could hope to play my part.
Think first, fight afterwards—the soldier's art:
　One taste of the old time sets all to rights!

Not it! I fancied Cuthbert's reddening face
   Beneath its garniture of curly gold,
   Dear fellow, till I almost felt him fold
An arm in mine to fix me to the place,
That way he used. Alas, one night's disgrace!
   Out went my heart's new fire and left it cold.

Giles, then, the soul of honour—there he stands
   Frank as ten years ago when knighted first.
   What honest man should dare (he said) he durst.
Good—but the scene shifts—faugh! what hangman's hands
Pin to his breast a parchment? his own bands
   Read it. Poor traitor, spit upon and curst!

Better this present than a past like that;
   Back therefore to my darkening path again!
   No sound, no sight as far as eye could strain.
Will the night send a howlet or a bat?
I asked: when something on the dismal flat
   Come to arrest my thoughts and change their train.

A sudden little river crossed my path
   As unexpected as a serpent comes.
   No sluggish tide congenial to the glooms—
This, as it frothed by, might have been a bath
For the fiend's glowing hoof—to see the wrath
   Of its black eddy bespate with flakes and spumes.

So petty yet so spiteful! all along,
   Low scrubby alders kneeled down over it;
   Drenched willows flung them headlong in a fit
Of mute despair, a suicidal throng:
The river which had done them all the wrong,
   Whate'er that was, rolled by, deterred no whit.

Which, while I forded,—good saints, how I feared
 To set my foot upon a dead man's cheek,
 Each step, or feel the spear I thrust to seek
For hollows, tangled in his hair or beard!
—It may have been a water-rat I speared,
 But, ugh! it sounded like a baby's shriek.

Glad was I when I reached the other bank.
 Now for a better country. Vain presage!
 Who were the strugglers, what war did they wage
Whose savage trample thus could pad the dank
Soil to a plash? toads in a poisoned tank,
 Or wild cats in a red-hot iron cage—

The fight must so have seemed in that fell cirque.
 What penned them there, with all the plain to choose?
 No foot-print leading to that horrid mews,
None out of it. Mad brewage set to work
Their brains, no doubt, like galley-slaves the Turk
 Pits for his pastime, Christians against Jews.

And more than that—a furlong on—why, there!
 What bad use was that engine for, that wheel,
 Or brake, not wheel—that harrow fit to reel
Men's bodies out like silk? with all the air
Of Tophet's tool, on earth left unaware,
 Or brought to sharpen its rusty teeth of steel.

Then came a bit of stubbed ground, once a wood,
 Next a marsh, it would seem, and now mere earth
 Desperate and done with; (so a fool finds mirth,
Makes a thing and then mars it, till his mood
Changes and off he goes!) within a rood—
 Bog, clay and rubble, sand and stark black dearth.

Now blotches rankling, coloured gay and grim,
  Now patches where some leanness of the soil's
  Broke into moss or substances like boils;
Then came some palsied oak, a cleft in him
Like a distorted mouth that splits its rim
  Gaping at death, and dies while it recoils.

And just as far as ever from the end!
  Nought in the distance but the evening, nought
  To point my footstep further! At the thought,
A great black bird, Apollyon's bosom-friend,
Sailed past, nor beat his wide wing dragon-penned
  That brushed my cap—perchance the guide I sought.

For, looking up, aware I somehow grew,
  'Spite of the dusk, the plain had given place
  All round to mountains—with such name to grace
Mere ugly heights and heaps now stolen in view.
How thus they had surprised me,—solve it, you!
  How to get from them was no clearer case.

Yet half I seemed to recognise some trick
  Of mischief happened to me, God knows when—
  In a bad dream perhaps. Here ended, then,
Progress this way. When, in the very nick
Of giving up, one time more, came a click
  As when a trap shuts—you're inside the den!

Burningly it came on me all at once,
  This was the place! those two hills on the right,
  Crouched like two bulls locked horn in horn in fight;
While to the left, a tall scalped mountain . . . Dunce,
Dotard, a-dozing at the very nonce,
  After a life spent training for the sight!

What in the midst lay but the Tower itself?
　The round squat turret, blind as the fool's heart,
　Built of brown stone, without a counterpart
In the whole world. The tempest's mocking elf
Points to the shipman thus the unseen shelf
　He strikes on, only when the timbers start.

Not see? because of night perhaps?—Why, day
　Came back again for that! before it left,
　The dying sunset kindled through a cleft:
The hills, like giants at a hunting, lay,
Chin upon hand, to see the game at bay,—
　"Now stab and end the creature—to the heft!"

Not hear? when noise was everywhere! it tolled
　Increasing like a bell. Names in my ears,
　Of all the lost adventurers my peers,—
How such a one was strong, and such was bold,
And such was fortunate, yet each of old
　Lost, lost! one moment knelled the woe of years.

There they stood, ranged along the hillsides, met
　To view the last of me, a living frame
　For one more picture! in a sheet of flame
I saw them and I knew them all. And yet
Dauntless the slug-horn to my lips I set,
　And blew. *"Childe Roland to the Dark Tower came."*

ROBERT BROWNING

One day in 1847, while they were living at Pisa, Mrs. Browning timidly placed in her husband's hands the manuscript of these Sonnets, and left the room. He read them with thrilling excitement and declared them to be the finest sonnets written since Shakespeare. However that may be, they are certainly among the best sonnets and the best love-poems in English. The title was thought of by Browning because of her poem called *Catarina to Camoens*.

From SONNETS FROM THE PORTUGUESE

I

I THOUGHT once how Theocritus had sung
Of the sweet years, the dear and wished-for years,
Who each one in a gracious hand appears
To bear a gift for mortals, old or young:
And, as I mused it in his antique tongue,
I saw, in gradual vision through my tears,
The sweet, sad years, the melancholy years,
Those of my own life, who by turns had flung
A shadow across me. Straightway I was 'ware,
So weeping, how a mystic Shape did move
Behind me, and drew me backward by the hair;
And a voice said in mastery, while I strove,—
"Guess now who holds thee?"—"Death!" I said.
　　But, there,
The silver answer rang,—"Not Death, but Love."

V

I LIFT my heavy heart up solemnly,
As once Electra her sepulchral urn,
And, looking in thine eyes, I overturn
The ashes at thy feet. Behold and see
What a great heap of grief lay hid in me,

And how the red wild sparkles dimly burn
Through the ashen grayness. If thy foot in scorn
Could tread them out to darkness utterly,
It might be well perhaps. But if instead
Thou wait beside me for the wind to blow
The grey dust up, . . . those laurels on thine head,
O my Belovèd, will not shield thee so,
That none of all the fires shall scorch and shred
The hair beneath. Stand farther off then! Go.

VI

Go from me. Yet I feel that I shall stand
Henceforward in thy shadow. Nevermore
Alone upon the threshold of my door
Of individual life, I shall command
The uses of my soul, nor lift my hand
Serenely in the sunshine as before,
Without the sense of that which I forbore—
Thy touch upon the palm. The widest land
Doom takes to part us, leaves thy heart in mine
With pulses that beat double. What I do
And what I dream include thee, as the wine
Must taste of its own grapes. And when I sue
God for myself, He hears that name of thine,
And sees within my eyes the tears of two.

VII

THE face of all the world is changed, I think,
Since first I heard the footsteps of thy soul
Move still, oh, still, beside me, as they stole
Betwixt me and the dreadful outer brink
Of obvious death, where I, who thought to sink,
Was caught up into love, and taught the whole
Of life in a new rhythm. The cup of dole

God gave for baptism, I am fain to drink,
And praise its sweetness, Sweet, with thee anear.
The names of country, heaven, are changed away
For where thou art or shalt be, there or here;
And this . . . this lute and song . . . loved yesterday,
(The singing angels know) are only dear
Because thy name moves right in what they say.

VIII

WHAT can I give thee back, O liberal
And princely giver, who hast brought thee gold
And purple of thine heart, unstained, untold,
And laid them on the outside of the wall
For such as I to take or leave withal,
In unexpected largesse? am I cold,
Ungrateful, that for these most manifold
High gifts, I render nothing back at all?
Not so; not cold,—but very poor instead.
Ask God who knows. For frequent tears have run
The colours from my life, and left so dead
And pale a stuff, it were not fitly done
To give the same as pillow to thy head.
Go farther! let it serve to trample on.

XV

ACCUSE me not, beseech thee, that I wear
Too calm and sad a face in front of thine;
For we two look two ways, and cannot shine
With the same sunlight on our brow and hair.
On me thou lookest with no doubting care,
As on a bee shut in a crystalline;
Since sorrow hath shut me safe in love's divine,
And to spread wing and fly in the outer air
Were most impossible failure, if I strove

To fail so. But I look on thee—on thee—
Beholding, besides love, the end of love,
Hearing oblivion beyond memory;
As one who sits and gazes from above,
Over the rivers to the bitter sea.

XVIII

I NEVER gave a lock of hair away
To a man, Dearest, except this to thee,
Which now upon my fingers thoughtfully,
I ring out to the full brown length and say
"Take it." My day of youth went yesterday;
My hair no longer bounds to my foot's glee,
Nor plant I it from rose or myrtle-tree,
As girls do, any more: it only may
Now shade on two pale cheeks the mark of tears,
Taught drooping from the head that hangs aside
Through sorrow's trick. I thought the funeral-shear
Would take this first, but Love is justified,—
Take it thou,—finding pure, from all those years,
The kiss my mother left here when she died.

XX

BELOVED, my Belovèd, when I think
That thou wast in the world a year ago,
What time I sat alone here in the snow
And saw no footprint, heard the silence sink
No moment at thy voice, but, link by link,
Went counting all my chains as if that so
They never could fall off at any blow
Struck by thy possible hand,—why, thus I drink
Of life's great cup of wonder! Wonderful,
Never to feel thee thrill the day or night
With personal act or speech,—nor ever cull

Some prescience of thee with the blossoms white
Thou sawest growing! Atheists are as dull,
Who cannot guess God's presence out of sight.

XXIV

LET the world's sharpness, like a clasping knife,
Shut in upon itself and do no harm
In this close hand of Love, now soft and warm,
And let us hear no sound of human strife
After the click of the shutting. Life to life—
I lean upon thee, Dear, without alarm,
And feel as safe as guarded by a charm
Against the stab of worldlings, who if rife
Are weak to injure. Very whitely still
The lilies of our lives may reassure
Their blossoms from their roots, accessible
Alone to heavenly dews that drop not fewer,
Growing straight, out of man's reach, on the hill.
God only, who made us rich, can make us poor.

XXVII

MY own Belovèd, who hast lifted me
From this drear flat of earth where I was thrown,
And, in betwixt the languid ringlets, blown
A life-breath, till the forehead hopefully
Shines out again, as all the angels see,
Before thy saving kiss! My own, my own,
Who camest to me when the world was gone,
And I who looked for only God, found *thee!*
I find thee; I am safe, and strong, and glad.
As one who stands in dewless asphodel
Looks backward on the tedious time he had
In the upper life,—so I, with bosom-swell,
Make witness, here, between the good and bad,
That Love, as strong as Death, retrieves as well.

XXVIII

My letters! all dead paper, mute and white!
And yet they seem alive and quivering
Against my tremulous hands which loose the string
And let them drop down on my knee tonight.
This said,—he wished to have me in his sight
Once, as a friend: this fixed a day in spring
To come and touch my hand . . . a simple thing,
Yet I wept for it!—this, . . . the paper's light . . .
Said, *Dear, I love thee;* and I sank and quailed
As if God's future thundered on my past.
This said, *I am thine*—and so its ink has paled
With lying at my heart that beat too fast.
And this . . . O Love, thy words have ill availed
If, what this said, I dared repeat at last!

XXXVIII

First time he kissed me, he but only kissed
The fingers of this hand wherewith I write;
And ever since, it grew more clean and white,
Slow to world-greetings, quick with its "Oh, list,"
When the angels speak. A ring of amethyst
I could not wear here, plainer to my sight,
Than that first kiss. The second passed in height
The first, and sought the forehead, and half missed,
Half falling on the hair. O beyond meed!
That was the chrism of love, which love's own crown,
With sanctifying sweetness, did precede.
The third upon my lips was folded down
In perfect, purple state; since when, indeed,
I have been proud and said, "My love, my own."

XLIII

How do I love thee? Let me count the ways.
I love thee to the depth and breadth and height
My soul can reach, when feeling out of sight
For the ends of Being and ideal Grace.
I love thee to the level of everyday's
Most quiet need, by sun and candle-light.
I love thee freely, as men strive for Right;
I love thee purely, as they turn from Praise.
I love thee with the passion put to use
In my old griefs, and with my childhood's faith.
I love thee with a love I seemed to lose
With my lost saints,—I love thee with the breath,
Smiles, tears, of all my life!—and, if God choose,
I shall but love thee better after death.

ELIZABETH BARRETT BROWNING

These two poems are part of the Hebrew Melodies, perhaps the best known of Byron's lyrics. Byron's "tempest-anger, tempest-mirth," and romantic genius are best displayed in his long poems. Strange that the most popular romantic poet of his time should also have been the ablest satirist. Byron did not regard the Hebrew Melodies highly. He wrote them for music, to please a friend. *She Walks in Beauty* was written at 3 A.M., Byron's favourite hour for composition, on returning from a ball-room, where he had seen a lady dressed in mourning, with spangles.

The Destruction of Sennacherib

THE Assyrian came down like the wolf on the fold,
And his cohorts were gleaming in purple and gold;
And the sheen of their spears was like stars on the sea,
When the blue wave rolls nightly on deep Galilee.

[191]

Like the leaves of the forest when Summer is green,
That host with their banners at sunset were seen:
Like the leaves of the forest when Autumn hath blown,
That host on the morrow lay wither'd and strown.

For the Angel of Death spread his wings on the blast,
And breathed in the face of the foe as he pass'd;
And the eyes of the sleepers waxed deadly and chill,
And their hearts but once heaved, and for ever grew still!

And there lay the steed with his nostril all wide,
But through it there roll'd not the breath of his pride;
And the foam of his gasping lay white on the turf,
And cold as the spray of the rock-beating surf.

And there lay the rider distorted and pale,
With the dew on his brow, and the rust on his mail:
And the tents were all silent, the banners alone,
The lances unlifted, the trumpet unblown.

And the widows of Ashur are loud in their wail,
And the idols are broke in the temple of Baal;
And the might of the Gentile, unsmote by the sword,
Hath melted like snow in the glance of the Lord!

LORD BYRON

She Walks in Beauty

She walks in beauty, like the night
  Of cloudless climes and starry skies;
And all that's best of dark and bright
  Meet in her aspect and her eyes:
Thus mellow'd to that tender light
  Which heaven to gaudy day denies.

[192]

One shade the more, one ray the less,
  Had half impair'd the nameless grace
Which waves in every raven tress,
  Or softly lightens o'er her face;
Where thoughts serenely sweet express
How pure, how dear their dwelling-place.

And on that cheek, and o'er that brow,
  So soft, so calm, yet eloquent,
The smiles that win, the tints that glow,
  But tell of days in goodness spent,
A mind at peace with all below,
A heart whose love is innocent!

LORD BYRON

No one knows how long a time Gray spent on the composition of the *Elegy*. It is often stated that it took him seven years to write it; but there is no proof of this. It is certain he had it in his mind or on his mind for some years; and it was finally published in February 1751, and sold for sixpence. It became instantly popular and has never known any decline in public favour. It expresses in language of exquisite beauty thoughts common to all mankind. Doctor Johnson, who disliked Gray, admired this poem, and was especially fond of the stanza beginning

But who to dumb forgetfulness a prey

probably because of his own terror of death.

The rich were buried in the church; the poor in the churchyard.

It was perhaps characteristic of Matthew Arnold that he preferred the stilted and pedantic later *Odes* to the splendid *Elegy*.

[193]

ELEGY

WRITTEN IN A COUNTRY CHURCHYARD

THE curfew tolls the knell of parting day,
The lowing herd wind slowly o'er the lea,
The ploughman homeward plods his weary way,
And leaves the world to darkness and to me.

Now fades the glimmering landscape on the sight,
And all the air a solemn stillness holds,
Save where the beetle wheels his droning flight,
And drowsy tinklings lull the distant folds;

Save that from yonder ivy-mantled tower
The moping owl does to the moon complain
Of such, as wandering near her secret bower,
Molest her ancient solitary reign.

Beneath those rugged elms, that yew-tree's shade,
Where heaves the turf in many a mouldering heap,
Each in his narrow cell for ever laid,
The rude forefathers of the hamlet sleep.

The breezy call of incense-breathing morn,
The swallow twittering from the straw-built shed,
The cock's shrill clarion, or the echoing horn,
No more shall rouse them from their lowly bed.

For them no more the blazing hearth shall burn,
Or busy housewife ply her evening care:
No children run to lisp their sire's return,
Or climb his knees the envied kiss to share.

Oft did the harvest to their sickle yield,
Their furrow oft the stubborn glebe has broke;
How jocund did they drive their team afield!
How bowed the woods beneath their sturdy stroke!

Let not ambition mock their useful toil,
Their homely joys, and destiny obscure;
Nor grandeur hear with a disdainful smile,
The short and simple annals of the poor.

The boast of heraldry, the pomp of power,
And all that beauty, all that wealth e'er gave,
Awaits alike th' inevitable hour:
The paths of glory lead but to the grave.

Nor you, ye proud, impute to these the fault,
If memory o'er their tomb no trophies raise,
Where thro' the long-drawn aisle and fretted vault
The pealing anthem swells the note of praise.

Can storied urn or animated bust
Back to its mansion call the fleeting breath?
Can honour's voice provoke the silent dust,
Or flattery soothe the dull cold ear of death?

Perhaps in this neglected spot is laid
Some heart once pregnant with celestial fire;
Hands, that the rod of empire might have sway'd,
Or waked to extasy the living lyre.

But knowledge to their eyes her ample page
Rich with the spoils of time did ne'er unroll;
Chill penury repress'd their noble rage,
And froze the genial current of the soul.

Full many a gem of purest ray serene
The dark unfathom'd caves of ocean bear:
Full many a flower is born to blush unseen,
And waste its sweetness on the desert air.

Some village-Hampden, that with dauntless breast
The little tyrant of his fields withstood;
Some mute inglorious Milton here may rest,
Some Cromwell, guiltless of his country's blood.

Th' applause of listening senates to command,
The threats of pain and ruin to despise,
To scatter plenty o'er a smiling land,
And read their history in a nation's eyes,

Their lot forbade: nor circumscribed alone
Their growing virtues, but their crimes confined;
Forbade to wade through slaughter to a throne,
And shut the gates of mercy on mankind;

The struggling pangs of conscious truth to hide,
To quench the blushes of ingenuous shame,
Or heap the shrine of luxury and pride
With incense kindled at the Muse's flame.

Far from the madding crowd's ignoble strife
Their sober wishes never learn'd to stray;
Along the cool sequester'd vale of life
They kept the noiseless tenour of their way.

Yet ev'n these bones from insult to protect
Some frail memorial still erected nigh,
With uncouth rhymes and shapeless sculpture decked
Implores the passing tribute of a sigh.

Their name, their years, spelt by th' unletter'd muse,
The place of fame and elegy supply:
And many a holy text around she strews,
That teach the rustic moralist to die.

For who, to dumb forgetfulness a prey,
This pleasing anxious being e'er resign'd,
Left the warm precincts of the cheerful day,
Nor cast one longing lingering look behind?

On some fond breast the parting soul relies,
Some pious drops the closing eye requires;
Ev'n from the tomb the voice of nature cries,
Ev'n in our ashes live their wonted fires.

For thee, who, mindful of th' unhonour'd dead,
Dost in these lines their artless tale relate;
If chance, by lonely contemplation led,
Some kindred spirit shall inquire thy fate,—

Haply some hoary-headed swain may say,
'Oft have we seen him at the peep of dawn
Brushing with hasty steps the dews away
To meet the sun upon the upland lawn.

'There at the foot of yonder nodding beech
That wreathes its old fantastic roots so high,
His listless length at noontide would he stretch,
And pore upon the brook that babbles by.

'Hard by yon wood, now smiling as in scorn
Muttering his wayward fancies he would rove;
Now drooping, woeful wan, like one forlorn,
Or crazed with care, or cross'd in hopeless love.

'One morn I missed him on the custom'd hill,
Along the heath and near his favourite tree;
Another came; nor yet beside the rill,
Nor up the lawn, nor at the wood was he;

'The next, with dirges due in sad array
Slow thro' the church-way path we saw him borne;—
Approach and read (for thou can'st read) the lay,
Graved on the stone beneath yon aged thorn.'

The Epitaph

Here rests his head upon the lap of Earth,
A youth, to fortune and to fame unknown:
Fair science frown'd not on his humble birth,
And melancholy mark'd him for her own.

Large was his bounty, and his soul sincere,
Heav'n did a recompense as largely send:
He gave to misery (all he had) a tear,
He gained from Heav'n ('twas all he wish'd) a friend.

No farther seek his merits to disclose,
Or draw his frailties from their dread abode,
(There they alike in trembling hope repose,)
The bosom of his Father and his God.

THOMAS GRAY

Of all the famous living poets of England, Watson is now the oldest in years, and the least appreciated. He cannot be said to have survived his reputation, but his name is rarely mentioned and I am afraid he is not so widely read as in the early days of the present century. Yet there is no one today who is more authentically a Poet.

Nearly half a century has passed since he wrote *Wordsworth's Grave;* and perhaps there has never been an instance where literary criticism has been more admirably combined with poetic expression.

His Epigrams exhibit remarkable gifts of conciseness and penetration.

The poem *How Weary Is Our Heart* is a passionate plea for the rights of little people.

How Weary Is Our Heart

Of kings and courts; of kingly, courtly ways
In which the life of man is bought and sold;
How weary is our heart these many days!

Of ceremonious embassies that hold
Parley with Hell in fine and silken phrase,
How weary is our heart these many days!

Of wavering counsellors neither hot nor cold,
Whom from His mouth God speweth, be it told
How weary is our heart these many days!

Yea, for the ravelled night is round the lands,
And sick are we of all the imperial story.
The tramp of Power, and its long trail of pain;
The mighty brows in meanest arts grown hoary;
The mighty hands,

That in the dear, affronted name of Peace
Bind down a people to be racked and slain;
The emulous armies waxing without cease,
All-puissant all in vain;
The pacts and leagues to murder by delays,
And the dumb throngs that on the deaf thrones gaze;
The common loveless lust of territory;
The lips that only babble of their mart,
While to the night the shrieking hamlets blaze;
The bought allegiance, and the purchased praise,
False honour, and shameful glory;—
Of all the evil whereof this is part,
How weary is our heart,
How weary is our heart these many days!

WILLIAM WATSON

———

Time and fashion have been rather cruel to *One More
Unfortunate* but they have only strengthened the pathos
and tragedy of *The Song of the Shirt.*

THE SONG OF THE SHIRT

WITH fingers weary and worn,
    With eyelids heavy and red,
A woman sat, in unwomanly rags,
    Plying her needle and thread—
Stitch! stitch! stitch!
    In poverty, hunger, and dirt,
And still with a voice of dolorous pitch
    She sang the "Song of the Shirt."

[200]

"Work! work! work!
  While the cock is crowing aloof!
And work—work—work,
  Till the stars shine through the roof!
It's Oh! to be a slave
  Along with the barbarous Turk,
Where woman has never a soul to save,
  If this is Christian work!

"Work—work—work,
  Till the brain begins to swim;
Work—work—work,
  Till the eyes are heavy and dim!
Seam, and gusset, and band,
Band, and gusset, and seam,
Till over the buttons I fall asleep,
  And sew them on in a dream!

"Oh, Men, with Sisters dear!
  Oh, Men, with Mothers and Wives!
It is not linen you're wearing out
  But human creatures' lives!
Stitch—stitch—stitch,
  In poverty, hunger, and dirt,
Sewing at once, with a double thread,
  A Shroud as well as a Shirt.

"But why do I talk of Death?
  That Phantom of grisly bone,
I hardly fear its terrible shape,
  It seems so like my own—
It seems so like my own,
  Because of the fasts I keep;
Oh, God! that bread should be so dear,
  And flesh and blood so cheap!

"Work—work—work!
  My labour never flags;
And what are its wages? A bed of straw,
  A crust of bread—and rags.
That shattered roof—this naked floor—
  A table—a broken chair—
And a wall so blank, my shadow I thank
  For sometimes falling there!

"Work—work—work!
  From weary chime to chime,
Work—work—work,
  As prisoners work for crime!
Band, and gusset, and seam,
  Seam, and gusset, and band,
Till the heart is sick, and the brain benumbed,
  As well as the weary hand.

"Work—work—work,
  In the dull December light,
And work—work—work,
  When the weather is warm and bright—
While underneath the eaves
  The brooding swallows cling
As if to show me their sunny backs
  And twit me with the spring.

"Oh! but to breathe the breath
  Of the cowslip and primrose sweet—
With the sky above my head,
  And the grass beneath my feet;
For only one short hour
  To feel as I used to feel,
Before I knew the woes of want
  And the walk that costs a meal.

"Oh! but for one short hour!
 A respite however brief!
No blessèd leisure for Love or Hope,
 But only time for Grief!
A little weeping would ease my heart,
 But in their briny bed
My tears must stop, for every drop
 Hinders needle and thread!"

With fingers weary and worn,
 With eyelids heavy and red,
A woman sat, in unwomanly rags,
 Plying her needle and thread—
Stitch! stitch! stitch!
 In poverty, hunger, and dirt,
And still with a voice of dolorous pitch,—
Would that its tone could reach the Rich!—
 She sang this "Song of the Shirt!"

THOMAS HOOD

In this group of poems, the author of *The Red Badge
of Courage* and *Maggie* and *The Monster* is a "prodigal
in thought, an economist in words."

The Violets

THERE was a land where lived no violets.
A traveller at once demanded: "Why?"
The people told him:
"Once the violets of this place spoke thus:
'Until some woman freely gives her lover
To another woman
We will fight in bloody scuffle.'"
Sadly the people added:
"There are no violets here."

STEPHEN CRANE

[203]

THE WAYFARER

THE wayfarer,
Perceiving the pathway to truth,
Was struck with astonishment.
It was thickly grown with weeds.
"Ha," he said,
"I see that none has passed here
In a long time."
Later he saw that each weed
Was a singular knife.
"Well," he mumbled at last,
"Doubtless there are other roads."

STEPHEN CRANE

ANCESTRY

ONCE I saw mountains angry,
And ranged in battle-front.
Against them stood a little man;
Ay, he was no bigger than my finger.
I laughed, and spoke to one near me,
"Will he prevail?"
"Surely," replied this other;
"His grandfathers beat them many times."
Then did I see much virtue in grandfathers,—
At least, for the little man
Who stood against the mountains.

STEPHEN CRANE

When a great poem is published, who can set any limit to the range of its influence?

In the year 1908 I saw for the first time the Grand

Canyon of the Colorado. I have not seen all the wonders of the world, but I can say confidently that the most sublime natural spectacle I have seen is this Grand Canyon. After several days there, I was sitting in the smoking car of the tiny switch-train that takes tourists back to Williams, when the fireman of the locomotive, who had a day off, came in and sat beside me. We fell into conversation, and I asked him if he were impressed with the majesty of the Canyon. I told him that this had been my first sight of it, and that I was completely overcome; but he, who made four trips a day thither, did it still impress him, or was it just part of the daily job? He asked, "Do you want to know how it impresses me? I will tell you." Then he quoted without missing a word the whole of Bryant's poem *Thanatopsis*.

The word "Thanatopsis" is from two Greek words, *Thanatos*, meaning death, and *opsis*, meaning sight. Thus the title of the poem means "A consideration of death."

There is no poem in American literature about which so many false statements have been made as about *Thanatopsis*. The majority of works on English literature say that it was written when Bryant was in his teens, and most of them give the age seventeen for its composition. Bryant himself said he did not know when it was written.

It was first printed in *The North American Review* for September 1817. Bryant was then twenty-three. This first edition of the poem is very far from being a masterpiece. The magnificent beginning, seventeen lines, did not appear at all; and the noble, stately conclusion, of nine lines, is also absent. Presumably he had not written them.

Some beautiful individual lines in the poem were also added later, and there were some very bad lines which he afterward cancelled, for example:

> The tittering world
> Dance to the grave.

At the beginning of the poem in the 1817 version there were four introductory rhymed stanzas, in a short metre, which are utterly commonplace.

In 1821, when Bryant was twenty-seven, *Thanatopsis* was published substantially as we have it now.

Thus it is clear that, although *Thanatopsis* is a great poem, it was not written by a boy, and the first edition was not in any way remarkable. Bryant's revisions, however, are very remarkable.

THANATOPSIS

To him who in the love of Nature holds
Communion with her visible forms, she speaks
A various language; for his gayer hours
She has a voice of gladness, and a smile
And eloquence of beauty, and she glides
Into his darker musings, with a mild
And healing sympathy, that steals away
Their sharpness, ere he is aware. When thoughts
Of the last bitter hour come like a blight
Over thy spirit, and sad images
Of the stern agony, and shroud, and pall,
And breathless darkness, and the narrow house,
Make thee to shudder, and grow sick at heart;—
Go forth, under the open sky, and list
To Nature's teachings, while from all around—
Earth and her waters, and the depths of air—
Comes a still voice—

Yet a few days, and thee
The all-beholding sun shall see no more
In all his course; nor yet in the cold ground,
Where thy pale form was laid, with many tears,
Nor in the embrace of ocean, shall exist

Thy image. Earth, that nourished thee, shall claim
Thy growth, to be resolved to earth again,
And, lost each human trace, surrendering up
Thine individual being, shalt thou go
To mix forever with the elements,
To be a brother to the insensible rock
And to the sluggish clod, which the rude swain
Turns with his share, and treads upon. The oak
Shall send his roots abroad, and pierce thy mould.

Yet not to thine eternal resting-place
Shalt thou retire alone, nor couldst thou wish
Couch more magnificent. Thou shalt lie down
With patriarchs of the infant world—with kings,
The powerful of the earth—the wise, the good,
Fair forms, and hoary seers of ages past,
All in one mighty sepulchre. The hills
Rock-ribbed and ancient as the sun,—the vales
Stretching in pensive quietness between;
The venerable woods—rivers that move
In majesty, and the complaining brooks
That make the meadows green; and, poured round all,
Old Ocean's gray and melancholy waste,—
Are but the solemn decorations all
Of the great tomb of man. The golden sun,
The planets, all the infinite host of heaven,
Are shining on the sad abodes of death,
Through the still lapse of ages. All that tread
The globe are but a handful to the tribes
That slumber in its bosom.—Take the wings
Of morning, pierce the Barcan wilderness,
Or lose thyself in the continuous woods
Where rolls the Oregon, and hears no sound,
Save his own dashings—yet the dead are there:
And millions in those solitudes, since first

The flight of years began, have laid them down
In their last sleep—the dead reign there alone.
So shalt thou rest, and what if thou withdraw
In silence from the living, and no friend
Take note of thy departure? All that breathe
Will share thy destiny. The gay will laugh
When thou art gone, the solemn brood of care
Plod on, and each one as before will chase
His favourite phantom; yet all these shall leave
Their mirth and their employments, and shall come
And make their bed with thee. As the long train
Of ages glide away, the sons of men,
The youth in life's fresh spring, and he who goes
In the full strength of years, matron and maid,
The speechless babe, and the gray-headed man—
Shall one by one be gathered to thy side,
By those, who in their turn shall follow them.

So live, that when thy summons comes to join
The innumerable caravan, which moves
To that mysterious realm, where each shall take
His chamber in the silent halls of death,
Thou go not, like the quarry-slave at night,
Scourged to his dungeon, but, sustained and soothed
By an unfaltering trust, approach thy grave,
Like one who wraps the drapery of his couch
About him, and lies down to pleasant dreams.

WILLIAM CULLEN BRYANT

Lessons which Emerson taught by example as well as by precept.

FABLE

THE mountain and the squirrel
Had a quarrel,
And the former called the latter "Little Prig";
Bun replied,
'You are doubtless very big;
But all sorts of things and weather
Must be taken in together,
To make up a year
And a sphere.
And I think it no disgrace
To occupy my place.
If I'm not so large as you,
You are not so small as I,
And not half so spry.
I'll not deny you make
A very pretty squirrel track;
Talents differ; all is well and wisely put;
If I cannot carry forests on my back,
Neither can you crack a nut.'

RALPH WALDO EMERSON

FORBEARANCE

HAST thou named all the birds without a gun?
Loved the wood-rose, and left it on its stalk?
At rich men's tables eaten bread and pulse?
Unarmed, faced danger with a heart of trust?
And loved so well a high behaviour
In man or maid, that thou from speech refrained,
Nobility more nobly to repay?
O, be my friend, and teach me to be thine!

RALPH WALDO EMERSON

[209]

These two poems illustrate the more tranquil mood in which Miss Branch reveals intense feeling. The love of nature and the love of home. Elsewhere in this volume will be found illustrations of her dynamic power.

HER WORDS

MY mother has the prettiest tricks
    Of words and words and words.
Her talk comes out as smooth and sleek
    As breasts of singing birds.

She shapes her speech all silver fine
    Because she loves it so.
And her own eyes begin to shine
    To hear her stories grow.

And if she goes to make a call
    Or out to take a walk,
We leave our work when she returns
    And run to hear her talk.

We had not dreamed these things were so
    Of sorrow and of mirth.
Her speech is as a thousand eyes
    Through which we see the earth.

God wove a web of loveliness,
    Of clouds and stars and birds,
But made not anything at all
    So beautiful as words.

They shine around our simple earth
    With golden shadowings,
And every common thing they touch
    Is exquisite with wings.

There's nothing poor and nothing small
    But is made fair with them.
They are the hands of living faith
    That touch the garment's hem.

They are as fair as bloom or air,
    They shine like any star,
And I am rich who learned from her
    How beautiful they are.

ANNA HEMPSTEAD BRANCH

The Silence of the Poets

I BETTER like that shadowed side of things
In which the Poets wrote not; when they went
Unto the fullness of their great content
Like moths into the grass with folded wings.
The silence of the Poets with it brings
The other side of moons, and it is spent
In love, in sorrow, or in wonderment.
After the silence, maybe a bird sings.
I have heard call, as Summer calls the swallow,
A leisure, bidding unto ways serene
To be a child of winds and the blue hazes.
"Dream"—quoth the Dreamer—and 'tis sweet to follow!
So Keats watched stars rise from his meadows green,
And Chaucer spent his hours among the daisies.

ANNA HEMPSTEAD BRANCH

Sabine Baring-Gould died in 1924, ninety years old. His autobiography is full of interest; and his hymns will be sung in centuries to come. Although *Onward, Christian Soldiers* is perhaps the most widely known, I think the following is his best.

Now the Day Is Over

Now the day is over,
Night is drawing nigh;
Shadows of the evening
Steal across the sky.

Jesus, give the weary
Calm and sweet repose;
With Thy tenderest blessing
May our eyelids close.

Grant to little children,
Visions bright of Thee;
Guard the sailors tossing
On the deep blue sea.

Comfort every sufferer
Watching late in pain;
Those who plan some evil
From their sins restrain.

Through the long night-watches
May Thine angels spread
Their white wings above me,
Watching round my bed.

When the morning wakens,
Then may I arise
Pure, and fresh, and sinless
In Thy holy eyes.

SABINE BARING-GOULD

In the first, last, and only issue of *The North Street Gazette*, edited by Maurice Baring and Hilaire Belloc in 1908, appeared an article advocating votes for monkeys, an announcement that the journal was written for the rich by the poor, that all communications accompanied by stamps would be confiscated, that all public scandals would be fearlessly exposed except those that might be lucrative to the editors or injure them and their friends; while this poetic masterpiece came from Mr. Belloc.

EAST AND WEST

THE dog is a faithful, intelligent friend,
    But his hide is covered with hair.
The cat will inhabit a house to the end,
    But her hide is covered with hair.

The camel excels in a number of ways,
    The Arab accords him continual praise;
He can go without drinking for several days—
    But his hide is covered with hair.

The hide of the mammoth is covered with wool,
    The hide of the porpoise is sleek and cool,
But you find if you look at that gambolling fool—
    That his hide is covered with hair.

The men that sit on the Treasury Bench,
Their hide is covered with hair, etc.

Chorus

Oh! I thank my God for this at the least,
I was born in the west and not in the east:
And he made me a human instead of a beast,
Whose HIDE IS COVERED WITH HAIR.

HILAIRE BELLOC

———

Observe that though this poem is in rhyme, the lack of emphasis at the unaccented end of the lines gives almost the effect of blank verse.

It is a study in human testimony. All we know of the late Duchess is from the lips of her worst enemy—her husband; and through his depreciation of her we feel the real charm of her character and the deliberate cruelty of his. It is the story of Andromeda without Perseus.

MY LAST DUCHESS

FERRARA

THAT's my last Duchess painted on the wall,
Looking as if she were alive. I call
That piece a wonder, now: Frà Pandolf's hands
Worked busily a day, and there she stands.
Will't please you sit and look at her? I said
"Frà Pandolf" by design, for never read
Strangers like you that pictured countenance,
The depth and passion of its earnest glance,

But to myself they turned (since none puts by
The curtain I have drawn for you, but I)
And seemed as they would ask me, if they durst,
How such a glance came there; so, not the first
Are you to turn and ask thus. Sir, 'twas not
Her husband's presence only, called that spot
Of joy into the Duchess' cheek: perhaps
Frà Pandolf chanced to say "Her mantle laps
Over my lady's wrist too much," or "Paint
Must never hope to reproduce the faint
Half-flush that dies along her throat:" such stuff
Was courtesy, she thought, and cause enough
For calling up that spot of joy. She had
A heart—how shall I say?—too soon made glad,
Too easily impressed; she liked whate'er
She looked on, and her looks went everywhere.
Sir, 'twas all one! My favour at her breast,
The dropping of the daylight in the West,
The bough of cherries some officious fool
Broke in the orchard for her, the white mule
She rode with round the terrace—all and each
Would draw from her alike the approving speech,
Or blush, at least. She thanked men,—good! but thanked
Somehow—I know not how—as if she ranked
My gift of a nine-hundred-years-old name
With anybody's gift. Who'd stoop to blame
This sort of trifling? Even had you skill
In speech—(which I have not)—to make your will
Quite clear to such an one, and say, "Just this
Or that in you disgusts me; here you miss,
Or there exceed the mark"—and if she let
Herself be lessoned so, nor plainly set
Her wits to yours, forsooth, and made excuse,
—E'en then would be some stooping; and I choose
Never to stoop. Oh sir, she smiled, no doubt,

Whene'er I passed her; but who passed without
Much the same smile? This grew; I gave commands;
Then all smiles stopped together. There she stands
As if alive. Will't please you rise? We'll meet
The company below, then. I repeat,
The Count your master's known munificence
Is ample warrant that no just pretence
Of mine for dowry will be disallowed;
Though his fair daughter's self, as I avowed
At starting, is my object. Nay, we'll go
Together down, sir. Notice Neptune, though,
Taming a sea-horse, thought a rarity,
Which Claus of Innsbruck cast in bronze for me!

ROBERT BROWNING

John Farrar wrote his own poems before publishing those
of others; and success attended both adventures.

A Comparison

APPLE blossoms look like snow,
They're different, though.
Snow falls softly, but it brings
Noisy things:
Sleighs and bells, forts and fights,
Cosy nights.

But apple blossoms when they go,
White and slow,
Quiet all the orchard space,
Till the place
Hushed with falling sweetness seems
Filled with dreams.

JOHN FARRAR

Poet, parodist, anthologist, critic, Louis Untermeyer has shown by precept and example what poetry is, and what it can accomplish.

PRAYER

GOD, though this life is but a wraith,
Although we know not what we use,
Although we grope with little faith,
Give me the heart to fight—and lose.

Ever insurgent let me be,
Make me more daring than devout;
From sleek contentment keep me free,
And fill me with a bouyant doubt.

Open my eyes to visions girt
With beauty, and with wonder lit—
But let me always see the dirt,
And all that spawn and die in it.

Open my ears to music; let
Me thrill with Spring's first flutes and drums—
But never let me dare forget
The bitter ballads of the slums.

From compromise and things half-done,
Keep me, with stern and stubborn pride.
And when, at last the fight is won.
God, keep me still unsatisfied.

LOUIS UNTERMEYER

POEMS ON TREES

Every tree is itself a poem. Ever since I read *The Wood-landers*, Hardy's novel where the trees are living characters, every tree has seemed to me to have a personality. The most beautiful poem I know on this general subject is A. E. Housman's lyric on the cherry-blooms. Joyce Kilmer will be remembered for centuries because of two lines in his poem; Robert Frost's *Birches* is characteristic of its author's meditative spirit; Lanier's ballad is full of feeling; and Tennyson's *The Oak*, written when he was eighty, compares the life of a man to a tree in different seasons. Observe that the shape of the poem as printed is like the bole of a tree.

LOVELIEST OF TREES

LOVELIEST of trees, the cherry now
Is hung with bloom along the bough,
And stands about the woodland ride
Wearing white for Eastertide.

Now, of my threescore years and ten,
Twenty will not come again,
And take from seventy springs a score,
It only leaves me fifty more.

And since to look at things in bloom
Fifty springs are little room,
About the woodlands I will go
To see the cherry hung with snow.

A. E. HOUSMAN

TREES

I THINK that I shall never see
A poem lovely as a tree.

A tree whose hungry mouth is prest
Against the earth's sweet-flowing breast;

A tree that looks at God all day,
And lifts her leafy arms to pray;

A tree that may in summer wear
A nest of robins in her hair;

Upon whose bosom snow has lain;
Who intimately lives with rain.

Poems are made by fools like me,
But only God can make a tree.

JOYCE KILMER

BIRCHES

WHEN I see birches bend to left and right
Across the line of straighter darker trees,
I like to think some boy's been swinging them.
But swinging doesn't bend them down to stay.
Ice-storms do that. Often you must have seen them
Loaded with ice a sunny winter morning
After a rain. They click upon themselves
As the breeze rises, and turn many-coloured
As the stir cracks and crazes their enamel.
Soon the sun's warmth makes them shed crystal shells
Shattering and avalanching on the snow-crust—
Such heaps of broken glass to sweep away

You'd think the inner dome of heaven had fallen.
They are dragged to the withered bracken by the load,
And they seem not to break; though, once they are bowed
So low for long, they never right themselves:
You may see their trunks arching in the woods
Years afterwards, trailing their leaves on the ground
Like girls on hands and knees that throw their hair
Before them over their heads to dry in the sun.
But I was going to say when Truth broke in
With all her matter-of-fact about the ice-storm
I should prefer to have some boy bend them
As he went out and in to fetch the cows—
Some boy too far from town to learn baseball,
Whose only play was what he found himself,
Summer or winter, and could play alone.
One by one he subdued his father's trees
By riding them down over and over again
Until he took the stiffness out of them,
And not one but hung limp, not one was left
For him to conquer. He learned all there was
To learn about not launching out too soon
And so not carrying the tree away
Clear to the ground. He always kept his poise
To the top branches, climbing carefully
With the same pains you use to fill a cup
Up to the brim, and even above the brim.
Then he flung outward, feet first, with a swish,
Kicking his way down through the air to the ground.

So was I once myself a swinger of birches;
And so I dream of going back to be.
It's when I'm weary of considerations,
And life is too much like a pathless wood
Where your face burns and tickles with the cobwebs
Broken across it, and one eye is weeping

From a twig's having lashed across it open.
I'd like to get away from earth awhile
And then come back to it and begin over.

May no fate wilfully misunderstand me
And half grant what I wish and snatch me away
Not to return. Earth's the right place for love:
I don't know where it's likely to go better.
I'd like to go by climbing a birch-tree,
And climb black branches up a snow-white trunk
Towards heaven, till the tree could bear no more,
But dipped its top and set me down again.
That would be good both going and coming back.
One could do worse than be a swinger of birches.

ROBERT FROST

A Ballad of Trees and the Master

Into the woods my Master went,
Clean forspent, forspent.
Into the woods my Master came,
Forspent with love and shame.
But the olives they were not blind to Him,
The little gray leaves were kind to Him:
The thorn-tree had a mind to Him
When into the woods He came.

Out of the woods my Master went,
And he was well content.
Out of the woods my Master came,
Content with death and shame.
When Death and Shame would woo Him last,
From under the trees they drew Him last:
'Twas on a tree they slew Him—last
When out of the woods he came.

SIDNEY LANIER

THE OAK

Live thy Life,
  Young and old,
Like yon oak,
Bright in spring,
  Living gold;

Summer-rich
  Then; and then
Autumn-changed,
Soberer-hued
  Gold again.

All his leaves
  Fall'n at length,
Look, he stands,
Trunk and bough,
  Naked strength.

ALFRED TENNYSON

THE LONELY TREE

A twisted ash, a ragged fir,
A silver birch with leaves astir.

Men talk of forests broad and deep,
Where summer long the shadows sleep.

Though I love forests deep and wide,
The lone tree on the bare hillside,

The brave, wind-beaten, lonely tree
Is rooted in the heart of me.

A twisted ash, a ragged fir,
A silver birch with leaves astir.

WILFRID WILSON GIBSON

[222]

SHAKESPEARE'S SONGS AND SONNETS

Shakespeare was the best dramatist, the best sonneteer, the best song-writer in the English language. He defeated every specialist at his own game. No other man has ever used words with such ease, beauty, and precision.

We know that Shakespeare left the excitement of London life for the peace of his native village, Stratford, in 1610 or 1611; and no one knows why he did this; he was only about forty-six, yet his work was done. My own conjecture is, that it was because of the publication of his Sonnets. They were printed in 1609, and they are filled with such tremendous passion and are so amazingly intimate in their allusions, that he may have found it awkward to remain in London.

The Songs of Shakespeare have that airy, unconscious grace that was the peculiar gift of the Elizabethans. Nothing has ever given the spirit of Winter in the country-side better than the Song from *Love's Labour's Lost*. And the affectionate allusions to Tom, Dick, Marian, and greasy Joan, are in the manner of the true aristocrat, who is accustomed to the ministrations of house-servants, and understands how to treat them.

⸻

WHERE THE BEE SUCKS

WHERE the bee sucks, there suck I,
In a cowslip's bell I lie;
There I couch when owls do cry.
On the bat's back I do fly
After summer merrily.
Merrily, merrily, shall I live now
Under the blossom that hangs on the bough.

WILLIAM SHAKESPEARE

[223]

O Mistress Mine

O, Mistress mine, where are you roaming?
O, stay and hear; your true love's coming,
  That can sing both high and low:
Trip no further, pretty sweeting,
Journeys end in lovers meeting,
  Every wise man's son doth know.

What is love? 'tis not hereafter;
Present mirth hath present laughter;
  What's to come is still unsure:
In delay there lies no plenty;
Then come kiss me, sweet and twenty,
  Youth's a stuff will not endure.

WILLIAM SHAKESPEARE

Come Unto These Yellow Sands

Come unto these yellow sands,
  And then take hands:
Curtsied when you have, and kissed,—
  The wild waves whist,—
Foot it featly here and there;
And sweet sprites, the burden bear.
    Hark, hark!
      Bow, wow.
    The watch-dogs bark:
      Bow, wow.
    Hark, hark! I hear
The strain of strutting Chanticleer
  Cock-a-diddle-dow.

WILLIAM SHAKESPEARE

TAKE, O, TAKE THOSE LIPS AWAY

TAKE, O, take those lips away,
    That so sweetly were forsworn;
And those eyes, the break of day,
    Lights that do mislead the morn:
But my kisses bring again,
            Bring again;
Seals of love, but sealed in vain,
            Sealed in vain!

WILLIAM SHAKESPEARE

HARK, HARK! THE LARK

HARK, hark! the lark at heaven's gate sings,
    And Phœbus 'gins arise,
His steeds to water at those springs
    On chaliced flowers that lies;
And winking mary-buds begin
    To ope their golden eyes:
With every thing that pretty is,
    My lady sweet, arise!
        Arise, arise!

WILLIAM SHAKESPEARE

FULL FATHOM FIVE THY FATHER LIES

FULL fathom five thy father lies;
    Of his bones are coral made:
Those are pearls that were his eyes:
    Nothing of him that doth fade,
But doth suffer a sea-change
Into something rich and strange.
Sea-nymphs hourly ring his knell;
            Ding-dong.
Hark! now I hear them,—Ding-dong, bell.

WILLIAM SHAKESPEARE

WHEN ICICLES HANG BY THE WALL

WHEN icicles hang by the wall,
    And Dick the shepherd blows his nail,
And Tom bears logs into the hall,
    And milk comes frozen home in pail,
When blood is nipped and ways be foul,
Then nightly sings the staring owl,
"Tu-whit, tu-who!" a merry note,
While greasy Joan doth keel the pot.

When all aloud the wind doth blow,
    And coughing drowns the parson's saw,
And birds sit brooding in the snow,
    And Marian's nose looks red and raw,
When roasted crabs hiss in the bowl,
Then nightly sings the staring owl,
"Tu-whit, tu-who!" a merry note,
While greasy Joan doth keel the pot.

WILLIAM SHAKESPEARE

SONNETS

18

SHALL I compare thee to a summer's day?
Thou art more lovely and more temperate:
Rough winds do shake the darling buds of May,
And summer's lease hath all too short a date:
Sometime too hot the eye of heaven shines,
And often is his gold complexion dimmed;
And every fair from fair sometime declines,
By chance or nature's changing course untrimmed;
But thy eternal summer shall not fade

Nor lose possession of that fair thou owest;
Nor shall Death brag thou wander'st in his shade,
When in eternal lines to time thou growest:
So long as men can breathe or eyes can see,
So long lives this and this gives life to thee.

29

When in disgrace with fortune and men's eyes,
I all alone beweep my outcast state,
And trouble deaf heaven with my bootless cries,
And look upon myself, and curse my fate,
Wishing me like to one more rich in hope,
Featured like him, like him with friends possessed,
Desiring this man's art, and that man's scope,
With what I most enjoy contented least;
Yet in these thoughts myself almost despising,
Haply I think on thee,—and then my state,
Like to the lark at break of day arising
From sullen earth, sings hymns at heaven's gate;
For thy sweet love remembered such wealth brings
That then I scorn to change my state with kings.

30

When to the sessions of sweet silent thought
I summon up remembrance of things past,
I sigh the lack of many a thing I sought,
And with old woes new wail my dear time's waste:
Then can I drown an eye, unused to flow,
For precious friends hid in death's dateless night,
And weep afresh love's long since cancelled woe,
And moan the expense of many a vanished sight:
Then can I grieve at grievances foregone,
And heavily from woe to woe tell o'er

The sad account of fore-bemoanèd moan,
Which I new pay as if not paid before.
But if the while I think on thee, dear friend,
All losses are restored and sorrows end.

33

FULL many a glorious morning have I seen
Flatter the mountain tops with sovereign eye,
Kissing with golden face the meadows green,
Gilding pale streams with heavenly alchemy;
Anon permit the basest clouds to ride
With ugly rack on his celestial face,
And from the forlorn world his visage hide,
Stealing unseen to west with this disgrace:
Even so my sun one early morn did shine,
With all-triumphant splendour on my brow;
But, out! alack! he was but one hour mine,
The region cloud hath masked him from me now.
Yet him for this my love no whit disdaineth;
Suns of the world may stain when heaven's sun staineth.

64

WHEN I have seen by Time's fell hand defaced
The rich-proud cost of outworn buried age;
When sometime lofty towers I see down-razed
And brass eternal slave to mortal rage;
When I have seen the hungry ocean gain
Advantage on the kingdom of the shore,
And the firm soil win of the watery main,
Increasing store with loss, and loss with store;
When I have seen such interchange of state,
Or state itself confounded to decay;

Ruin hath taught me thus to ruminate—
That Time will come and take my love away.
This thought is as a death, which cannot choose
But weep to have that which it fears to lose.

71

No longer mourn for me when I am dead
Than you shall hear the surly sullen bell
Give warning to the world that I am fled
From this vile world, with vilest worms to dwell:
Nay, if you read this line, remember not
The hand that writ it; for I love you so
That I in your sweet thoughts would be forgot
If thinking on me then should make you woe.
O, if, I say, you look upon this verse
When I perhaps compounded am with clay,
Do not so much as my poor name rehearse,
But let your love even with my life decay.
Lest the wise world should look into your moan
And mock you with me after I am gone.

73

THAT time of year thou mayst in me behold
When yellow leaves, or none, or few, do hang
Upon those boughs which shake against the cold,
Bare ruined choirs, where late the sweet birds sang.
In me thou see'st the twilight of such day
As after sunset fadeth in the west,
Which by and by black night doth take away,
Death's second self, that seals up all in rest.
In me thou see'st the glowing of such fire
That on the ashes of his youth doth lie,
As the death-bed whereon it must expire,
Consumed with that which it was nourished by.
This thou perceiv'st, which makes thy love more strong,
To love that well which thou must leave ere long.

90

THEN hate me when thou wilt; if ever, now;
Now, while the world is bent my deeds to cross,
Join with the spite of fortune, make me bow,
And do not drop in for an after-loss:
Ah, do not, when my heart has scaped this sorrow,
Come in the rearward of a conquered woe,
Give not a windy night a rainy morrow,
To linger out a purposed overthrow.
If thou wilt leave me, do not leave me last,
When other petty griefs have done their spite,
But in the onset come; so I shall taste
At first the very worst of fortune's might;
And other strains of woe, which now seem woe,
Compared with loss of thee will not seem so.

106

WHEN in the chronicle of wasted time
I see descriptions of the fairest wights,
And beauty making beautiful old rime
In praise of ladies dead and lovely knights,
Then, in the blazon of sweet beauty's best.
Of hand, of foot, of lip, of eye, of brow,
I see their antique pen would have expressed
Even such a beauty as you master now.
So all their praises are but prophecies
Of this our time, all you profiguring:
And, for they looked but with divining eyes,
They had not skill enough your worth to sing:
For we, which now behold these present days,
Have eyes to wonder, but lack tongues to praise.

WILLIAM SHAKESPEARE

The best passages in this unearthly poem combine profound thought with ravishing melody. Enchantment by a magician.

CHRISTABEL

PART I

'TIS the middle of night by the castle clock,
And the owls have awakened the crowing cock,
Tu—whit!——Tu—whoo!
And hark, again! the crowing cock,
How drowsily it crew.

Sir Leoline, the Baron rich,
Hath a toothless mastiff bitch;
From her kennel beneath the rock
She maketh answer to the clock,
Four for the quarters, and twelve for the hour;
Ever and aye, by shine and shower,
Sixteen short howls, not over loud;
Some say, she sees my lady's shroud.

Is the night chilly and dark?
The night is chilly, but not dark.
The thin grey cloud is spread on high,
It covers but not hides the sky.
The moon is behind, and at the full;
And yet she looks both small and dull.
The night is chill, the cloud is gray:
'Tis a month before the month of May,
And the Spring comes slowly up this way.

The lovely lady, Christabel,
Whom her father loves so well,
What makes her in the wood so late,
A furlong from the castle gate?

She had dreams all yesternight
Of her own betrothèd knight;
And she in the midnight wood will pray
For the weal of her lover that's far away.

She stole along, she nothing spoke,
The sighs she heaved were soft and low,
And naught was green upon the oak
But moss and rarest mistletoe:
She kneels beneath the huge oak tree,
And in silence prayeth she.

The lady sprang up suddenly,
The lovely lady, Christabel!
It moaned as near, as near can be,
But what it is she cannot tell.—
On the other side it seems to be,
Of the huge, broad-breasted, old oak tree.

The night is chill; the forest bare;
Is it the wind that moaneth bleak?
There is not wind enough in the air
To move away the ringlet curl
From the lovely lady's cheek—
There is not wind enough to twirl
The one red leaf, the last of its clan,
That dances as often as dance it can,
Hanging so light, and hanging so high,
On the topmost twig that looks up at the sky.

Hush, beating heart of Christabel!
Jesu, Maria, shield her well!
She folded her arms beneath her cloak,
And stole to the other side of the oak.
   What sees she there?

There she sees a damsel bright,
Drest in a silken robe of white,
That shadowy in the moonlight shone:
The neck that made that white robe wan,
Her stately neck, and arms were bare;
Her blue-veined feet unsandaled were,
And wildly glittered here and there
The gems entangled in her hair.
I guess, 't was frightful there to see
A lady so richly clad as she—
Beautiful exceedingly!

"Mary mother, save me now!"
(Said Christabel), "And who art thou?"

The lady strange made answer meet,
And her voice was faint and sweet:—
"Have pity on my sore distress,
I scarce can speak for weariness:
Stretch forth thy hand, and have no fear!"

  .   .   .   .

Sweet Christabel her feet doth bare,
And jealous of the listening air
They steal their way from stair to stair,
Now in glimmer, and now in gloom,
And now they pass the Baron's room,
As still as death, with stifled breath!
And now have reached her chamber door;
And now doth Geraldine press down
The rushes of the chamber floor

The moon shines dim in the open air,
And not a moonbeam enters here.
But they without its light can see
The chamber carved so curiously,

[233]

Carved with figures strange and sweet,
All made out of the carver's brain,
For a lady's chamber meet:
The lamp with twofold silver chain
Is fastened to an angel's feet.

The silver lamp burns dead and dim;
But Christabel the lamp will trim.
She trimmed the lamp, and made it bright,
And left it swinging to and fro,
While Geraldine, in wretched plight,
Sank down upon the floor below.

. . . .

THE CONCLUSION TO PART I

It was a lovely sight to see
The lady Christabel, when she
Was praying at the old oak tree.
　　Amid the jaggèd shadows
　　Of mossy leafless boughs,
　　Kneeling in the moonlight,
　　To make her gentle vows;

Her slender palms together prest,
Heaving sometimes on her breast;
Her face resigned to bliss or bale—
Her face, oh call it fair not pale,
And both blue eyes more bright than clear,
Each about to have a tear.

With open eyes (ah woe is me!)
Asleep, and dreaming fearfully,
Fearfully dreaming, yet, I wis,
Dreaming that alone, which is—

O sorrow and shame! Can this be she,
The lady, who knelt at the old oak tree?
And lo! the worker of these harms,
That holds the maiden in her arms,
Seems to slumber still and mild,
As a mother with her child.

A star hath set, a star hath risen,
O Geraldine! since arms of thine
Have been the lovely lady's prison.
O Geraldine! one hour was thine—
Thou'st had thy will! By tairn and rill,
The night-birds all that hour were still.
But now they are jubilant anew,
From cliff and tower, tu—whoo! tu—whoo!
Tu—whoo! tu—whoo! from wood and fell!

And see! the lady Christabel
Gathers herself from out her trance;
Her limbs relax, her countenance
Grows sad and soft; the smooth thin lids
Close o'er her eyes; and tears she sheds—
Large tears that leave the lashes bright!
And oft the while she seems to smile
As infants at a sudden light!

Yea, she doth smile, and she doth weep,
Like a youthful hermitess,
Beauteous in a wilderness,
Who, praying always, prays in sleep.
And, if she move unquietly,
Perchance, 't is but the blood so free
Comes back and tingles in her feet.
No doubt, she hath a vision sweet.
What if her guardian spirit 't were,

What if she knew her mother near?
But this she knows, in joys and woes,
That saints will aid if men will call:
For the blue sky bends over all!

. . . .

So quickly she rose, and quickly arrayed
Her maiden limbs, and having prayed
That He, who on the cross did groan,
Might wash away her sins unknown,
She forthwith led fair Geraldine
To meet her sire, Sir Leoline.

The lovely maid and lady tall
Are pacing both into the hall,
And pacing on through page and groom,
Enter the Baron's presence-room.

The Baron rose, and while he prest
His gentle daughter to his breast,
With cheerful wonder in his eyes
The lady Geraldine espies,
And gave such welcome to the same,
As might beseem so bright a dame!

But when he heard the lady's tale,
And when she told her father's name,
Why waxed Sir Leoline so pale,
Murmuring o'er the name again,
Lord Roland de Vaux of Tryermaine?

Alas! they had been friends in youth;
But whispering tongues can poison truth;
And constancy lives in realms above;
And life is thorny; and youth is vain;
And to be wroth with one we love
Doth work like madness in the brain.

[236]

And thus it chanced, as I divine,
With Roland and Sir Leoline.
Each spake words of high disdain
And insult to his heart's best brother:
They parted—ne'er to meet again!
But never either found another
To free the hollow heart from paining—
They stood aloof, the scars remaining,
Like cliffs which had been rent asunder;
A dreary sea now flows between;—
But neither heat, nor frost, nor thunder,
Shall wholly do away, I ween,
The marks of that which once hath been.

Sir Leoline, a moment's space,
Stood gazing on the damsel's face:
And the youthful Lord of Tryermaine
    Came back upon his heart again.

O then the Baron forgot his age,
His noble heart swelled high with rage;
He swore by the wounds in Jesu's side
He would proclaim it far and wide,
With trump and solemn heraldry,
That they, who thus had wronged the dame,
Were base as spotted infamy!
"And if they dare deny the same,
My herald shall appoint a week,
And let the recreant traitors seek
My tourney court—that there and then
I may dislodge their reptile souls
From the bodies and forms of men!"
He spake: his eye in lightning rolls!
For the lady was ruthlessly seized; and he kenned
In the beautiful lady the child of his friend!

And now the tears were on his face,
And fondly in his arms he took
Fair Geraldine, who met the embrace,
Prolonging it with joyous look.
Which when she viewed, a vision fell
Upon the soul of Christabel,
The vision of fear, the touch and pain!
She shrunk and shuddered, and saw again—
(Ah, woe is me! Was it for thee,
Thou gentle maid! such sights to see?)

. . . .

THE CONCLUSION TO PART II

A little child, a limber elf,
Singing, dancing to itself,
A fairy thing with red round cheeks,
That always finds, and never seeks,
Makes such a vision to the sight
As fills a father's eyes with light;
And pleasures flow in so thick and fast
Upon his heart, that he at last
Must needs express his love's excess
With words of unmeant bitterness.
Perhaps 't is pretty to force together
Thoughts so all unlike each other;
To mutter and mock a broken charm,
To dally with wrong that does no harm.
Perhaps 't is tender too and pretty
At each wild word to feel within
A sweet recoil of love and pity.
And what, if in a world of sin
(O sorrow and shame should this be true!)
Such giddiness of heart and brain
Comes seldom save from rage and pain,
So talks as it 's most used to do.

SAMUEL TAYLOR COLERIDGE

[238]

DELIGHT IN DISORDER

Smooth-running as is this lyric of Ben Jonson's, it has not the ease of the other Elizabethans; it foretells the new age. With this should be read Herrick's *Delight in Disorder*.

SIMPLEX MUNDITIIS

STILL to be neat, still to be drest,
As you were going to a feast;
Still to be powdered, still perfumed:
Lady, it is to be presumed,
Though art's hid causes are not found,
All is not sweet, all is not sound.

Give me a look, give me a face,
That makes simplicity a grace;
Robes loosely flowing, hair as free:
Such sweet neglect more taketh me
Than all the adulteries of art;
They strike mine eyes, but not my heart.

BEN JONSON

DELIGHT IN DISORDER

A SWEET disorder in the dress
Kindles in clothes a wantonness.
A lawn about the shoulders thrown
Into a fine distraction;
An erring lace, which here and there
Enthralls the crimson stomacher;
A cuff neglectful, and thereby
Ribbands to flow confusedly;
A winning wave, deserving note,
In the tempestuous petticoat;
A careless shoestring, in whose tie
I see a wild civility;—
Do more bewitch me, than when art
Is too precise in every part.

ROBERT HERRICK

It is probable that Bret Harte's verses will live as long as his stories, and that both will survive men now living.

PLAIN LANGUAGE FROM TRUTHFUL JAMES

WHICH I wish to remark,
And my language is plain,
That for ways that are dark
And for tricks that are vain,
The heathen Chinee is peculiar,
Which the same I would rise to explain.

Ah Sin was his name;
And I shall not deny,
In regard to the same,
What that name might imply;
But his smile, it was pensive and childlike,
As I frequent remarked to Bill Nye.

'Twas August the third,
And quite soft was the skies;
Which it might be inferred
That Ah Sin was likewise;
Yet he played it that day upon William
And me in a way I despise.

Which we had a small game,
And Ah Sin took a hand:
It was Euchre. The same
He did not understand;
But he smiled as he sat by the table,
With a smile that was childlike and bland.

Yet the cards they were stocked
  In a way that I grieve,
And my feelings were shocked
  At the state of Nye's sleeve,
Which was stuffed full of aces and bowers,
  And the same with intent to deceive.

But the hands that were played
  By that heathen Chinee,
And the points that he made,
  Were quite frightful to see,—
Till at last he put down a right bower
  Which the same Nye had dealt unto me.

Then I looked up at Nye,
  And he gazed upon me;
And he rose with a sigh,
  And said, "Can this be?
We are ruined by Chinese cheap labour,"—
  And he went for that heathen Chinee.

In the scene that ensued
  I did not take a hand,
But the floor it was strewed
  Like the leaves on the strand
With the cards that Ah Sin had been hiding,
  In the game "he did not understand."

In his sleeves, which were long,
  He had twenty-four jacks,—
Which was coming it strong,
  Yet I state but the facts;
And we found on his nails, which were taper,
  What is frequent in tapers,—that's wax.

[241]

Which is why I remark,
    And my language is plain,
That for ways that are dark
    And for tricks that are vain,
The heathen Chinee is peculiar,—
    Which the same I am free to maintain.

BRET HARTE

I like *Dorothy Q.* much better than the declamatory *Nautilus*. This poem and *The Last Leaf* have Holmes's characteristic combination of humour and pathos.

DOROTHY Q.

A FAMILY PORTRAIT

[The portrait was an actual one, of Holmes's great-grandmother, Dorothy Quincy. His own note reads: "Dorothy was the daughter of Judge Edmund Quincy, and the niece of Josiah Quincy, Junior, the young patriot and orator, who died just before the American Revolution. . . . The son of the latter, Josiah Quincy, [was] the first mayor of Boston bearing that name."]

GRANDMOTHER's mother: her age, I guess,
Thirteen summers, or something less;
Girlish bust, but womanly air;
Smooth, square forehead with uprolled hair,
Lips that lover has never kissed;
Taper fingers and slender wrist;
Hanging sleeves of stiff brocade;
So they painted the little maid.

On her hand a parrot green
Sits unmoving and broods serene.
Hold up the canvas full in view,—
Look! there's a rent the light shines through,
Dark with a century's fringe of dust,—
That was a Red-Coat's rapier-thrust!
Such is the tale the lady old,
Dorothy's daughter's daughter, told.

Who the painter was none may tell,—
One whose best was not over well;
Hard and dry, it must be confessed,
Flat as a rose that has long been pressed;
Yet in her cheek the hues are bright,
Dainty colours of red and white,
And in her slender shape are seen
Hint and promise of stately mien.

Look not on her with eyes of scorn,—
Dorothy Q. was a lady born!
Ay! since the galloping Normans came,
England's annals have known her name;
And still to the three-hilled rebel town
Dear is that ancient name's renown,
For many a civic wreath they won,
The youthful sire and the gray-haired son.

O Damsel Dorothy! Dorothy Q.!
Strange is this gift that I owe to you;
Such a gift as never a king
Save to daughter or son might bring,—
All my tenure of heart and hand,
All my title to house and land;
Mother and sister and child and wife
And joy and sorrow and death and life!

What if a hundred years ago
Those close-shut lips had answered No,
When forth the tremulous question came
That cost the maiden her Norman name,
And under the folds that look so still
The bodice swelled with the bosom's thrill?
Should I be I, or would it be
One-tenth another, to nine-tenths me?

Soft is the breath of a maiden's Yes:
Not the light gossamer stirs with less;
But never a cable that holds so fast
Through all the battles of wave and blast,
And never an echo of speech or song
That lives in the babbling air so long!
There were tones in the voice that whispered then
You may hear today in a hundred men.

O lady and lover, how faint and far
Your images hover,—and here we are,
Solid and stirring in flesh and bone,—
Edward's and Dorothy's—all their own,—
A goodly record for Time to show
Of a syllable spoken so long ago!—
Shall I bless you, Dorothy, or forgive
For the tender whisper that bade me live?

It shall be a blessing, my little maid!
I will heal the stab of the Red-Coat's blade,
And freshen the gold of the tarnished frame,
And gild with a rhyme your household name;
So you shall smile on us brave and bright
As first you greeted the morning's light,
And live untroubled by woes and fears
Through a second youth of a hundred years.

OLIVER WENDELL HOLMES

THE LAST LEAF

I saw him once before,
As he passed by the door,
And again

[244]

The pavement stones resound,
As he totters o'er the ground
    With his cane.

They say that in his prime,
Ere the pruning-knife of Time
    Cut him down,
Not a better man was found
By the Crier on his round
    Through the town.

But now he walks the streets,
And he looks at all he meets
    Sad and wan,
And he shakes his feeble head,
That it seems as if he said,
    "They are gone."

The mossy marbles rest
On the lips that he has prest
    In their bloom,
And the names he loved to hear
Have been carved for many a year
    On the tomb.

My grandmamma has said—
Poor old lady, she is dead
    Long ago—
That he had a Roman nose,
And his cheek was like a rose
    In the snow;

But now his nose is thin,
And it rests upon his chin
    Like a staff,

And a crook is in his back,
And a melancholy crack
   In his laugh.

I know it is a sin
For me to sit and grin
   At him here;
But the old three-cornered hat,
And the breeches, and all that,
   Are so queer!

And if I should live to be
The last leaf upon the tree
   In the spring,
Let them smile, as I do now,
At the old forsaken bough
   Where I cling.

OLIVER WENDELL HOLMES

James Whitcomb Riley came nearer to being the heir of Longfellow than any other poet. His books sold by the hundred thousand, and their expression of sentiment, the passion of the past, homelife, childhood, is always sincere. Furthermore, although he wrote no plays, he was essentially a dramatist; he created many living characters, and had amazing skill in making their speech absolutely true to their individualities.

LITTLE ORPHANT ANNIE

LITTLE Orphant Annie's come to our house to stay,
An' wash the cups and saucers up, an' brush the crumbs
   away,

An' shoo the chickens off the porch, an' dust the hearth, an'
    sweep,
An' make the fire, an' bake the bread, an' earn her board-
    an'-keep;
An' all us other children, when the supper things is done,
We set around the kitchen fire an' has the mostest fun
A-list'nin' to the witch-tales 'at Annie tells about,
An' the Gobble-uns 'at gits you
               Ef you
           Don't
               Watch
                Out!

Onc't they was a little boy who wouldn't say his pray'rs—
An' when he went to bed at night, away up stairs,
His mammy heerd him holler, an' his daddy heerd him bawl,
An' when they turn't the kivvers down, he wasn't there at
    all!
An' they seeked him in the rafter-room, an' cubby-hole, an'
    press,
An' seeked him up the chimbly-flue, an' ever'wheres, I guess;
But all they ever found was thist his pants an' roundabout!
An' the Gobble-uns 'll git you
               Ef you
           Don't
               Watch
                Out!

An' one time a little girl 'ud allus laugh and grin,
An' make fun of ever' one, an' all her blood-an'-kin;
An' onc't when they was "company," an' ole folks was there,
She mocked 'em an' shocked 'em, an' said she didn't care!
An' thist as she kicked her heels, an 'turn't to run an' hide,
They was two great big Black Things a-standin' by her side,

An' they snatched her through the ceilin' 'fore she knowed
    what she's about!
An' the Gobble-uns 'll git you
        Ef you
           Don't
               Watch
                  Out!

An' little Orphant Annie says, when the blaze is blue,
An' the lampwick sputters, an' the wind goes woo-oo!
An' you hear the crickets quit, an' the moon is gray,
An' the lightnin'-bugs in dew is all squenched away,—
You better mind yer parents, and yer teachers fond and
    dear,
An' churish them 'at loves you, an' dry the orphant's tear,
An' he'p the pore an' needy ones 'at clusters all about,
Er the Gobble-uns 'll git you
        Ef you
           Don't
               Watch
                  Out!

                          JAMES WHITCOMB RILEY

━━

This poem, by the author of *Lorna Doone*, with the sig-
nature "R. D. B. in memoriam M. F. G.," first appeared in
the *University Magazine* in 1879. The author's name was
kept an absolute secret until July 1909. In *The Athenæum*
for 3 July 1909, was printed an interesting letter from
Agnes E. Cook, by which we learn that Blackmore actually
dreamed this poem, in its exact language and metre.
The letter from the author which was published in the same
Athenæum article, gives the facts connected with this
extraordinary dream.

Teddⁿ Jany 5th 1879.

My Dear Sir.

Having lately been at the funeral of a most dear relation I was there again (in a dream) last night, and heard the mourners sing the lines enclosed, which impressed me so that I was able to write them without change of a word this morning. I never heard or read them before to my knowledge. They do not look so well on paper as they sounded; but if you like to print them, here they are. Only please not to put my name beyond initials or send me money for them. With all good wishes to Mrs. Cook and yourself

Very truly yours
R. D. BLACKMORE.

K. Cook, Esqre LL.D.

DOMINUS ILLUMINATIO MEA

1

In the hour of death, after this life's whim,
When the heart beats low, and the eyes grow **dim**,
And pain has exhausted every limb—
  The lover of the Lord shall trust in Him.

2

When the will has forgotten the life-long aim,
And the mind can only disgrace its fame,
And a man is uncertain of his own name,
  The power of the Lord shall fill this frame.

3

When the last sigh is heaved and the last tear shed,
And the coffin is waiting beside the bed,
And the widow and child forsake the dead,
  The angel of the Lord shall lift this head.

4

For even the purest delight may pall,
The power must fail, and the pride must fall,
And the love of the dearest friends grow small—
But the glory of the Lord is all in all.

R. D. BLACKMORE

As in all Arnold's love-poems, the expression of passion is restrained. As we know from his remarks on the love-letters of Keats, he thought even a lover should be dignified. But although meditation and passion kept him in equilibrium, he was in both moods sincere.

DOVER BEACH

THE sea is calm tonight.
The tide is full, the moon lies fair
Upon the straits;—on the French coast the light
Gleams and is gone; the cliffs of England stand,
Glimmering and vast, out in the tranquil bay.
Come to the window, sweet is the night-air!
Only, from the long line of spray
Where the sea meets the moon-blanch'd land,
Listen! you hear the grating roar
Of pebbles which the waves draw back, and fling,
At their return, up the high strand,
Begin, and cease, and then again begin,
With tremulous cadence slow, and bring
The eternal note of sadness in.

Sophocles long ago
Heard it on the Ægæan, and it brought
Into his mind the turbid ebb and flow
Of human misery; we
Find also in the sound a thought,
Hearing it by this distant northern sea.

The Sea of Faith
Was once, too, at the full, and round earth's shore
Lay like the folds of a bright girdle furl'd.
But now I only hear
Its melancholy, long, withdrawing roar,
Retreating, to the breath
Of the night-wind, down the vast edges drear
And naked shingles of the world.

Ah, love, let us be true
To one another! for the world, which seems
To lie before us like a land of dreams,
So various, so beautiful, so new,
Hath really neither joy, nor love, nor light,
Nor certitude, nor peace, nor help for pain;
And we are here as on a darkling plain
Swept with confused alarms of struggle and flight,
Where ignorant armies clash by night.

MATTHEW ARNOLD

This is the only one of Arnold's poems that is obscure,
but he never wrote anything more purely poetical. It is
indeed the very spirit of poetry. It would be as superfluous
and as unfortunate to attempt to explain this reach of the
imagination, as it would be to edit a dream with intro-
duction and notes.

THE FORSAKEN MERMAN

COME, dear children, let us away;
Down and away below.
Now my brothers call from the bay;
Now the great winds shorewards blow;
Now the salt tides seawards flow;
Now the wild white horses play,
Champ and chafe and toss in the spray.
Children dear, let us away.
This way, this way.

Call her once before you go.
Call once yet.
In a voice that she will know:
"Margaret! Margaret!"
Children's voices should be dear
(Call once more) to a mother's ear:
Children's voices, wild with pain.
Surely she will come again.
Call her once and come away.
This way, this way.
"Mother dear, we cannot stay."
The wild white horses foam and fret.
Margaret! Margaret!
Come, dear children, come away down.

Call no more.
One last look at the white-wall'd town,
And the little grey church on the windy shore.
Then come down.
She will not come though you call all day
Come away, come away.

THE FORSAKEN MERMAN

Children dear, was it yesterday
We heard the sweet bells over the bay?
In the caverns where we lay,
Through the surf and through the swell
The far-off sound of a silver bell?
Sand-strewn caverns, cool and deep,
Where the winds are all asleep;
Where the spent lights quiver and gleam;
Where the salt weed sways in the stream;
Where the sea-beasts rang'd all round,
Feed in the ooze of their pasture-ground;
Where the sea-snakes coil and twine,
Dry their mail and bask in the brine;
Where great whales come sailing by,
Sail and sail, with unshut eye,
Round the world forever and aye?
When did music come this way?
Children dear, was it yesterday?

Children dear, was it yesterday
(Call yet once) that she went away?
Once she sate with you and me,
On a gold throne in the heart of the sea,
And the youngest sate on her knee,
She comb'd its bright hair, and she tended it well,
When down swung the sound of the far-off bell.
She sigh'd, she look'd up through the clear green sea.
She said: "I must go, for my kinsfolk pray
In the little grey church on the shore today.
'Twill be Easter-time in the world—ah me!
And I lose my poor soul, Merman, here with thee."
I said: "Go up, dear heart, through the waves.
Say thy prayer, and come back to the kind sea-caves."
She smil'd, she went up through the surf in the bay.
Children dear, was it yesterday?

[253]

Children dear, were we long alone?
"The sea grows stormy, the little ones moan.
Long prayers," I said, "in the world they say.
Come," I said, and we rose through the surf in the bay.
We went up the beach, by the sandy down
Where the sea-stocks bloom, to the white-wall'd town.
Through the narrow pav'd streets, where all was still,
To the little grey church on the windy hill.
From the church came a murmur of folk at their prayers,
But we stood without in the cold blowing airs.
We climb'd on the graves, on the stones, worn with rains,
And we gaz'd up the aisle through the small leaded panes.
She sat by the pillar; we saw her clear:
"Margaret, hist! come quick, we are here.
Dear heart," I said, "we are long alone.
The sea grows stormy, the little ones moan."
But, ah, she gave me never a look.
For her eyes were seal'd to the holy book.
Loud prays the priest; shut stands the door.
Come away, children, call no more.
Come away, come down, call no more.

Down, down, down.
    Down to the depths of the sea.
She sits at her wheel in the humming town,
Singing most joyfully.
Hark, what she sings; "O joy, O joy,
For the humming street, and the child with its toy.
For the priest, and the bell, and the holy well.
For the wheel where I spun.
And the blessed light of the sun."
And so she sings her fill,
Singing most joyfully,
Till the shuttle falls from her hand,
And the whizzing wheel stands still.

She steals to the window, and looks at the sand;
And over the sand at the sea;
And her eyes are set in a stare;
And anon there breaks a sigh,
And anon there drops a tear,
From a sorrow-clouded eye,
And a heart sorrow-laden,
A long, long sigh,
For the cold strange eyes of a little Mermaiden,
And the gleam of her golden hair.

Come away, away children.
Come children, come down.
The hoarse wind blows colder;
Lights shine in the town.
She will start from her slumber
When gusts shake the door;
She will hear the winds howling,
Will hear the waves roar.
We shall see, while above us
The waves roar and whirl,
A ceiling of amber,
A pavement of pearl.
Singing, "Here came a mortal,
But faithless was she.
And alone dwell for ever
The kings of the sea."

But, children, at midnight,
When soft the winds blow;
When clear falls the moonlight;
When spring-tides are low:
When sweet airs come seaward
From heaths starr'd with broom;
And high rocks throw mildly

On the blanch'd sands a gloom:
Up the still, glistening beaches,
Up the creeks we will hie;
Over banks of bright seaweed
The ebb-tide leaves dry.
We will gaze, from the sand-hills,
At the white, sleeping town;
At the church on the hill-side—
And then come back down.
Singing, "There dwells a lov'd one,
But cruel is she!
She left lonely for ever
The kings of the sea."

MATTHEW ARNOLD

But the Spirit of the Lord departed from Saul, and an evil spirit troubled him.

And Saul's servants said unto him, Behold now, an evil spirit from God troubleth thee.

Let our lord now command thy servants, which are before thee, to seek out a man, who is a cunning player on an harp: and it shall come to pass, when the evil spirit from God is upon thee, that he shall play with his hand, and thou shalt be well.

And Saul said unto his servants, Provide me now a man that can play well, and bring him to me.

Then answered one of the servants, and said, Behold, I have seen a son of Jesse the Beth-lehemite, that is cunning in playing, and a mighty valiant man, and a man of war, and prudent in matters, and a comely person, and the Lord is with him. . . .

And David came to Saul, and stood before him: and he loved him greatly; and he became his armourbearer.

And Saul sent to Jesse, saying, Let David, I pray thee, stand before me; for he hath found favour in my sight.

And it came to pass, when the evil spirit from God was upon Saul, that David took an harp, and played with his hand: so Saul was refreshed, and was well, and the evil spirit departed from him. I *Samuel* 16:14–23.

SAUL

I

SAID Abner, "At last thou art come! Ere I tell, ere thou
    speak,
Kiss my cheek, wish me well!" Then I wished it, and did
    kiss his cheek.
And he: "Since the King, O my friend, for thy countenance
    sent,
Neither drunken nor eaten have we; nor until from his tent
Thou return with the joyful assurance the King liveth yet,
Shall our lip with the honey be bright, with the water be
    wet.
For out of the black mid-tent's silence, a space of three
    days,
Not a sound hath escaped to thy servants, of prayer nor of
    praise,
To betoken that Saul and the Spirit have ended their strife,
And that, faint in his triumph, the monarch sinks back
    upon life.

II

"Yet now my heart leaps, O beloved! God's child with his
    dew
On thy gracious gold hair, and those lilies still living and
    blue
Just broken to twine round thy harpstrings, as if no wild
    heat
Were now raging to torture the desert!"

III

Then I, as was meet,
Knelt down to the God of my fathers, and rose on my feet,
And ran o'er the sand burnt to powder. The tent was un-
looped;
I pulled up the spear that obstructed, and under I stooped;
Hands and knees on the slippery grass-patch, all withered
and gone,
That extends to the second enclosure, I groped my way on
Till I felt where the foldskirts fly open. Then once more I
prayed,
And opened the foldskirts and entered, and was not afraid
But spoke, "Here is David, thy servant!" And no voice re-
plied.
At the first I saw naught but the blackness: but soon I
descried
A something more black than the blackness—the vast, the
upright
Main prop which sustains the pavilion: and slow into sight
Grew a figure against it, gigantic and blackest of all.
Then a sunbeam, that burst through the tent-roof, showed
Saul.

IV

He stood as erect as that tent-prop, both arms stretched out
wide
On the great cross-support in the centre, that goes to each
side;
He relaxed not a muscle, but hung there as, caught in his
pangs
And waiting his change, the king-serpent all heavily hangs,
Far away from his kind, in the pine, till deliverance come
With the spring-time,—so agonized Saul, drear and stark,
blind and dumb.

V

Then I tuned my harp,—took off the lilies we twine round
  its chords
Lest they snap 'neath the stress of the noon-tide—those
  sunbeams like swords!
And I first played the tune all our sheep know, as, one after
  one,
So docile they come to the pen-door till folding be done.
They are white and untorn by the bushes, for lo, they have
  fed
Where the long grasses stifle the water within the stream's
  bed;
And now one after one seeks its lodging, as star follows star
Into eve and the blue far above us,—so blue and so far!

VI

—Then the tune for which quails on the cornland will each
  leave his mate
To fly after the player; then, what makes the crickets elate
Till for boldness they fight one another; and then, what has
  weight
To set the quick jerboa a-musing outside his sand house—
There are none such as he for a wonder, half bird and half
  mouse!
God made all the creatures and gave them our love and our
  fear,
To give sign, we and they are his children, one family here.

VII

Then I played the help-tune of our reapers, their wine-
  song, when hand
Grasps at hand, eye lights eye in good friendship, and
  great hearts expand

And grow one in the sense of this world's life.——And then,
    the last song
When the dead man is praised on his journey——"Bear, bear
    him along,
With his few faults shut up like dead flowerets! Are balm
    seeds not here
To console us? The land has none left such as he on the
    bier.
Oh, would we might keep thee, my brother!"——And then,
    the glad chant
Of the marriage,——first go the young maidens, next, she
    whom we vaunt
As the beauty, the pride of our dwelling.——And then, the
    great march
Wherein man runs to man to assist him and buttress an arch
Naught can break; who shall harm them, our friends?
    Then, the chorus intoned
As the Levites go up to the altar in glory enthroned.
But I stopped here: for here in the darkness Saul groaned.

VIII

And I paused, held my breath in such silence, and listened
    apart;
And the tent shook, for mighty Saul shuddered: and spar-
    kles 'gan dart
From the jewels that woke in his turban, at once, with a
    start,
All its lordly male-sapphires, and rubies courageous at
    heart.
So the head: but the body still moved not, still hung there
    erect.
And I bent once again to my playing, pursued it unchecked,
As I sang:——

IX

"Oh, our manhood's prime vigour!
No spirit feels waste,
Not a muscle is stopped in its playing nor sinew unbraced.
Oh, the wild joys of living! the leaping from rock up to
rock,
The strong rending of boughs from the fir-tree, the cool
silver shock
Of the plunge in a pool's living water, the hunt of the bear,
And the sultriness showing the lion is couched in his lair.
And the meal, the rich dates yellowed over with gold dust
divine,
And the locust-flesh steeped in the pitcher, the full draught
of wine,
And the sleep in the dried river-channel where bulrushes tell
That the water was wont to go warbling so softly and well.
How good is man's life, the mere living! how fit to employ
All the heart and the soul and the senses forever in joy!
Hast thou loved the white locks of thy father, whose sword
thou didst guard
When he trusted thee forth with the armies, for glorious
reward?
Didst thou see the thin hands of thy mother, held up as
men sung
The low song of the nearly-departed, and hear her faint
tongue
Joining in while it could to the witness, "Let one more
attest,
I have lived, seen God's hand through a lifetime, and all
was for best?"
Then they sung through their tears in strong triumph, not
much, but the rest.
And thy brothers, the help and the contest, the working
whence grew

[261]

Such result as, from seething grape-bundles, the spirit
strained true:
And the friends of thy boyhood—that boyhood of wonder
and hope,
Present promise and wealth of the future beyond the eye's
scope,—
Till lo, thou art grown to a monarch; a people is thine;
And all gifts which the world offers singly, on one head
combine!
On one head, all the beauty and strength, love and rage
(like the throe
That, a-work in the rock, helps its labour and lets the gold
go)
High ambition and deeds which surpass it, fame crowning
them,—all
Brought to blaze on the head of one creature—King Saul!"

X

And lo, with that leap of my spirit,—heart, hand, harp,
and voice,
Each lifting Saul's name out of sorrow, each bidding rejoice
Saul's fame in the light it was made for—as when, dare I
say,
The Lord's army, in rapture of service, strains through its
array,
And upsoareth the cherubim-chariot—"Saul!" cried I, and
stopped,
And waited the thing that should follow. Then Saul, who
hung propped
By the tent's cross-support in the centre, was struck by his
name.
Have ye seen when Spring's arrowy summons goes right to
the aim,
And some mountain, the last to withstand her, that held (he
alone,

While the vale laughed in freedom and flowers) on a broad
    bust of stone
A year's snow bound about for a breast-plate,—leaves grasp
    of the sheet?
Fold on fold all at once it crowds thunderously down to his
    feet,
And there fronts you, stark, black, but alive yet, your
    mountain of old,
With his rents, the successive bequeathing of ages untold—
Yea, each harm got in fighting your battles, each furrow
    and scar
Of his head thrust 'twixt you and the tempest—all hail,
    there they are!
—Now again to be softened with verdure, again hold the
    nest
Of the dove, tempt the goat and its young to the green on
    his crest
For their food in the ardours of summer. One long shudder
    thrilled
All the tent till the very air tingled, then sank and was
    stilled
At the King's self left standing before me, released and
    aware.
What was gone, what remained? All to traverse 'twixt hope
    and despair,
Death was past, life not come: so he waited. Awhile his
    right hand
Held the brow, helped the eyes left too vacant forthwith to
    remand
To their place what new objects should enter: 'twas Saul,
    as before.
I looked up and dared gaze at those eyes, nor was hurt any
    more
Than by slow pallid sunsets in autumn, ye watch from the
    shore,

At their sad level gaze o'er the ocean—a sun's slow decline
Over hills which, resolved in stern silence, o'erlap and en-
    twine
Base with base to knit strength more intensely: so, arm
    folded arm
O'er the chest whose slow heavings subsided.

.   .   .   .

XVIII

"I believe it! 'Tis thou, God, that givest, 'tis I who re-
    ceive:
In the first is the last, in thy will is my power to believe.
All's one gift: thou canst grant it moreover, as prompt to
    my prayer,
As I breathe out this breath, as I open these arms to the air.
From thy will stream the worlds, life and nature, thy dread
    Sabaoth:
I will?—the mere atoms despise me! Why am I not loth
To look that, even that in the face too? Why is it I dare
Think but lightly of such impuissance? What stops my
    despair?
This;—'tis not what man Does which exalts him, but what
    man Would do!
See the King—I would help him but cannot, the wishes fall
    through.
Could I wrestle to raise him from sorrow, grow poor to
    enrich,
To fill up his life, starve my own out, I would—knowing
    which,
I know that my service is perfect. Oh, speak through me
    now!
Would I suffer for him that I love? So wouldst thou—so
    wilt thou!
So shall crown thee the topmost, ineffablest, uttermost
    crown—

And thy love fill infinitude wholly, nor leave up nor down
One spot for the creature to stand in! It is by no breath,
Turn of eye, wave of hand, that salvation joins issue with
    death!
As thy Love is discovered almighty, almighty be proved
Thy power, that exists with and for it, of being Beloved!
He who did most, shall bear most; the strongest shall stand
    the most weak.
'Tis the weakness in strength, that I cry for! my flesh, that
    I seek
In the Godhead! I seek and I find it. O Saul, it shall be
A Face like my face that receives thee; a Man like to me,
Thou shalt love and be loved by, forever: a Hand like this
    hand
Shall throw open the gates of new life to thee! See the
    Christ stand!"

XIX

I know not too well how I found my way home in the night.
There were witnesses, cohorts about me, to left and to right,
Angels, powers, the unuttered, unseen, the alive, the aware:
I repressed, I got through them as hardly, as strugglingly
    there,
As a runner beset by the populace famished for news—
Life or death. The whole earth was awakened, hell loosed
    with her crews;
And the stars of night beat with emotion, and tingled and
    shot
Out in fire the strong pain of pent knowledge: but I fainted
    not,
For the Hand still impelled me at once and supported, sup-
    pressed
All the tumult, and quenched it with quiet, and holy behest,
Till the rapture was shut in itself, and the earth sank to
    rest.

Anon at the dawn, all the trouble had withered from earth—
Not so much, but I saw it die out in the day's tender birth;
In the gathered intensity brought to the grey of the hills;
In the shuddering forests' held breath; in the sudden wind-
thrills;
In the startled wild beasts that bore off, each with eye sidling
still
Though averted with wonder and dread; in the birds stiff
and chill
That rose heavily, as I approached them, made stupid with
awe:
E'en the serpent that slid away silent,—he felt the new law.
The same stared in the white humid faces upturned by the
flowers;
The same worked in the heart of the cedar and moved the
vine-bowers:
And the little brooks witnessing murmured, persistent and
low,
With their obstinate, all but hushed voices—"E'en so, it
is so!"

ROBERT BROWNING

This English poet, James Elroy Flecker, who died young
in 1915, might have gone far had he enjoyed good health.
He wrote the best English translation of Goethe's *Kennst
du das Land* that has ever appeared. He also stated very
well the purpose of the poet, when he said that the business
of the poet is not to save men's souls, but to make them
worth saving.

"It is not the poet's business to save man's soul but to
make it worth saving. . . . However few poets have written with a clear theory of art for art's sake, it is by that
theory alone that their work has been, or can be, judged;

—and rightly so if we remember that art embraces all life
and all humanity, and sees in the temporary and fleeting
doctrines of conservative or revolutionary only the human
grandeur or passion that inspires them."

His own volume had been written "with the single inten-
tion of creating beauty."

THE OLD SHIPS

I HAVE seen old ships sail like swans asleep
Beyond the village which men still call Tyre,
With leaden age o'ercargoed, dipping deep
For Famagusta and the hidden sun
That rings black Cyprus with a lake of fire;
And all those ships were certainly so old
Who knows how oft with squat and noisy gun,
Questing brown slaves or Syrian oranges,
The pirate Genoese
Hell raked them till they rolled
Blood, water, fruit, and corpses up the hold.
But now through friendly seas they softly run,
Painted the mid-sea blue or the shore-sea green,
Still patterned with the vine and grapes in gold.

But I have seen
Pointing her shapely shadows from the dawn
And image tumbled on a rose-swept bay
A drowsy ship of some yet older day;
And, wonder's breath indrawn,
Thought I—who knows—who knows—but in that same
(Fished up beyond Aeaea, patched up new
—Stern painted brighter blue—)
That talkative, bald-headed seaman came
(Twelve patient comrades sweating at the oar)

From Troy's doom-crimson shore,
And with great lies about his wooden horse
Set the crew laughing, and forgot his course.
It was so old a ship—who knows—who knows?
—And yet so beautiful, I watched in vain
To see the mast burst open with a rose,
And the whole deck put on its leaves again.

JAMES ELROY FLECKER

After the appearance of *Trilby* which gave new life to this sentimental song, English was angry whenever he was reminded of it; he thought his membership in Congress was more important!

BEN BOLT

DON'T you remember sweet Alice, Ben Bolt,—
  Sweet Alice whose hair was so brown,
Who wept with delight when you gave her a smile,
  And trembled with fear at your frown?
In the old churchyard in the valley, Ben Bolt,
  In a corner obscure and alone,
They have fitted a slab of the granite so gray,
  And Alice lies under the stone.

Under the hickory tree, Ben Bolt,
  Which stood at the foot of the hill,
Together we've lain in the noonday shade,
  And listened to Appleton's mill.
The mill-wheel has fallen to pieces, Ben Bolt,
  The rafters have tumbled in,
And a quiet which crawls round the walls as you gaze
  Has followed the olden din.

Do you mind of the cabin of logs, Ben Bolt,
   At the edge of the pathless wood,
And the button-ball tree with its motley limbs,
   Which nigh by the doorstep stood?
The cabin to ruin has gone, Ben Bolt,
   The tree you would seek for in vain;
And where once the lords of the forest waved,
   Are grass and the golden grain.

And don't you remember the school, Ben Bolt,
   With the master so cruel and grim,
And the shaded nook in the running brook
   Where the children went to swim?
Grass grows on the master's grave, Ben Bolt,
   The spring of the brook is dry,
And of all the boys who were schoolmates then
   There are only you and I.

There is change in the things I loved, Ben Bolt,
   They have changed from the old to the new;
But I feel in the depths of my spirit the truth,
   There never was change in you.
Twelvemonths twenty have passed, Ben Bolt,
   Since first we were friends—yet I hail
Your presence a blessing, your friendship a truth,
   Ben Bolt of the salt-sea gale.

                 THOMAS DUNN ENGLISH

One will most enjoy these poems of Robert Frost if one hears the author read them.

AFTER APPLE-PICKING

My long two-pointed ladder's sticking through a tree
Toward heaven still,
And there's a barrel that I didn't fill
Beside it, and there may be two or three
Apples I didn't pick upon some bough.
But I am done with apple-picking now.
Essence of winter sleep is on the night,
The scent of apples: I am drowsing off.
I cannot rub the strangeness from my sight
I got from looking through a pane of glass
I skimmed this morning from the drinking trough
And held against the world of hoary grass.
It melted, and I let it fall and break.
But I was well
Upon my way to sleep before it fell,
And I could tell
What form my dreaming was about to take.
Magnified apples appear and disappear,
Stem end and blossom end,
And every fleck of russet showing clear.
My instep arch not only keeps the ache,
It keeps the pressure of a ladder-round.
I feel the ladder sway as the boughs bend.
And I keep hearing from the cellar bin
The rumbling sound
Of load on load of apples coming in.
For I have had too much
Of apple-picking: I am overtired
Of the great harvest I myself desired.

There were ten thousand thousand fruit to touch,
Cherish in hand, lift down, and not let fall.
For all
That struck the earth,
No matter if not bruised or spiked with stubble,
Went surely to the cider-apple heap
As of no worth.
One can see what will trouble
This sleep of mine, whatever sleep it is.
Were he not gone,
The woodchuck could say whether it's like his
Long sleep, as I describe its coming on,
Or just some human sleep.

ROBERT FROST

MENDING WALL

SOMETHING there is that doesn't love a wall,
That sends the frozen ground-swell under it,
And spills the upper boulders in the sun;
And makes gaps even two can pass abreast.
The work of hunters is another thing:
I have come after them and made repair
Where they have left not one stone on stone,
But they would have the rabbit out of hiding,
To please the yelping dogs. The gaps I mean,
No one has seen them made or heard them made,
But at spring mending-time we find them there.
I let my neighbour know beyond the hill;
And on a day we meet to walk the line
And set the wall between us once again.
We keep the wall between us as we go.
To each the boulders that have fallen to each.
And some are loaves and some so nearly balls
We have to use a spell to make them balance:

"Stay where you are until our backs are turned!"
We wear our fingers rough with handling them.
Oh, just another kind of outdoor game,
One on a side. It comes to little more:
There where it is we do not need the wall:
He is all pine and I am apple orchard.
My apple trees will never get across
And eat the cones under his pines, I tell him.
He only says, "Good fences make good neighbours."
Spring is the mischief in me, and I wonder
If I could put a notion in his head:
"Why do they make good neighbours? Isn't it
Where there are cows? But here there are no cows.
Before I built a wall I'd ask to know
What I was walling in or walling out,
And to whom I was like to give offense.
Something there is that doesn't love a wall,
That wants it down." I could say "Elves" to him.
But it's not elves exactly, and I'd rather
He said it for himself. I see him there
Bringing a stone grasped firmly by the top
In each hand, like an old stone savage armed.
He moves in darkness as it seems to me,
Not of woods only and the shade of trees.
He will not go behind his father's saying,
And he likes having thought of it so well
He says again, "Good fences make good neighbours."

ROBERT FROST

THE SNOW-STORM

Not the description of the storm, as in Whittier; but rather its effect on the observer's mind.

THE SNOW-STORM

ANNOUNCED by all the trumpets of the sky,
Arrives the snow, and, driving o'er the fields,
Seems nowhere to alight: the whited air
Hides hills and woods, the river, and the heaven,
And veils the farm-house at the garden's end.
The sled and traveller stopped, the courier's feet
Delayed, all friends shut out, the housemates sit
Around the radiant fireplace, enclosed
In a tumultuous privacy of storm.

Come see the north wind's masonry.
Out of an unseen quarry evermore
Furnished with tile, the fierce artificer
Curves his white bastions with projected roof
Round every windward stake, or tree, or door.
Speeding, the myriad-handed, his wild work
So fanciful, so savage, nought cares he
For number or proportion. Mockingly,
On coop or kennel he hangs Parian wreaths;
A swan-like form invests the hidden thorn;
Fills up the farmer's lane from wall to wall,
Maugre the farmer's sighs; and at the gate
A tapering turret overtops the work.
And when his hours are numbered, and the world
Is all his own, retiring, as he were not,
Leaves, when the sun appears, astonished Art
To mimic in slow structures, stone by stone,
Built in an age, the mad wind's night-work,
The frolic architecture of the snow.

RALPH WALDO EMERSON

[273]

All of Mr. Ficke's verses contain ideas.

I Am Weary of Being Bitter

I am weary of being bitter and weary of being wise,
  And the armour and the mask of these fall from me, after
    long.
I would go where the islands sleep, or where the sea-dawns
    rise,
  And lose my bitter wisdom in the wisdom of a song.

There are magics in melodies, unknown of the sages;
  The powers of purest wonder on secret wings go by.
Doubtless out of the silence of dumb preceding ages
  Song woke the chaos-world—and light swept the sky.

All that we know is idle; idle is all we cherish;
  Idle the will that takes loads that proclaim it strong.
For the knowledge, the strength, the burden—all shall
    perish:
  One thing only endures, one thing only—song.

ARTHUR DAVISON FICKE

━━

Two of the great Hymns of the Church.

Walking with God

Oh! for a closer walk with God,
A calm and heavenly frame;
A light to shine upon the road
That leads me to the Lamb!

Where is the blessèdness I knew
When first I saw the Lord?
Where is the soul-refreshing view
Of Jesus and his word?

What peaceful hours I once enjoyed!
How sweet their memory still!
But they have left an aching void
The world can never fill.

Return, O holy Dove, return,
Sweet messenger of rest!
I hate the sins that made thee mourn
And drove thee from my breast.

The dearest idol I have known,
Whate'er that idol be,
Help me to tear it from thy throne,
And worship only thee.

So shall my walk be close with God,
Calm and serene my frame;
So purer light shall mark the road
That leads me to the Lamb.
WILLIAM COWPER

LIGHT SHINING OUT OF DARKNESS

GOD moves in a mysterious way
    His wonders to perform;
He plants his footsteps in the sea,
    And rides upon the storm.

Deep in unfathomable mines
    Of never-failing skill,
He treasures up his bright designs,
    And works his sovereign will.

Ye fearful saints, fresh courage take,
　The clouds ye so much dread
Are big with mercy, and shall break
　In blessings on your head.

Judge not the Lord by feeble sense,
　But trust him for his grace:
Behind a frowning providence
　He hides a smiling face.

His purposes will ripen fast,
　Unfolding every hour;
The bud may have a bitter taste,
　But sweet will be the flower.

Blind unbelief is sure to err,
　And scan his work in vain:
God is his own interpreter,
　And he will make it plain.

WILLIAM COWPER

Archibald MacLeish saw service in the war: *hinc illæ lacrimæ*.

MEMORIAL RAIN

AMBASSADOR PUSER the ambassador
reminds himself in French, felicitous tongue,
what these (young men no longer) lie here for
in rows that once, and somewhere else, were young—

All night in Brussels the wind had tugged at my door:
I had heard the wind at my door and the trees strung
taut, and to me who had been before
in that country it was a strange wind blowing

[276]

steadily, stiffening the walls, the floor,
the roof of my room. I had not slept for knowing
he too, dead, was a stranger in that land
and felt beneath the earth in the wind's flowing
a tightening of roots and would not understand,
remembering lake winds in Illinois,
that strange wind. I had felt his bones in the
sand listening.

        —reflects that these enjoy
their country's gratitude, that deep repose,
that peace no pain can break, no hurt destroy,
that rest, that sleep—

        At Ghent the wind rose.
There was a smell of rain and a heavy drag
of wind in the hedges but not as the wind blows
over fresh water when the waves lag
foaming and the willows huddle and it will rain:
I felt him waiting.

        —indicates the flag
which (may he say) enisles in Flanders' plain
this little field these happy, happy dead
have made America—

        In the ripe grain
the wind coiled glistening, darted, fled,
dragging its heavy body; at Waereghem
the wind coiled in the grass above his head:
waiting—listening—

        —dedicates to them
this earth their bones have hallowed, this last gift
a grateful country—

WHAT I LIKE

 Under the dry grass stem
the words are blurred, are thickened, the words sift
confused by the rasp of the wind, by the thin grating
of ants under the grass, the minute shift
and tumble of dusty sand separating
from dusty sand. The roots of the grass strain,
tighten, the earth is rigid, waits—he is waiting—

And suddenly, and all at once, the rain !

The people scatter, they run into houses, the wind
is trampled under the rain, shakes free, is again
trampled. The rain gathers, running in thinned
spurts of water that ravel in the dry sand
seeping into the sand under the grass roots seeping
between cracked boards to the bones of a clenched hand:
the earth relaxes, loosens; he is sleeping,
he rests, he is quiet, he sleeps in a strange land.

ARCHIBALD MACLEISH

So long as many persons feel like this, communism cannot
become universal.

An Old Woman of the Roads

O, to have a little house!
To own the hearth and stool and all!
The heaped up sods upon the fire,
The pile of turf against the wall!

To have a clock with weights and chains
And pendulum swinging up and down!
A dresser filled with shining delph,
Speckled and white and blue and brown!

I could be busy all the day
Clearing and sweeping hearth and floor,
And fixing on their shelf again
My white and blue and speckled store!

I could be quiet there at night
Beside the fire and by myself,
Sure of a bed and loth to leave
The ticking clock and the shining delph!

Och! but I'm weary of mist and dark,
And roads where there's never a house nor bush,
And tired I am of bog and road,
And the crying wind and the lonesome hush!

And I am praying to God on high,
And I am praying Him night and day,
For a little house—a house of my own—
Out of the wind's and the rain's way.

PADRAIC COLUM

———

This man of peace wrote one of the greatest of all poems celebrating military valour; I suppose his love of freedom overcame his hatred of violence.

CONCORD HYMN

*Sung at the completion of the Battle Monument,
April 19, 1836*

By the rude bridge that arched the flood,
    Their flag to April's breeze unfurled,
Here once the embattled farmers stood,
    And fired the shot heard round the world.

The foe long since in silence slept;
  Alike the conqueror silent sleeps;
And Time the ruined bridge has swept
  Down the dark stream which seaward creeps.

On this green bank, by this soft stream,
  We set today a votive stone;
That memory may their deed redeem,
  When, like our sires, our sons are gone.

Spirit, that made those heroes dare
  To die, and leave their children free,
Bid Time and Nature gently spare
  The shaft we raise to them and thee.

RALPH WALDO EMERSON

The first two lines and the remark on the repetition sung by the thrush have made this poem one of the best-known in English literature. Naturalists had observed that the thrush always gave an encore; Browning gave the poetical reason for it.

HOME-THOUGHTS, FROM ABROAD

I

Oh, to be in England
Now that April's there,
And whoever wakes in England
Sees, some morning, unaware,
That the lowest boughs and the brush-wood sheaf
Round the elm-tree bole are in tiny leaf,
While the chaffinch sings on the orchard bough
In England—now!

II

And after April, when May follows,
And the whitethroat builds, and all the swallows!
Hark, where my blossomed pear-tree in the hedge
Leans to the field and scatters on the clover
Blossoms and dewdrops—at the bent spray's edge—
That's the wise thrush; he sings each song twice over,
Lest you should think he never could recapture
The first fine careless rapture!
And though the fields look rough with hoary dew,
All will be gay when noontide wakes anew
The buttercups, the little children's dower
—Far brighter than this gaudy melon-flower!

ROBERT BROWNING

The second line is the keynote. Old age is better than
youth. The poem was written probably in opposition to the
teaching of Omar Khayyam, which had recently appeared
in the beautiful version of Fitzgerald. If Browning could
have known then how, twenty-five years later, he would hate
Old Fitz!

RABBI BEN EZRA

Grow old along with me!
The best is yet to be,
The last of life, for which the first was made:
Our times are in his hand
Who saith, "A whole I planned,
Youth shows but half; trust God: see all, nor be afraid!"

Not that, amassing flowers,
Youth sighed, "Which rose make ours,
Which lily leave and then as best recall?"
Not that, admiring stars,
It yearned, "Nor Jove, nor Mars;
Mine be some figured flame which blends, transcends them
all!"

[281]

Not for such hopes and fears
Annulling youth's brief years,
Do I remonstrate: folly wide the mark!
Rather I prize the doubt
Low kinds exist without,
Finished and finite clouds, untroubled by a spark.

Poor vaunt of life indeed,
Were man but formed to feed
On joy, to solely seek and find and feast:
Such feasting ended, then
As sure an end to men;
Irks care the crop-full bird? Frets doubt the maw-
 crammed beast?

Rejoice we are allied
To That which doth provide
And not partake, effect and not receive!
A spark disturbs our clod;
Nearer we hold of God
Who gives, than of his tribes that take, I must believe.

Then, welcome each rebuff
That turns earth's smoothness rough,
Each sting that bids nor sit nor stand but go!
Be our joys three-parts pain!
Strive, and hold cheap the strain:
Learn, nor account the pang; dare, never grudge the
 throe!

For thence,—a paradox
Which comforts while it mocks,—
Shall life succeed in that it seems to fail:
What I aspired to be,
And was not, comforts me:
A brute I might have been, but would not sink i' the scale.

What is he but a brute
Whose flesh hath soul to suit,
Whose spirit works lest arms and legs want play?
To man, propose this test—
Thy body at its best,
How far can that project thy soul on its lone way?

Yet gifts should prove their use:
I own the Past profuse
Of power each side, perfection every turn:
Eyes, ears took in their dole,
Brain treasured up the whole;
Should not the heart beat once "How good to live and
   learn"?

Not once beat "Praise be thine!
I see the whole design,
I, who saw power, see now Love perfect too:
Perfect I call thy plan:
Thanks that I was a man!
Maker, remake, complete,—I trust what thou shalt do!"

For pleasant is this flesh;
Our soul, in its rose-mesh
Pulled ever to the earth, still yearns for rest;
Would we some prize might hold
To match those manifold
Possessions of the brute,—gain most, as we did best!

Let us not always say,
"Spite of this flesh today
I strove, made head, gained ground upon the whole!"
As the bird wings and sings,
Let us cry, "All good things
Are ours, nor soul helps flesh more, now, than flesh helps
   soul!"

Therefore I summon age
To grant youth's heritage,
Life's struggle having so far reached its term:
Thence shall I pass, approved
A man, for aye removed
From the developed brute; a God though in the germ.

And I shall thereupon
Take rest, ere I be gone
Once more on my adventure brave and new:
Fearless and unperplexed,
When I wage battle next,
What weapons to select, what armour to indue.

Youth ended, I shall try
My gain or loss thereby;
Leave the fire ashes, what survives is gold:
And I shall weigh the same,
Give life its praise or blame:
Young, all lay in dispute; I shall know, being old.

For note, when evening shuts,
A certain moment cuts
The deed off, calls the glory from the grey:
A whisper from the west
Shoots—"Add this to the rest,
Take it and try its worth: here dies another day."

So, still within this life,
Though lifted o'er its strife,
Let me discern, compare, pronounce at last,
"This rage was right i' the main,
That acquiescence vain:
The Future I may face now I have proved the Past."

For more is not reserved
To man, with soul just nerved
To act tomorrow what he learns today:
Here, work enough to watch
The Master work, and catch
Hints of the proper craft, tricks of the tool's true play.

As it was better, youth
Should strive, through acts uncouth,
Toward making, than repose on aught found made:
So, better, age, exempt
From strife, should know, than tempt
Further. Thou waitedst age: wait death nor be afraid!

Enough now, if the Right
And Good and Infinite
Be named here, as thou callest thy hand thine own,
With knowledge absolute,
Subject to no dispute
From fools that crowded youth, nor let thee feel alone.

Be there, for once and all,
Severed great minds from small,
Announced to each his station in the Past!
Was I, the world arraigned,
Were they, my soul disdained,
Right? Let age speak the truth and give us peace at last!

Now, who shall arbitrate?
Ten men love what I hate,
Shun what I follow, slight what I receive;
Ten, who in ears and eyes
Match me: we all surmise,
They this thing, and I that: whom shall my soul believe?

Not on the vulgar mass
Called "work," must sentence pass,
Things done, that took the eye and had the price;
O'er which, from level stand,
The low world laid its hand,
Found straightway to its mind, could value in a trice:

But all, the world's coarse thumb
And finger failed to plumb,
So passed in making up the main account;
All instincts immature,
All purposes unsure,
That weighed not as his work, yet swelled the man's
    amount:

Thoughts hardly to be packed
Into a narrow act,
Fancies that broke through language and escaped;
All I could never be,
All, men ignored in me,
This, I was worth to God, whose wheel the pitcher shaped.

Ay, note that Potter's wheel,
That metaphor! and feel
Why time spins fast, why passive lies our clay,—
Thou, to whom fools propound,
When the wine makes its round,
"Since life fleets, all is change; the Past gone, seize
    today!"

Fool! All that is, at all,
Lasts ever, past recall;
Earth changes, but thy soul and God stand sure:
What entered into thee,
That was, is, and shall be:
Time's wheel runs back or stops: Potter and clay endure.

He fixed thee 'mid this dance
Of plastic circumstance,
This Present, thou, forsooth, would fain arrest:
Machinery just meant
To give thy soul its bent,
Try thee and turn thee forth, sufficiently impressed.

What though the earlier grooves
Which ran the laughing loves
Around thy base, no longer pause and press?
What though, about thy rim,
Skull-things in order grim
Grow out, in graver mood, obey the sterner stress?

Look not thou down but up!
To uses of a cup,
The festal board, lamp's flash and trumpet's peal,
The new wine's foaming flow,
The Master's lips aglow!
Thou, heaven's consummate cup, what needst thou with
    earth's wheel?

But I need, now as then,
Thee, God, who mouldest men;
And since, not even while the whirl was worst,
Did I—to the wheel of life
With shapes and colours rife,
Bound dizzily—mistake my end, to slake thy thirst:

So, take and use thy work:
Amend what flaws may lurk,
What strain o' the stuff, what warpings past the aim!
My times be in thy hand!
Perfect the cup as planned!
Let age approve of youth, and death complete the same!

ROBERT BROWNING

This sixteenth-century farce, *Gammer Gurton's Needle*, played at an English university, contains the finest drinking song I have ever seen. Whether one drinks or not, the song should be enthusiastic. Of all the anti-climaxes in the world's literature, the worst is that of Bryant's exhortation:

"Fill up the cup from the brook that glides"

which is as depressing as it is no doubt healthful. Whoever wrote this old English drinking-song had the right spirit for the occasion.

ALE SONG

I CANNOT eat but little meat,
 My stomach is not good;
But, sure, I think that I can drink
 With him that wears a hood.
Though I go bare, take ye no care,
 I am nothing a-cold,
I stuff my skin so full within
 Of jolly good ale and old.

Chorus

Back and side, go bare, go bare;
 Both foot and hand, go cold:
But, belly, God send thee good ale enough,
 Whether it be new or old.

I love no roast, but a nut-brown toast
 And a crab laid in the fire;
A little bread shall do me stead,
 Much bread I not desire.
No frost nor snow, no wind, I trow,
 Can hurt me if I would,
I am so wrapt and throughly lapt
 Of jolly good ale and old.

And Tib my wife, that as her life
 Loveth well good ale to seek,
Full oft drinks she till ye may see
 The tears run down her cheek;
Then doth she trowl to me the bowl,
 Even as a malt-worm should,
And saith, 'Sweetheart, I took my part
 Of this jolly good ale and old.'

Now let them drink till they nod and wink,
 Even as good fellows should do;
They shall not miss to have the bliss
 Good ale doth bring men to.
And all poor souls that have scoured bowls,
 Or have them lustily trowled,
God save the lives of them and their wives,
 Whether they be young or old.

ANONYMOUS

A contemporary English poet is A. E. Coppard, who successfully combines humour and romance.

The Trespasser

When winter springs were flowing,
 And the lane was full of water,
I climbed the bank by Rixon's farm
 And there met Rixon's girl:
"Now who be you and what's your style
 Come traipsing o'er our meadow?"
Says she to me, and her sweet eyes
 Gloomed like the moon in shadow.

[289]

Though half the world is full of care
    The other half is lively;
She held a dead goose by its neck,
    For Christmas sport was nigh:
"I'm no'," says I, "a trespasser,
    And I was ne'er a rover;
It was those puddles by your hedge
    That set me gadding over!"

Her hair was like the hueless wave
    The blackest night uncovers,
And like a filly full of pride
    She bridled at my talk;
So huffed she was, so proud she was,
    I had a mind to scoffing,
But soon came frolic to her eyes
    And then I fell a-chaffing.

"Go back your ways, nor come again,
    This path is no' for public!"
"I'll not," says I, "depart from you,
    For private is my wish."
"The like o' you," said Rixon's girl,
    "Are best to keep at distance."
But I walked with her, I talked with her,
    And light was her resistance.

A. E. COPPARD

Nothing could show the revolution in English literature in the eighteenth century better than the contrast between Pope and Blake. The towering reputation of Blake in the twentieth century is significant. We can see farther by one flash of his lightning than in the steady sunlight of some other poets.

PIPING DOWN THE VALLEYS WILD

PIPING down the valleys wild,
 Piping songs of pleasant glee,
On a cloud I saw a child,
 And he laughing said to me:

"Pipe a song about a Lamb!"
 So I piped with merry cheer,
"Piper, pipe that song again";
 So I piped: he wept to hear.

"Drop that pipe, thy happy pipe;
 Sing thy songs of happy cheer!"
So I sung the same again,
 While he wept with joy to hear.

"Piper, sit thee down and write
 In a book that all may read."
So he vanish'd from my sight;
 And I pluck'd a hollow reed,

And I made a rural pen,
 And I stain'd the water clear,
And I wrote my happy songs
 Every child may joy to hear.

WILLIAM BLAKE

THE TIGER

TIGER! Tiger! burning bright
In the forests of the night,
What immortal hand or eye
Could frame thy fearful symmetry?

In what distant deeps or skies
Burnt the fire of thine eyes?
On what wings dare he aspire?
What the hand dare seize the fire?

And what shoulder, and what art,
Could twist the sinews of thy heart?
And when thy heart began to beat,
What dread hand? and what dread feet?

What the hammer? what the chain?
In what furnace was thy brain?
What the anvil? what dread grasp
Dare its deadly terrors clasp?

When the stars threw down their spears,
And watered heaven with their tears,
Did He smile His work to see?
Did He who made the lamb make thee?

Tiger! Tiger! burning bright
In the forests of the night,
What immortal hand or eye
Dare frame thy fearful symmetry?

WILLIAM BLAKE

THE LAMB

LITTLE Lamb, who made thee?
Dost thou know who made thee?
Gave thee life, and bid thee feed
By the stream and o'er the mead;
Gave thee clothing of delight,
Softest clothing, woolly, bright;
Gave thee such a tender voice,
Making all the vales rejoice?
Little Lamb, who made thee?
Dost thou know who made thee?

Little Lamb, I'll tell thee,
Little Lamb, I'll tell thee:
He is callèd by thy name,
For he calls Himself a Lamb.
He is meek, and He is mild;
He became a little child.
I a child, and thou a lamb,
We are callèd by His name.
Little Lamb, God bless thee!
Little Lamb, God bless thee!

WILLIAM BLAKE

THE CHIMNEY SWEEPER

A LITTLE black thing among the snow,
Crying "weep! weep!" in notes of woe!
"Where are thy father and mother, say?"—
"They are both gone up to the church to pray.

"Because I was happy upon the heath
And smiled among the winter's snow,
They clothèd me in the clothes of death,
And taught me to sing the notes of woe.

"And because I am happy and dance and sing,
They think they have done me no injury,
And are gone to praise God and his priest and king,
Who make up a heaven of our misery."

WILLIAM BLAKE

A. E. (George W. Russell) is a poet, painter, journalist, statesman, farmer, novelist, essayist, philosopher, mystic. He told me once that the highest poetry is always the poetry of transfiguration. The poet fuses his mind with a fact or an idea or an observation; and out of that fusion comes the flame. "It takes two currents to make the electric light," said he. Hence lyric poetry is always greater than narrative verse. His own poems illustrate perfectly the transfiguration.

CHILDHOOD

How I could see through and through you!
So unconscious, tender, kind,
More than ever was known to you
Of the pure ways of your mind.

We who long to rest from strife
Labour sternly as a duty;
But a magic in your life
Charms, unknowing of its beauty.

We are pools whose depths are told;
You are like a mystic fountain,
Issuing ever pure and cold
From the hollows of the mountain.

[294]

We are men by anguish taught
To distinguish false from true;
Higher wisdom we have not;
But a joy within guides you.

A. E.

BY THE MARGIN OF THE GREAT DEEP

WHEN the breath of twilight blows to flame the misty skies,
All its vaporous sapphire, violet glow and silver gleam
With their magic flood me through the gateway of the eyes;
    I am one with the twilight's dream.
When the trees and skies and fields are one in dusky mood,
Every heart of man is rapt within the mother's breast:
Full of peace and sleep and dreams in the vasty quietude,
    I am one with their hearts at rest.

From our immemorial joys of hearth and home and love
Strayed away along the margin of the unknown tide,
All its reach of soundless calm can thrill me far above
    Word or touch from the lips beside.

Aye, and deep and deep and deeper let me drink and draw
From the olden fountain more than light or peace or dream,
Such primeval being as o'erfills the heart with awe,
    Growing one with its silent stream.

A. E.

Crashaw and Hopkins, two centuries apart, had the same timeless inspiration.

TWO WENT UP TO THE TEMPLE TO PRAY

Two went to pray? Oh, rather say
One went to brag, the other to pray;

[295]

One stands up close and treads on high
Where the other dares not send his eye;

One nearer to God's altar trod,
The other to the altar's God.

RICHARD CRASHAW

HEAVEN-HAVEN

A Nun Takes the Veil

I HAVE desired to go
　Where springs not fail,
To fields where flies no sharp and sided hail,
　And a few lilies blow.

And I have asked to be
　Where no storms come,
Where the green swell is in the havens dumb,
　And out of the swing of the sea.

GERARD MANLEY HOPKINS

———

Holmes is among our greatest writers of hymns. He called *Lord of all being* his Sun-day hymn.

HYMN OF TRUST

O LOVE Divine, that stooped to share
　Our sharpest pang, our bitterest tear,
On Thee we cast each earth-born care,
　We smile at pain while Thou art near!

[296]

Though long the weary way we tread,
   And sorrow crown each lingering year,
No path we shun, no darkness dread,
   Our hearts still whispering, Thou art near!

When drooping pleasure turns to grief,
   And trembling faith is changed to fear,
The murmuring wind, the quivering leaf,
   Shall softly tell us, Thou art near!

On Thee we fling our burdening woe,
   O Love Divine, forever dear,
Content to suffer while we know,
   Living and dying, Thou art near!

OLIVER WENDELL HOLMES

A Sun-Day Hymn

Lord of all being! throned afar,
Thy glory flames from sun and star;
Centre and soul of every sphere,
Yet to each loving heart how near!

Sun of our life, thy quickening ray
Sheds on our path the glow of day;
Star of our hope, thy softened light
Cheers the long watches of the night.

Our midnight is thy smile withdrawn;
Our noontide is thy gracious dawn;
Our rainbow arch thy mercy's sign;
All, save the clouds of sin, are thine!

Lord of all life, below, above,
Whose light is truth, whose warmth is love,
Before thy ever-blazing throne
We ask no lustre of our own.

Grant us thy truth to make us free,
And kindling hearts that burn for thee,
Till all thy living altars claim
One holy light, one heavenly flame!

OLIVER WENDELL HOLMES

Every year in August, Mr. Guest and I, with a whole troop of children, visit in Michigan the Huron County Fair, held at the county seat, the town of Bad Axe. It is certain that no child enjoys the occasion more than we do.

THE BAD AXE FAIR

"It's all too big and wonderful," said Billy Phelps to me.
The county fair at Bad Axe is the one I want to see.
Chicago has the marvelous things, but when the summer's
   done
It's into Bad Axe we will go to have our day of fun.
Then you and I and Dr. Charles will take the kids along
To see the horses and the cows and mingle with the throng.

We'll wander through the cattle sheds, the winners to
admire.
We'll chat with friendly farming folk and talk of dam and
sire.
We'll tread once more that crowded hall where women folk
display
The things they've made throughout the year since we have
been away.
And then we'll do the poultry show and hear the roosters
crow
And live again the boyhood dreams we had so long ago.

We'll eat hot dogs and ice cream cones and wash them down
with pop.
At every loud-voiced barker's stand our merry group will
stop.
We'll venture every game of chance for blankets pink and
blue.
We'll purchase numbers on a wheel, and should we win a
few
We'll give them to the farmers' wives, and then with hearts
elate
We'll squander dimes upon a man to guess the children's
weight.

We'll hear that red-garbed little band which never seems
to rest.
We'll stand in awe to see a man break rocks upon his chest.
We'll ride the squeaking Ferris wheel; pitch rings at
trinkets gay
And miss the gaudy prize we want, and tired at close of day
We'll march our youthful army home and solemnly declare
No show upon the earth excels that Bad Axe County Fair.

EDGAR A. GUEST

[299]

There have been many poems written on the fairies; but with the exception of those by Shakespeare, my favourite poem on the little people is this one. When I read it aloud to a professor of English, he said "No woman could possibly have written it; it is the work of a man." The author, Rose Fyleman, is a concert singer and one of the few women who regularly contribute to *Punch*.

The Fairies Have Never a Penny to Spend

THE fairies have never a penny to spend,
They haven't a thing to put by,
But theirs is a dower of bird and flower
And theirs is the earth and sky.
And though you should live in a palace of gold
Or sleep in a dried-up ditch,
You could never be poor as the fairies are,
And never as rich.

Since ever and ever the world began
They have danced like a ribbon of flame,
They have sung their song through the centuries long
And yet it is never the same.
And though you be foolish or though you be wise,
With air of silver or gold,
You can never be young as the fairies are,
And never as old.

ROSE FYLEMAN

Emily Dickinson's father was a Congressman, her mother a model housewife. Emily spent her productive years as a recluse, going out at dusk to look at her plants. With her poems she was like a miser with money; the public did not know she was rich. Few persons have ever left such unsuspected wealth to mankind. Only three or four poems were published during her life; and she died in 1886. In 1892 a selection appeared that won instant acclaim; and in 1924 came the Complete Poems.

THE RAILWAY TRAIN

I LIKE to see it lap the miles,
And lick the valleys up,
And stop to feed itself at tanks;
And then, prodigious, step

Around a pile of mountains,
And, supercilious, peer
In shanties by the sides of roads;
And then a quarry pare

To fit its sides, and crawl between,
Complaining all the while
In horrid, hooting stanza;
Then chase itself down hill

And neigh like Boanerges;
Then, punctual as a star,
Stop—docile and omnipotent—
At its own stable door.

EMILY DICKINSON

I Never Saw a Moor

I never saw a moor,
I never saw the sea;
Yet know I how the heather looks,
And what a wave must be.

I never spoke with God,
Nor visited in heaven;
Yet certain am I of the spot
As if the chart were given.

EMILY DICKINSON

Autumn

The morns are meeker than they were
The nuts are getting brown;
The berry's cheek is plumper,
The rose is out of town.

The maple wears a gayer scarf,
The field a scarlet gown.
Lest I should be old-fashioned,
I'll put a trinket on.

EMILY DICKINSON

This was Emerson's own favourite, not mine.

Days

Daughters of Time, the hypocritic Days,
Muffled and dumb like barefoot dervishes,
And marching single in an endless file,
Bring diadems and fagots in their hands.

[302]

To each they offer gifts after his will,
Bread, kingdoms, stars, and sky that holds them all.
I, in my pleached garden, watched the pomp,
Forgot my morning wishes, hastily
Took a few herbs and apples, and the Day
Turned and departed silent. I, too late,
Under her solemn fillet saw the scorn.

RALPH WALDO EMERSON

Mouthed by a million schoolboys, this poem survives.

ABOU BEN ADHEM

ABOU BEN ADHEM (may his tribe increase!)
Awoke one night from a deep dream of peace,
And saw, within the moonlight in his room,
Making it rich, and like a lily in bloom,
An angel writing in a book of gold:—
Exceeding peace had made Ben Adhem bold,
And to the presence in the room he said,
"What writest thou?"—The vision raised its head,
And with a look made of all sweet accord,
Answered, "The names of those who love the Lord."
"And is mine one?" said Abou. "Nay, not so,"
Replied the angel. Abou spoke more low,
But cheerly still; and said, "I pray thee, then,
Write me as one that loves his fellow-men."

The angel wrote, and vanished. The next night
It came again with a great wakening light,
And showed the names whom love of God had blessed,
And, lo! Ben Adhem's name led all the rest!

LEIGH HUNT

This great writer of hymns, Frederick William Faber, died in 1863 at the age of forty-nine. When he told his friend Wordsworth that he had become rector of a church, Wordsworth replied, "I do not say you are wrong, but England loses a poet." In 1845 he became a Roman Catholic, and was ordained priest in 1847. In his last illness, after receiving Extreme Unction, he asked how long he had to live, and on being told about an hour, he said "Then I can hear *David Copperfield*." Accordingly he spent his last moments listening to the genius of Dickens.

FAITH OF OUR FATHERS

FAITH of our fathers, living still,
   In spite of dungeon, fire and sword,
O how our hearts beat high with joy
   When-e'er we hear that glorious word!

Our fathers, chained in prisons dark,
   Were still in heart and conscience free:
How sweet would be their children's fate,
   If they, like them, could die for thee!

Faith of our fathers, we will strive
   To win all nations unto thee;
And through the truth that comes from God,
   Mankind shall then indeed be free.

Faith of our fathers, we will love
   Both friend and foe in all our strife,
And preach thee, too, as love knows how
   By kindly words and virtuous life.

Faith of our fathers! holy faith!
We will be true to thee till death!

FREDERICK WILLIAM FABER

HARK, HARK, MY SOUL!

HARK, hark, my soul! Angelic songs are swelling
　O'er earth's green fields and ocean's wave-beat shore;
How sweet the truth those blessed strains are telling
　Of that new life when sin shall be no more.

Onward we go, for still we hear them singing,
　"Come, weary souls, for Jesus bids you come";
And through the dark, its echoes sweetly ringing,
　The music of the gospel leads us home.

Far, far away, like bells at evening pealing;
　The voice of Jesus sounds o'er land and sea,
And laden souls by thousands meekly stealing,
　Kind Shepherd, turn their weary steps to Thee.

Angels, sing on, your faithful watches keeping;
　Sing us sweet fragments of the songs above,
Till morning's joy shall end the night of weeping,
　And life's long shadows break in cloudless love.

FREDERICK WILLIAM FABER

FLOWER IN THE CRANNIED WALL

　FLOWER in the crannied wall,
　I pluck you out of the crannies,
　I hold you here, root and all, in my hand,
　Little flower—but *if* I could understand
　What you are, root and all, and all in all,
　I should know what God and man is.

ALFRED TENNYSON

The best of all poems on such a theme. If the author had not been a humorist, he might have slipped in such dangerous footing. As it is, I am sorry for any one who can read *Little Boy Blue* without emotion.

LITTLE BOY BLUE

THE little toy dog is covered with dust,
    But sturdy and stanch he stands;
The little toy soldier is red with rust,
    And his musket moulds in his hands.
Time was when the little toy dog was new,
    And the soldier was passing fair;
And that was the time when our Little **Boy Blue**
    Kissed them and put them there.

"Now don't you go till I come," he said,
    "And don't you make any noise!"
So, toddling off to his trundle bed,
    He dreamt of his pretty toys;
And, as he was dreaming, an angel song
    Awakened our Little Boy Blue—
Oh, the years are many, the years are long,
    But the little toy friends are true!

Ay, faithful to Little Boy Blue they stand,
    Each in the same old place,
Awaiting the touch of a little hand,
    The smile of a little face;
And they wonder, as waiting the long years through
    In the dust of that little chair,
What has become of our Little Boy Blue
    Since he kissed them and put them there.

EUGENE FIELD

Sarah Flower and her sister Eliza were respectively seven and nine years older than Browning; as a boy, he delighted in their company, and had a boyish love for Eliza, who probably inspired his sonnet *Eyes Calm Beside Thee* and certainly exerted an influence in the composition of *Pauline*.

The hymn *Nearer, My God, to Thee* was composed by Sarah in 1841, and first heard in public, when the two sisters sang it as a duet in church. (Read *Genesis* 28:10–22.)

Sarah was married to William Bridges Adams, the inventor of "fish-joint" for uniting ends of rails; he made many improvements in machinery, and wrote scientific and technical works.

NEARER, MY GOD, TO THEE

NEARER, my God, to Thee,
Nearer to Thee!
E'en though it be a cross
That raiseth me,
Still all my song shall be,
Nearer, my God, to Thee.

Though like the wanderer,
The sun gone down,
Darkness be over me,
My rest a stone;
Yet in my dreams I'd be
Nearer, my God, to Thee.

There let the way appear
Steps unto heaven;
All that Thou sendest me
In mercy given;
Angels to beckon me
Nearer, my God, to Thee.

Then, with my waking thoughts
  Bright with Thy praise,
Out of my stony griefs,
  Bethel I'll raise;
So by my woes to be
  Nearer, my God, to Thee.

Or if on joyful wing,
  Cleaving the sky,
Sun, moon, and stars forgot
  Upward I fly,
Still all my song shall be
  Nearer, my God, to Thee.

SARAH FLOWER

═══

Robert Frost was born in San Francisco, made his reputation in England, and writes about New England. He loves to sit up all night in conversation; hence his affectionate wonder at those who go to bed early.

Good Hours

I HAD for my winter evening walk—
No one at all with whom to talk,
But I had the cottages in a row
Up to their shining eyes in snow.

And I thought I had the folk within:
I had the sound of a violin;
I had a glimpse through curtain laces
Of youthful forms and youthful faces.

I had such company outward bound.
I went till there were no cottages found.
I turned and repented, but coming back
I saw no window but that was black.

Over the snow my creaking feet
Disturbed the slumbering village street
Like profanation, by your leave,
At ten o'clock of a winter eve.

ROBERT FROST

━━

When Henry James heard Tennyson read one of his poems, he said that Tennyson had taken out of the poem more than he had put into it. Well, there is much for the silent reader in Mr. Gibson's verse; they actually sound better in the mind than when read aloud.

THE ORPHANS

At five o'clock one April morn
I met them making tracks,
Young Benjamin and Abel Horn,
With bundles on their backs.

Young Benjamin is seventy-five,
Young Abel, seventy-seven—
The oldest innocents alive
Beneath that April heaven.

I asked them why they trudged about
With crabby looks and sour—
"And does your mother know you're out
At this unearthly hour?"

They stopped: and scowling up at me,
Each shook a grizzled head,
And swore; and then spat bitterly,
As with one voice they said:

"Homeless, about the country-side
We never thought to roam;
But mother, she has gone and died,
And broken up the home."

WILFRID WILSON GIBSON

NORTHUMBERLAND

HEATHERLAND and bent-land—
Black land and white,
God bring me to Northumberland,
The land of my delight.

Land of singing waters,
And winds from off the sea,
God bring me to Northumberland,
The land where I would be.

Heatherland and bent-land,
And valleys rich with corn,
God bring me to Northumberland,
The land where I was born.

WILFRID WILSON GIBSON

AFTER

"How fared you when you mortal were?
   What did you see on my peopled star?"
"Oh, well enough," I answered her,
   "It went for me where mortals are!

"I saw blue flowers and the merlin's flight
   And the rime on the wintry tree,
Blue doves I saw and summer light
   On the wings of the cinnamon bee."

RALPH HODGSON

━━━

This poem expresses accurately the difference between the ground-scenery of England and that of France, as beheld from above.

LONDON TO PARIS, BY AIR

THE droning roar is quickened, and we lift
On steady wing, like upward sweep of air,
Into the fleece-strewn heaven. The great plane
Draws to herself the leagues; onward we bear
In one resistless eddy towards the south,
Over the English fields, trim-hedged and square,
And countless, winding lanes, a vast expanse
Of flattened green: huge shapes of shadow float
Inconsequent as bubbles: haunts of men
Stripped of their cherished privacy we note,
And crawling multitudes within a town—
On all we rangers of the wind look down.

[311]

The coast-line swings to us; beneath our feet
The grey-green carpet of the sliding sea
Stretches afar, on it small, busy ships
Whose comet-tails in foamy whiteness flee:
We lift, and snowy cloudlets roam below,
Frail, wistful spirits of pure charity
Blessing the waters: like green marble veined,
The waves roll in upon the yellowing sand,
Then break to myriad, filmy curves of lace
Where they eternally caress the land:
Now low lies France—the kingdom of the breeze
Parts not the nations like the severing seas.

Down the wide river, jauntily outspread,
A fishing fleet comes seaward, to our eyes
Mere walnut shells with autumn leaves for sails:
And now a fellow pilgrim of the skies,
Like a big insect droning past our flank,
Cruises to England home: before us lies
The rolling plain, with its great, hedgeless strips
Of close-tilled fields, red roofs, and painted trees.
The feathered arrows of the long French roads,
And all the stretch of quiet harmonies:
Then heaven shows, and downward to earth's breast,
Like homing bird, we wheel and sink to rest.

LORD GORELL

Herrick's volume of beautiful songs called *Hesperides* was published in London in 1648 and there was no second edition until the nineteenth century. In the Great Civil War the blast of trumpets o'er-crowed his country reedpipe; but his timeless lyrics belong to eternity. Thomas Bailey Aldrich said

"What mighty epics have been wrecked by time
 Since Herrick launched his cockleshells of rhyme!"

HESPERIDES

I SING of brooks, of blossoms, birds, and flowers,
Of April, May, of June and July flowers.
I sing of Maypoles, hock-carts, wassails, wakes,
Of bridegrooms, brides, and of their bridal-cakes.
I write of youth, of love, and have access
By these to sing of cleanly wantonness.
I sing of dews, of rains, and, piece by piece,
Of balm, of oil, of spice, and ambergris.
I sing of times trans-shifting, and I write
How roses first came red and lilies white.
I write of groves, of twilights, and I sing
The court of Mab and of the fairy king.
I write of hell; I sing, and ever shall,
Of heaven, and hope to have it after all.

ROBERT HERRICK

CHERRY-RIPE

"CHERRY-RIPE, ripe, ripe!" I cry;
"Full and fair ones; come and buy!"
If so be you ask me where
They do grow, I answer, "There,
Where my Julia's lips do smile;
There's the land, or cherry-isle,
Whose plantations fully show
All the year where cherries grow."

ROBERT HERRICK

[313]

To Daffodils

FAIR daffodils, we weep to see
  You haste away so soon;
As yet the early-rising sun
  Has not attained his noon.
    Stay, stay,
  Until the hasting day
    Has run
  But to the even-song;
And, having prayed together, we
  Will go with you along.

We have short time to stay as you:
  We have as short a spring,
As quick a growth to meet decay
  As you or anything.
    We die
  As your hours do, and dry
    Away
  Like to the summer's rain;
Or as the pearls of morning's dew,
  Ne'er to be found again.

ROBERT HERRICK

How Roses Came Red

ROSES at first were white,
  Till they could not agree
Whether my Sapho's breast
  Or they more white should be.

But being vanquished quite,
  A blush their cheeks bespread;
Since which, believe the rest,
  The roses first came red.

ROBERT HERRICK

CORINNA'S GOING A-MAYING

GET up, get up for shame, the blooming morn
Upon her wings presents the god unshorn.
   See how Aurora throws her fair
   Fresh-quilted colours through the air.
   Get up, sweet slug-a-bed, and see
   The dew bespangling herb and tree.
Each flower has wept and bowed towards the east
Above an hour since, yet you not dressed;
   Nay, not so much as out of bed,
   When all the birds have matins said
   And sung their thankful hymns? 'Tis sin,
   Nay, profanation to keep in,
Whenas a thousand virgins on this day
Spring, sooner than the lark, to fetch in May.

Rise, and put on your foliage, and be seen
To come forth, like the spring-time, fresh and green,
   And sweet as Flora. Take no care
   For jewels for your gown or hair;
   Fear not, the leaves will strew
   Gems in abundance upon you;
Besides, the childhood of the day has kept,
Against you come, some orient pearls unwept;
   Come and receive them while the light
   Hangs on the dew-locks of the night,
   And Titan on the eastern hill
   Retires himself, or else stands still
Till you come forth. Wash, dress, be brief in praying:
Few beads are best when once we go a-Maying.

Come, my Corinna, come; and, coming, mark
How each field turns a street, each street a park
   Made green, and trimmed with trees; see how

Devotion gives each house a bough
Or branch: each porch, each door ere this
An ark, a tabernacle is,
Made up of white-thorn neatly interwove,
As if here were those cooler shades of love.
Can such delights be in the street
And open fields, and we not see 't?
Come, we'll abroad; and let's obey
The proclamation made for May,
And sin no more, as we have done, by staying;
But, my Corinna, come, let's go a-Maying.

There's not a budding boy or girl this day
But is got up and gone to bring in May;
A deal of youth, ere this, is come
Back, and with white-thorn laden, home.
Some have despatched their cakes and cream
Before that we have left to dream;
And some have wept, and wooed, and plighted troth,
And chose their priest, ere we can cast off sloth.
Many a green-gown has been given,
Many a kiss, both odd and even;
Many a glance, too, has been sent
From out the eye, love's firmament;
Many a jest told of the keys betraying,
This night, and locks picked; yet we're not a-Maying.

Come, let us go while we are in our prime,
And take the harmless folly of the time.
We shall grow old apace, and die
Before we know our liberty.
Our life is short, and our days run
As fast away as does the sun;
And as a vapour or a drop of rain,
Once lost, can ne'er be found again,

So when or you or I are made
A fable, song, or fleeting shade,
All love, all liking, all delight
Lies drowned with us in endless night.
Then while time serves, and we are but decaying,
Come, my Corinna, come, let's go a-Maying.

ROBERT HERRICK

Sally Cleghorn lives in a Vermont village; she hates in-
justice and cruelty with a fierce hatred; occasionally she
writes a poem like this, indicating a preference for the religion of Martha over that of Mary.

A SAINT'S HOURS

Her matins
IN the still cold before the sun,
   Her brothers and her sisters small
She woke, and washed and dressed each one.

Prime
And through the morning hours all
   Singing above her broom she stood
And swept the house from hall to hall

Tierce
Then out she ran with tidings good,
   Across the field and down the lane,
To share them with the neighbourhood.

Sexts
Four miles she walked, and home again,
   To sit through half the afternoon
And hear a feeble crone complain.

Nones
But when she saw the frosty moon
   And lakes of shadow on the hill,
Her maiden dreams grew bright as noon.

[317]

Vespers

She threw her pitying apron frill
Over a little trembling mouse
When the sleek cat yawned on the sill

Even song

In the late hours and drowsy house.
At last, too tired, beside her bed
She fell asleep—her prayers half said.

SARAH CLEGHORN

The poem expresses exactly the general attitude towards life characteristic of its author. Neither optimistic nor pessimistic, but perplexed in the extreme. All we know is that we are sailing under sealed orders.

WHERE LIES THE LAND?

WHERE lies the land to which the ship would go?
Far, far ahead, is all her seamen know.
And where the land she travels from? Away,
Far, far behind, is all that they can say.

On sunny noons upon the deck's smooth face,
Linked arm in arm, how pleasant here to pace;
Or, o'er the stern reclining, watch below
The foaming wake far widening as we go.

On stormy nights when wild northwesters rave,
How proud a thing to fight with wind and wave!
The dripping sailor on the reeling mast
Exults to bear, and scorns to wish it past.

Where lies the land to which the ship would go?
Far, far ahead, is all her seamen know.
And where the land she travels from? Away,
Far, far behind, is all that they can say.

ARTHUR HUGH CLOUGH

—

If Ben Jonson had not written lyrics, no one would have thought he could. The rhinoceros becomes dainty, the elephant graceful.

To Celia

Drink to me only with thine eyes,
　　And I will pledge with mine;
Or leave a kiss but in the cup,
　　And I'll not look for wine.
The thirst that from the soul doth rise,
　　Doth ask a drink divine:
But might I of Jove's nectar sup,
　　I would not change for thine.

I sent thee late a rosy wreath,
　　Not so much honouring thee
As giving it a hope that there
　　It could not withered be.
But thou thereon didst only breathe,
　　And sent'st it back to me:
Since when it grows, and smells, I swear,
　　Not of itself, but thee.

BEN JONSON

[319]

HYMN TO DIANA

QUEEN and huntress, chaste and fair,
Now the sun is laid to sleep,
Seated in thy silver chair,
State in wonted manner keep:
   Hesperus entreats thy light,
   Goddess excellently bright.

Earth, let not thy envious shade
Dare itself to interpose;
Cynthia's shining orb was made
Heaven to clear when day did close:
   Bless us then with wishèd sight,
   Goddess excellently bright.

Lay thy bow of pearl apart
And thy crystal-shining quiver;
Give unto the flying hart
Space to breathe, how short soever:
   Thou that mak'st a day of night,
   Goddess excellently bright.

BEN JONSON

Browning's lyrical poem, *Never the Time and the Place*, was written when he was past seventy; the title has become a proverbial expression.

NEVER THE TIME AND THE PLACE

NEVER the time and the place
   And the loved one all together!
This path—how soft to pace!

This May—what magic weather!
Where is the loved one's face?
In a dream that loved one's face meets mine,
   But the house is narrow, the place is bleak
Where, outside, rain and wind combine
   With a furtive ear, if I strive to speak,
   With a hostile eye at my flushing cheek,
With a malice that marks each word, each sign!
O enemy sly and serpentine,
   Uncoil thee from the waking man!
     Do I hold the Past
     Thus firm and fast
Yet doubt if the Future hold I can?
This path so soft to pace shall lead
Through the magic of May to herself indeed!
Or narrow if needs the house must be,
Outside are the storms and strangers: we—
Oh, close, safe, warm sleep I and she,
   —I and she!

                  ROBERT BROWNING

═══

An American novelist, Allan Updegraff. When he was an undergraduate, he wrote a poem inspired by the lyric of Browning.

THE TIME AND THE PLACE

WILL you not come? The pines are gold with evening
   And breathe their old-time fragrance by the sea;
   You loved so well their spicy exhalation,—
So smiled to smell it and old ocean's piquancy;
   And those weird tales of winds and waves' relation—
Could you forget? Will you not come to me?

See, 'tis the time: the last long gleams are going,
  The pine-spires darken, mists rise waveringly;
  The gloaming brings the old familiar longing
To be re-crooned by twilight voices of the sea.
  And just such tinted wavelets shoreward thronging—
  Could you forget things once so dear—and me?

Whatever of the waves is ceaseless longing,
  And of the twilight immortality:
  The urge of some wild, inchoate aspiration
Akin to afterglow and stars and winds and sea:
  This hour makes full and pours out in libation,—
  Could you forget? Will you not come to me?

What golden galleons sailed into the sunset
  Not to come home unto eternity:
  What souls went outward hopeful of returning,
This time and tide might well call back across the sea.
  Did we not dream so while old Wests were burning?
  Could you forget such once-dear things—and me?

From the dimmed sky and long grey waste of waters,
  Lo, one lone sail on all the lonely sea
  A moment blooms to whiteness like a lily,
As sudden fades, is gone, yet half-seems still to be;
  And you,—though that last time so strange and stilly,—
  Though you are dead, will you not come to me?

                                    ALLAN UPDEGRAFF

Narrative poetry is, as the Irishman A. E. says, usually second-rate; but it may be redeemed by genius.

THE EVE OF SAINT AGNES

I

St. Agnes' Eve—Ah, bitter chill it was!
The owl, for all his feathers, was a-cold;
The hare limped trembling through the frozen grass,
And silent was the flock in woolly fold:
Numb were the Beadsman's fingers, while he told
His rosary, and while his frosted breath,
Like pious incense from a censer old,
Seemed taking flight for heaven, without a death,
Past the sweet Virgin's picture, while his prayer he saith.

II

His prayer he saith, this patient, holy man;
Then takes his lamp, and riseth from his knees,
And back returneth, meagre, barefoot, wan,
Along the chapel aisle by slow degrees:
The sculptured dead, on each side, seem to freeze,
Emprisoned in black, purgatorial rails:
Knights, ladies, praying in dumb orat'ries,
He passeth by; and his weak spirit fails
To think how they may ache in icy hoods and mails.

III

Northward he turneth through a little door,
And scarce three steps, ere Music's golden tongue
Flattered to tears this agèd man and poor;
But no—already had his deathbell rung:
The joys of all his life were said and sung:

[323]

His was harsh penance on St. Agnes' Eve:
Another way he went, and soon among
Rough ashes sat he for his soul's reprieve,
And all night kept awake, for sinners' sake to grieve.

IV

That ancient Beadsman heard the prelude soft;
And so it chanced, for many a door was wide,
From hurry to and fro. Soon, up aloft,
The silver, snarling trumpets 'gan to chide:
The level chambers, ready with their pride,
Were glowing to receive a thousand guests:
The carvèd angels, ever eager-eyed,
Stared, where upon their heads the cornice rests,
With hair blown back, and wings put crosswise on their
  breasts.

V

At length burst in the argent revelry,
With plume, tiara, and all rich array,
Numerous as shadows haunting faerily
The brain, new stuffed, in youth, with triumphs gay
Of old romance. These let us wish away,
And turn, sole-thoughted, to one Lady there,
Whose heart had brooded, all that wintry day,
On love, and winged St. Agnes' saintly care,
As she had heard old dames full many times declare.

VI

They told her how, upon St. Agnes' Eve,
Young virgins might have visions of delight,
And soft adorings from their loves receive
Upon the honeyed middle of the night,
If ceremonies due they did aright;

As, supperless to bed they must retire,
And couch supine their beauties, lily white;
Nor look behind, nor sideways, but require
Of Heaven with upward eyes for all that they desire.

VII

Full of this whim was thoughtful Madeline:
The music, yearning like a God in pain,
She scarcely heard: her maiden eyes divine,
Fixed on the floor, saw many a sweeping train
Pass by—she heeded not at all: in vain
Came many a tiptoe, amorous cavalier,
And back retired; not cooled by high disdain,
But she saw not: her heart was otherwhere:
She sighed for Agnes' dreams, the sweetest of the year.

VIII

She danced along with vague, regardless eyes,
Anxious her lips, her breathing quick and short:
The hallowed hour was near at hand: she sighs
Amid the timbrels, and the thronged resort
Of whisperers in anger, or in sport;
'Mid looks of love, defiance, hate, and scorn,
Hoodwinked with faery fancy; all amort,
Save to St. Agnes and her lambs unshorn,
And all the bliss to be before to-morrow morn.

IX

So, purposing each moment to retire,
She lingered still. Meantime, across the moors,
Had come young Porphyro, with heart on fire
For Madeline. Beside the portal doors,

Buttressed from moonlight, stands he, and implores
All saints to give him sight of Madeline,
But for one moment in the tedious hours,
That he might gaze and worship all unseen;
Perchance speak, kneel, touch, kiss—in sooth such things
    have been.

X

He ventures in: let no buzzed whisper tell:
All eyes be muffled, or a hundred swords
Will storm his heart, Love's fev'rous citadel:
For him, those chambers held barbarian hordes,
Hyena foemen, and hot-blooded lords,
Whose very dogs would execrations howl
Against his lineage: not one breast affords
Him any mercy, in that mansion foul,
Save one old beldame, weak in body and in soul.

XI

Ah, happy chance! the agèd creature came,
Shuffling along with ivory-headed wand,
To where he stood, hid from the torch's flame,
Behind a broad hall-pillar, far beyond
The sound of merriment and chorus bland:
He startled her; but soon she knew his face,
And grasped his fingers in her palsied hand,
Saying, "Mercy, Porphyro! hie thee from this place:
They are all here tonight, the whole blood-thirsty race!

XII

"Get hence! get hence! there's dwarfish Hildebrand;
He had a fever late, and in the fit
He cursèd thee and thine, both house and land:
Then there's that old Lord Maurice, not a whit
More tame for his grey hairs—Alas me! flit!

[326]

Flit like a ghost away."—"Ah, Gossip dear,
We're safe enough; here in this arm-chair sit,
And tell me how"—"Good Saints! not here, not here;
Follow me, child, or else these stones will be thy bier."

XIII

He followed through a lowly archèd way,
Brushing the cobwebs with his lofty plume,
And as she muttered "Well-a—well-a-day!"
He found him in a little moonlight room,
Pale, latticed, chill, and silent as a tomb.
"Now tell me where is Madeline," said he,
"O tell me, Angela, by the holy loom
Which none but secret sisterhood may see,
When they St. Agnes' wool are weaving piously."

XIV

"St. Agnes! Ah! it is St. Agnes' Eve—
Yet men will murder upon holy days:
Thou must hold water in a witch's sieve,
And be liege-lord of all the Elves and Fays,
To venture so: it fills me with amaze
To see thee, Porphyro!—St. Agnes' Eve!
God's help! my lady fair the conjuror plays
This very night: good angels her deceive!
But let me laugh awhile, I've mickle time to grieve."

XV

Feebly she laugheth in the languid moon,
While Porphyro upon her face doth look,
Like puzzled urchin on an agèd crone
Who keepeth closed a wond'rous riddlebook,
As spectacled she sits in chimney nook.

[327]

But soon his eyes grew brilliant, when she told
His lady's purpose; and he scarce could brook
Tears, at the thought of those enchantments cold,
And Madeline asleep in lap of legends old.

XVI

Sudden a thought came like a full-blown rose,
Flushing his brow, and in his painèd heart
Made purple riot: then doth he propose
A stratagem, that makes the beldame start:
"A cruel man and impious thou art:
Sweet lady, let her pray, and sleep, and dream
Alone with her good angels, far apart
From wicked men like thee. Go, go!—I deem
Thou canst not surely be the same that thou didst seem."

XVII

"I will not harm her, by all saints I swear,"
Quoth Porphyro: "O may I ne'er find grace
When my weak voice shall whisper its last prayer,
If one of her soft ringlets I displace,
Or look with ruffian passion in her face:
Good Angela, believe me by these tears;
Or I will, even in a moment's space,
Awake, with horrid shout, my foemen's ears,
And beard them, though they be more fanged than wolves
    and bears."

XVIII

"Ah! why wilt thou affright a feeble soul?
A poor, weak, palsy-stricken, churchyard thing,
Whose passing-bell may ere the midnight toll;
Whose prayers for thee, each morn and evening,
Were never missed."—Thus plaining, doth she bring

[328]

A gentler speech from burning Porphyro;
So woeful, and of such deep sorrowing,
That Angela gives promise she will do
Whatever he shall wish, betide her weal or woe.

XIX

Which was, to lead him, in close secrecy,
Even to Madeline's chamber, and there hide
Him in a closet, of such privacy
That he might see her beauty unespied,
And win perhaps that night a peerless bride,
While legioned faeries paced the coverlet,
And pale enchantment held her sleepy-eyed.
Never on such a night have lovers met,
Since Merlin paid his Demon all the monstrous debt.

XX

"It shall be as thou wishest," said the Dame:
"All cates and dainties shall be storèd there
Quickly on this feast-night: by the tambour frame
Her own lute thou wilt see: no time to spare,
For I am slow and feeble, and scarce dare
On such a catering trust my dizzy head.
Wait here, my child, with patience; kneel in prayer
The while: Ah! thou must needs the lady wed,
Or may I never leave my grave among the dead."

XXI

So saying, she hobbled off with busy fear.
The lover's endless minutes slowly passed;
The dame returned, and whispered in his ear
To follow her; with agèd eyes aghast
From fright of dim espial. Safe at last,

[329]

Through many a dusky gallery, they gain
The maiden's chamber, silken, hushed, and chaste;
Where Porphyro took covert, pleased amain.
His poor guide hurried back with agues in her brain.

XXII

Her falt'ring hand upon the balustrade,
Old Angela was feeling for the stair,
When Madeline, St. Agnes' charmèd maid,
Rose, like a missioned spirit, unaware:
With silver taper's light, and pious care,
She turned, and down the agèd gossip led
To a safe level matting. Now prepare,
Young Porphyro, for gazing on that bed;
She comes, she comes again, like ring-dove frayed and fled.

XXIII

Out went the taper as she hurried in;
Its little smoke, in pallid moonshine, died:
She closed the door, she panted, all akin
To spirits of the air, and visions wide:
No uttered syllable, or, woe betide!
But to her heart, her heart was voluble,
Paining with eloquence her balmy side;
As though a tongueless nightingale should swell
Her throat in vain, and die, heart-stifled, in her dell.

XXIV

A casement high and triple-arched there was,
All garlanded with carven imag'ries
Of fruits, and flowers, and bunches of knotgrass,
Innumerable of stains and splendid dyes,
As are the tiger-moth's deep-damasked wings;

And in the midst, 'mong thousand heraldries,
And twilight saints, and dim emblazonings,
A shielded scutcheon blushed with blood of queens and
    kings.

XXV

Full on this casement shone the wintry moon,
And threw warm gules on Madeline's fair breast,
As down she knelt for heaven's grace and boon;
Rose-bloom fell on her hands, together prest,
And on her silver cross soft amethyst,
And on her hair a glory, like a saint:
She seemed a splendid angel, newly drest,
Save wings, for heaven:—Porphyro grew faint:
She knelt, so pure a thing, so free from mortal taint.

XXVI

Anon his heart revives: her vespers done,
Of all its wreathèd pearls her hair she frees;
Unclasps her warmèd jewels one by one;
Loosens her fragrant bodice; by degrees
Her rich attire creeps rustling to her knees:
Half-hidden, like a mermaid in sea-weed,
Pensive awhile she dreams awake, and sees,
In fancy, fair St. Agnes in her bed,
But dares not look behind, or all the charm is fled.

XXVII

Soon, trembling in her soft and chilly nest,
In sort of wakeful swoon, perplexed she lay,
Until the poppied warmth of sleep oppressed
Her soothèd limbs, and soul fatigued away;
Flown, like a thought, until the morrow-day;

Blissfully havened both from joy and pain;
Clasped like a missal where swart Paynims pray;
Blinded alike from sunshine and from rain,
As though a rose should shut, and be a bud again.

XXVIII

Stol'n to this paradise, and so entranced,
Porphyro gazed upon her empty dress,
And listened to her breathing, if it chanced
To wake into a slumberous tenderness;
Which when he heard, that minute did he bless,
And breathed himself: then from the closet crept,
Noiseless as fear in a wide wilderness,
And over the hushed carpet, silent, stept,
And 'tween the curtains peeped, where, lo!—how fast she
    slept.

XXIX

Then by the bed-side, where the faded moon
Made a dim, silver twilight, soft he set
A table, and, half anguished, threw thereon
A cloth of woven crimson, gold, and jet:—
O for some drowsy Morphean amulet!
The boisterous, midnight, festive clarion,
The kettle-drum, and far-heard clarinet,
Affray his ears, though but in dying tone:—
The hall door shuts again, and all the noise is gone.

XXX

And still she slept an azure-lidded sleep,
In blanchèd linen, smooth, and lavendered,
While he from forth the closet brought a heap
Of candied apple, quince, and plum, and gourd;
With jellies soother than the creamy curd,

And lucent syrops, tinct with cinnamon;
Manna and dates, in argosy transferred
From Fez; and spicèd dainties, every one,
From silken Samarcand to cedared Lebanon.

XXXI

These delicates he heaped with glowing hand
On golden dishes and in baskets bright
Of wreathèd silver: sumptuous they stand
In the retirèd quiet of the night,
Filling the chilly room with perfume light.—
"And now, my love, my seraph fair, awake!
Thou art my heaven, and I thine eremite:
Open thine eyes, for meek St. Agnes' sake,
Or I shall drowse beside thee, so my soul doth ache."

XXXII

Thus whispering, his warm, unnervèd arm
Sank in her pillow. Shaded was her dream
By the dusk curtains:—'t was a midnight charm
Impossible to melt as icèd stream:
The lustrous salvers in the moonlight gleam;
Broad golden fringe upon the carpet lies:
It seemed he never, never could redeem
From such a stedfast spell his lady's eyes;
So mused awhile, entoiled in woofèd phantasies.

XXXIII

Awakening up, he took her hollow lute,—
Tumultuous,—and, in chords that tenderest be,
He played an ancient ditty, long since mute,
In Provence called, "La belle dame sans mercy:"
Close to her ear touching the melody;—

Wherewith disturbed, she uttered a soft moan:
He ceased—she panted quick—and suddenly
Her blue affrayèd eyes wide open shone:
Upon his knees he sank, pale as smooth-sculptured stone.

XXXIV

Her eyes were open, but she still beheld,
Now wide awake, the vision of her sleep:
There was a painful change, that night expelled
The blisses of her dream so pure and deep,
At which fair Madeline began to weep,
And moan forth witless words with many a sigh;
While still her gaze on Porphyro would keep;
Who knelt, with joinèd hands and piteous eye,
Fearing to move or speak, she looked so dreamingly.

XXXV

"Ah, Porphyro!" said she, "but even now
Thy voice was at sweet tremble in mine ear,
Made tuneable with every sweetest vow;
And those sad eyes were spiritual and clear:
How changed thou art! how pallid, chill, and drear!
Give me that voice again, my Porphyro,
Those looks immortal, those complainings dear!
Oh leave me not in this eternal woe,
For if thou diest, my Love, I know not where to go."

XXXVI

Beyond a mortal man impassioned far
At these voluptuous accents, he arose,
Ethereal, flushed, and like a throbbing star
Seen mid the sapphire heaven's deep repose;
Into her dream he melted, as the rose

Blendeth its odour with the violet,—
Solution sweet: meantime the frost-wind blows
Like Love's alarum pattering the sharp sleet
Against the window-panes; St. Agnes' moon hath set.

XXXVII

'T is dark: quick pattereth the flaw-blown sleet:
"This is no dream, my bride, my Madeline!"
'T is dark: the icèd gusts still rave and beat:
"No dream, alas! alas! and woe is mine!
Porphyro will leave me here to fade and pine.—
Cruel! what traitor could thee hither bring?
I curse not, for my heart is lost in thine,
Though thou forsakest a deceivèd thing;—
A dove forlorn and lost with sick unprunèd wing."

XXXVIII

"My Madeline! sweet dreamer! lovely bride!
Say, may I be for aye thy vassal blest?
Thy beauty's shield, heart-shaped and vermeil **dyed?**
Ah, silver shrine, here will I take my rest
After so many hours of toil and quest,
A famished pilgrim,—saved by miracle.
Though I have found, I will not rob thy nest
Saving of thy sweet self; if thou think'st well
To trust, fair Madeline, to no rude infidel.

XXXIX

"Hark! 't is an elfin-storm from faery land,
Of haggard seeming, but a boon indeed:
Arise—arise! the morning is at hand;—
The bloated wassaillers will never heed:—
Let us away, my love, with happy speed;
There are no ears to hear, or eyes to see,—

[335]

Drowned all in Rhenish and the sleepy mead:
Awake! arise! my love, and fearless be,
For o'er the southern moors I have a home for thee."

XL

She hurried at his words, beset with fears,
For there were sleeping dragons all around,
At glaring watch, perhaps, with ready spears—
Down the wide stairs a darkling way they found.—
In all the house was heard no human sound.
A chain-drooped lamp was flickering by each door;
The arras, rich with horseman, hawk, and hound,
Fluttered in the besieging wind's uproar;
And the long carpets rose along the gusty floor.

XLI

They glide, like phantoms, into the wide hall;
Like phantoms, to the iron porch, they glide;
Where lay the Porter, in uneasy sprawl,
With a huge empty flaggon by his side:
The wakeful bloodhound rose, and shook his hide,
But his sagacious eye an inmate owns:
By one, and one, the bolts full easy slide:—
The chains lie silent on the footworn stones;—
The key turns, and the door upon its hinges groans.

XLII

And they are gone: aye, ages long ago
These lovers fled away into the storm.
That night the Baron dreamt of many a woe,
And all his warrior-guests, with shade and form
Of witch, and demon, and large coffin-worm,
Were long be-nightmared. Angela the old
Died palsy-twitched, with meagre face deform:
The Beadsman, after thousand aves told,
For aye unsought for slept among his ashes cold.

JOHN KEATS

In the Baltimore Symphony Orchestra, Lanier played the flute.

THE MOCKING BIRD

SUPERB and sole, upon a plumèd spray
That o'er the general leafage boldly grew,
He summ'd the woods in song; or typic drew
The watch of hungry hawks, the lone dismay
Of languid doves when long their lovers stray,
And all birds' passion-plays that sprinkle dew
At morn in brake or bosky avenue.
Whate'er birds did or dreamed, this bird could say.
Then down he shot, bounced airily along
The sward, twitched in a grasshopper, made song
Midflight, perched, prinked, and to his art again.
Sweet Science, this large riddle read me plain:
How may the death of that dull insect be
The life of yon trim Shakspere on the tree?

SIDNEY LANIER

This poem appeared in the novel called *Secret Service Operator 13,* published shortly after the death of Robert W. Chambers. It is my understanding that the poem was written by Mr. Chambers. It deserves to rank with the best of its kind.

WHEN I'SE FIGHTIN' FOH DE LAWD

WHEN I'se fightin' foh de Lawd
Lyin' dyin' whar I lay,
Will de onliest Son o' Gawd
Come to meet me on de way?
Whar de golden chariots rattle,

Will yuh meet me in de battle,
Will yuh meet me in de battle,
Will yuh meet me on that day?

I will meet yuh on that day!

Will de shoutin' Angels greet me?
Will de shoutin' Angels pray?
Oh Lawd Jesus will yuh meet me,
Will yuh lif' me whar I lay?
Whar de golden chariots rattle,
Will yuh meet me in de battle,
Will yuh meet me in de battle?
Will yuh meet me on that day?

I will meet yuh on that day!

ROBERT W. CHAMBERS

When he was about thirty years old, John Henry Newman was in a vessel becalmed on the Mediterranean; the lines in this hymn came into his head and he wrote them down, giving them originally the title *The Pillar and the Cloud*. I do not know of any greater hymn in the English language; like the Lord's Prayer, it can be sincerely uttered by any one who has any religious aspiration, without reference to any particular form of belief.

LEAD, KINDLY LIGHT

LEAD, kindly Light, amid th' encircling gloom,
Lead Thou me on.
The night is dark, and I am far from home;
Lead Thou me on.
Keep Thou my feet; I do not ask to see
The distant scene; one step enough for me.

I was not ever thus, nor prayed that Thou
       Shouldst lead me on.
I loved to choose and see my path, but now
       Lead Thou me on.
I loved the garish day, and, spite of fears,
Pride ruled my will; remember not past years.

So long Thy power hath blest me, sure it still
       Will lead me on,
O'er moor and fen, o'er crag and torrent, till
       The night is gone.
And with the morn those angel faces smile
Which I have loved long since, and lost awhile.

JOHN HENRY NEWMAN

Mrs. Thomas Sergeant Perry was a professional painter, who wrote poetry as a recreation.

LIFE AND DEATH

O YE who see with other eyes than ours,
And speak with tongues we are too deaf to hear,
Whose touch we cannot feel yet know ye near,
When, with a sense of yet undreamed-of powers,
We sudden pierce the cloud of sense that lowers,
Enwrapping us as 't were our spirit's tomb,
And catch some sudden glory through the gloom,
As Arctic sufferers dream of sun and flowers!
Do ye not sometimes long for power to speak
To our dull ears, and pierce their shroud of clay
With a loud cry, "Why, then, this grief at 'death'?
We are the living, you the dead today!
This truth you soon shall see, dear hearts, yet weak,
In God's bright mirror cleared from mortal breath!"

LILLA CABOT PERRY

I have never been able to discover the name of the author of the following poem; it is of course not a translation of the famous Latin hymn. But it is a beautiful poem and most effective in its universal application.

STABAT MATER

JEWS were wrought to cruel madness,
Christians fled in fear and sadness,
    Mary stood the cross beside:
At its foot her feet she planted,
By the dreadful scene undaunted,
    Till the gentle sufferer died.

Poets oft have told her story,
Painters decked her brow with glory,
    Priests her name have deified:
But no worship, song, or glory,
Touches like the simple story,
    Mary stood the cross beside.

So when crushed by fierce oppression,
Goodness suffers like transgression,
    Christ again is crucified:
But if Love be there true-hearted,
By no grief or terror parted,
    We may stand the cross beside.

ANONYMOUS

This genial Irishman, James Stephens, novelist and poet, has a style both in prose and in verse, that is all his own. The denunciation in *Righteous Anger* is given with joy; and his imagination is full of glee.

Righteous Anger

THE lanky hank of a she in the inn over there
Nearly killed me for asking the loan of a glass of beer;
May the devil grip the whey-faced slut by the hair,
And beat bad manners out of her skin for a year.

That parboiled imp, with the hardest jaw you will see
On virtue's path, and a voice that would rasp the dead,
Came roaring and raging the minute she looked at me,
And threw me out of the house on the back of my head!

If I asked her master he'd give me a cask a day;
But she, with the beer at hand, not a gill would arrange!
May she marry a ghost and bear him a kitten, and may
The High King of Glory permit her to get the mange!

JAMES STEPHENS

After Business Hours

WHEN I sit down with thee at last alone,
  Shut out the wrangle of the clashing day,
  The scrape of petty jars that fret and fray,
  The snarl and yelp of brute beasts for a bone;
When thou and I sit down at last alone,
  And through the dusk of rooms divinely grey
  Spirit to spirit finds its voiceless way,
  As tone melts meeting in accordant tone,—
Oh, then our souls, far in the vast of sky,
  Look from a tower, too high for sound of strife
  Or any violation of the town,

Where the great vacant winds of God go by,
And over the huge misshapen city of life
Love pours his silence and his moonlight down.

RICHARD HOVEY

In an age when the writing of sonnets was very common, neither Browning nor Tennyson cared much for it. Tennyson wrote comparatively few sonnets. Browning wrote only two, one at the beginning and one nearly at the end of his career and suppressed both. Yet I am particularly fond of the early one. Of course it may have been only an ideal he had in mind; but there is some reason to think it was addressed to Eliza Flower. She and her sister Sarah were intimate friends of his youth; and just enough older to receive boyish adoration. Browning was twenty-two when this sonnet appeared in *The Monthly Repository*.

EYES CALM

EYES calm beside thee (Lady, could'st thou know!)
May turn away thick with fast-gathering tears;
I glance not where all gaze: thrilling and low
Their passionate praises reach thee—my cheek wears
Alone no wonder when thou passest by;
Thy tremulous lids bent and suffused reply
To the irrepressible homage which doth glow
On every lip but mine: if in thine ears
Their accents linger—and thou dost recall
Me as I stood, still, guarded, very pale,
Beside each votarist whose lighted brow
Wore worship like an aureole, "O'er them all
My beauty," thou wilt murmur, "did prevail
Save that one only":—Lady, could'st thou know!

ROBERT BROWNING

Professor Leonard's volume *Two Lives* placed him in the front rank of living American poets. I have taken nothing from that, as its sequence should not be interrupted. Here are two poems from the book called *The Vaunt of Man*.

THE VAGABOND

AROUND the world I've been in many a guise,
In cape, or furs, or oilskin, fronting Fate;
Down rainy seas, through many a stormy strait,
By upland forests, over hills that rise
White, green, or crimson, in the season skies:
Through civic arch and eagle-crested gate,
Imperial boulevards and halls of state;
And asked for Fame—and failed of every prize.

Except, except the experienced eye and free,
And these impregnable old sides of mirth;
Except, except, a glorious wisdom, worth
All the poor scorn these tatters bring to me:
Some feeling for the massy bulk of earth,
Some still monitions of mortality.

WILLIAM ELLERY LEONARD

I FEEL ME NEAR TO SOME HIGH THING

I FEEL me near to some High Thing
That earth awaits from me,
But cannot find in all my journeying
What it may be.

I get no hint from hall or street,
From forest, hill, or plain,
Save now a sudden quickening of my feet,
Now some wild pain.

[343]

I only feel it should be done,
As Something great and true,
And that my hands could build it in the sun,
If I but knew.

WILLIAM ELLERY LEONARD

—

Alfred Noyes has written epics, dramas, ballads, long and short poems; he is probably the best living reader of his works. And this poem was written to be chanted.

THE HIGHWAYMAN

PART ONE

THE wind was a torrent of darkness among the gusty trees,
The moon was a ghostly galleon tossed upon cloudy seas,
The road was a ribbon of moonlight over the purple moor,
And the highwayman came riding—
    Riding—riding—
The highwayman came riding, up to the old inn-door.

He'd a French cocked-hat on his forehead, a bunch of lace
    at his chin,
A coat of the claret velvet, and breeches of brown doe-
    skin;
They fitted with never a wrinkle: his boots were up to the
    thigh!
And he rode with a jeweled twinkle,
    His pistol butts a-twinkle,
His rapier hilt a-twinkle, under the jeweled sky.

Over the cobbles he clattered and clashed in the dark inn-
    yard,
And he tapped with his whip on the shutters, but all was
    locked and barred;

[344]

He whistled a tune to the window, and who should be wait-
    ing there
But the landlord's black-eyed daughter,
   Bess, the landlord's daughter,
Plaiting a dark red love-knot into her long black hair.

And dark in the dark old inn-yard a stable-wicket creaked
Where Tim the ostler listened; his face was white and
    peaked;
His eyes were hollows of madness, his hair like mouldy hay,
But he loved the landlord's daughter,
   The landlord's red-lipped daughter,
Dumb as a dog he listened, and he heard the robber say—

"One kiss, my bonny sweetheart, I'm after a prize to-night,
But I shall be back with the yellow gold before the morning
    light;
Yet, if they press me sharply, and harry me through the
    day,
Then look for me by moonlight,
   Watch for me by moonlight,
I'll come to thee by moonlight, though hell should bar the
    way."

He rose upright in the stirrups; he scarce could reach her
    hand,
But she loosened her hair i' the casement! His face burnt
    like a brand
As the black cascade of perfume came tumbling over his
    breast;
And he kissed its waves in the moonlight,
   (Oh, sweet black waves in the moonlight!)
Then he tugged at his rein in the moonlight, and galloped
    away to the West.

PART TWO

He did not come in the dawning; he did not come at noon;
And out o' the tawny sunset, before the rise o' the moon,
When the road was a gipsy's ribbon, looping the purple
  moor,
A red-coat troop came marching—
  Marching—marching—
King George's men came marching, up to the old inn-door.

They said no word to the landlord, they drank his ale in-
  stead,
But they gagged his daughter and bound her to the foot of
  her narrow bed;
Two of them knelt at her casement, with muskets at their
  side!
There was death at every window;
  And hell at one dark window;
For Bess could see, through her casement, the road that *he*
  would ride.

They had tied her up to attention, with many a sniggering
  jest;
They had bound a musket beside her, with the barrel be-
  neath her breast!
"Now keep good watch!" and they kissed her.
  She heard the dead man say—
Look out for me by moonlight;
  Watch for me by moonlight;
I'll come to thee by moonlight, though hell should bar the
  way!

She twisted her hands behind her; but all the knots held
  good!

She writhed her hands till her fingers were wet with sweat
  or blood!
They stretched and strained in the darkness, and the hours
  crawled by like years,
Till, now, on the stroke of midnight,
  Cold, on the stroke of midnight,
The tip of one finger touched it! The trigger at least was
  hers!

The tip of one finger touched it; she strove no more for the
  rest!
Up, she stood up to attention, with the barrel beneath her
  breast,
She would not risk their hearing; she would not strive
  again;
For the road lay bare in the moonlight;
  Blank and bare in the moonlight;
And the blood of her veins in the moonlight throbbed to her
  love's refrain.

Tlot-tlot; tlot-tlot! Had they heard it? The horse-hoofs
  ringing clear;
Tlot-tlot, tlot-tlot, in the distance? Were they deaf that
  they did not hear?
Down the ribbon of moonlight, over the brow of the hill,
The highwayman came riding,
  Riding, riding!
The red-coats looked to their priming! She stood up,
  straight and still!

Tlot-tlot, in the frosty silence! *Tlot-tlot,* in the echoing
  night!
Nearer he came and nearer! Her face was like a light!
Her eyes grew wide for a moment; she drew one last deep
  breath,

Then her finger moved in the moonlight,
  Her musket shattered the moonlight,
Shattered her breast in the moonlight and warned him—
  with her death.

He turned; he spurred to the West; he did not know who
  stood
Bowed, with her head o'er the musket, drenched with her
  own red blood!
Not till the dawn he heard it, his face grew grey to hear
How Bess, the landlord's daughter,
  The landlord's black-eyed daughter,
Had watched for her love in the moonlight, and died in the
  darkness there.

Back, he spurred like a madman, shrieking a curse to the
  sky,
With the white road smoking behind him and his rapier
  brandished high!
Blood-red were his spurs i' the golden noon: wine-red was
  his velvet coat,
When they shot him down on the highway,
  Down like a dog in the highway,
And he lay in his blood on the highway, with the bunch of
  lace at his throat.

. . . .

And still of a winter's night, they say, when the wind is in
  the trees,
When the moon is a ghostly galleon tossed upon cloudy seas,
When the road is a ribbon of moonlight over the purple
  moor,
A highwayman comes riding—
  Riding—riding
A highwayman comes riding, up to the old inn-door.

Over the cobbles he clatters and clangs in the dark inn-
    yard;
He taps with his whip on the shutters, but all is locked and
    barred;
He whistles a tune to the window, and who should be wait-
    ing there
But the landlord's black-eyed daughter,
    Bess, the landlord's daughter,
Plaiting a dark red love-knot into her long black hair.

                                        ALFRED NOYES

George Woodberry's mastery of language made him come
nearer to the ideal of accurate expression than most of his
contemporaries.

THE ROSE OF STARS

WHEN Love, our great Immortal,
    Put on mortality,
And down from Eden's portal
    Brought this sweet life to be,
At the sublime archangel
    He laughed with veilèd eyes,
For he bore within his bosom
    The seed of Paradise.

He hid it in his bosom,
    And there such warmth it found,
It brake in bud and blossom,
    And the rose fell on the ground;
As the green light on the prairie,
    As the red light on the sea,
Through fragrant belts of summer
    Came this sweet life to be.

[349]

And the grave archangel seeing
    Spread his mighty wings for flight,
But the glow hung round him fleeing
    Like the rose of an Arctic night;
And sadly moving heavenward
    By Venus and by Mars,
He heard the joyful planets
    Hail Earth, the Rose of Stars.

GEORGE WOODBERRY

She wrote many poems, stories, essays; she had force and fervour. It was inevitable that this poem should be set to music. The words themselves are music.

SHEEP AND LAMBS

ALL in the April evening,
    April airs were abroad;
The sheep with their little lambs
    Passed me by on the road.

The sheep with their little lambs
    Passed me by on the road;
All in the April evening,
    I thought on the Lamb of God.

The lambs were weary, and crying
    With a weak human cry,
I thought on the Lamb of God,
    Going meekly to die.

Up in the blue, blue mountains
    Dewy pastures are sweet;
Rest for the little bodies,
    Rest for the little feet.

Rest for the Lamb of God
Upon the hill-top green,
Only a cross of shame
Two stark crosses between.

All in the April evening,
April airs were abroad,
I saw the sheep with their lambs,
And thought on the Lamb of God.

KATHARINE TYNAN

A Spaniard, George Santayana, without a drop of alien
blood, is a consummate master of English prose. Early in
life he wrote poems that belong to literature.

SONNETS

A WALL, a wall around my garden rear,
And hedge me in from the disconsolate hills;
Give me but one of all the mountain rills,
Enough of ocean in its voice I hear.
Come no profane insatiate mortal near
With the contagion of his passionate ills;
The smoke of battle all the valley fills,
Let the eternal sunlight greet me here.
This spot is sacred to the deeper soul
And to the piety that mocks no more.
In nature's inmost heart is no uproar,
None in this shrine; in peace the heavens roll,
In peace the slow tides pulse from shore to shore,
And ancient quiet broods from pole to pole.

GEORGE SANTAYANA

O WORLD, thou choosest not the better part!
It is not wisdom to be only wise,
And on the inward vision close the eyes,
But it is wisdom to believe the heart.
Columbus found a world, and had no chart,
Save one that faith deciphered in the skies;
To trust the soul's invincible surmise
Was all his science and his only art.
Our knowledge is a torch of smoky pine
That lights the pathway but one step ahead
Across a void of mystery and dread.
Bid, then, the tender light of faith to shine
By which alone the mortal heart is led
Unto the thinking of the thought divine.

GEORGE SANTAYANA

ON A VOLUME OF SCHOLASTIC PHILOSOPHY

WHAT chilly cloister or what lattice dim
Cast painted light upon this careful page?
What thought compulsive held the patient sage
Till sound of matin bell or evening hymn?
Did visions of the Heavenly Lover swim
Before his eyes in youth, or did stern rage
Against rash heresy keep green his age?
Had he seen God, to write so much of Him?
Gone is that irrecoverable mind
With all its phantoms, senseless to mankind
As a dream's trouble or the speech of birds.
The breath that stirred his lips he soon resigned
To windy chaos, and we only find
The garnered husks of his disusèd words.

GEORGE SANTAYANA

[352]

Charles G. D. Roberts, one of the foremost poets in Canadian literary history, published his first volume in 1880.

THE SWEET O' THE YEAR

THE upland hills are green again;
The river runs serene again;
    All down the miles
    Of orchard aisles
The pink-lip blooms are seen again;
    To garden close
      And dooryard plot
    Comes back the rose
      And bergamot.

The ardent blue leans near again;
The far-flown swallow is here again;
    To his thorn-bush
    Returns the thrush,
And the painted-wings appear again;
    In young surprise
      The meadows run
    All starry eyes
      To meet the sun.

Warm runs young blood in the veins again,
And warm love floods in the rains again.
    Earth, all aflush
    With the fecund rush,
To her Heart's Desire attains again;
    While stars outbeat
      The exultant word—
    "Death's in defeat,
      And Love is Lord."

CHARLES G. D. ROBERTS

In an age of experimentation, when many would-be poets found it easier to differ from the great poets than to resemble them, Sara Teasdale kept steadfastly to the conventional metres of English lyrical poetry. Her love-songs are as passionate in their revelation of feeling as they are restrained in expression.

BARTER

LIFE has loveliness to sell,
  All beautiful and splendid things,
Blue waves whitened on a cliff,
  Soaring fire that sways and sings,
And children's faces looking up
Holding wonder like a cup.

Life has loveliness to sell,
  Music like a curve of gold,
Scent of pine trees in the rain,
  Eyes that love you, arms that hold,
And for your spirit's still delight,
Holy thoughts that star the night.

SARA TEASDALE

PITY

THEY never saw my lover's face,
  They only know our love was brief,
Wearing awhile a windy grace
  And passing like an autumn leaf.

They wonder why I do not weep,
  They think it strange that I can sing,
They say, "Her love was scarcely deep
  Since it has left so slight a sting."

They never saw my love nor knew
That in my heart's most secret place
I pity them as angels do
Men who have never seen God's face.

SARA TEASDALE

To the Cuckoo

O BLITHE New-comer! I have heard,
I hear thee and rejoice:
O Cuckoo! shall I call thee Bird,
Or but a wandering Voice?

While I am lying on the grass
Thy twofold shout I hear;
From hill to hill it seems to pass,
At once far off and near.

Though babbling only to the Vale
Of sunshine and of flowers,
Thou bringest unto me a tale
Of visionary hours.

Thrice welcome, darling of the Spring!
Even yet thou art to me
No bird, but an invisible thing,
A voice, a mystery;

The same whom in my school-boy days
I listen'd to; that Cry
Which made me look a thousand ways
In bush, and tree, and sky.

WHAT I LIKE

To seek thee did I often rove
Through woods and on the green;
And thou wert still a hope, a love;
Still longed for, never seen!

And I can listen to thee yet;
Can lie upon the plain
And listen, till I do beget
That golden time again.

O blessèd Bird! the earth we pace
Again appears to be
An unsubstantial, faery place;
That is fit home for Thee!

WILLIAM WORDSWORTH

In his first volume of poems (1934) called *Requiem for the Living*, Mr. Tenney shows abundant promise.

BOUQUET FOR JUDAS

BECAUSE you have been kind to me
With words you meant in scorn
I send this rose that you may see
My blood upon the thorn.
And from the tree of fertile grief
Your faithlessness has made
I send you back this single leaf
Who rest within its shade.

CHARLES HENRY TENNEY

It is his prose, not his verse, that keeps Synge alive; for there is more poetry in his prose than there ever was in his rhymes. Yet his verse glows with indignation and with humour.

THE CURSE

To a sister of an enemy of the author's who disapproved of "The Playboy"

LORD, confound this surly sister,
Blight her brow with blotch and blister,
Cramp her larynx, lung, and liver,
In her guts a galling give her.

Let her live to earn her dinners
In Mountjoy with seedy sinners:
Lord, this judgment quickly bring,
And I'm your servant, John M. Synge.

JOHN M. SYNGE

The late Stephen Phillips suffered from too extravagant praise at the outset of his career in the 'nineties; the English critics compared him to Milton. But *Marpessa, Christ in Hades,* and some of his dramas will always have a place in literature; furthermore, there are individual lines in nearly all his poems that are impressive.

Phillips always had a high aim in poetry, and believed that poetry should always be written in an exalted and noble style. He compared the traffic policeman to an orchestral conductor, directing with uplifted hand the polyphonic music of the crowded thoroughfare.

GLADSTONE

THE saint and poet dwell apart; but thou
Wast holy in the furious press of men,
And choral in the central rush of life.
Yet didst thou love old branches and a book,
And Roman verses on an English lawn. . . .

Yet not for all thy breathing charm remote,
Nor breach tremendous in the forts of Hell,
Not for these things we praise thee, though these things
Are much; but more, because thou didst discern
In temporal policy the eternal will;

Thou gav'st to party strife the epic note,
And to debate the thunder of the Lord;
To meanest issues fire of the Most High.

STEPHEN PHILLIPS

———

The most ruthless and destructive of all critics, Time,
has played havoc with many nineteenth century names;
many that seemed immortal have shared the common fate.
But after all these years, Poe stands higher than ever before. The one hundred and twenty-fifth anniversary of his
birth, in this very year of 1934, was celebrated by a nation-
ally representative assembly.

TO HELEN

HELEN, thy beauty is to me
    Like those Nicéan barks of yore,
That gently, o'er a perfumed sea,
    The weary, way-worn wanderer bore
    To his own native shore.

[358]

On desperate seas long wont to roam,
   Thy hyacinth hair, thy classic face,
Thy Naiad airs have brought me home
   To the glory that was Greece,
   And the grandeur that was Rome.

Lo! in yon brilliant window-niche
   How statue-like I see thee stand,
The agate lamp within thy hand!
   Ah, Psyche, from the regions which
   Are Holy-Land!

EDGAR ALLAN POE

ANNABEL LEE

IT was many and many a year ago,
   In a kingdom by the sea,
That a maiden there lived whom you may know
   By the name of Annabel Lee;—
And this maiden she lived with no other thought
   Than to love and be loved by me.

She was a child and *I* was a child,
   In this kingdom by the sea,
But we loved with a love that was more than love—
   I and my Annabel Lee—
With a love that the wingèd seraphs of heaven
   Coveted her and me.

And this was the reason that, long ago,
   In this kingdom by the sea,
A wind blew out of a cloud by night
   Chilling my Annabel Lee;
So that her highborn kinsmen came
   And bore her away from me,
To shut her up in a sepulchre
   In this kingdom by the sea.

The angels, not half so happy in heaven,
    Went envying her and me—
Yes! that was the reason (as all men know,
    In this kingdom by the sea)
That the wind came out of the cloud, chilling
    And killing my Annabel Lee.

But our love it was stronger by far than the love
    Of those who were older than we—
    Of many far wiser than we—
And neither the angels in heaven above,
    Nor the demons down under the sea,
Can ever dissever my soul from the soul
    Of the beautiful Annabel Lee:

For the moon never beams without bringing me dreams
    Of the beautiful Annabel Lee;
And the stars never rise but I feel the bright eyes
    Of the beautiful Annabel Lee;
And so, all the night-tide, I lie down by the side
Of my darling—my darling—my life and my bride,
    In her sepulchre there by the sea—
    In her tomb by the side of the sea.

EDGAR ALLAN POE

THE RAVEN

ONCE upon a midnight dreary, while I pondered, weak and
    weary,
Over many a quaint and curious volume of forgotten lore,—
While I nodded, nearly napping, suddenly there came a
    tapping,
As of some one gently rapping, rapping at my chamber
    door.
" 'Tis some visitor," I muttered, "tapping at my chamber
    door:
        Only this and nothing more."

Ah, distinctly I remember it was in the bleak December,
And each separate dying ember wrought its ghost upon the
floor.
Eagerly I wished the morrow;—vainly I had sought to
borrow
From my books surcease of sorrow—sorrow for the lost
Lenore,
For the rare and radiant maiden whom the angels name
Lenore:
Nameless *here* for evermore.

And the silken, sad, uncertain rustling of each purple
curtain
Thrilled me—filled me with fantastic terrors never felt
before;
So that now, to still the beating of my heart, I stood re-
peating
" 'Tis some visitor entreating entrance at my chamber door,
Some late visitor entreating entrance at my chamber door:
This it is and nothing more."

Presently my soul grew stronger; hesitating then no longer,
"Sir," said I, "or Madam, truly your forgiveness I implore;
But the fact is I was napping, and so gently you came
rapping,
And so faintly you came tapping, tapping at my chamber
door,
That I scarce was sure I heard you"—here I opened wide
the door:—
Darkness there and nothing more!

Deep into that darkness peering, long I stood there wondering, fearing,
Doubting, dreaming dreams no mortal ever dared to dream
before:

But the silence was unbroken, and the stillness gave no
    token,
And the only word there spoken was the whispered word,
    "Lenore!"
This I whispered, and an echo murmured back the word,
    "Lenore!"
        Merely this and nothing more.

Back into the chamber turning, all my soul within me
    burning,
Soon again I heard a tapping somewhat louder than before.
"Surely," said I, "surely that is something at my window
    lattice;
Let me see, then, what thereat is, and this mystery explore:
Let my heart be still a moment and this mystery explore:
        'Tis the wind and nothing more!"

Open here I flung the shutter, when, with many a flirt and
    flutter,
In there stepped a stately Raven of the saintly days of
    yore;
Not the least obeisance made he; not a minute stopped or
    stayed he;
But, with mien of lord or lady, perched above my chamber
    door,
Perched upon a bust of Pallas just above my chamber door:
        Perched, and sat, and nothing more.

Then this ebony bird beguiling my sad fancy into smiling,
By the grave and stern decorum of the countenance it
    wore,—
"Though thy crest be shorn and shaven, thou," I said, "art
    sure no craven,
Ghastly grim and ancient Raven wandering from the
    Nightly shore:

Tell me what thy lordly name is on the Night's Plutonian
    shore!"
        Quoth the Raven, "Nevermore."

Much I marvelled this ungainly fowl to hear discourse so
    plainly,
Though its answer little meaning—little relevancy bore;
For we cannot help agreeing that no living human being
Ever yet was blessed with seeing bird above his chamber
    door,
Bird or beast upon the sculptured bust above his chamber
    door,
        With such name as "Nevermore."

But the Raven, sitting lonely on the placid bust, spoke only
That one word, as if his soul in that one word he did out-
    pour.
Nothing further then he uttered, not a feather then he
    fluttered,
Till I scarcely more than muttered,—"Other friends have
    flown before;
On the morrow *he* will leave me, as my Hopes have flown
    before."
        Then the bird said, "Nevermore."

Startled at the stillness broken by reply so aptly spoken,
"Doubtless," said I, "what it utters is its only stock and
    store,
Caught from some unhappy master whom unmerciful Dis-
    aster
Followed fast and followed faster till his songs one burden
    bore:
Till the dirges of his Hope that melancholy burden bore
        Of 'Never—nevermore.'"

But the Raven still beguiling my sad fancy into smiling,
Straight I wheeled a cushioned seat in front of bird and
bust and door;
Then upon the velvet sinking, I betook myself to linking
Fancy unto fancy, thinking what this ominous bird of yore,
What this grim, ungainly, ghastly, gaunt, and ominous
bird of yore
Meant in croaking "Nevermore."

This I sat engaged in guessing, but no syllable expressing
To the fowl whose fiery eyes now burned into my bosom's
core;
This and more I sat divining, with my head at ease re-
clining
On the cushion's velvet lining that the lamplight gloated
o'er,
But whose velvet-violet lining with the lamplight gloating
o'er
She shall press, ah, nevermore!

Then, methought, the air grew denser, perfumed from an
unseen censer
Swung by seraphim whose foot-falls tinkled on the tufted
floor.
"Wretch," I cried, "thy God hath lent thee—by these
angels he hath sent thee
Respite—respite and nepenthe from thy memories of Le-
nore!
Quaff, oh quaff this kind nepenthe, and forget this lost
Lenore!"
Quoth the Raven, "Nevermore."

"Prophet!" said I, "thing of evil! prophet still, if bird or
devil!
Whether Tempter sent, or whether tempest tossed thee here
ashore,

Desolate yet all undaunted, on this desert land enchanted—
On this home by Horror haunted—tell me truly, I implore:
Is there—*is* there balm in Gilead?—tell me—tell me, I
  implore!"
> Quoth the Raven, "Nevermore."

"Prophet!" said I, "thing of evil—prophet still, if bird or
  devil!
By that Heaven that bends above us, by that God we both
  adore,
Tell this soul with sorrow laden if, within the distant
  Aidenn,
It shall clasp a sainted maiden whom the angels name
  Lenore:
Clasp a rare and radiant maiden whom the angels name
  Lenore!"
> Quoth the Raven, "Nevermore."

"Be that word our sign of parting, bird or fiend!" I
  shrieked, upstarting:
"Get thee back into the tempest and the Night's Plutonian
  shore!
Leave no black plume as a token of that lie thy soul hath
  spoken!
Leave my loneliness unbroken! quit the bust above my door!
Take thy beak from out my heart, and take thy form from
  off my door!"
> Quoth the Raven, "Nevermore."

And the Raven, never flitting, still is sitting, still is sitting
On the pallid bust of Pallas just above my chamber door;
And his eyes have all the seeming of a demon that is dream-
  ing,
And the lamplight o'er him streaming throws his shadow on
  the floor:

And my soul from out that shadow that lies floating on the
floor
      Shall be lifted—nevermore!

EDGAR ALLAN POE

———

The early death of this American poet was a severe loss
to literature. He was making a steady intellectual advance,
and gaining mastery of poetic expression.

GLOUCESTER MOORS

A MILE behind is Gloucester town
Where the fishing fleets put in,
A mile ahead the land dips down
And the woods and farms begin.
Here, where the moors stretch free
In the high blue afternoon,
Are the marching sun and talking sea,
And the racing winds that wheel and flee
On the flying heels of June.

Jill-o'-er-the-ground is purple blue,
Blue is the quaker-maid,
The wild geranium holds its dew
Long in the boulder's shade.
Wax-red hangs the cup
From the huckleberry boughs,
In barberry bells the grey moths sup,
Or where the choke-cherry lifts high up
Sweet bowls for their carouse.

Over the shelf of the sandy cove
Beach-peas blossom late.
By copse and cliff the swallows rove
Each calling to his mate.
Seaward the sea-gulls go,
And the land-birds all are here;
That green-gold flash was a vireo,
And yonder flame where the marsh-flags grow
Was a scarlet tanager.

This earth is not the steadfast place
We landsmen build upon;
From deep to deep she varies pace,
And while she comes is gone.
Beneath my feet I feel
Her smooth bulk heave and dip;
With velvet plunge and soft upreel
She swings and steadies to her keel
Like a gallant, gallant ship.

These summer clouds she sets for sail,
The sun is her masthead light,
She tows the moon like a pinnace frail
Where her phosphor wake churns bright.
Now hid, now looming clear,
On the face of the dangerous blue
The star fleets tack and wheel and veer,
But on, but on does the old earth steer
As if her port she knew.

God, dear God! Does she know her port,
Though she goes so far about?
Or blind astray, does she make her sport
To brazen and chance it out?
I watched when her captains passed:

She were better captainless.
Men in the cabin, before the mast,
But some were reckless and some aghast,
And some sat gorged at mess.

By her battened hatch I leaned and caught
Sounds from the noisome hold,—
Cursing and sighing of souls distraught
And cries too sad to be told.
Then I strove to go down and see;
But they said, "Thou art not of us!"
I turned to those on the deck with me
And cried, "Give help!" But they said, "Let be:
Our ship sails faster thus."

Jill-o'er-the-ground is purple blue,
Blue is the quaker-maid,
The alder-clump where the brook comes through,
Breeds cresses in its shade.
To be out of the moiling street
With its swelter and its sin!
Who has given to me this sweet,
And given my brother dust to eat?
And when will his wage come in?

Scattering wide or blown in ranks,
Yellow and white and brown,
Boats and boats from the fishing banks
Come home to Gloucester town.
There is cash to purse and spend,
There are wives to be embraced,
Hearts to borrow and hearts to lend,
And hearts to take and keep to the end,—
O little sails, make haste!

But thou, vast outbound ship of souls,
What harbour town for thee?
What shapes, when thy arriving tolls,
Shall crowd the banks to see?
Shall all the happy shipmates then
Stand singing brotherly?
Or shall a haggard ruthless few
Warp her over and bring her to,
While the many broken souls of men
Fester down in the slaver's pen,
And nothing to say or do?

WILLIAM VAUGHN MOODY

This hard-bitten, disillusioned poet, author of the Devil's Parody of Gray's *Elegy*, has the penetration of acid. His cynicism is sometimes too heavy a load for Pegasus. But when he gives his imagination full play, he soars.

BERT KESSLER

I WINGED my bird,
Though he flew toward the setting sun;
But just as the shot rang out, he soared
Up and up through the splinters of golden light,
Till he turned right over, feathers ruffled,
With some of the down of him floating near,
And fell like a plummet into the grass.
I tramped about, parting the tangles,
Till I saw a splash of blood on a stump,
And the quail lying close to the rotten roots.
I reached my hand, but saw no brier,
But something pricked and stunned and numbed it.
And then, in a second, I spied the rattler—

[369]

The shutters wide in his yellow eyes,
The head of him arched, sunk back in the rings of him,
A circle of filth, the color of ashes,
Or oak leaves bleached under layers of leaves,
I stood like a stone as he shrank and uncoiled
And started to crawl beneath the stump,
When I fell limp in the grass.

EDGAR LEE MASTERS

===

Doctor Eugene Edmund Murphey, of Augusta, Georgia, is a physician, a poet, and ornithologist. And these three poems on birds have the element of transfiguration.

BOBOLINKS

HIGH over the valley, in the cool nights of September
One hears the call notes of migrating Bobolinks
Falling like golden coins gently dropped
On slabs of porphyry.
Clink-clink, Clink-clink,
Now here, now there, pausing, receding,
As wave after wave of invisible birds
Sweep over us.
Oh valiant wings of Faith that bear them
Through the starlit dim immensity!
They know that when the night is over
There comes a dawn with reedy banks and
Grass-fields, where they may rest
Unhunted and content.
Dear God! Do something to the futile
Hearts of men
Who in their time must turn

Like homing birds
To Thee, from whence they came.
Still their poor senseless fears
And make them know
That after weary nights must come
A dawn unearthly
And beyond all mortal ken
When they shall rest in
Unimagined fields,
Unharried and content.
Give them the Faith, O Lord, of migrant Bobolinks,
The courage and the prescience
Of Thy little birds.

EUGENE EDMUND MURPHEY

BROWN-HEADED NUTHATCH

I AM sprawled in the sunshine
Watching a Nuthatch,
A Brown-headed Nuthatch
Working his way
Down a storm-riven pine.
His thin clarineting
Seems to my senses
Pleasantly fit
To the haze of October.
But to the grub, cowering deep
In the crypts of the pine-bark,
This faint little trumpet,
Elfin, attenuate,
Comes as the ultimate
Trumpet o' doom.
Who knows but that now
As I drowse in the sunlight
Fed and contented,

Some God may be hanging
Head-down like a Nuthatch
From out of his Heaven,
Inflating himself
To sound his trump
For me.

EUGENE EDMUND MURPHEY

The Barn Owl

CHAPTER I

READING far into the night
At my grandfather's farm-house,
A night filled with luminous fog
When all sounds carry clearly,
I heard from afar down the road
The rapid staccato of footsteps.
A negro farm-hand came gasping
Into the lamp-light
Face ashen with terror.
"Massa, you know de old house
In de field by de river
Where de overseer lived
In de time of yo' gran'pa?
Old folks say he poisoned his wife
Because she was sickly.
Dat house is ha'nted!
I passed dere tonight
On my way from de Praise House.
I was lightin' my pipe
When out of de up-above window
Floated a something—white,
With a face like a little ole 'oman.
As soon as I seen it
I lit out of dere

And run here to tell you
Dat house is ha'nted!"
"Well, let's go and look at it."
So taking my gun and one of those
Newfangled flashlights,
Followed by Jim
With his arms full of lightwood,
We went to the place,
Pushed through the dust and the cobwebs,
Ascended the stairs
To the sound that old timbers
Give out at night-time,
And there in the corner
Over the rafters
Two beautiful Barn Owls
Were feeding their young.
So Jim's ha'nt was laid
But all the way home
Our talk was of Spirits.

CHAPTER II

But in this old City
Numbers of houses are really
Haunted.
I seldom go near them.
In one I have seen
A hard-faced and leech-minded mother
Giving her daughter,
Her beauty and girlhood, to a
Senile, lustic, glabrous and
Lecherous gargoyle
Because he had money.
After five years,
Four of them spent in paretic impotence,
He at length had the grace

[373]

To go sleep with his fathers.
But out of her eyes
The ghost of lost girlhood
Wistfully peers through clouded corneæ
Invoking our pity.
In another a man—
I sat there and saw him—
Bartered his word and the thing we call honour
For tawdry preferment,
And though he is dead
The ghost of his honour
Stalks through his house
And will never be quiet.
And yet in another
The friendship of decades
Was slain for a phrase
For the laughter of strangers.
The ghost of dead friendship
Is also persistent.
I know an old mansion set deep in a garden
Shaded by oak-trees.
All night little figures
Pluck at the door-latch, pry at the shutters,
Peer down the chimneys—
The thin little ghosts of
Dead happy hours
Crying to enter.
Poor little spirits, no one may help them.
The people who live there
Think that these noises are merely the night-wind,
But I who am wiser know better.
I see them.
And oft at my sleeve
When I walk in the moonlight
There comes a faint tugging,

The ghosts of illusions I loved in my boyhood
That are dead long ago,
I may never regain them.
Why is it so easy to banish the spirits
For ignorant negroes
When no one can quiet
My own ghosts for me?

EUGENE EDMUND MURPHEY

Our foremost living American woman poet, Edna St.
Vincent Millay, has shown extraordinary versatility. She
writes dramas, songs, meditative verse, satires; and her
collection of Sonnets, called (after Donne) *Fatal Interview*,
contains some of her best work.

AFTERNOON ON A HILL

I WILL be the gladdest thing
  Under the sun!
I will touch a hundred flowers
  And not pick one.

I will look at cliffs and clouds
  With quiet eyes,
Watch the wind bow down the grass,
  And the grass rise.

And when lights begin to show
  Up from the town,
I will mark which must be mine,
  And then start down!

EDNA ST. VINCENT MILLAY

WHEN THE YEAR GROWS OLD

I CANNOT but remember
   When the year grows old—
October—November—
   How she disliked the cold!

She used to watch the swallows
   Go down across the sky,
And turn from the window
   With a little sharp sigh.

And often when the brown leaves
   Were brittle on the ground,
And the wind in the chimney
   Made a melancholy sound,

She had a look about her
   That I wish I could forget—
The look of a scared thing
   Sitting in a net!

Oh, beautiful at nightfall
   The soft spitting snow!
And beautiful the bare boughs
   Rubbing to and fro!

But the roaring of the fire,
   And the warmth of fur,
And the boiling of the kettle
   Were beautiful to her!

I cannot but remember
   When the year grows old—
October—November—
   How she disliked the cold!

EDNA ST. VINCENT MILLAY

[376]

Beauty, tenderness, sympathy, piety, and high humility are characteristics of Alice Meynell.

THE SHEPHERDESS

SHE walks—the lady of my delight—
A shepherdess of sheep.
Her flocks are thoughts. She keeps them white;
She guards them from the steep;
She feeds them on the fragrant height,
And folds them in for sleep.

She roams maternal hills and bright,
Dark valleys safe and deep.
Into that tender breast at night
The chastest stars may peep.
She walks—the lady of my delight—
A shepherdess of sheep.

She holds her little thoughts in sight,
Though gay they run and leap.
She is so circumspect and right;
She has her soul to keep.
She walks—the lady of my delight—
A shepherdess of sheep.

ALICE MEYNELL

RAIN

THE rain is raining all around,
It falls on field and tree,
It rains on the umbrellas here,
And on the ships at sea.

ROBERT LOUIS STEVENSON

When Masefield rounded the Horn as an able-bodied sea-man, could anything have seemed to him more improbable than his becoming Poet Laureate? Yet although he knew the worst of nature and the worst of man, he kept a shrine in his heart.

SEA-FEVER

I MUST go down to the seas again, to the lonely sea and the sky,
And all I ask is a tall ship and a star to steer her by,
And the wheel's kick and the wind's song and the white sail's shaking,
And a grey mist on the sea's face, and a grey dawn breaking.

I must go down to the seas again, for the call of the running tide
Is a wild call and a clear call that may not be denied;
And all I ask is a windy day with the white clouds flying,
And the flung spray and the blown spume, and the sea-gulls crying.

I must go down to the seas again, to the vagrant gypsy life,
To the gull's way and the whale's way where the wind's like a whetted knife;
And all I ask is a merry yarn from a laughing fellow-rover,
And quiet sleep and a sweet dream when the long trick's over.

JOHN MASEFIELD

BEAUTY

I HAVE seen dawn and sunset on moors and windy hills
Coming in solemn beauty like slow old tunes in Spain:
I have seen the lady April bringing the daffodils,
Bringing the springing grass and the soft warm April rain.

I have heard the song of the blossoms and the old chant of
the sea,
And seen strange lands from under the arched white sails of
ships;
But the loveliest things of beauty God ever has showed to
me
Are her voice, and her hair, and eyes, and the dear red
curve of her lips.
JOHN MASEFIELD

CARGOES

QUINQUIREME of Nineveh from distant Ophir,
Rowing home to haven in sunny Palestine,
   With a cargo of ivory
   And apes and peacocks,
Sandalwood, cedarwood, and sweet, white wine.

Stately Spanish galleon coming from the Isthmus,
Dipping through the Tropics by the palm-green shores
   With a cargo of diamonds,
   Emeralds, amethysts,
Topazes, and cinnamon, and gold moidores.

Dirty British coaster with a salt-caked smoke stack,
Butting through the channel in the mad March days
   With a cargo of Tyne coal,
   Road rails, pig lead,
Firewood, ironware, and cheap tin trays.
JOHN MASEFIELD

He was the mediæval minstrel reincarnated. He walked from Florida to New Jersey reciting his poems and again from Illinois to New Mexico. He was a prophet, priest, and poet. He had a flaming imagination; at his best, he was sublime; at his worst, he was grotesque. But he was always original, and "the air seems bright with his past presence yet."

COLUMBUS

WOULD that we had the fortunes of Columbus,
Sailing his caravels a trackless way,
He found a Universe—he sought Cathay.
God give such dawns, as when, his venture o'er,
The Sailor looked upon San Salvador.
God lead us past the setting of the sun
To wizard islands, of august surprise;
God make our blunders wise.

VACHEL LINDSAY

GENERAL WILLIAM BOOTH ENTERS INTO HEAVEN

(To be sung to the tune of "The Blood of the Lamb" with indicated instruments)

I

(Bass drum beaten loudly.)
BOOTH led boldly with his big bass drum—
(Are you washed in the blood of the Lamb?)
The Saints smiled gravely and they said: "He's come."
(Are you washed in the blood of the Lamb?)
Walking lepers followed, rank on rank,
Lurching bravos from the ditches dank,

Drabs from the alleyways and drug fiends pale—
Minds still passion-ridden, soul-powers frail:—
Vermin-eaten saints with mouldy breath,
Unwashed legions with the ways of Death—
(Are you washed in the blood of the Lamb?)

(*Banjos.*)
Every slum had sent its half-a-score
The round world over. (Booth had groaned for more.)
Every banner that the wide world flies
Bloomed with glory and transcendent dyes.
Big-voiced lasses made their banjos bang,
Tranced, fanatical they shrieked and sang:—
"Are you washed in the blood of the Lamb?"
Hallelujah! It was queer to see
Bull-necked convicts with that land make free.
Loons with trumpets blowed a blare, blare, blare
On, on upward thro' the golden air!
(Are you washed in the blood of the Lamb?)

II

(*Bass drum slower and softer.*)
Booth died blind and still by faith he trod,
Eyes still dazzled by the ways of God.
Booth led boldly, and he looked the chief,
Eagle countenance in sharp relief,
Beard a-flying, air of high command
Unabated in that holy land.

(*Sweet flute music.*)
Jesus came from out the court-house door,
Stretched his hands above the passing poor.

[381]

Booth saw not, but led his queer ones there
Round and round the mighty court-house square.
Yet in an instant all that blear review
Marched on spotless, clad in raiment new.
The lame were straightened, withered limbs uncurled
And blind eyes opened on a new, sweet world.

(Bass drum louder.)
Drabs and vixens in a flash made whole!
Gone was the weasel-head, the snout, the jowl!
Sages and sibyls now, and athletes clean,
Rulers of empires, and of forests green!

*(Grand chorus of all instruments. Tambourines to the fore-
        ground.)*
The hosts were sandaled, and their wings were fire
(Are you washed in the blood of the Lamb?)
But their noise played havoc with the angel-choir.
(Are you washed in the blood of the Lamb?)
Oh, shout Salvation! It was good to see
Kings and Princes by the Lamb set free.
The banjos rattled and the tambourines
Jing-jing-jingled in the hands of Queens.

(Reverently sung, no instruments.)
And when Booth halted by the curb for prayer
He saw his Master thro' the flag-filled air.
Christ came gently with a robe and crown
For Booth the soldier, while the throng knelt down.
He saw King Jesus. They were face to face,
And he knelt a-weeping in that holy place.
Are you washed in the blood of the Lamb?

VACHEL LINDSAY

When the Frost Is on the Punkin

When the frost is on the punkin and the fodder's in the
    shock,
And you hear the kyouck and gobble of the struttin' turkey-
    cock,
And the clackin' of the guineys, and the cluckin' of the hens,
And the rooster's hallylooyer as he tiptoes on the fence;
O, it's then's the time a feller is a-feelin' at his best,
With the risin' sun to greet him from a night of peaceful
    rest,
As he leaves the house, bareheaded, and goes out to feed the
    stock,
When the frost is on the punkin and the fodder's in the
    shock.

They's something kind o' harty-like about the atmusfere
When the heat of summer's over and the coolin' fall is
    here—
Of course we miss the flowers, and the blossoms on the trees,
And the mumble of the hummin'-birds and buzzin' of the
    bees;
But the air's so appetizin'; and the landscape through the
    haze
Of a crisp and sunny morning of the airly autumn days
Is a pictur' that no painter has the colourin' to mock—
When the frost is on the punkin and the fodder's in the
    shock.

The husky, rusty russel of the tossels of the corn,
And the raspin' of the tangled leaves as golden as the morn;
The stubble in the furries—kind o' lonesome-like, but still
A-preachin' sermuns to us of the barns they growed to fill;
The strawstack in the medder, and the reaper in the shed;

WHAT I LIKE

The hosses in theyr stalls below—the clover overhead!—
O, it sets my hart a-clickin' like the tickin' of a clock,
When the frost is on the punkin and the fodder's in the
    shock.

Then your apples all is gethered, and the ones a feller keeps
Is poured around the cellar-floor in red and yaller heaps;
And your cider-makin's over, and your wimmen-folks is
    through
With theyr mince and apple-butter, and theyr souse and
    sausage too! . . .
I don't know how to tell it—but if such a thing could be
As the angels wantin' boardin', and they'd call around on
    me—
I'd want to 'commodate 'em—all the whole-indurin' flock—
When the frost is on the punkin and the fodder's in the
    shock.

                       JAMES WHITCOMB RILEY

A LIFE LESSON

THERE! little girl; don't cry!
  They have broken your doll, I know;
    And your tea-set blue,
    And your playhouse, too,
  Are things of the long ago;
    But childish troubles will soon pass by.—
    There! little girl; don't cry!

There! little girl; don't cry!
  They have broken your slate, I know;
    And the glad, wild ways
    Of your schoolgirl days
  Are things of the long ago;
    But life and love will soon come by.—
    There! little girl; don't cry!

There! little girl; don't cry!
They have broken your heart, I know;
And the rainbow gleams
Of your youthful dreams
Are things of the long ago;
But heaven holds all for which you sigh.—
There! little girl; don't cry!

JAMES WHITCOMB RILEY

The foremost living American poet is also the least talkative. Like Ralph Hodgson and A. E. Housman in England, Edwin Arlington Robinson lets his poetry speak for itself, and shares their aversion for "publicity." He has done everything possible to avoid attracting attention, but his work is so good that all his efforts are in vain. Furthermore, after years of production that gave him a reputation chiefly as an intellectual and analytical writer, he revealed in *Tristram* (1927) an unsuspected capacity for passion.

THE DEAD VILLAGE

HERE there is death. But even here, they say,
Here where the dull sun shines this afternoon
As desolate as ever the dead moon
Did glimmer on dead Sardis, men were gay;
And there were little children here to play,
With small soft hands that once did keep in tune
The strings that stretch from heaven, till too soon
The change came, and the music passed away.
Now there is nothing but the ghosts of things,—
No life, no love, no children, and no men;

And over the forgotten place there clings
The strange and unrememberable light
That is in dreams. The music failed, and then
God frowned, and shut the village from His sight.

EDWIN ARLINGTON ROBINSON

FOR A DEAD LADY

No more with overflowing light
Shall fill the eyes that now are faded,
Nor shall another's fringe with night
Their woman-hidden world as they did.
No more shall quiver down the days
The flowing wonder of her ways,
Whereof no language may requite
The shifting and the many-shaded.

The grace, divine, definitive,
Clings only as a faint forestalling;
The laugh that love could not forgive
Is hushed, and answers to no calling;
The forehead and the little ears
Have gone where Saturn keeps the years;
The breast where roses could not live
Has done with rising and with falling.

The beauty, shattered by the laws
That have creation in their keeping,
No longer trembles at applause,
Or over children that are sleeping;
And we who delve in beauty's lore
Know all that we have known before
Of what inexorable cause
Makes Time so vicious in his reaping.

EDWIN ARLINGTON ROBINSON

THE HOUSE ON THE HILL

THEY are all gone away,
The House is shut and still,
There is nothing more to say.

Through broken walls and grey
The winds blow bleak and shrill;
They are all gone away.
Nor is there one today
To speak them good or ill;
There is nothing more to say.

Why is it then we stray
Around that sunken sill?
They are all gone away.

And our poor fancy-play
For them is wasted skill:
There is nothing more to say.

There is ruin and decay
In the House on the Hill:
They are all gone away;
There is nothing more to say.

EDWIN ARLINGTON ROBINSON

A picture of Canadian winter.

A January Morning

The glittering roofs are still with frost; each worn
Black chimney builds into the quiet sky
Its curling pile to crumble silently.
Far out to the westward on the edge of morn,

The slender misty city towers up-borne
Glimmer faint rose against the pallid blue;
And yonder on those northern hills, the hue
Of amethyst, hang fleeces dull as horn.

And here behind me come the woodmen's sleighs
With shouts and clamorous squeakings; might and main
Up the steep slope the horses stamp and strain,
Urged on by hoarse-tongued drivers—cheeks ablaze,
Iced beards and frozen eyelids—team by team,
With frost-fringed flanks, and nostrils jetting steam.

ARCHIBALD LAMPMAN

Ulysses

It little profits that an idle king,
By this still hearth, among these barren crags,
Match'd with an aged wife, I mete and dole
Unequal laws unto a savage race,
That hoard, and sleep, and feed, and know not me.
I cannot rest from travel: I will drink
Life to the lees: all times I have enjoy'd
Greatly, have suffer'd greatly, both with those
That loved me, and alone; on shore, and when

Thro' scudding drifts the rainy Hyades
Vext the dim sea: I am become a name;
For always roaming with a hungry heart
Much have I seen and known; cities of men
And manners, climates, councils, governments,
Myself not least, but honour'd of them all;
And drunk delight of battle with my peers,
Far on the ringing plains of windy Troy.
I am a part of all that I have met;
Yet all experience is an arch wherethro'
Gleams that untravell'd world, whose margin fades
For ever and for ever when I move.
How dull it is to pause, to make an end,
To rust unburnish'd, not to shine in use!
As tho' to breathe were life. Life piled on life
Were all too little, and of one to me
Little remains: but every hour is saved
From that eternal silence, something more,
A bringer of new things; and vile it were
For some three suns to store and hoard myself,
And this grey spirit yearning in desire
To follow knowledge like a sinking star,
Beyond the utmost bound of human thought.
　　This is my son, mine own Telemachus,
To whom I leave the sceptre and the isle—
Well-loved of me, discerning to fulfil
This labour, by slow prudence to make mild
A rugged people, and thro' soft degrees
Subdue them to the useful and the good.
Most blameless is he, centred in the sphere
Of common duties, decent not to fail
In offices of tenderness, and pay
Meet adoration to my household gods,
When I am gone. He works his work, I mine.
　　There lies the port; the vessel puffs her sail:

[389]

There gloom the dark broad seas. My mariners,
Souls that have toil'd, and wrought, and thought with me—
That ever with a frolic welcome took
The thunder and the sunshine, and opposed
Free hearts, free foreheads—you and I are old;
Old age hath yet his honour and his toil;
Death closes all: but something ere the end,
Some work of noble note, may yet be done,
Not unbecoming men that strove with Gods.
The lights begin to twinkle from the rocks:
The long day wanes: the slow moon climbs: the deep
Moans round with many voices. Come, my friends,
'Tis not too late to seek a newer world.
Push off, and sitting well in order smite
The sounding furrows; for my purpose holds
To sail beyond the sunset, and the baths
Of all the western stars, until I die.
It may be that the gulfs will wash us down:
It may be we shall touch the Happy Isles,
And see the great Achilles, whom we knew.
Tho' much is taken, much abides; and tho'
We are not now that strength which in old days
Moved earth and heaven; that which we are, we are;
One equal temper of heroic hearts,
Made weak by time and fate, but strong in will
To strive, to seek, to find, and not to yield.

ALFRED TENNYSON

L'Envoi

Now in the thought, now in a shadowed word,
Now in a voice that thrills eternity,
Ever there comes an onward phrase to me
Of some transcendent music I have heard;
No piteous thing by soft hands dulcimered,
No trumpet crash of blood-sick victory,
But a glad strain of some vast harmony
That no brief mortal touch has ever stirred.
There is no music in the world like this,
No character wherewith to set it down,
No kind of instrument to make it sing.
No kind of instrument? Ah, yes, there is;
And after time and place are overthrown,
God's touch will keep its one chord quivering.

EDWIN ARLINGTON ROBINSON

Although it is certain that Kipling's best work, both in
prose and verse, was written before the end of the nineteenth
century, what difference does that make? He wrote enough
to make his chances for survival greater than those of any
other author now living.

The Song of the Banjo

You couldn't pack a Broadwood half a mile—
  You mustn't leave a fiddle in the damp—
You couldn't raft an organ up the Nile,
  And play it in an Equatorial swamp.
I travel with the cooking-pots and pails—
  I'm sandwiched 'tween the coffee and the pork—
And when the dusky column checks and tails,
  You should hear me spur the rearguard to a walk!

[391]

With my *"Pilly-willy-winky-winky popp!"*
    [Oh, it's any tune that comes into my head!]
So I keep 'em moving forward till they drop;
    So I play 'em up to water and to bed.

In the silence of the camp before the fight,
    When it's good to make your will and say your prayer,
You can hear my *strumpty-tumpty* overnight,
    Explaining ten to one was always fair.
I'm the Prophet of the Utterly Absurd,
    Of the Patently Impossible and Vain—
And when the Thing that Couldn't has occurred,
    Give me time to change my leg and go again.

        With my *"Tumpa-tumpa-tumpa-tum-pa tump!"*
        In the desert where the dung-fed camp-smoke curled
    There was never voice before us till I led our lonely
        chorus,
        I—the war-drum of the White Man round the world!

By the bitter road the Younger Son must tread,
    Ere he win to hearth and saddle of his own,—
'Mid the riot of the shearers at the shed,
    In the silence of the herder's hut alone—
In the twilight, on a bucket upside down,
    Hear me babble what the weakest won't confess—
I am Memory and Torment—I am Town!
    I am all that ever went with evening dress!

        With my *"Tunk-a tunka-tunka-tunka tunk!"*
        [So the lights—the London Lights—grow near and
        plain!]
    So I rowel 'em afresh towards the Devil and the Flesh,
        Till I bring my broken rankers home again.

In desire of many marvels over sea,
 Where the new-raised tropic city sweats and roars,
I have sailed with Young Ulysses from the quay
 Till the anchor rumbled down on stranger shores.
He is blooded to the open and the sky,
 He is taken in a snare that shall not fail,
He shall hear me singing strongly, till he die,
 Like the shouting of a backstay in a gale.

 With my *"Hya! Heeya! Heeya! Hullah! Haul!"*
 [O the green that thunders aft along the deck!]
 Are you sick o' towns and men? You must sign and
 sail again,
 For it's "Johnny Bowlegs, pack your kit and trek!"

Through the gorge that gives the stars at noonday clear—
 Up the pass that packs the scud beneath our wheel—
Round the bluff that sinks her thousand fathom sheer—
 Down the valley with our guttering brakes asqueal:
Where the trestle groans and quivers in the snow,
 Where the many-shedded levels loop and twine,
Hear me lead my reckless children from below
 Till we sing the Song of Roland to the pine.

 With my *"Tinka-tinka-tinka-tinka-tink!"*
 [Oh the axe has cleared the mountain, croup and
 crest!]
 And we ride the iron stallions down to drink,
 Through the cañons to the waters of the West!

And the tunes that mean so much to you alone—
 Common tunes that make you choke and blow your nose,
Vulgar tunes that bring the laugh that brings the groan—
 I can rip your very heartstrings out with those;
With the feasting, and the folly, and the fun—

And the lying, and the lusting, and the drink,
And the merry play that drops you, when you're done,
  To the thoughts that burn like irons if you think.

  With my *"Plunka-lunka-lunka-lunka-lunk!"*
    Here's a trifle on account of pleasure past,
      Ere the wit that made you win gives you eyes to see
        your sin
      And—the heavier repentance at the last!

Let the organ moan her sorrow to the roof —
  I have told the naked stars the Grief of Man!
Let the trumpet snare the foeman to the proof —
  I have known Defeat, and mocked it as we ran!
My bray ye may not alter nor mistake
  When I stand to jeer the fatted Soul of Things,
But the Song of Lost Endeavour that I make,
  Is it hidden in the twanging of the strings?

    With my *"Ta-ra-rara-rara-ra-ra-rrrp!"*
      [Is it naught to you that hear and pass me by?]
      But the word — the word is mine, when the order
        moves the line
      And the lean, locked ranks go roaring down to die!

The grandam of my grandam was the Lyre—
  [O the blue below the little fisher-huts!]
That the Stealer stooping beachward filled with fire,
  Till she bore my iron head and ringing guts!
By the wisdom of the centuries I speak —
  To the tune of yestermorn I set the truth —
I, the joy of life unquestioned — I, the Greek —
  I, the everlasting Wonder-song of Youth!

With my *"Tinka-tinka-tinka-tinka-tink!"*
   [What d' ye lack, my noble masters? What d' ye
     lack?]
So I draw the world together link by link:
   Yea, from Delos up to Limerick and back!

RUDYARD KIPLING

RECESSIONAL

GOD of our fathers, known of old,
   Lord of our far-flung battle-line,
Beneath whose awful Hand we hold
   Dominion over palm and pine —
Lord God of Hosts, be with us yet,
Lest we forget — lest we forget!

The tumult and the shouting dies;
   The captains and the kings depart:
Still stands Thine ancient sacrifice,
   An humble and a contrite heart.
Lord God of Hosts, be with us yet,
Lest we forget — lest we forget!

Far-called, our navies melt away;
   On dune and headland sinks the fire:
Lo, all our pomp of yesterday
   Is one with Nineveh and Tyre!
Judge of the Nations, spare us yet,
Lest we forget — lest we forget!

If, drunk with sight of power, we loose
   Wild tongues that have not Thee in awe,
Such boasting as the Gentiles use,
   Or lesser breeds without the Law—
Lord God of Hosts, be with us yet,
Lest we forget — lest we forget!

[395]

For heathen heart that puts her trust
    In reeking tube and iron shard,
All valiant dust that builds on dust
    And, guarding, calls not Thee to guard,
For frantic boast and foolish word —
Thy Mercy on Thy People, Lord! Amen.

RUDYARD KIPLING

We do not need to be told that this is Elizabethan. It has an added poignancy from the tragic disorder of its author's life.

SWEET ARE THE THOUGHTS THAT SAVOUR OF CONTENT

SWEET are the thoughts that savour of content;
    The quiet mind is richer than a crown;
Sweet are the nights in careless slumber spent;
    The poor estate scorns fortune's angry frown:
Such sweet content, such minds, such sleep, such bliss,
Beggars enjoy, when princes oft do miss.

The homely house that harbours quiet rest;
    The cottage that affords no pride nor care;
    The mean that 'grees with country music best;
    The sweet consort of mirth and music's fare;
Obscurèd life sets down a type of bliss:
A mind content both crown and kingdom is.

ROBERT GREENE

Stephen Foster was a genius; the greatest of American song-writers.

MASSA'S IN DE COLD, COLD GROUND

ROUND de meadows am a-ringing
    De darkies' mournful song,
While de mocking-bird am singing,
    Happy as de day am long.
Where de ivy am a-creeping,
    O'er de grassy mound,
Dere old massa am a-sleeping,
    Sleeping in de cold, cold ground.

    Down in de corn-field
      Hear dat mournful sound:
    All de darkies am a-weeping,—
      Massa's in de cold, cold ground.

When de autumn leaves were falling,
    When de days were cold,
'T was hard to hear old massa calling,
    Cayse he was so weak and old.
Now de orange tree am blooming
    On de sandy shore,
Now de summer days am coming,—
    Massa nebber calls no more.

Massa make de darkies love him,
    Cayse he was so kind;
Now dey sadly weep above him,
    Mourning cayse he leave dem behind.
I cannot work before tomorrow,
    Cayse de tear-drop flow;
I try to drive away my sorrow,
    Pickin' on de old banjo.

Down in de corn-field
Hear dat mournful sound:
All de darkies am a-weeping,—
Massa's in de cold, cold ground.

STEPHEN COLLINS FOSTER

OLD FOLKS AT HOME

WAY down upon de Swanee Ribber,
Far, far away,
Dere's wha my heart is turning ebber,
Dere's wha de old folks stay.
All up and down de whole creation
Sadly I roam,
Still longing for de old plantation,
And for de old folks at home.

All de world am sad and dreary,
Eberywhere I roam;
Oh, darkies, how my heart grows weary,
Far from de old folks at home!

All round de little farm I wandered
When I was young,
Den many happy days I squandered,
Many de songs I sung.
When I was playing wid my brudder
Happy was I;
Oh, take me to my kind old mudder!
Dere let me live and die.

One little hut among de bushes,
One dat I love,
Still sadly to my memory rushes,
No matter where I rove.

When will I see de bees a-humming
All round de comb?
When will I hear de banjo tumming,
Down in my good old home?

All de world am sad and dreary,
Eberywhere I roam,
Oh, darkies, how my heart grows weary,
Far from de old folks at home!

STEPHEN COLLINS FOSTER

MY OLD KENTUCKY HOME, GOOD-NIGHT

THE sun shines bright in the old Kentucky home;
'Tis summer, the darkies are gay;
The corn-top's ripe, and the meadow's in the bloom,
While the birds make music all the day.
The young folks roll on the little cabin floor,
All merry, all happy and bright;
By-'n'-by hard times comes a-knocking at the door:—
Then my old Kentucky home, good-night!

Weep no more, my lady,
O, weep no more today!
We will sing one song for the old Ken-
tucky home,
For the old Kentucky home, far away.

They hunt no more for the possum and the coon,
On the meadow, the hill, and the shore;
They sing no more by the glimmer of the moon,
On the bench by the old cabin door.
The day goes by like a shadow o'er the heart,
With sorrow, where all was delight;
The time has come when the darkies have to part:—
Then my old Kentucky home, good-night!

[399]

The head must bow, and the back will have to bend,
  Wherever the darkey may go;
A few more days, and the trouble all will end,
  In the field where the sugar-canes grow.
A few more days for to tote the weary load,—
  No matter, 't will never be light;
A few more days till we totter on the road:—
  Then my old Kentucky home, good-night!

Weep no more, my lady,
O, weep no more today!
We will sing one song for the old Ken-
  tucky home,
For the old Kentucky home, far away.

STEPHEN COLLINS FOSTER

Emerson seldom went far away from home for his observations and parables. Every observation caused a reflexion. "Emotion remembered in tranquillity."

TWO RIVERS

THY summer voice, Musketaquit,
Repeats the music of the rain;
But sweeter rivers pulsing flit
Through thee, as thou through Concord Plain.

Thou in thy narrow banks art pent:
The stream I love unbounded goes
Through flood and sea and firmament;
Through light, through life it forward flows.

[400]

SONG

I see the inundation sweet,
I hear the spending of the stream
Through years, through men, through Nature fleet,
Through love and thought, through power and dream.

Musketaquit, a goblin strong,
Of shard and flint makes jewels gay;
They lose their grief who hear his song,
And where he winds is the day of day.

So forth and brighter fares my stream,—
Who drinks it shall not thirst again;
No darkness stains its equal gleam
And ages drop in it like rain.

RALPH WALDO EMERSON

Ben Jonson told Drummond that Donne, after he became
a Doctor of Divinity, "repenteth highly and seeketh to destroy his poems." Fortunately he could not; there is an
ecstasy of passion in his best poems with a sincerity height-
ened by its individuality of expression. Dean Briggs used to
say that Donne's lines flash light "into the darkest places of
the soul, like torches in the catacombs." The tremendous
exaggeration of the language in his love poems is absolutely
sincere; for what language can possibly overwrite such feeling?

I have often the curious sensation immediately after reading one of his lyrics that I have after gazing at a bright
light and then extinguishing it. The light still shines in
the darkness.

SONG

Go and catch a falling star,
  Get with child a mandrake root,
Tell me where all past years are,

Or who cleft the devil's foot;
Teach me to hear mermaids singing,
Or to keep off envy's stinging,
    And find
    What wind
Serves to advance an honest mind.

If thou be'st born to strange sights,
    Things invisible go see,
Ride ten thousand days and nights
    Till Age snow white hairs on thee;
Thou, when thou return'st, wilt tell me
All strange wonders that befell thee,
    And swear
    No where
Lives a woman true and fair.

If thou find'st one, let me know;
    Such a pilgrimage were sweet.
Yet do not; I would not go,
    Though at next door we might meet.
Though she were true when you met her,
And last till you write your letter,
    Yet she
    Will be
False, ere I come, to two or three.

JOHN DONNE

LOVE'S DEITY

I LONG to talk with some old lover's ghost,
    Who died before the god of Love was born:
I cannot think that he, who then loved most,
    Sunk so low, as to love one who did scorn.
But since this god produced a destiny,
And that vice-nature, custom, lets it be,
    I must love her that loves not me.

Sure they, which made him god, meant not so much,
  Nor he in his young godhead practised it;
But when an even flame two hearts did touch,
  His office was indulgently to fit
Actives to passives, correspondency
Only his subject was; it cannot be
  Love, if I love who loves not me.

But every modern god will now extend
  His vast prerogative as far as Jove;
To rage, to lust, to write to, to commend,
  All is the purlieu of the god of Love.
Oh were we wakened by this tyranny
To ungod this child again, it could not be
  I should love her, who loves not me.

Rebel and atheist too, why murmur I
  As though I felt the worst that love could do?
Love may make me leave loving, or might try
  A deeper plague, to make her love me too,
Which, since she loves before, I'm loath to see;
Falsehood is worse than hate; and that must be,
  If she whom I love, should love me.

                              JOHN DONNE

THE DREAM

DEAR love, for nothing less than thee
Would I have broke this happy dream,
          It was a theme
For reason, much too strong for phantasy,
Therefore thou waked'st me wisely; yet
My Dream thou brok'st not, but continued'st it,
Thou art so truth, that thoughts of thee suffice,
To make dreams truths; and Fables histories;
Enter these arms, for since thou thoughtst it best,
Not to dream all my dream, let's act the rest.

As lightning, or a Taper's light,
Thine eyes, and not thy noise wak'd me;
      Yet I thought thee
(For thou lovest truth) an Angel, at first sight,
But when I saw thou sawest my heart,
And knew'st my thoughts, beyond an Angel's art,
Then thou knew'st what I dreamt, when thou knew'st when
Excess of joy would wake me, and cam'st then,
I must confess, it could not choose but be
Profane, to think thee any thing but thee.

Coming and staying show'd thee, thee,
But rising makes me doubt, that now,
      Thou art not thou.
That love is weak, where fear's as strong as he;
'Tis not all spirit, pure, and brave,
If mixture it of *Fear, Shame, Honour*, have.
Perchance as torches which must ready be,
Men light and put out, so thou deal'st with me,
Thou cam'st to kindle, goest to come; Then I
Will dream that hope again, but else would die.

JOHN DONNE

The Relic

When my grave is broke up again
Some second guest to entertain,
   (For graves have learn'd that woman-head
To be to more than one a bed)
     And he that digs it, spies
A bracelet of bright hair about the bone,
   Will he not let us alone,
And think that there a loving couple lies,
Who thought that this device might be some way
To make their souls, at the last busy day,
Meet at this grave, and make a little stay?

If this fall in a time, or land,
Where mass-devotion doth command,
Then, he that digs us up, will bring
Us, to the Bishop, and the King,
     To make us Relics; then
Thou shalt be a Mary Magdalen, and I
     A something else thereby;
All women shall adore us, and some men;
And since at such time, miracles are sought,
I would have that age by this paper taught
What miracles we harmless lovers wrought.

First, we lov'd well and faithfully,
Yet knew not what we lov'd, nor why,
Difference of sex no more we knew,
Than our Guardian Angels do;
     Coming and going, we
Perchance might kiss, but not between those meals;
     Our hands ne'r toucht the seals,
Which nature, injur'd by late law, sets free:
These miracles we did; but now alas,
All measure, and all language, I should pass,
Should I tell what a miracle she was.

JOHN DONNE

THE EAGLE

HE clasps the crag with crooked hands;
Close to the sun in lonely lands,
Ring'd with the azure world he stands.

The wrinkled sea beneath him crawls;
He watches from his mountain walls,
And like a thunderbolt he falls.

ALFRED TENNYSON

Payne's life was like a fairy-tale. He founded and edited a newspaper at the age of fourteen. This song was first sung in his opera *Clari* in London, 1823.

HOME, SWEET HOME!

MID pleasures and palaces though we may roam,
Be it ever so humble, there's no place like home;
A charm from the sky seems to hallow us there,
Which, seek through the world, is ne'er met with elsewhere.
        Home, Home, sweet, sweet Home!
There's no place like Home! there's no place like Home!

An exile from home, splendour dazzles in vain;
O, give me my lowly thatched cottage again!
The birds singing gayly, that came at my call,—
Give me them,—and the peace of mind, dearer than all!
        Home, Home, sweet, sweet Home!
There's no place like Home! there's no place like Home!

How sweet 't is to sit 'neath a fond father's smile,
And the cares of a mother to soothe and beguile!
Let others delight mid new pleasures to roam,
But give me, oh, give me, the pleasures of home!
        Home! Home! sweet, sweet Home!
There's no place like Home! there's no place like Home!

To thee I'll return, overburdened with care;
The heart's dearest solace will smile on me there;
No more from that cottage again will I roam;
Be it ever so humble, there's no place like home.
        Home! Home! sweet, sweet Home!
There's no place like Home! there's no place like Home!

                                        JOHN HOWARD PAYNE

A good anthology of Canadian verse would be a revelation to England and to the United States.

OFF RIVIÈRE DU LOUP

OH, ship incoming from the sea,
   With all your cloudy tower of sail,
Dashing the water to the lee,
   And leaning grandly to the gale;
The sunset pageant in the West
   Has filled your canvas curves with rose,
And jewelled every toppling crest
   That crashes into silver snows.

You know the joy of coming home,
   After long leagues to France or Spain,
You feel the clear Canadian foam,
   And the gulf water heave again.

Between the sombre purple hills
   That cool the sunset's molten bars,
You will go on as the wind wills
   Beneath the river's roof of stars.

You will toss onward towards the lights
   That spangle over the lonely pier,
By hamlets glimmering on the heights,
   By level islands black and clear.

You will go on beyond the tide,
   Through brimming plains of olive sedge,
Through paler shadows light and wide,
   The rapids piled along the ledge.

[407]

At evening off some reedy bay
  You will swing slowly on your chain,
And catch the scent of dewy hay
  Soft blowing from the pleasant plain.

DUNCAN CAMPBELL SCOTT

=====

I know Edwin Markham is not a one-poem man, but still
I like this popular favourite the most.

THE MAN WITH THE HOE

(Written after seeing Millet's world-famous painting)

BOWED by the weight of centuries he leans
Upon his hoe and gazes on the ground,
The emptiness of ages in his face,
And on his back the burden of the world.
Who made him dead to rapture and despair,
A thing that grieves not and that never hopes,
Stolid and stunned, a brother to the ox?
Who loosened and let down this brutal jaw?
Whose was the hand that slanted back this brow?
Whose breath blew out the light within this brain?

Is this the Thing the Lord God made and gave
To have dominion over sea and land;
To trace the stars and search the heavens for power;
To feel the passion of Eternity?
Is this the dream He dreamed who shaped the suns
And marked their ways upon the ancient deep?
Down all the caverns of Hell to their last gulf

THE MAN WITH THE HOE

There is no shape more terrible than this—
More tongued with censure of the world's blind greed—
More filled with signs and portents for the soul—
More packt with danger to the universe.

What gulfs between him and the seraphim!
Slave of the wheel of labor, what to him
Are Plato and the swing of Pleiades?
What the long reaches of the peaks of song,
The rift of dawn, the reddening of the rose?
Through this dread shape the suffering ages look;
Time's tragedy is in that aching stoop;
Through this dread shape humanity betrayed,
Plundered, profaned and disinherited,
Cries protest to the Judges of the World,
A protest that is also prophecy.

O masters, lords and rulers in all lands,
Is this the handiwork you give to God,
This monstrous thing, distorted and soul-quenched?
How will you ever straighten up this shape;
Touch it again with immortality;
Give back the upward looking and the light;
Rebuild in it the music and the dream;
Make right the immemorial infamies,
Perfidious wrongs, immedicable woes?

O masters, lords and rulers in all lands,
How will the future reckon with this man?
How answer his brute question in that hour
When whirlwinds of rebellion shake the world?
How will it be with kingdoms and with kings—
With those who shaped him to the thing he is—
When this dumb terror shall appeal to God,
After the silence of the centuries?

EDWIN MARKHAM

[409]

This contemporary English poet combines fancy and fact.

MILK FOR THE CAT

WHEN the tea is brought at five o'clock,
And all the neat curtains are drawn with care,
The little black cat with bright green eyes
Is suddenly purring there.

At first she pretends, having nothing to do,
She has come in merely to blink by the grate,
But, though tea may be late or the milk may be sour,
She is never late.

And presently her agate eyes
Take a soft large milky haze,
And her independent casual glance
Becomes a stiff hard gaze.

Then she stamps her claws or lifts her ears
Or twists her tail and begins to stir,
Till suddenly all her lithe body becomes
One breathing trembling purr.

The children eat and wriggle and laugh;
The two old ladies stroke their silk:
But the cat is grown small and thin with desire,
Transformed to a creeping lust for milk.

The white saucer like some full moon descends
At last from the clouds of the table above;
She sighs and dreams and thrills and glows,
Transfigured with love.

She nestles over the shining rim,
Buries her chin in the creamy sea;
Her tail hangs loose; each drowsy paw
Is doubled under each bending knee.

A long dim ecstasy holds her life;
Her world is an infinite shapeless white,
Till her tongue has curled the last holy drop,
Then she sinks back into the night,

Draws and dips her body to heap
Her sleepy nerves in the great arm chair,
Lies defeated and buried deep
Three or four hours unconscious there.

HAROLD MONRO

Bernice Kenyon is a poet steadily growing in authority of expression. This picture of imagined old age is not what I want for myself, but——

Old Age

When I am old I shall sit quietly
With folded hands, under the noonday sun;
And never let the past drift back to me,
And never hope for years not yet begun;

But watch, as I do today, ants in the grass,
And spiders patiently renewing webs,
And the unweary flight of gulls that pass
Along the river while the slow tide ebbs;

And see how bees take honey and wing out
In perilous winds, back to their secret hive;
And watch the flowers opening all about,
And clouds of gnats that dance to be alive;

Until I find myself grown less than these,
Heedless as they, and happy, at high noon.
Where, all unmindful of grim mysteries,
I can forget that death must take me soon.

BERNICE KENYON

Longfellow is the most popular poet in the English
language, except Shakespeare. One of the best writers of
sonnets. An excellent composer of ballads. His *Serenade* is
one of the best songs in American literature. A poet of the
home and of domestic life.

THE DAY IS DONE

THE day is done, and the darkness
Falls from the wings of Night,
As a feather is wafted downward
From an eagle in his flight.

I see the lights of the village
Gleam through the rain and the mist,
And a feeling of sadness comes o'er me
That my soul cannot resist:

A feeling of sadness and longing,
That is not akin to pain,
And resembles sorrow only
As the mist resembles the rain.

[412]

Come, read to me some poem,
  Some simple and heartfelt lay,
That shall soothe this restless feeling,
  And banish the thoughts of day.

Not from the grand old masters,
  Not from the bards sublime,
Whose distant footsteps echo
  Through the corridors of Time.

For, like strains of martial music,
  Their mighty thoughts suggest
Life's endless toil and endeavor;
  And tonight I long for rest.

Read from some humbler poet,
  Whose songs gushed from his heart,
As showers from the clouds of summer,
  Or tears from the eyelids start;

Who, through long days of labor,
  And nights devoid of ease,
Still heard in his soul the music
  Of wonderful melodies.

Such songs have power to quiet
  The restless pulse of care,
And come like the benediction
  That follows after prayer.

Then read from the treasured volume
  The poem of thy choice,
And lend to the rhyme of the poet
  The beauty of thy voice.

And the night shall be filled with music,
  And the cares, that infest the day,
Shall fold their tents, like the Arabs,
  And as silently steal away.

             HENRY WADSWORTH LONGFELLOW

THE SKELETON IN ARMOUR

SPEAK! speak! thou fearful guest!
Who, with thy hollow breast
Still in rude armour drest,
  Comest to daunt me!
Wrapt not in Eastern balms,
But with thy fleshless palms
  Why dost thou haunt me?

Then, from those cavernous eyes
Pale flashes seemed to rise,
As when the Northern skies
  Gleam in December;
And, like the water's flow
Under December's snow,
Came a dull voice of woe
  From the heart's chamber.

"I was a Viking old!
My deeds, though manifold,
No Skald in song has told,
  No Saga taught thee!
Take heed, that in thy verse
Thou dost the tale rehearse,
Else dread a dead man's curse;
  For this I sought thee.

"Far in the Northern Land,
By the wild Baltic's strand,
I, with my childish hand,
   Tamed the gerfalcon;
And, with my skates fast-bound,
Skimmed the half-frozen Sound,
That the poor whimpering hound
   Trembled to walk on.

"Oft to his frozen lair
Tracked I the grisly bear,
While from my path the hare
   Fled like a shadow;
Oft through the forest dark
Followed the were-wolf's bark,
Until the soaring lark
   Sang from the meadow.

"But when I older grew,
Joining a corsair's crew,
O'er the dark sea I flew
   With the marauders.
Wild was the life we led;
Many the souls that sped,
Many the hearts that bled,
   By our stern orders.

"Many a wassail-bout
Wore the long Winter out;
Often our midnight shout
   Set the cocks crowing,
As we the Berserk's tale
Measured in cups of ale,
Draining the oaken pail,
   Filled to o'erflowing.

"Once as I told in glee
Tales of the stormy sea,
Soft eyes did gaze on me,
   Burning yet tender;
And as the white stars shine
On the dark Norway pine,
On that dark heart of mine
   Fell their soft splendour.

"I wooed the blue-eyed maid,
Yielding, yet half afraid,
And in the forest's shade
   Our vows were plighted.
Under its loosened vest
Fluttered her little breast,
Like birds within their nest
   By the hawk frighted.

"Bright in her father's hall
Shields gleamed upon the wall,
Loud sang the minstrels all,
   Chanting his glory;
When of old Hildebrand
I asked his daughter's hand,
Mute did the minstrels stand
   To hear my story.

"While the brown ale he quaffed,
Loud then the champion laughed,
And as the wind-gusts waft
   The sea-foam brightly,
So the loud laugh of scorn,
Out of those lips unshorn,
From the deep drinking-horn
   Blew the foam lightly.

"She was a Prince's child,
I but a Viking wild,
And though she blushed and smiled,
    I was discarded!
Should not the dove so white
Follow the sea-mew's flight,
Why did they leave that night
    Her nest unguarded?

"Scarce had I put to sea,
Bearing the maid with me,
Fairest of all was she
    Among the Norsemen!
When on the white sea-strand,
Waving his armèd hand,
Saw we old Hildebrand,
    With twenty horsemen.

"Then launched they to the blast,
Bent like a reed each mast,
Yet we were gaining fast,
    When the wind failed us;
And with a sudden flaw
Came round the gusty Skaw,
So that our foe we saw
    Laugh as he hailed us.

"And as to catch the gale
Round veered the flapping sail,
'Death!' was the helmsman's hail,
    'Death without quarter!'
Mid-ships with iron keel
Struck we her ribs of steel;
Down her black hulk did reel
    Through the black water!

"As with his wings aslant,
Sails the fierce cormorant,
Seeking some rocky haunt,
   With his prey laden,—
So towards the open main,
Beating to sea again,
Through the wild hurricane,
   Bore I the maiden.

"Three weeks we westward bore,
And when the storm was o'er,
Cloud-like we saw the shore
   Stretching to leeward;
There for my lady's bower
Built I the lofty tower,
Which, to this very hour,
   Stands looking seaward.

"There lived we many years;
Time dried the maiden's tears;
She had forgot her fears,
   She was a mother;
Death closed her mild blue eyes,
Under that tower she lies;
Ne'er shall the sun arise
   On such another!

"Still grew my bosom then,
Still as a stagnant fen!
Hateful to me were men,
   The sunlight hateful!
In the vast forest here,
Clad in my warlike gear,
Fell I upon my spear,
   Oh, death was grateful!

"Thus, seamed with many scars,
Bursting these prison bars,
Up to its native stars
   My soul ascended!
There from the flowing bowl
Deep drinks the warrior's soul,
Skoal! to the Northland! *skoal!*"
   Thus the tale ended.

                    HENRY WADSWORTH LONGFELLOW

At Sunium Byron's carved autograph is still plainly legible.

THE ISLES OF GREECE

THE isles of Greece, the isles of Greece!
   Where burning Sappho loved and sung,
Where grew the arts of war and peace,—
   Where Delos rose, and Phœbus sprung!
Eternal summer gilds them yet,
But all, except their sun, is set.

The Scian and the Teian muse,
   The hero's harp, the lover's lute,
Have found the fame your shores refuse:
   Their place of birth alone is mute
To sounds which echo further west
Than your sires' "Islands of the Blest."

The mountains look on Marathon—
   And Marathon looks on the sea;
And musing there an hour alone,
   I dream'd that Greece might still be free;
For standing on the Persians' grave,
I could not deem myself a slave.

[419]

A king sate on the rocky brow
   Which looks o'er sea-born Salamis;
And ships, by thousands, lay below,
   And men in nations;—all were his!
He counted them at break of day—
And when the sun set, where were they?

And where are they? and where art thou,
   My country? On thy voiceless shore
The heroic lay is tuneless now—
   The heroic bosom beats no more!
And must thy lyre, so long divine,
Degenerate into hands like mine?

'Tis something, in the dearth of fame,
   Though link'd among a fetter'd race,
To feel at least a patriot's shame,
   Even as I sing, suffuse my face;
For what is left the poet here?
For Greeks a blush—for Greece a tear.

Must *we* but weep o'er days more blest?
   Must *we* but blush?—Our fathers bled.
Earth! render back from out thy breast
   A remnant of our Spartan dead!
Of the three hundred grant but three,
To make a new Thermopylæ!

What, silent still? and silent all?
   Ah, no;—the voices of the dead
Sound like a distant torrent's fall,
   And answer, "Let one living head,
But one arise,—we come, we come!"
'Tis but the living who are dumb.

In vain—in vain: strike other chords ·
   Fill high the cup with Samian wine!
Leave battles to the Turkish hordes,
   And shed the blood of Scio's vine!
Hark! rising to the ignoble call—
How answers each bold Bacchanal!

You have the Pyrrhic dance as yet;
   Where is the Pyrrhic phalanx gone?
Of two such lessons, why forget
   The nobler and the manlier one?
You have the letters Cadmus gave—
Think ye he meant them for a slave?

Fill high the bowl with Samian wine!
   We will not think of themes like these!
It made Anacreon's song divine;
   He served—but served Polycrates—
A tyrant; but our masters then
Were still, at least, our countrymen.

The tyrant of the Chersonese
   Was freedom's best and bravest friend;
That tyrant was Miltiades!
   Oh! that the present hour would lend
Another despot of the kind!
Such chains as his were sure to bind.

Fill high the bowl with Samian wine!
   On Suli's rock, and Parga's shore,
Exists the remnant of a line
   Such as the Doric mothers bore;
And there, perhaps, some seed is sown,
The Heracleidan blood might own.

[421]

Trust not for freedom to the Franks,
  They have a king who buys and sells;
In native swords and native ranks,
  The only hope of courage dwells:
But Turkish force, and Latin fraud,
Would break your shield, however broad.

Fill high the bowl with Samian wine!
  Our virgins dance beneath the shade—
I see their glorious black eyes shine;
  But gazing on each glowing maid,
My own the burning tear-drop laves,
To think such breasts must suckle slaves.

Place me on Sunium's marbled steep,
  Where nothing, save the waves and I,
May hear our mutual murmurs sweep;
  There, swan-like, let me sing and die:
A land of slaves shall ne'er be mine—
Dash down yon cup of Samian wine!

LORD BYRON

CAVALIER TUNES

These are perfect examples of the *dramatic* lyric; they are songs representing sentiments exactly the opposite of those of the composer.

I. MARCHING ALONG

I

KENTISH Sir Byng stood for his King,
Bidding the crop-headed Parliament swing:

And, pressing a troop unable to stoop
And see the rogues flourish and honest folk droop,
Marched them along, fifty-score strong,
Great-hearted gentlemen, singing this song.

II

God for King Charles! Pym and such carles
To the Devil that prompts 'em their treasonous parles!
Cavaliers, up! Lips from the cup,
Hands from the pasty, nor bite take nor sup
Till you're—
 CHORUS.
  Marching along, fifty-score strong,
  Great-hearted gentlemen, singing this song.

III

Hampden to hell, and his obsequies' knell
Serve Hazelrig, Fiennes, and young Harry as well!
England, good cheer! Rupert is near!
Kentish and loyalists, keep we not here
 CHORUS.
  Marching along, fifty-score strong,
  Great-hearted gentlemen, singing this song.

IV

Then, God for King Charles! Pym and his snarls
To the Devil that pricks on such pestilent carles!
Hold by the right, you double your might;
So, onward to Nottingham, fresh for the fight,
 CHORUS.
  March we along, fifty-score strong,
  Great-hearted gentlemen, singing this song!

II. GIVE A ROUSE

I

KING CHARLES, and who'll do him right now?
King Charles, and who's ripe for fight now?
Give a rouse: here's, in hell's despite now,
King Charles!

II

Who gave me the goods that went since?
Who raised me the house that sank once?
Who helped me to gold I spent since?
Who found me in wine you drank once?
  CHORUS.
      King Charles, and who'll do him right now?
      King Charles, and who's ripe for fight now?
      Give a rouse: here's, in hell's despite now,
      King Charles!

III

To whom used my boy George quaff else,
By the old fool's side that begot him?
For whom did he cheer and laugh else,
While Noll's damned troopers shot him?
  CHORUS.
      King Charles, and who'll do him right now?
      King Charles, and who's ripe for fight now?
      Give a rouse: here's, in hell's despite now,
      King Charles!

[424]

III. BOOT AND SADDLE

I

Boot, saddle, to horse, and away!
Rescue my castle before the hot day
Brightens to blue from its silvery grey,
    CHORUS.
        Boot, saddle, to horse, and away!

II

Ride past the suburbs, asleep as you'd say;
Many's the friend there, will listen and pray
"God's luck to gallants that strike up the lay—
    CHORUS.
        Boot, saddle, to horse, and away!"

III

Forty miles off, like a roebuck at bay,
Flouts Castle Brancepeth the Roundheads' array:
Who laughs, "Good fellows ere this, by my fay,
    CHORUS.
        Boot, saddle, to horse, and away!"

IV

Who? My wife Gertrude; that, honest and gay,
Laughs when you talk of surrendering, "Nay!
I've better counsellors; what counsel they?
    CHORUS.
        Boot, saddle, to horse, and away!"

ROBERT BROWNING

Bliss Carman, Canadian disciple of Browning, has been producing poetry for forty years. Like other Canadian poets he glorifies Winter.

VESTIGIA

I TOOK a day to search for God,
And found Him not. But as I trod
By rocky ledge, through woods untamed,
Just where one scarlet lily flamed,
I saw His footprint in the sod.

Then suddenly, all unaware,
Far off in the deep shadows, where
A solitary hermit thrush
Sang through the holy twilight hush—
I heard His voice upon the air.

And even as I marvelled how
God gives us Heaven here and now,
In a stir of wind that hardly shook
The poplar leaves beside the brook—
His hand was light upon my brow.

At last with evening as I turned
Homeward, and thought what I had learned
And all that there was still to probe—
I caught the glory of His robe
Where the last fires of sunset burned.

Back to the world with quickening start
I looked and longed for any part
In making saving Beauty be.
And from that kindling ecstasy
I knew God dwelt within my heart.

BLISS CARMAN

WINTER

WHEN the winter comes along the river line
And Earth has put away her green attire,
With all the pomp of her autumnal pride,
The world is made a sanctuary old,
Where Gothic trees uphold the arch of grey,
And gaunt stone fences on the ridge's crest
Stand like carved screens before a crimson shrine,
Showing the sunset glory through the chinks.
There, like a nun with frosty breath, the soul,
Uplift in adoration, sees the world
Transfigured to a temple of her Lord;
While down the soft blue-shadowed aisles of snow
Night, like a sacristan with silent step,
Passes to light the tapers of the stars.

BLISS CARMAN

THE NIGHTINGALE NEAR THE HOUSE

HERE is the soundless cypress on the lawn:
It listens, listens. Taller trees beyond
Listen. The moon at the unruffled pond
    Stares. And you sing, you sing.

The star-enchanted song falls through the air
From lawn to lawn down terraces of sound,
Darts in white arrows on the shadowed ground;
    And all through the night you sing.

My dreams are flowers to which you are a bee
As all night long I listen, and my brain
Receives your song; then loses it again
    In moonlight on the lawn.

[427]

Now is your voice a marble high and white,
Then like a mist on fields of paradise,
Now is a raging fire, then is like ice,
    Then breaks, and it is dawn.

                            HAROLD MONRO

A flower from a garden in Canada.

THE ROSE

THE Rose was given to man for this:
    He, suddenly seeing it in later years,
Should swift remember Love's first lingering kiss
    And Grief's last lingering tears;

Or, being blind, should feel its yearning soul
    Knit all its piercing perfume round his own,
Till he should see on memory's ample scroll
    All roses he had known;

Or, being hard, perchance his finger-tips
    Careless might touch the satin of its cup,
And he should feel a dead babe's budding lips
    To his lips lifted up;

Or, being deaf and smitten with its star,
    Should, on a sudden, almost hear a lark
Rush singing up—the nightingale afar
    Sing through the dew-bright dark;

Or, sorrow-lost in paths that round and round
    Circle old graves, its keen and vital breath
Should call to him within the yew's bleak bound
    Of Life, and not of Death.

                    ISABELLA VALANCY CRAWFORD

[428]

Invisible presences are the most real.

WINTER DUSK

DARK frost was in the air without,
　　The dusk was still with cold and gloom,
When less than even a shadow came
　　And stood within the room.

But of the three around the fire,
　　None turned a questioning head to look.
Still read a clear voice, on and on,
　　Still stooped they o'er their book.

The children watched their mother's eyes
　　Moving on softly line to line;
It seemed to listen too—that shade,
　　Yet made no outward sign.

The fire-flames crooned a tiny song,
　　No cold wind moved the wintry tree;
The children both in Faërie dreamed
　　Beside their mother's knee.

And nearer yet that spirit drew
　　Above that heedless one, intent
Only on what the simple words
　　Of her small story meant.

No voiceless sorrow grieved her mind,
　　No memory her bosom stirred,
Nor dreamed she, as she read to two,
　　'Twas surely three who heard.

Yet when, the story done, she smiled
   From face to face, serene and clear,
A love, half dread, sprang up, as she
   Leaned close and drew them near.

WALTER DE LA MARE

OLD SUSAN

WHEN Susan's work was done she'd sit,
With one fat guttering candle lit,
And window opened wide to win
The sweet night air to enter in;
There, with a thumb to keep her place
She'd read, with stern and wrinkled face,
Her mild eyes gliding very slow
Across the letters to and fro,
While wagged the guttering candle flame
In the wind that through the window came.
And sometimes in the silence she
   Would mumble a sentence audibly,
Or shake her head as if to say,
"You silly souls, to act this way!"
And never a sound from night I'd hear,
Unless some far-off cock crowed clear;
Or her old shuffling thumb should turn
Another page; and rapt and stern,
Through her great glasses bent on me
She'd glance into reality;
And shake her round old silvery head,
With—"You!—I thought you was in bed!"—
Only to tilt her book again,
And rooted in Romance remain.

WALTER DE LA MARE

[430]

The Bells of Heaven

'Twould ring the bells of Heaven
The wildest peal for years,
If Parson lost his senses
And people came to theirs,
And he and they together
Knelt down with angry prayers
For tamed and shabby tigers
And dancing dogs and bears,
And wretched, blind pit ponies,
And little hunted hares.

RALPH HODGSON

Stupidity Street

I saw with open eyes
    Singing birds sweet
Sold in the shops
    For the people to eat,
Sold in the shops of
    Stupidity Street.

I saw in vision
    The worm in the wheat,
And in the shops nothing
    For people to eat;
Nothing for sale in
    Stupidity Street.

RALPH HODGSON

Christina Rossetti, Elizabeth Barrett Browning, Emily Brontë, Emily Dickinson—contemporaries all, and no woman poet today equal to any one of them! I wonder if there was anything about the suppression of "females" in Victorian days that kept the home-fires burning? Now women are free, many of them write free verse instead of poetry. And in these days so often called skeptical, cynical, and unbelieving, the poetry of that ardent Roman Catholic, Christina Rossetti, is more appreciated than when she was on earth.

Up-Hill

Does the road wind up-hill all the way?
    Yes, to the very end.
Will the day's journey take the whole long day?
    From morn to night, my friend.

But is there for the night a resting-place?
    A roof for when the slow dark hours begin.
May not the darkness hide it from my face?
    You cannot miss that inn.

Shall I meet other wayfarers at night?
    Those who have gone before.
Then must I knock, or call when just in sight?
    They will not keep you standing at that door.

Shall I find comfort, travel-sore and weak?
    Of labour you shall find the sum.
Will there be beds for me and all who seek?
    Yea, beds for all who come.

CHRISTINA ROSSETTI

Stevenson's stories, essays, poems, and letters will live forever. In every one of these four kinds of literature he is a favourite with more than a few readers.

Bed in Summer

In winter I get up at night
And dress by yellow candle-light.
In summer, quite the other way,
I have to go to bed by day.

I have to go to bed and see
The birds still hopping on the tree,
Or hear the grown-up people's feet
Still going past me in the street.

And does it not seem hard to you,
When all the sky is clear and blue,
And I should like so much to play,
To have to go to bed by day?

ROBERT LOUIS STEVENSON

Whole Duty of Children

A child should always say what's true
And speak when he is spoken to,
And behave mannerly at table;
At least as far as he is able.

ROBERT LOUIS STEVENSON

My Shadow

I HAVE a little shadow that goes in and out with me,
And what can be the use of him is more than I can see.
He is very, very like me from the heels up to the head;
And I see him jump before me, when I jump into my bed.

The funniest thing about him is the way he likes to grow—
Not at all like proper children, which is always very slow;
For he sometimes shoots up taller like an india-rubber ball,
And he sometimes gets so little that there's none of him at
    all.

He hasn't got a notion of how children ought to play,
And can only make a fool of me in every sort of way.
He stays so close beside me, he's a coward you can see;
I'd think shame to stick to nursie as that shadow sticks to
    me!

One morning, very early, before the sun was up,
I rose and found the shining dew on every buttercup;
But my lazy little shadow, like an arrant sleepy-head,
Had stayed at home behind me and was fast asleep in bed.

ROBERT LOUIS STEVENSON

A Lad That Is Gone

SING me a song of a lad that is gone
    Say, could that lad be I?
Merry of soul he sailed on a day
    Over the sea to Skye.

Mull was astern, Rum on the port,
Egg on the starboard bow;
Glory of youth glowed in his soul:
Where is that glory now?

Sing me a song of a lad that is gone,
Say, could that lad be I?
Merry of soul he sailed on a day
Over the sea to Skye.

Give me again all that was there,
Give me the sun that shone!
Give me the eyes, give me the soul,
Give me the lad that's gone!

Sing me a song of a lad that is gone,
Say, could that lad be I?
Merry of soul he sailed on a day
Over the sea to Skye.

Billow and breeze, islands and seas,
Mountains of rain and sun,
All that was good, all that was fair,
All that was me is gone.

ROBERT LOUIS STEVENSON

HAPPY THOUGHT

THE world is so full of a number of things,
I'm sure we should all be as happy as kings.

ROBERT LOUIS STEVENSON

CHRISTMAS AT SEA

THE sheets were frozen hard, and they cut the naked hand;
The decks were like a slide, where a seaman scarce could
stand;
The wind was a nor'-wester, blowing squally off the sea;
And cliffs and spouting breakers were the only things a-lee.

They heard the surf a-roaring before the break of day;
But 'twas only with the peep of light we saw how ill we lay.
We tumbled every hand on deck instanter, with a shout,
And we gave her the maintops'l, and stood by to go about.

All day we tacked and tacked between the South Head and
the North;
All day we hauled the frozen sheets, and got no further
forth;
All day as cold as charity, in bitter pain and dread,
For very life and nature we tacked from head to head.

We gave the South a wider berth, for there the tide-race
roared;
But every tack we made we brought the North Head close
aboard:
So's we saw the cliff and houses and the breakers running
high,
And the coastguard in his garden, with his glass against
his eye.

The frost was on the village roofs as white as ocean foam;
The good red fires were burning bright in every longshore
home;
The windows sparkled clear, and the chimneys volleyed out;
And I vow we sniffed the victuals as the vessel went about.

The bells upon the church were rung with a mighty jovial
  cheer;
For it's just that I should tell you how (of all days in the
  year)
This day of our adversity was blessèd Christmas morn,
And the house above the coastguard's was the house where I
  was born.

O well I saw the pleasant room, the pleasant faces there,
My mother's silver spectacles, my father's silver hair;
And well I saw the firelight, like a flight of homely elves,
Go dancing round the china plates that stand upon the
  shelves.

And well I knew the talk they had, the talk that was of me,
Of the shadow on the household and the son that went to sea;
And O the wicked fool I seemed, in every kind of way,
To be here and hauling frozen ropes on blessèd Christmas
  Day.

They lit the high sea-light, and the dark began to fall.
"All hands to loose topgallant sails," I heard the captain call.
"By the Lord, she'll never stand it," our first mate, Jackson,
  cried.
. . . "It's the one way or the other, Mr. Jackson," he
  replied.

She staggered to her bearings, but the sails were new and
  good,
And the ship smelt up to windward just as though she
  understood,
As the winter's day was ending, in the entry of the night,
We cleared the weary headland, and passed below the light.

And they heaved a mighty breath, every soul on board but
    me,
As they saw her nose again pointing handsome out to sea;
But all that I could think of, in the darkness and the cold,
Was just that I was leaving home and my folks were grow-
    ing old.

ROBERT LOUIS STEVENSON

The master of melody. I take delight in his familiar
songs, which never become hackneyed to me. And I heard
Patti sing this one!

'TIS THE LAST ROSE OF SUMMER

'Tis the last rose of summer
    Left blooming alone;
All her lovely companions
    Are faded and gone;
No flower of her kindred,
    No rose-bud is nigh,
To reflect back her blushes,
    Or give sigh for sigh.

I'll not leave thee, thou lone one,
    To pine on the stem;
Since the lovely are sleeping,
    Go, sleep thou with them.
Thus kindly I scatter
    Thy leaves o'er the bed,
Where the mates of the garden
    Lie scentless and dead.

[438]

So soon may I follow,
    When friendships decay,
And from Love's shining circle
    The gems drop away.
When true hearts lie withered,
    And fond ones are flown,
Oh! who would inhabit
    This bleak world alone?

THOMAS MOORE

———

Although the Reverend Charles Kingsley was a famous preacher and pastor, an exponent of what was called "muscular Christianity," a debater on the Protestant side of a theological argument, a novelist of immense reputation, a writer of a popular book for children—I believe that some of his songs will outlive everything else he did or wrote.

THE SANDS OF DEE

"O MARY, go and call the cattle home,
    And call the cattle home,
    And call the cattle home,
    Across the sands of Dee:"
The western wind was wild and dank with foam,
    And all alone went she.

The western tide crept up along the sand,
    And o'er and o'er the sand,
    And round and round the sand,
    As far as eye could see:
The rolling mist came down and hid the land,
    And never home came she.

[439]

"Oh! is it weed, or fish, or floating hair,
   A tress of golden hair,
   A drownèd maiden's hair
   Above the nets at sea?
Was never salmon yet that shone so fair
   Among the stakes at Dee."

They rowed her in across the rolling foam,
   The cruel crawling foam,
   The cruel hungry foam
   To her grave beside the sea:
But still the boatmen hear her call the cattle home
   Across the sands of Dee!

CHARLES KINGSLEY

A contemporary American poet who affirms the glory of life.

THE LETTER

THE night is measureless, no voice, no cry
Pierces the dark in which the planet swings—
It is the shadow of her bulk that flings
So deep a gloom on the enormous sky;
This timorous dust, this phantom that is I
Cowers in shelter, while the evening brings
A sense of mystery and how all things
Waver like water and are gliding by.

Now, while the stars in heaven like blowing sand
Drift to their darkness, while oblivion
Hushes the fire of some fading sun,
I turn the page again—and there they stand,
Traced by love's fleeting but victorious hand,
The words: "My darling, my belovèd one."

JOHN HALL WHEELOCK

Noon: Amagansett Beach

GLORY—glory to God in the highest—and on earth,
  Glory! The everlasting sun
Has laid his hand upon the harp-string, with the music of
    his mirth
  Heaven and ocean are one chord, in unison.

He has spoken—he has spoken—from his midmost throne
  In the blue hollow of noon he has spoken! Heaven has
      heard
The sound of the song of his shining; he has made known
  To listening space his wonder, and revealed his word—

Who sheds his light upon the earth, and upon the dark
    place,
  Light! And upon the waters of the sea,
Light! O Father, pour down thy light upon me—touch
    my face!
  Hallow me, my Father—even me.

Here, where the long ranges of the dunes roll
  Their tawny billows to the south and to the north, and
      against the sky
Flutters the pale sea-grass, fresh is the wind—and the whole
  Clear hollow of heaven is full of the wine of thy glory,
      even as I.

The waves curve upward—they fail—they fall—
  Dragging, dragging, along the dim sea-reach,
The heavy hem of the garment of the waters; rhythmical,
    rhythmical
  Is the rustle of the sea's robe upon the beach.

Along the shallows, along the far shore-line
    They burst in thunder and light—where the grey
        shingles gleam,
The tongue of the foam is a tongue of fire: the hollows of
    the breakers shine,
    Darken—and are shattered as a dream.

But out where the further waters have their sleep,
    On the pale meadows of ocean, on the barren fields and
        bare,
That the sea-bird wanders, that the sea-wind wanders—on
    the illimitable Deep,
    Silence. The silence of the immensity is like a prayer.

Interminable—interminable—interminable—the void sea—
    The many ways, the many waves. In the huge round
Of the sorrowful heavens, in the hushed vacancy,
    No voice. . . . Vastness without bound.

This is my heart's country. These lonely lands
    Are on with my wild, lonely heart; these winds and waves
        that roam
Old, desolate ways forever—they are one with me—these
    sterile sands
    And bitter waters. Here is my heart's home.

Amid these large horizons and spaces that she loves,
    My spirit's thought, on lorn adventurings
And inconsolable quests intent, endlessly moves—
    And spreads upon the eternal solitude her fleeting wings:

Even as a sea-bird on the changeless, changing,
    Pale pastures lost, as a sea-bird on the wild waste astray,
Searching the everlasting reaches—failing—faltering—like
    a sea-bird ranging—
    Wandering, wandering the wide way.

  . . . .

Loneliness—loneliness forever. Dune beyond dune,
  Stretches the infinite loneliness—pale sand and pale
    sea-grass,

Pale beaches, mile upon mile. In the immensity of noon
  A hawk moves upon the wind. Clouds darken, and pass.
The sound of the breathing of the sea is hushed, on the
  far shore
Her robe lies fallen; the white waves, one by one,
Subside into slumber, and cease into slumber: from the blue
  vault to the blue floor
Heaven is a shining room filled full of the sun.

He hallows the waters. The benediction of his light is shed
  Upon the proud waters. Emerald—turquoise—chryso-
    prase—
Glitter the waters! The garment of his glory is spread
  Upon the everlasting waters, upon the everlasting ways.
JOHN HALL WHEELOCK

THE FISH-HAWK

On the large highway of the awful air that flows
  Unbounded between sea and heaven, while twilight
    screened
The sorrowful distances, he moved and had repose;
  On the huge wind of the immensity he leaned
His steady body in long lapse of flight—and rose

Gradual, through broad gyres of ever-climbing rest,
  Up the clear stair of the eternal sky, and stood
Throned on the summit. Slowly, with his widening breast,
  Widened around him the enormous solitude,
From the grey rim of ocean to the glowing west.

Headlands and capes forlorn of the far coast, the land
  Rolling her barrens toward the south, he, from his throne
Upon the gigantic wind, beheld: he hung—he fanned

[443]

The abyss for mighty joy, to feel beneath him strown
Pale pastures of the sea, with heaven on either hand—

The world with all her winds and waters, earth and air,
  Fields, folds, and moving clouds. The awful and adored
Arches and endless aisles of vacancy, the fair
  Void of sheer heights and hollows hailed him as her lord
And lover in the highest, to whom all heaven lay bare.

Till from that tower of ecstasy, that baffled height,
  Stooping, he sank; and slowly on the world's wide way
Walked, with great wing on wing, the merciless proud
      Might,
  Hunting the huddled and lone reaches for his prey
Down the dim shore—and faded in the crumbling light.

Slowly the dusk covered the land. Like a great hymn
  The sound of moving winds and waters was; the sea
Whispered a benediction, and the west grew dim
  Where evening lifted her clear candles quietly . . .
Heaven, crowded with stars, trembled from rim to rim.

JOHN HALL WHEELOCK

Doctor Murphey of Augusta is a physician and a natural-
ist and a man of letters.

LINES TO ACCOMPANY A FLAGON OF GEORGIA'S FAMOUS PRODUCT ON ITS WAY TO CALIFORNIA

ON the hills of California and the sunny slopes of France
The heavy headed purple grapes hang earthward in a
      trance,
But in the fields of Georgia from the mountains to the sea
The stalwart stalks of Indian Corn stand up most valiantly.

And when the grapes are ripened they yield their juices
    sweet
To the soft and even pressure of the peasants' naked feet,
But the corn is more resistant, it will yield itself alone
To the firm relentless grinding of two mighty wheels of
    stone.

And so its parents' weakness is renascent in the wine.
Its effect is soft and clinging like the tendrils of the vine,
But if you lust for action or would lead a hope forlorn,
You will find the force that's needed in the Spirit of the
    Corn.

                EUGENE EDMUND MURPHEY

━━

    Wordsworth in his sonnet on the sonnet, beginning
"Scorn not the Sonnet," closes with a tribute to Milton.

                in his hand
    The Thing became a trumpet; whence he blew
    Soul-animating strains—alas, too few!

Milton's sonnets are indeed few in number, and they are in
the first rank of English poems.

ON HIS BLINDNESS

WHEN I consider how my light is spent
Ere half my days in this dark world and wide,
And that one talent which is death to hide
Lodged with me useless, though my soul more bent
To serve therewith my Maker, and present
My true account, lest He, returning, chide,

"Doth God exact day-labour, light denied?"
I fondly ask. But Patience, to prevent
That murmur, soon replies, "God doth not need
Either man's work or his own gifts. Who best
Bear His mild yoke, they serve Him best. His state
Is kingly: thousands at His bidding speed,
And post o'er land and ocean without rest;
They also serve who only stand and wait."

JOHN MILTON

ON THE LATE MASSACRE IN PIEDMONT

AVENGE, O Lord, Thy slaughtered saints, whose bones
Lie scattered on the Alpine mountains cold;
Even them who kept Thy truth so pure of old
When all our fathers worshipped stocks and stones,
Forget not: in Thy book record their groans
Who were Thy sheep, and in their ancient fold
Slain by the bloody Piedmontese, that rolled
Mother with infant down the rocks. Their moans
The vales redoubled to the hills, and they
To heaven. Their martyred blood and ashes sow
O'er all the Italian fields, where still doth sway
The triple Tyrant; that from these may grow
A hundredfold, who, having learnt Thy way,
Early may fly the Babylonian woe.

JOHN MILTON

Meaning The Cheerful Man and The Thoughtful Man. The greatness of these poems may be indicated by the fact that if one attempted to select individual lines for citation, one would have to quote both poems entire. Incidentally, the second poem had an enormous influence on the Romantic Movement in England in the middle of the eighteenth century.

L'Allegro

Hence, loathèd Melancholy,
    Of Cerberus and blackest Midnight born
In Stygian cave forlorn,
    'Mongst horrid shapes, and shrieks, and sights unholy!
Find out some uncouth cell,
    Where brooding darkness spreads his jealous wings
And the night-raven sings;
    There, under ebon shades and low-browed rocks,
As ragged as thy locks,
    In dark Cimmerian desert ever dwell.
But come, thou goddess fair and free,
In heaven yclept Euphrosyne,
And by men heart-easing Mirth;
Whom lovely Venus, at a birth,
With two sister Graces more,
To ivy-crownèd Bacchus bore;
Or whether—as some sager sing—
The frolic wind that breathes the spring,
Zephyr, with Aurora playing,
As he met her once a-Maying,
There, on beds of violets blue,
And fresh-blown roses washed in dew,
Filled her with thee, a daughter fair,
So buxom, blithe, and debonair.
Haste thee, nymph, and bring with thee
Jest and youthful Jollity,

Quips and cranks and wanton wiles,
Nods and becks and wreathèd smiles,
Such as hang on Hebe's cheek
And love to live in dimple sleek;
Sport, that wrinkled Care derides,
And Laughter holding both his sides.
Come, and trip it, as ye go,
On the light, fantastic toe;
And in thy right hand lead with thee
The mountain-nymph, sweet Liberty.
And if I give thee honour due,
Mirth, admit me of thy crew,
To live with her, and live with thee,
In unreprovèd pleasures free:
To hear the lark begin his flight,
And, singing, startle the dull night,
From his watch-tower in the skies,
Till the dappled dawn doth rise;
Then to come in spite of sorrow,
And at my window bid good-morrow,
Through the sweetbriar or the vine
Or the twisted eglantine.
While the cock, with lively din,
Scatters the rear of darkness thin,
And to the stack or the barn door
Stoutly struts his dames before;
Oft listening how the hounds and horn
Cheerly rouse the slumbering morn,
From the side of some hoar hill,
Through the high wood echoing shrill;
Sometime walking, not unseen,
By hedgerow elms, on hillocks green,
Right against the eastern gate
Where the great sun begins his state,
Robed in flames and amber light,

The clouds in thousand liveries dight;
While the ploughman, near at hand,
Whistles o'er the furrowed land,
And the milkmaid singeth blithe,
And the mower whets his scythe,
And every shepherd tells his tale
Under the hawthorn in the dale.
Straight mine eyes hath caught new pleasures
Whilst the landskip round it measures:
Russet lawns and fallows grey,
Where the nibbling flocks do stray;
Mountains on whose barren breast
The labouring clouds do often rest;
Meadows trim, with daisies pied;
Shallow brooks and rivers wide;
Towers and battlements it sees
Bosomed high in tufted trees,
Where perhaps some beauty lies,
The cynosure of neighbouring eyes.
Hard by a cottage chimney smokes
From betwixt two agèd oaks,
Where Corydon and Thyrsis met,
Are at their savoury dinner set
Of herbs and other country messes,
Which the neat-handed Phyllis dresses;
And then in haste her bower she leaves
With Thestylis to bind the sheaves;
Or, if the earlier season lead,
To the tanned haycock in the mead.
Sometimes, with secure delight,
The upland hamlets will invite,
When the merry bells ring round,
And the jocund rebecks sound
To many a youth and many a maid
Dancing in the chequered shade;

And young and old come forth to play
On a sunshine holiday,
Till the livelong daylight fail;
Then to the spicy, nut-brown ale,
With stories told of many a feat:
How faery Mab the junkets eat;
She was pinched and pulled, she said;
And he, by friar's lanthorn led,
Tells how the drudging goblin sweat
To earn his cream-bowl duly set,
When in one night, ere glimpse of morn,
His shadowy flail hath threshed the corn
That ten day-labourers could not end;
Then lies him down the lubber fiend,
And, stretched out all the chimney's length,
Basks at the fire his hairy strength,
And, crop-full, out of doors he flings
Ere the first cock his matin rings.
Thus done the tales, to bed they creep,
By whispering winds soon lulled asleep.
Towered cities please us then,
And the busy hum of men,
Where throngs of knights and barons bold,
In weeds of peace, high triumphs hold,
With store of ladies, whose bright eyes
Rain influence, and judge the prize
Of wit or arms, while both contend
To win her grace whom all commend.
There let Hymen oft appear
In saffron robe, with taper clear,
And pomp and feast and revelry,
With mask and antique pageantry:
Such sights as youthful poets dream
On summer eves by haunted stream.
Then to the well-trod stage anon

If Jonson's learnèd sock be on,
Or sweetest Shakespeare, Fancy's child,
Warble his native wood-notes wild.
And ever, against eating cares,
Lap me in soft Lydian airs,
Married to immortal verse,
Such as the meeting soul may pierce,
In notes with many a winding bout
Of linkèd sweetness long drawn out
With wanton heed and giddy cunning,
The melting voice through mazes running,
Untwisting all the chains that tie
The hidden soul of harmony;
That Orpheus' self may heave his head
From golden slumber on a bed
Of heaped Elysian flowers, and hear
Such strains as would have won the ear
Of Pluto to have quite set free
His half-regained Eurydice.
These delights if thou canst give,
Mirth, with thee I mean to live.   JOHN MILTON

IL PENSEROSO

HENCE, vain, deluding joys,
    The brood of Folly without father bred!
How little you bested,
    Or fill the fixèd mind with all your toys!
Dwell in some idle brain,
    And fancies fond with gaudy shapes possess,
As thick and numberless
    As the gay motes that people the sunbeams,
Or likest hovering dreams,
    The fickle pensioners of Morpheus' train.

[451]

But hail, thou goddes sage and holy!
Hail, divinest Melancholy!
Whose saintly visage is too bright
To hit the sense of human sight,
And therefore to our weaker view
O'erlaid with black, staid Wisdom's hue;
Black, but such as in esteem
Prince Memnon's sister might beseem,
Or that starred Ethiop queen that strove
To set her beauty's praise above
The sea-nymphs, and their powers offended.
Yet thou art higher far descended:
Thee bright-haired Vesta long of yore
To solitary Saturn bore;
His daughter she; in Saturn's reign
Such mixture was not held a stain.
Oft in glimmering bowers and glades
He met her, and in secret shades
Of woody Ida's inmost grove,
While yet there was no fear of Jove.
Come, pensive nun, devout and pure,
Sober, steadfast, and demure,
All in a robe of darkest grain,
Flowing with majestic train,
And sable stole of cypress lawn
Over thy decent shoulders drawn.
Come, but keep thy wonted state,
With even step and musing gait
And looks commercing with the skies,
Thy rapt soul sitting in thine eyes;
There, held in holy passion still,
Forget thyself to marble, till
With a sad, leaden, downward cast
Thou fix them on the earth as fast.
And join with thee calm Peace and Quiet,

Spare Fast, that oft with gods doth diet,
And hears the Muses in a ring
Aye round about Jove's altar sing;
And add to these retirèd Leisure,
That in trim gardens takes his pleasure;
But, first and chiefest, with thee bring
Him that yon soars on golden wing,
Guiding the fiery-wheelèd throne,
The cherub Contemplation;
And the mute Silence hist along,
'Less Philomel will deign a song
In her sweetest, saddest plight,
Smoothing the rugged brow of night,
While Cynthia checks her dragon yoke
Gently o'er the accustomed oak.
Sweet bird, that shunn'st the noise of folly,
Most musical, most melancholy!
Thee, chauntress, oft the woods among
I woo, to hear thy even-song;
And, missing thee, I walk unseen
On the dry, smooth-shaven green,
To behold the wandering moon,
Riding near her highest noon,
Like one that had been led astray
Through the heaven's wide, pathless way,
And oft, as if her head she bowed,
Stooping through a fleecy cloud.
Oft, on a plat of rising ground,
I hear the far-off curfew sound
Over some wide-watered shore,
Swinging slow with sullen roar;
Or, if the air will not permit,
Some still, removèd place will fit,
Where glowing embers through the room
Teach light to counterfeit a gloom,

Far from all resort of mirth
Save the cricket on the hearth
Or the bellman's drowsy charm
To bless the doors from nightly harm.
Or let my lamp at midnight hour
Be seen in some high, lonely tower,
Where I may oft outwatch the Bear,
With thrice-great Hermes, or unsphere
The spirit of Plato to unfold
What worlds or what vast regions hold
The immortal mind that hath forsook
Her mansion in this fleshly nook;
And of these demons that are found
In fire, air, flood, or under ground,
Whose power hath a true consent
With planet or with element.
Sometime let gorgeous Tragedy
In sceptered pall come sweeping by,
Presenting Thebes, or Pelops' line,
Or the tale of Troy divine,
Or what—though rare—of later age
Ennobled hath the buskined stage.
But, O sad virgin, that thy power
Might raise Musæus from his bower;
Or bid the soul of Orpheus sing
Such notes, as warblèd to the string,
Drew iron tears down Pluto's cheek,
And made hell grant what love did seek;
Or call up him that left half told
The story of Cambuscan bold,
Of Camball, and of Algarsife,
And who had Canace to wife,
That owned the virtuous ring and glass,
And of the wondrous horse of brass
On which the Tartar king did ride;

And if aught else great bards beside
In sage and solemn tunes have sung,
Of tourneys and of trophies hung,
Of forests and enchantments drear,
Where more is meant than meets the ear.
Thus, Night, oft see me in thy pale career,
Till civil-suited Morn appear,
Not tricked and frounced, as she was wont
With the Attic boy to hunt,
But kerchiefed in a comely cloud,
While rocking winds are piping loud,
Or ushered with a shower still,
When the gust hath blown his fill,
Ending on the rustling leaves,
With minute-drops from off the eaves.
And when the sun begins to fling
His flaring beams, me, goddess, bring
To archèd walks of twilight groves,
And shadows brown, that Sylvan loves,
Of pine or monumental oak,
Where the rude axe with heavèd stroke
Was never heard the nymphs to daunt,
Or fright them from their hallowed haunt.
There in close covert by some brook,
Where no profaner eye may look,
Hide me from day's garish eye,
While the bee with honied thigh,
That at her flowery work doth sing,
And the waters murmuring,
With such consort as they keep,
Entice the dewy-feathered Sleep.
And let some strange, mysterious dream
Wave at his wings, in airy stream
Of lively portraiture displayed,
Softly on my eyelids laid;

And, as I wake, sweet music breathe
Above, about, or underneath,
Sent by some Spirit to mortals good,
Or the unseen Genius of the wood.
But let my due feet never fail
To walk the studious cloister's pale,
And love the high embowèd roof,
With antique pillars massy-proof,
And storied windows richly dight,
Casting a dim religious light.
There let the pealing organ blow,
To the full-voiced choir below,
In service high and anthems clear,
As may with sweetness, through mine ear,
Dissolve me into ecstasies,
And bring all Heaven before mine eyes.
And may at last my weary age
Find out the peaceful hermitage,
The hairy gown and mossy cell,
Where I may sit and rightly spell
Of every star that Heaven doth shew,
And every herb that sips the dew,
Till old experience do attain
To something like prophetic strain.
These pleasures, Melancholy, give;
And I with thee will choose to live.

JOHN MILTON

Swinburne had a gift of musical expression that would have placed him among the greatest of English poets, if he had had more to express.

A Forsaken Garden

In a coign of the cliff between lowland and highland,
  At the sea-down's edge between windward and lee,
Walled round with rocks as an inland island,
  The ghost of a garden fronts the sea.
A girdle of brushwood and thorn encloses
  The steep square slope of the blossomless bed
Where the weeds that grew green from the graves of its
    roses
        Now lie dead.

The fields fall southward, abrupt and broken,
  To the low last edge of the long lone land.
If a step should sound or a word be spoken,
  Would a ghost not rise at the strange guest's hand?
So long have the grey bare walks lain guestless,
  Through branches and briers if a man make way,
He shall find no life but the sea-wind's restless
        Night and day.

The dense hard passage is blind and stifled
  That crawls by a track none turn to climb
To the strait waste place that the years have rifled
  Of all but the thorns that are touched not of time.
The thorns he spares when the rose is taken;
  The rocks are left when he wastes the plain;
The wind that wanders, the weeds wind-shaken,
        These remain.

Not a flower to be pressed of the foot that falls not;
  As the heart of a dead man the seed-plots are dry;
From the thicket of thorns whence the nightingale calls not,
  Could she call, there were never a rose to reply.
Over the meadows that blossom and wither
  Rings but the note of a sea-bird's song;
Only the sun and the rain come hither
      All year long.

The sun burns sere and the rain dishevels
  One gaunt bleak blossom of scentless breath.
Only the wind here hovers and revels
  In a round where life seems barren as death.
Here there was laughing of old, there was weeping,
  Haply, of lovers none ever will know,
Whose eyes went seaward a hundred sleeping
      Years ago.

Heart handfast in heart as they stood, "Look thither,"
  Did he whisper? "look forth from the flowers to the sea;
For the foam-flowers endure when rose-blossoms wither,
  And men that love lightly may die—but we?"
And the same wind sang and the same waves whitened,
  And or ever the garden's last petals were shed,
In the lips that had whispered, the eyes that had lightened,
      Love was dead.

Or they loved their life through, and then went whither?
  And were one to the end—but what end who knows?
Love deep as the sea as a rose must wither,
  As the rose-red seaweed that mocks the rose.
Shall the dead take thought for the dead to love them?
  What love was ever as deep as a grave?
They are loveless now as the grass above them
      Or the wave.

All are one now, roses and lovers,
  Not known of the cliffs and the fields and the sea.
Not a breath of the time that has been hovers
  In the air now soft with a summer to be.
Not a breath shall there sweeten the seasons hereafter
  Of the flowers or the lovers that laugh now or weep,
When as they that are free now of weeping and laughter,
      We shall sleep.

Here death may deal not again for ever:
  Here change may come not till all change end.
From the graves they have made they shall rise up never,
  Who have left nought living to ravage and rend.
Earth, stones, and thorns of the wild ground growing,
  While the sun and the rain live, these shall be:
Till a last wind's breath upon all these blowing
      Roll the sea.

Till the slow sea rise and the sheer cliff crumble,
  Till terrace and meadow the deep gulfs drink,
Till the strength of the waves of the high tides humble
  The fields that lessen, the rocks that shrink,
Here now in his triumph where all things falter,
  Stretched out on the spoils that his own hand spread,
As a god self-slain on his own strange altar,
      Death lies dead.
                    ALGERNON CHARLES SWINBURNE

WHEN THE HOUNDS OF SPRING

(*Chorus from Atalanta in Calydon*)

WHEN the hounds of spring are on winter's traces,
  The mother of months in meadow or plain
Fills the shadows and windy places

With lisp of leaves and ripple of rain;
And the brown bright nightingale amorous
Is half assuaged for Itylus,
For the Thracian ships and the foreign faces,
The tongueless vigil, and all the pain.

Come with bows bent and with emptying of quivers,
    Maiden most perfect, lady of light,
With a noise of winds and many rivers,
    With a clamour of waters, and with might;
Bind on thy sandals, O thou most fleet,
Over the splendour and speed of thy feet;
For the faint east quickens, the wan west shivers,
    Round the feet of the day and the feet of the night.

Where shall we find her, how shall we sing to her,
    Fold our hands round her knees, and cling?
O that man's heart were as fire and could spring to her,
    Fire, or the strength of the streams that spring!
For the stars and the winds are unto her
As raiment, as songs of the harp-player;
For the risen stars and the fallen cling to her,
    And the southwest-wind and the west-wind sing.

For winter's rains and ruins are over,
    And all the season of snows and sins;
The days dividing lover and lover,
    The light that loses, the night that wins;
And time remembered is grief forgotten,
And frosts are slain and flowers begotten,
And in green underwood and cover
    Blossom by blossom the spring begins.

The full streams feed on flower of rushes,
    Ripe grasses trammel a travelling foot,

The faint fresh flame of the young year flushes
  From leaf to flower and flower to fruit;
And fruit and leaf are as gold and fire,
And the oat is heard above the lyre,
And the hoofèd heel of a satyr crushes
  The chestnut-husk at the chestnut-root.

And Pan by noon and Bacchus by night,
  Fleeter of foot than the fleet-foot kid,
Follows with dancing and fills with delight
  The Mænad and the Bassarid;
And soft as lips that laugh and hide
The laughing leaves of the trees divide,
And screen from seeing and leave in sight
  The god pursuing, the maiden hid.

The ivy falls with the Bacchanal's hair
  Over her eyebrows hiding her eyes;
The wild vine slipping down leaves bare
  Her bright breast shortening into sighs;
The wild vine slips with the weight of its leaves,
But the berried ivy catches and cleaves
To the limbs that glitter, the feet that scare
  The wolf that follows, the fawn that flies.

ALGERNON CHARLES SWINBURNE

This sturdy, incorruptible member of Parliament from Hull, most conscientious and industrious in the performance of his duties, occasionally escaped from politics into his garden.

THE GARDEN

How vainly men themselves amaze
To win the palm, the oak, or bays,
And their incessant labours see
Crowned from some single herb or tree,
Whose short and narrow-vergèd shade
Does prudently their toils upbraid;
While all flowers and all trees do close
To weave the garlands of repose.

Fair Quiet, have I found thee here,
And Innocence, thy sister dear?
Mistaken long, I sought you then
In busy companies of men.
Your sacred plants, if here below,
Only among the plants will grow;
Society is all but rude
To this delicious solitude.

No white nor red was ever seen
So amorous as this lovely green.
Fond lovers, cruel as their flame,
Cut in these trees their mistress' name:
Little, alas, they know or heed
How far these beauties hers exceed!
Fair trees, wheresoe'er your barks I wound,
No name shall but your own be found.

[462]

When we have run our passion's heat,
Love hither makes his best retreat.
The gods, that mortal beauty chase,
Still in a tree did end their race:
Apollo hunted Daphne so,
Only that she might laurel grow;
And Pan did after Syrinx speed,
Not as a nymph, but for a reed.

What wondrous life is this I lead!
Ripe apples drop about my head;
The luscious clusters of the vine
Upon my mouth do crush their wine;
The nectarine and curious peach
Into my hands themselves do reach;
Stumbling on melons, as I pass,
Ensnared with flowers, I fall on grass.

Meanwhile the mind, from pleasure less,
Withdraws into its happiness:
The mind, that ocean where each kind
Does straight its own resemblance find;
Yet it creates, transcending these,
Far other worlds and other seas,
Annihilating all that's made
To a green thought in a green shade.

Here at the fountain's sliding foot,
Or at some fruit-tree's mossy root,
Casting the body's vest aside,
My soul into the boughs does glide:
There, like a bird, it sits and sings,
Then whets and combs its silver wings,
And, till prepared for longer flight,
Waves in its plumes the various light.

Such was that happy garden-state
While man there walked without a mate:
After a place so pure and sweet,
What other help could yet be meet?
But 'twas beyond a mortal's share
To wander solitary there:
Two Paradises 'twere in one
To live in Paradise alone.

How well the skillful gardener drew,
Of flowers and herbs, this dial new;
Where, from above, the milder sun
Does through a fragrant zodiac run,
And, as it works, the industrious bee
Computes its time as well as we.
How could such sweet and wholesome hours
Be reckoned but with herbs and flowers!

ANDREW MARVELL

This is a garden of another kind.

THE GARDEN

THERE is a fenceless garden overgrown
With buds and blossoms and all sorts of leaves;
And once, among the roses and the sheaves,
The Gardener and I were there alone.
He led me to the plot where I had thrown
The fennel of my days on wasted ground,
And in that riot of sad weeds I found
The fruitage of a life that was my own.
My life! Ah, yes, there was my life, indeed!
And there were all the lives of humankind;

[464]

And they were like a book that I could read,
Whose every leaf, miraculously signed,
Outrolled itself from Thought's eternal seed,
Love-rooted in God's garden of the mind.

EDWIN ARLINGTON ROBINSON

Sometimes I think that of all the poems of Housman, this
is the one most difficult to forget.

EPITAPH ON AN ARMY OF MERCENARIES

THESE, in the day when heaven was falling,
  The hour when earth's foundations fled,
Followed their mercenary calling
  And took their wages and are dead.

Their shoulders held the sky suspended;
  They stood, and earth's foundations stay;
What God abandoned, these defended,
  And saved the sum of things for pay.

A. E. HOUSMAN

In the third stanza, the word *dividing* means "running
musical divisions."

A SONG

ASK me no more where Jove bestows,
When June is past, the fading rose;
For in your beauty's orient deep,
These flowers, as in their causes, sleep.

[465]

Ask me no more whither do stray
The golden atoms of the day;
For in pure love heaven did prepare
Those powders to enrich your hair.

Ask me no more whither dost haste
The nightingale when May is past;
For in your sweet dividing throat
She winters, and keeps warm her note.

Ask me no more where those stars light
That downwards fall in dead of night;
For in your eyes they sit, and there
Fixèd become, as in their sphere.

Ask me no more if east or west,
The phœnix builds her spicy nest;
For unto you at last she flies,
And in your fragrant bosom dies.

THOMAS CAREW

The best American triolet.

A Pitcher of Mignonette

A PITCHER of mignonette,
    In a tenement's highest casement:
Queer sort of flower-pot—yet
That pitcher of mignonette
Is a garden in heaven set,
    To the little sick child in the basement—
A pitcher of mignonette,
    In the tenement's highest casement.

HENRY C. BUNNER

Francis Thompson is one of the greatest religious poets of the nineteenth and twentieth centuries. And we have to go back to the Metaphysical poets of the early seventeenth century, Donne, Vaughan, Crashaw, to find anything resembling his passionate mysticism. His poetry is the poetry of transfiguration. The city street is the avenue to Paradise; the Thames is Genesaret; the angels are all visible. It may be that in the next life, as we look back on this, we shall wonder that we missed so many evidences.

Lilium Regis is the very spirit of prophecy; *The Veteran of Heaven* is the ecstasy of paradox; and *The Hound of Heaven* is the 139th Psalm set to the music of English verse. *Whither shall I flee from thy presence?*

After his death in 1907, the manuscript of *In No Strange Land* was found among his papers.

THE KINGDOM OF GOD

("In No Strange Land")

O WORLD invisible, we view thee,
O World intangible, we touch thee,
O World unknowable, we know thee,
Inapprehensible, we clutch thee!

Does the fish soar to find the ocean,
The eagle plunge to find the air—
That we ask of the stars in motion
If they have rumour of thee there?

Not where the wheeling systems darken,
And our benumbed conceiving soars!—
The drift of pinions, would we hearken,
Beats at our own clay-shuttered doors.

The angels keep their ancient places;—
Turn but a stone and start a wing!
'Tis ye, 'tis your estrangèd faces,
That miss the many-splendoured thing.

But (when so sad thou canst not sadder)
Cry,—and upon thy so sore loss
Shall shine the traffic of Jacob's ladder
Pitched betwixt Heaven and Charing Cross.

Yea, in the night, my Soul, my daughter,
Cry,—clinging Heaven by the hems;
And lo, Christ walking on the water
Not of Genesareth, but Thames!

FRANCIS THOMPSON

See *Revelation* XIX:xvi.

THE VETERAN OF HEAVEN

O CAPTAIN of the wars, whence won Ye so great scars?
  In what fight did Ye smite, and what manner was the foe?
Was it on a day of rout they compassed Thee about,
  Or gat Ye these adornings when Ye wrought their over-
    throw?

" 'Twas on a day of rout they girded me about,
  They wounded all My brow, and they smote Me through
    the side;
My hand held no sword when I met their armèd horde,
  And the conqueror fell down, and the conquered bruised
    his pride."

What is this, unheard before, that the unarmed make war,
　And the slain hath the gain, and the victor hath the rout?
What wars, then, are these, and what the enemies,
　　Strange Chief, with the scars of the conquest trenched
　　　about?

"The Prince I drave forth held the Mount of the North,
　Girt with the guards of flame that roll round the pole.
I drave him with My wars from all his fortress-stars,
　And the sea of death divided that My march might strike
　　its goal.

"In the keep of Northern Guard, many a great dæmonian
　　sword
　Burns as it turns round the Mount, occult, apart:
There is given him power and place still for some certain
　　days,
　And his Name would turn the Sun's blood back upon its
　　heart."

What is THY Name? O show!—"My Name ye may not
　know:
　'Tis a going forth with banners, and a baring of much
　　swords:
But my titles that are high, are they not upon my thigh?
　'King of Kings!' are the words, 'Lord of Lords':
　It is written 'King of Kings, Lord of Lords.' "

FRANCIS THOMPSON

THE HOUND OF HEAVEN

I FLED Him, down the nights and down the days;
　I fled Him, down the arches of the years;
I fled Him, down the labyrinthine ways
　Of my own mind; and in the mist of tears

I hid from Him, and under running laughter.
Up vistaed hopes I sped;
And shot, precipitated,
Adown Titanic glooms of chasmèd fears,
From those strong Feet that followed, followed after.
But with unhurrying chase,
And unperturbèd pace,
Deliberate speed, majestic instancy,
They beat—and a Voice beat
More instant than the Feet—
"All things betray thee, who betrayest Me."

I pleaded, outlaw-wise,
By many a hearted casement, curtained red,
Trellised with intertwining charities;
(For, though I knew His love Who followèd,
Yet was I sore adread
Lest, having Him, I must have naught beside.)
But, if one little casement parted wide,
The gust of His approach would clash it to:
Fear wist not to evade, as Love wist to pursue.
Across the margent of the world I fled,
And troubled the gold gateways of the stars,
Smiting for shelter on their clangèd bars;
Fretted to dulcet jars
And silvern chatter the pale ports o' the moon.
I said to Dawn: Be sudden—to Eve: Be soon;
With thy young skiey blossoms heap me over
From this tremendous Lover—
Float thy vague veil about me, lest He see!
I tempted all His servitors, but to find
My own betrayal in their constancy,
In faith to Him their fickleness to me,
Their traitorous trueness, and their loyal deceit.
To all swift things for swiftness did I sue;

Clung to the whistling mane of every wind.
  But whether they swept, smoothly fleet,
  The long savannahs of the blue;
      Or whether, Thunder-driven,
  They clanged his chariot 'thwart a heaven,
Plashy with flying lightnings round the spurn o' their
  feet:—
  Fear wist not to evade as Love wist to pursue.
      Still with unhurrying chase,
      And unperturbèd pace,
  Deliberate speed, majestic instancy,
      Came on the following Feet,
      And a Voice above their beat—
  "Naught shelters thee, who wilt not shelter Me."

I sought no more that after which I strayed
      In face of man or maid;
But still within the little children's eyes
      Seems something, something that replies,
They at least are for me, surely for me!
I turned me to them very wistfully;
But just as their young eyes grew sudden fair
      With dawning answers there,
Their angel plucked them from me by the hair.
"Come then, ye other children, Nature's—share
With me" (said I) "your delicate fellowship;
  Let me greet you lip to lip,
  Let me twine with you caresses,
      Wantoning
  With our Lady-Mother's vagrant tresses,
      Banqueting
  With her in her wind-walled palace,
  Underneath her azured daïs,
  Quaffing, as your taintless way is,
      From a chalice

Lucent-weeping out of the dayspring."
        So it was done:
I in their delicate fellowship was one—
Drew the bolt of Nature's secrecies.
    I knew all the swift importings
    On the wilful face of skies;
    I knew how the clouds arise
    Spumèd of the wild sea-snortings;
        All that's born or dies
    Rose and drooped with; made them shapers
Of mine own moods, or wailful or divine;
    With them joyed and was bereaven.
    I was heavy with the even,
    When she lit her glimmering tapers
    Round the day's dead sanctities.
    I laughed in the morning's eyes.
I triumphed and I saddened with all weather,
    Heaven and I wept together,
And its sweet tears were salt with mortal mine;
Against the red throb of its sunset-heart
    I laid my own to beat,
    And share commingling heat;
But not by that, by that, was eased my human smart.
In vain my tears were wet on Heaven's grey cheek.
For ah! we know not what each other says,
    These things and I; in sound *I* speak—
Their sound is but their stir, they speak by silences.
Nature, poor stepdame, cannot slake my drouth;
    Let her, if she would owe me,
Drop yon blue bosom-veil of sky, and show me
    The breasts o' her tenderness:
Never did any milk of hers once bless
        My thirsting mouth.
        Nigh and nigh draws the chase.
        With unperturbèd pace,

Deliberate speed, majestic instancy;
    And past those noisèd Feet
    A voice comes yet more fleet—
"Lo! naught contents thee, who content'st not Me."

Naked I wait Thy love's uplifted stroke!
My harness piece by piece Thou hast hewn from me,
    And smitten me to my knee;
    I am defenceless utterly.
    I slept, methinks, and woke,
And, slowly gazing, find me stripped in sleep.
In the rash lustihead of my young powers,
    I shook the pillaring hours
And pulled my life upon me; grimed with smears,
I stand amid the dust o' the mounded years—
My mangled youth lies dead beneath the heap.
My days have crackled and gone up in smoke,
Have puffed and burst as sun-starts on a stream.
    Yea, faileth now even dream
The dreamer, and the lute the lutanist;
Even the linked fantasies, in whose blossomy twist
I swung the earth a trinket at my wrist,
Are yielding; cords of all too weak account
For earth with heavy griefs so overplussed.
    Ah! is Thy love indeed
A weed, albeit an amaranthine weed,
Suffering no flowers except its own to mount?
    Ah! must—
    Designer infinite!—
Ah! must Thou char the wood ere Thou canst limn with
    it?
My freshness spent its wavering shower i' the dust;
And now my heart is as a broken fount,
Wherein tear-drippings stagnate, spilt down ever
    From the dank thoughts that shiver

[473]

Upon the sighful branches of my mind.
    Such is; what is to be?
The pulp so bitter, how shall taste the rind?
I dimly guess what Time in mists confounds;
Yet ever and anon a trumpet sounds
From the hid battlements of Eternity;
Those shaken mists a space unsettle, then
Round the half-glimpsèd turrets slowly wash again.
    But not ere him who summoneth
    I first have seen, enwound
With glooming robes purpureal, cypress-crowned;
His name I know, and what his trumpet saith.
Whether man's heart or life it be which yields
    Thee harvest, must Thy harvest-fields
    Be dunged with rotten death?

    Now of that long pursuit
    Comes on at hand the bruit;
That Voice is round me like a bursting sea:
    "And is thy earth so marred,
    Shattered in shard on shard?
Lo, all things fly thee, for thou fliest Me!
Strange, piteous, futile thing!
Wherefore should any set thee love apart?
Seeing none but I makes much of naught" (He said),
"And human love needs human meriting:
    How hast thou merited—
Of all man's clotted clay the dingiest clot?
    Alack, thou knowest not
How little worthy of any love thou art!
Whom wilt thou find to love ignoble thee,
    Save Me, save only Me?
All which I took from thee I did but take,
    Not for thy harms,

But just that thou might'st seek it in My arms.
    All which thy child's mistake
Fancies as lost, I have stored for thee at home:
    Rise, clasp My hand, and come!"

    Halts by me that footfall:
    Is my gloom, after all,
Shade of His hand, outstretched caressingly?
    "Ah! fondest, blindest, weakest,
    I am He Whom thou seekest!
Thou dravest love from thee, who dravest Me."

FRANCIS THOMPSON

Even the prose of Elinor Wylie was of imagination all compact; and grace seemed as natural to her as breathing.

VELVET SHOES

LET us walk in the white snow
    In a soundless space;
With footsteps quiet and slow,
    At a tranquil pace,
    Under veils of white lace.

I shall go shod in silk,
    And you in wool,
White as a white cow's milk,
    More beautiful
    Than the breast of a gull.

We shall walk through the still town
    In a windless peace;
We shall step upon white down,
    Upon silver fleece,
    Upon softer than these.

[475]

We shall walk in velvet shoes:
  Wherever we go
Silence will fall like dews
  On white silence below.
We shall walk in the snow.

ELINOR WYLIE

———

Immortal nonsense.

JABBERWOCKY

'Twas brillig, and the slithy toves
  Did gyre and gimble in the wabe:
All mimsy were the borogoves,
  And the mome raths outgrabe.

"Beware the Jabberwock, my son!
  The jaws that bite, the claws that catch!
Beware the Jubjub bird, and shun
  The frumious Bandersnatch!"

He took his vorpal sword in hand;
  Long time the manxome foe he sought—
So rested he by the Tumtum tree,
  And stood awhile in thought.

And, as in uffish thought he stood,
  The Jabberwock, with eyes of flame,
Came whiffing through the tulgey wood,
  And burbled as it came!

One, two! One, two! And through and through
  The vorpal blade went snicker-snack!
He left it dead, and with its head
  He went galumphing back.

"And hast thou slain the Jabberwock?
Come to my arms, my beamish boy!
O frabjous day! Callooh! Callay!"
He chortled in his joy.

'Twas brillig, and the slithy toves
Did gyre and gimble in the wabe:
All mimsy were the borogoves,
And the mome raths outgrabe.

LEWIS CARROLL

POEMS ON POETS

Some of the best criticism and most intelligent appreciation of the characteristics of individual poets have been expressed by members of their own guild; and expressed in poems that are themselves works of art. No one has ever interpreted the genius of Wordsworth more accurately than William Watson in *Wordsworth's Grave:* the sublime and the charming Milton have been appreciated respectively by Wordsworth and by Tennyson: before Browning had any general reputation, Landor placed him where he belonged, with Chaucer; Longfellow's finest sonnets are those that accompanied his translation of Dante; Rossetti in his sonnet on Shelley paid him the highest compliment that intellectual integrity can receive; Milton foretold the fame of Shakespeare, Arnold pointed out his uniqueness, and Ben Jonson in the most generous tribute ever made to a contemporary, said something that subsequent criticism has only repeated in less felicitous phrase.

After reading Ben's tribute to Shakespeare, one forgives him everything there might be to forgive. Edwin Booth said

[477]

a Christian was one who rejoiced in the superiority of a rival. If this be true, when Ben Jonson wrote his homage, he was not far from the Kingdom of God.

WORDSWORTH'S GRAVE

POET who sleepest by this wandering wave!
　　When thou wast born, what birth-gift hadst thou then?
To thee what wealth was that the Immortals gave,
　　The wealth thou gavest in thy turn to men?

Not Milton's keen, translunar music thine;
　　Not Shakespeare's cloudless, boundless human view;
Not Shelley's flush of rose on peaks divine;
　　Nor yet the wizard twilight Coleridge knew.

What hadst thou that could make so large amends
　　For all thou hadst not and thy peers possessed,
Motion and fire, swift means to radiant ends?—
　　Thou hadst, for weary feet, the gift of rest.

From Shelley's dazzling glow or thunderous haze,
　　From Byron's tempest-anger, tempest-mirth,
Men turned to thee and found—not blast and blaze,
　　Tumult of tottering heavens, but peace on earth.

Nor peace that grows by Lethe, scentless flower,
　　There in white languors to decline and cease;
But peace whose names are also rapture, power,
　　Clear sight, and love: for these are parts of peace.

WILLIAM WATSON

MEMORABILIA

AH, did you once see Shelley plain,
　　And did he stop and speak to you
And did you speak to him again?
　　How strange it seems and new!

[478]

But you were living before that,
　　And also you are living after;
And the memory I started at—
　　My starting moves your laughter.

I crossed a moor, with a name of its own
　　And a certain use in the world no doubt,
Yet a hand's-breadth of it shines alone
　　'Mid the blank miles round about:

For there I picked up on the heather
　　And there I put inside my breast
A moulted feather, an eagle-feather!
　　Well, I forget the rest.

ROBERT BROWNING

ON THE DEATH OF ROBERT BROWNING

HE held no dream worth waking: so he said,
　　He who stands now on death's triumphal steep,
　　Awakened out of life wherein we sleep
And dream of what he knows and sees, being dead.
But never death for him was dark or dread:
　　"Look forth," he bade the soul, and fear not. Weep,
　　All ye that trust not in his truth, and keep
Vain memory's vision of a vanished head
As all that lives of all that once was he
　　Save that which lightens from his word; but we,
　　Who, seeing the sunset-coloured waters roll,
Yet know the sun subdued not of the sea,
　　Nor weep nor doubt that still the spirit is whole,
　　And life and death but shadows of the soul.

ALGERNON CHARLES SWINBURNE

To Robert Browning

There is delight in singing, though none hear
Beside the singer; and there is delight
In praising, though the praiser sit alone
And see the praised far off him, far above.
Shakespeare is not our poet, but the world's,
Therefore on him no speech! and brief for thee,
Browning! Since Chaucer was alive and hale,
No man hath walkt along our roads with step
So active, so inquiring eye, or tongue
So varied in discourse. But warmer climes
Give brighter plumage, stronger wine: the breeze
Of Alpine heights thou playest with, borne on
Beyond Sorrento and Amalfi, where
The Siren waits thee, singing song for song.

WALTER SAVAGE LANDOR

London 1802

Milton! thou shouldst be living at this hour:
England hath need of thee; she is a fen
Of stagnant waters: altar, sword, and pen,
Fireside, the heroic wealth of hall and bower,
Have forfeited their ancient English dower
Of inward happiness. We are selfish men;
Oh! raise us up, return to us again;
And give us manners, virtue, freedom, power.
Thy soul was like a Star, and dwelt apart:
Thou hadst a voice whose sound was like the sea:
Pure as the naked heavens, majestic, free,
So didst thou travel on life's common way,
In cheerful godliness; and yet thy heart
The lowliest duties on herself did lay.

WILLIAM WORDSWORTH

ON SHAKESPEARE

WHAT needs my Shakespeare for his honoured bones
The labour of an age in pilèd stones?
Or that his hallowed relics should be hid
Under a star-ypointing pyramid?
Dear son of memory, great heir of fame,
What need'st thou such weak witness of thy name?
Thou, in our wonder and astonishment,
Hast built thyself a livelong monument.
For whilst to the shame of slow-endeavouring art
Thy easy numbers flow, and that each heart
Hath from the leaves of thy unvalued book
Those Delphic lines with deep impression took,
Then thou, our fancy of itself bereaving,
Dost make us marble with too much conceiving;
And, so sepulchred, in such pomp dost lie
That kings for such a tomb would wish to die.

JOHN MILTON

SHAKESPEARE

OTHERS abide our question. Thou art free.
We ask and ask: thou smilest and art still,
Out-topping knowledge. For the loftiest hill
That to the stars uncrowns his majesty,
Planting his stedfast footsteps in the sea,
Making the Heaven of Heavens his dwelling-place,
Spares but the cloudy border of his base
To the foil'd searching of mortality:
And thou, who didst the stars and sunbeams know,
Self-school'd, self-scann'd, self-honour'd, self-secure,
Didst walk on Earth unguess'd at. Better so!
All pains the immortal spirit must endure,
All weakness that impairs, all griefs that bow,
Find their sole voice in that victorious brow.

MATTHEW ARNOLD

[481]

To the Memory of My Beloved
Master William Shakespeare

To draw no envy, Shakespeare, on thy name,
Am I thus ample to thy book and fame;
While I confess thy writings to be such
As neither man, nor muse, can praise too much.
'T is true, and all men's suffrage. But these ways
Were not the paths I meant unto thy praise;
For silliest ignorance on these may light,
Which, when it sounds at best, but echoes right;
Or blind affection, which doth ne'er advance
The truth, but gropes, and urgeth all by chance;
Or crafty malice might pretend this praise,
And think to ruin, where it seemed to raise.
These are, as some infamous bawd or whore
Should praise a matron. What could hurt her more?
But thou art proof against them, and, indeed,
Above the ill fortune of them, or the need.
I therefore will begin. Soul of the age!
The applause, delight, the wonder of our stage!
My Shakespeare, rise! I will not lodge thee by
Chaucer, or Spenser, or bid Beaumont lie
A little further, to make thee a room:
Thou art a monument without a tomb,
And art alive still while thy book doth live
And we have wits to read and praise to give.
That I not mix thee so, my brain excuses,
I mean with great, but disproportioned Muses;
For if I thought my judgment were of years,
I should commit thee surely with thy peers,
And tell how far thou didst our Lyly outshine,
Or sporting Kyd, or Marlowe's mighty line.
And though thou hadst small Latin and less Greek,

From thence to honour thee, I would not seek
For names; but call forth thundering Æschylus,
Euripides, and Sophocles to us;
Pacuvius, Accius, him of Cordova dead,
To life again, to hear thy buskin tread,
And shake a stage; or, when thy socks were on,
Leave thee alone for the comparison
Of all that insolent Greece or haughty Rome
Sent forth, or since did from their ashes come.
Triumph, my Britain, thou hast one to show
To whom all scenes of Europe homage owe.
He was not of an age, but for all time!
And all the Muses still were in their prime,
When, like Apollo, he came forth to warm
Our ears, or like a Mercury to charm!
Nature herself was proud of his designs
And joyed to wear the dressing of his lines!
Which were so richly spun, and woven so fit,
As, since, she will vouchsafe no other wit.
The merry Greek, tart Aristophanes,
Neat Terence, witty Plautus, now not please;
But antiquated and deserted lie,
As they were not of Nature's family.
Yet must I not give Nature all; thy art,
My gentle Shakespeare, must enjoy a part.
For though the poet's matter nature be,
His art doth give the fashion; and, that he
Who casts to write a living line, must sweat,
(Such as thine are) and strike the second heat
Upon the Muses' anvil; turn the same
(And himself with it) that he thinks to frame,
Or, for the laurel, he may gain a scorn;
For a good poet's made, as well as born.
And such wert thou! Look how the father's face
Lives in his issue, even so the race

Of Shakespeare's mind and manners brightly shines
In his well turnèd, and true filèd lines;
In each of which he seems to shake a lance,
As brandished at the eyes of ignorance.
Sweet Swan of Avon! what a sight it were
To see thee in our waters yet appear,
And make those flights upon the banks of Thames,
That so did take Eliza, and our James!
But stay, I see thee in the hemisphere
Advanced, and made a constellation there!
Shine forth, thou Star of poets, and with rage
Or influence, chide or cheer the drooping stage,
Which, since thy flight from hence, hath mourned like night,
And despairs day, but for thy volume's light.

BEN JONSON

MILTON

AND did those feet in ancient time
    Walk upon England's mountains green?
And was the holy Lamb of God
    On England's pleasant pastures seen?

And did the Countenance Divine
    Shine forth upon our clouded hills?
And was Jerusalem builded here
    Among these dark Satanic Mills?

Bring me my bow of burning gold!
    Bring me my arrows of desire!
Bring me my spear! O clouds, unfold!
    Bring me my chariot of fire!

I will not cease from mental fight,
    Nor shall my sword sleep in my hand,
Till we have built Jerusalem
    In England's green and pleasant land.

WILLIAM BLAKE

MILTON

(ALCAICS)

O MIGHTY-MOUTH'D inventor of harmonies,
O skilled to sing of Time or Eternity,
  God-gifted organ-voice of England,
    Milton, a name to resound for ages;
Whose Titan angels, Gabriel, Abdiel,
Starr'd from Jehovah's gorgeous armouries,
  Tower, as the deep-domed empyrean
    Rings to the roar of an angel onset!
Me rather all that bowery loneliness,
The brooks of Eden mazily murmuring,
  And bloom profuse and cedar arches
    Charm, as a wanderer out in the ocean,
Where some refulgent sunset of India
  Streams o'er a rich ambrosial ocean isle,
    And crimson-hued the stately palm-woods
      Whisper in odorous heights of even.

ALFRED TENNYSON

PERCY BYSSHE SHELLEY

(INSCRIPTION FOR THE COUCH, STILL PRESERVED, ON WHICH HE PASSED THE LAST NIGHT OF HIS LIFE)

'TWIXT those twin worlds,—the world of Sleep, which gave
No dream to warm,—the tidal world of Death,
Which the earth's sea, as the earth, replenisheth,—
Shelley, Song's orient sun, to breast the wave,
Rose from this couch that morn. Ah! did he brave
Only the sea?—or did man's deed of hell
Engulf his bark 'mid mists impenetrable? . . .

No eye discerned, nor any power might save.
When that mist cleared, O Shelley! what dread veil
Was rent for thee, to whom far-darkling Truth
Reigned sovereign guide through thy brief ageless youth?
Was the Truth *thy* Truth, Shelley?—Hush! All-Hail,
Past doubt, thou gav'st it; and in Truth's bright sphere
Art first of praisers, being most praisèd here.

DANTE GABRIEL ROSSETTI

Rossetti's genius as a painter is seen in his poetry and his genius as a poet is seen in his painting. He wrote *The Blessed Damozel* when he was nineteen. His sonnet-sequence, *The House of Life*, places him among the great English sonneteers.

A Superscription

Look in my face; my name is Might-have-been;
I am also called No-more, Too-late, Farewell;
Unto thine ear I hold the dead-sea shell
Cast up thy Life's foam-fretted feet between;
Unto thine eyes the glass where that is seen
Which had Life's form and Love's, but by my spell
Is now a shaken shadow intolerable,
Of ultimate things unuttered the frail screen.
Mark me, how still I am! But should there dart
One moment through thy soul the soft surprise
Of that winged Peace which lulls the breath of sighs,—
Then shalt thou see me smile, and turn apart
Thy visage to mine ambush at thy heart,
Sleepless with cold commemorative eyes.

DANTE GABRIEL ROSSETTI

The Blessed Damozel

THE blessed damozel leaned out
   From the gold bar of Heaven;
Her eyes were deeper than the depth
   Of waters stilled at even;
She had three lilies in her hand,
   And the stars in her hair were seven.

Her robe, ungirt from clasp to hem,
   No wrought flowers did adorn,
But a white rose of Mary's gift,
   For service meetly worn;
Her hair that lay along her back
   Was yellow like ripe corn.

Her seemed she scarce had been a day
   One of God's choristers;
The wonder was not yet quite gone
   From that still look of hers;
Albeit, to them she left, her day
   Had counted as ten years.

(To one, it is ten years of years.
   . . . Yet now, and in this place,
Surely she leaned o'er me—her hair
   Fell all about my face. . . .
Nothing: the autumn fall of leaves.
   The whole year sets apace.)

It was the rampart of God's house
   That she was standing on;
By God built over the sheer depth
   The which is Space begun;
So high, that looking downward thence
   She scarce could see the sun.

It lies in Heaven, across the flood
　Of ether, as a bridge.
Beneath the tides of day and night
　With flame and darkness ridge
The void, as low as where this earth
　Spins like a fretful midge.

Around her, lovers, newly met
　'Mid deathless love's acclaims,
Spoke evermore among themselves
　Their heart-remembered names;
And the souls mounting up to God
　Went by her like thin flames.

And still she bowed herself and stooped
　Out of the circling charm;
Until her bosom must have made
　The bar she leaned on warm,
And the lilies lay as if asleep
　Along her bended arm.

From the fixed place of Heaven she saw
　Time like a pulse shake fierce
Through all the worlds. Her gaze still strove
　Within the gulf to pierce
Its path; and now she spoke as when
　The stars sang in their spheres.

The sun was gone now; the curled moon
　Was like a little feather
Fluttering far down the gulf; and now
　She spoke through the still weather.
Her voice was like the voice the stars
　Had when they sang together.

(Ah sweet! Even now, in that bird's song,
  Strove not her accents there,
Fain to be hearkened? When those bells
  Possessed the mid-day air,
Strove not her steps to reach my side
  Down all the echoing stair?)

"I wish that he were come to me,
  For he will come," she said.
"Have I not prayed in Heaven?—on earth,
  Lord, Lord, has he not pray'd?
Are not two prayers a perfect strength?
  And shall I feel afraid?

"When round his head the aureole clings,
  And he is clothed in white,
I'll take his hand and go with him
  To the deep wells of light;
As unto a stream we will step down,
  And bathe there in God's sight.

"We two will stand beside that shrine,
  Occult, withheld, untrod,
Whose lamps are stirred continually
  With prayer sent up to God;
And see our old prayers, granted, melt
  Each like a little cloud.

"We two will lie i' the shadow of
  That living mystic tree
Within whose secret growth the Dove
  Is sometimes felt to be,
While every leaf that His plumes touch
  Saith His Name audibly.

[489]

"And I myself will teach to him,
  I myself, lying so,
The songs I sing here; which his voice
  Shall pause in, hushed and slow,
And find some knowledge at each pause,
  Or some new thing to know."

(Alas! We two, we two, thou say'st!
  Yea, one wast thou with me
That once of old. But shall God lift
  To endless unity
The soul whose likeness with thy soul
  Was but its love for thee?)

"We two," she said, "will seek the groves
  Where the lady Mary is,
With her five handmaidens, whose names
  Are five sweet symphonies,
Cecily, Gertrude, Magdalen,
  Margaret and Rosalys.

"Circlewise sit they, with bound locks
  And foreheads garlanded;
Into the fine cloth white like flame
  Weaving the golden thread,
To fashion the birth-robes for them
  Who are just born, being dead.

"He shall fear, haply, and be dumb:
  Then will I lay my cheek
To his, and tell about our love,
  Not once abashed or weak:
And the dear Mother will approve
  My pride, and let me speak.

"Herself shall bring us, hand in hand,
 To Him round whom all souls
Kneel, the clear-ranged unnumbered heads
 Bowed with their aureoles:
And angels meeting us shall sing
 To their citherns and citoles.

"There will I ask of Christ the Lord
 Thus much for him and me:—
Only to live as once on earth
 With Love, only to be,
As then awhile, for ever now,
 Together, I and he."

She gazed and listened and then said,
 Less sad of speech than mild,—
"All this is when he comes." She ceased.
 The light thrilled towards her, fill'd
With angels in strong level flight.
 Her eyes prayed, and she smil'd.

(I saw her smile.) But soon their path
 Was vague in distant spheres:
And then she cast her arms along
 The golden barriers,
And laid her face between her hands,
 And wept. (I heard her tears.)

DANTE GABRIEL ROSSETTI

The Love-Letter

Warmed by her hand and shadowed by her hair
As close she leaned and poured her heart through thee,
Whereof the articulate throbs accompany

The smooth black stream that makes thy whiteness fair,—
Sweet fluttering sheet, even of her breath aware,—
Oh let thy silent song disclose to me
That soul wherewith her lips and eyes agree
Like married music in Love's answering air.
Fain had I watched her when, at some fond thought,
Her bosom to the writing closelier press'd,
And her breast's secrets poured into her breast;
When, through eyes raised an instant, her soul sought
My soul, and from the sudden confluence caught
The words that made her love the loveliest.

DANTE GABRIEL ROSSETTI

PROLOGUE TO THE TWO POETS OF CROISIC

SUCH a starved bank of moss
Till, that May-morn,
Blue ran the flash across:
Violets were born!

Sky—what a scowl of cloud
Till, near and far,
Ray on ray split the shroud:
Splendid, a star!

World—how it walled about
Life with disgrace
Till God's own smile came out:
That was thy face!

ROBERT BROWNING

Browning has caught in the language and rhythm, the silver-grey, quiet tone of Andrea's pictures. Browning did not dislike him because he was the son of a tailor; he disliked him because he was called the *faultless* painter. Things that are perfect cannot develop.

ANDREA DEL SARTO

(Called "The Faultless Painter.")

BUT do not let us quarrel any more,
No, my Lucrezia; bear with me for once:
Sit down and all shall happen as you wish.
You turn your face, but does it bring your heart?
I'll work then for your friend's friend, never fear,
Treat his own subject after his own way,
Fix his own time, accept too his own price,
And shut the money into this small hand
When next it takes mine. Will it? tenderly?
Oh, I'll content him,—but tomorrow, Love!
I often am much wearier than you think,
This evening more than usual, and it seems
As if—forgive now—should you let me sit
Here by the window with your hand in mine
And look a half-hour forth on Fiesole,
Both of one mind, as married people use,
Quietly, quietly the evening through,
I might get up tomorrow to my work
Cheerful and fresh as ever. Let us try.
Tomorrow, how you shall be glad for this!
Your soft hand is a woman of itself,
And mine the man's bared breast she curls inside.
Don't count the time lost, neither; you must serve
For each of the five pictures we require:
It saves a model. So! keep looking so—

My serpentining beauty, rounds on rounds!
—How could you ever prick those perfect ears,
Even to put the pearl there! oh, so sweet—
My face, my moon, my everybody's moon,
Which everybody looks on and calls his,
And, I suppose, is looked on by in turn,
While she looks—no one's: very dear, no less.
You smile? why, there's my picture ready made,
There's what we painters call our harmony!
A common greyness silvers everything,—
All in a twilight, you and I alike
—You, at the point of your first pride in me
(That's gone you know),—but I, at every point;
My youth, my hope, my art, being all toned down
To yonder sober pleasant Fiesole.
There's the bell clinking from the chapel-top;
That length of convent-wall across the way
Holds the trees safer, huddled more inside;
The last monk leaves the garden; days decrease,
And autumn grows, autumn in everything.
Eh? the whole seems to fall into a shape
As if I saw alike my work and self
And all that I was born to be and do,
A twilight-piece. Love, we are in God's hand.
How strange now looks the life he makes us lead;
So free we seem, so fettered fast we are!
I feel he laid the fetter: let it lie!
This chamber for example—turn your head—
All that's behind us! You don't understand
Nor care to understand about my art,
But you can hear at least when people speak:
And that cartoon, the second from the door
—It is the thing, Love! so such things should be—
Behold Madonna!—I am bold to say.
I can do with my pencil what I know,

What I see, what at bottom of my heart
I wish for, if I ever wish so deep—
Do easily, too—when I say perfectly,
I do not boast, perhaps: yourself are judge,
Who listened to the Legate's talk last week,
And just as much they used to say in France.
At any rate 'tis easy, all of it!
No sketches first, no studies, that's long past:
I do what many dream of, all their lives,
—Dream? strive to do, and agonise to do,
And fail in doing. I could count twenty such
On twice your fingers, and not leave this town,
Who strive—you don't know how the others strive
To paint a little thing like that you smeared
Carelessly passing with your robes afloat,—
Yet do much less, so much less, Someone says,
(I know his name, no matter)—so much less!
Well, less is more, Lucrezia: I am judged.
There burns a truer light of God in them,
In their vexed beating stuffed and stopped-up brain,
Heart, or whate'er else, than goes on to prompt
This low-pulsed forthright craftsman's hand of mine.
Their works drop groundward, but themselves, I know,
Reach many a time a heaven that's shut to me,
Enter and take their place there sure enough,
Though they come back and cannot tell the world.
My works are nearer heaven, but I sit here.
The sudden blood of these men! at a word—
Praise them, it boils, or blame them, it boils too.
I, painting from myself and to myself,
Know what I do, am unmoved by men's blame
Or their praise either. Somebody remarks
Morello's outline there is wrongly traced,
His hue mistaken; what of that? or else,
Rightly traced and well ordered; what of that?

Speak as they please, what does the mountain care?
Ah, but a man's reach should exceed his grasp,
Or what's a heaven for? All is silver-grey
Placid and perfect with my art: the worse!
I know both what I want and what might gain,
And yet how profitless to know, to sigh
"Had I been two, another and myself,
Our head would have o'erlooked the world!" No doubt.
Yonder's a work now, of that famous youth
The Urbinate who died five years ago.
('Tis copied, George Vasari sent it me.)
Well, I can fancy how he did it all,
Pouring his soul, with kings and popes to see,
Reaching, that heaven might so replenish him,
Above and through his art—for it gives way;
That arm is wrongly put—and there again—
A fault to pardon in the drawing's lines,
Its body, so to speak: its soul is right,
He means right—that, a child may understand.
Still, what an arm! and I could alter it:
But all the play, the insight and the stretch—
Out of me, out of me! And wherefore out?
Had you enjoined them on me, given me soul,
We might have risen to Rafael, I and you!
Nay, Love, you did give all I asked, I think—
More than I merit, yes, by many times.
But had you—oh, with the same perfect brow,
And perfect eyes, and more than perfect mouth,
And the low voice my soul hears, as a bird
The fowler's pipe, and follows to the snare—
Had you, with these the same, but brought a mind!
Some women do so. Had the mouth there urged
"God and the glory! never care for gain.
The present by the future, what is that?
Live for fame, side by side with Agnolo!

Rafael is waiting: up to God, all three!"
I might have done it for you. So it seems:
Perhaps not. All is as God over-rules.
Beside, incentives come from the soul's self;
The rest avail not. Why do I need you?
What wife had Rafael, or has Agnolo?
In this world, who can do a thing, will not;
And who would do it, cannot, I perceive:
Yet the will's somewhat—somewhat, too, the power—
And thus we half-men struggle. At the end,
God, I conclude, compensates, punishes.
'Tis safer for me, if the award be strict,
That I am something underrated here,
Poor this long while, despised, so speak the truth.
I dared not, do you know, leave home all day,
For fear of chancing on the Paris lords.
The best is when they pass and look aside;
But they speak sometimes; I must bear it all.
Well may they speak! That Francis, that first time,
And that long festal year at Fontainebleau!
I surely then could sometimes leave the ground,
Put on the glory, Rafael's daily wear,
In that humane great monarch's golden look,—
One finger in his beard or twisted curl
Over his mouth's good mark that made the smile,
One arm about my shoulder, round my neck,
The jingle of his gold chain in my ear,
I painting proudly with his breath on me,
All his court round him, seeing with his eyes,
Such frank French eyes, and such a fire of souls
Profuse, my hand kept plying by those hearts,—
And, best of all, this, this, this face beyond,
This in the background, waiting on my work,
To crown the issue with a last reward!
A good time, was it not, my kingly days?

And had you not grown restless . . . but I know—
'Tis done and past; 'twas right, my instinct said;
Too live the life grew, golden and not grey,
And I'm the weak-eyed bat no sun should tempt
Out of the grange whose four walls make his world.
How could it end in any other way?
You called me, and I came home to your heart.
The triumph was—to reach and stay there; since
I reached it ere the triumph, what is lost?
Let my hands frame your face in your hair's gold,
You beautiful Lucrezia that are mine!
"Rafael did this, Andrea painted that;
The Roman's is the better when you pray,
But still the other's Virgin was his wife—"
Men will excuse me. I am glad to judge
Both pictures in your presence; clearer grows
My better fortune, I resolve to think.
For, do you know, Lucrezia, as God lives,
Said one day Agnolo, his very self,
To Rafael . . . I have known it all these years . . .
(When the young man was flaming out his thoughts
Upon a palace-wall for Rome to see,
Too lifted up in heart because of it)
"Friend, there's a certain sorry little scrub
Goes up and down our Florence, none cares how,
Who, were he set to plan and execute
As you are, pricked on by your popes and kings,
Would bring the sweat into that brow of yours!"
To Rafael's!—And indeed the arm is wrong.
I hardly dare . . . yet, only you to see,
Give the chalk here—quick, thus the line should go!
Ay, but the soul! he's Rafael! rub it out!
Still, all I care for, if he spoke the truth,
(What he? why, who but Michel Agnolo?
Do you forget already words like those?)

If really there was a chance, so lost,—
Is, whether you're—not grateful—but more pleased.
Well, let me think so. And you smile indeed!
This hour has been an hour! Another smile?
If you would sit thus by me every night
I should work better, do you comprehend?
I mean that I should earn more, give you more.
See, it is settled dusk now; there's a star;
Morello's gone, the watch-lights show the wall,
The cue-owls speak the name we call them by.
Come from the window, love,—come in, at last,
Inside the melancholy little house
We built to be so gay with. God is just.
King Francis may forgive me: oft at nights
When I look up from painting, eyes tired out,
The walls become illumined, brick from brick
Distinct, instead of mortar, fierce bright gold,
That gold of his I did cement them with!
Let us but love each other. Must you go?
That Cousin here again? he waits outside?
Must see you—you, and not with me? Those loans?
More gaming debts to pay? you smiled for that?
Well, let smiles buy me! have you more to spend?
While hand and eye and something of a heart
Are left me, work's my ware, and what's it worth?
I'll pay my fancy. Only let me sit
The grey remainder of the evening out,
Idle, you call it, and muse perfectly
How I could paint, were I but back in France,
One picture, just one more—the Virgin's face,
Not yours this time! I want you at my side
To hear them—that is, Michel Agnolo—
Judge all I do and tell you of its worth.
Will you? Tomorrow, satisfy your friend.
I take the subjects for his corridor,

Finish the portrait out of hand—there, there,
And throw him in another thing or two
If he demurs; the whole should prove enough
To pay for this same Cousin's freak. Beside,
What's better and what's all I care about,
Get you the thirteen scudi for the ruff!
Love, does that please you? Ah, but what does he,
The Cousin! what does he to please you more?

I am grown peaceful as old age tonight.
I regret little, I would change still less.
Since there my past life lies, why alter it?
The very wrong to Francis!—it is true
I took his coin, was tempted and complied,
And built this house and sinned, and all is said.
My father and my mother died of want.
Well, had I riches of my own? you see
How one gets rich! Let each one bear his lot.
They were born poor, lived poor, and poor they died:
And I have laboured somewhat in my time
And not been paid profusely. Some good son
Paint my two hundred pictures—let him try!
No doubt, there's something strikes a balance. Yes,
You loved me quite enough, it seems tonight.
This must suffice me here. What would one have?
In heaven, perhaps, new chances, one more chance—
Four great walls in the New Jerusalem,
Meted on each side by the angel's reed,
For Leonard, Rafael, Agnolo and me
To cover—the three first without a wife,
While I have mine! So—still they overcome
Because there's still Lucrezia,—as I choose.

Again the Cousin's whistle! Go, my Love.

ROBERT BROWNING

[500]

He never meant to attack Wordsworth; but the latter's change from radical views to those of the extreme conservatives supplied the inspiration.

THE LOST LEADER

I

JUST for a handful of silver he left us,
  Just for a riband to stick in his coat—
Found the one gift of which fortune bereft us,
  Lost all the others she lets us devote;
They, with the gold to give, doled him out silver,
  So much was theirs who so little allowed:
How all our copper had gone for his service!
  Rags—were they purple, his heart had been proud!
We that had loved him so, followed him, honoured him,
  Lived in his mild and magnificent eye,
Learned his great language, caught his clear accents,
  Made him our pattern to live and to die!
Shakespeare was of us, Milton was for us,
  Burns, Shelley, were with us,—they watch from their
    graves!
He alone breaks from the van and the freemen,
  —He alone sinks to the rear and the slaves!

II

We shall march prospering,—not thro' his presence;
  Songs may inspirit us,—not from his lyre;
Deeds will be done,—while he boasts his quiescence,
  Still bidding crouch whom the rest bade aspire:
Blot out his name, then, record one lost soul more,
  One task more declined, one more footpath untrod,
One more devils'-triumph and sorrow for angels,
  One wrong more to man, one more insult to God!

[501]

Life's night begins: let him never come back to us!
    There would be doubt, hesitation and pain,
Forced praise on our part—the glimmer of twilight,
    Never glad confident morning again!
Best fight on well, for we taught him—strike gallantly,
    Menace our heart ere we master his own;
Then let him receive the new knowledge and wait us,
    Pardoned in heaven, the first by the throne!

ROBERT BROWNING

===

In the Uffizi gallery at Florence is Fra Lippo Lippi's great painting, The Coronation of the Virgin. It contains the combination of beauty and impudence that composed the character of the painter. This is the poem Browning read aloud to the company composed of Tennyson, Dante and William Rossetti, and Mrs. Browning.

FRA LIPPO LIPPI

I AM poor brother Lippo, by your leave!
You need not clap your torches to my face.
Zooks, what's to blame? you think you see a monk!
What, 'tis past midnight, and you go the rounds,
And here you catch me at an alley's end
Where sportive ladies leave their doors ajar?
The Carmine's my cloister: hunt it up,
Do,—harry out, if you must show your zeal,
Whatever rat, there, haps on his wrong hole,
And nip each softling of a wee white mouse,
Weke, weke, that's crept to keep him company!
Aha, you know your betters! Then, you'll take
Your hand away that's fiddling on my throat,
And please to know me likewise. Who am I?

[502]

Why, one, sir, who is lodging with a friend
Three streets off—he's a certain . . . how d'ye call?
Master—a . . . Cosimo of the Medici,
I' the house that caps the corner. Boh! you were best!
Remember and tell me, the day you're hanged,
How you affected such a gullet's-gripe!
But you, sir, it concerns you that your knaves
Pick up a manner nor discredit you:
Zooks, are we pilchards, that they sweep the streets
And count fair prize what comes into their net?
He's Judas to a tittle, that man is!
Just such a face! Why, sir, you make amends.
Lord, I'm not angry! Bid your hangdogs go
Drink out this quarter-florin to the health
Of the munificent House that harbours me
(And many more beside, lads! more beside!)
And all's come square again. I'd like his face—
His, elbowing on his comrade in the door
With the pike and lantern,—for the slave that holds
John Baptist's head a-dangle by the hair
With one hand ("Look you, now," as who should say)
And his weapon in the other, yet unwiped!
It's not your chance to have a bit of chalk,
A wood-coal or the like? or you should see!
Yes, I'm the painter, since you style me so.
What, brother Lippo's doings, up and down,
You know them and they take you? like enough!
I saw the proper twinkle in your eye—
'Tell you, I liked your looks at very first.
Let's sit and set things straight now, hip to haunch.
Here's spring come, and the nights one makes up bands
To roam the town and sing out carnival,
And I've been three weeks shut within my mew,
A-painting for the great man, saints and saints
And saints again. I could not paint all night—

Ouf! I leaned out of window for fresh air.
There came a hurry of feet and little feet,
A sweep of lute-strings, laughs, and whiffs of song,—
Flower o' the broom,
Take away love, and our earth is a tomb!
Flower o' the quince,
I let Lisa go, and what good in life since?
Flower o' the thyme—and so on. Round they went.
Scarce had they turned the corner when a titter
Like the skipping of rabbits by moonlight,—three slim
    shapes,
And a face that looked up . . . zooks, sir, flesh and blood,
That's all I'm made of! Into shreds it went,
Curtain and counterpane and coverlet,
All the bed-furniture—a dozen knots,
There was a ladder! Down I let myself,
Hands and feet, scrambling somehow, and so dropped,
And after them. I came up with the fun
Hard by Saint Laurence, hail fellow, well met,—
Flower o' the rose,
If I've been merry, what matter who knows?
And so as I was stealing back again
To get to bed and have a bit of sleep
Ere I rise up tomorrow and go work
On Jerome knocking at his poor old breast
With his great round stone to subdue the flesh,
You snap me of the sudden. Ah, I see!
Though your eye twinkles still, you shake your head—
Mine's shaved—a monk, you say—the sting's in that!
If Master Cosimo announced himself,
Mum's the word naturally; but a monk!
Come, what am I a beast for? tell us, now!
I was a baby when my mother died
And father died and left me in the street.
I starved there, God knows how, a year or two

[504]

On fig-skins, melon-parings, rinds and shucks,
Refuse and rubbish. One fine frosty day,
My stomach being empty as your hat,
The wind doubled me up and down I went.
Old Aunt Lapaccia trussed me with one hand,
(Its fellow was a stinger as I knew)
And so along the wall, over the bridge,
By the straight cut to the convent. Six words there,
While I stood munching my first bread that month:
"So, boy, you're minded," quoth the good fat father
Wiping his own mouth, 'twas refection-time,—
"To quit this very miserable world?
Will   you   renounce" . . . "the   mouthful   of   bread?"
       thought I;
By no means! Brief, they made a monk of me;
I did renounce the world, its pride and greed,
Palace, farm, villa, shop and banking-house,
Trash, such as these poor devils of Medici
Have given their hearts to—all at eight years old.
Well, sir, I found in time, you may be sure,
'Twas not for nothing—the good bellyful,
The warm serge and the rope that goes all round,
And day-long blessed idleness beside!
"Let's see what the urchin's fit for"—that came next.
Not overmuch their way, I must confess.
Such a to-do! They tried me with their books:
Lord, they'd have taught me Latin in pure waste!
Flower o' the clove,
All the Latin I construe is, "amo" I love!
But, mind you, when a boy starves in the streets
Eight years together, as my fortune was,
Watching folks' faces to know who will fling
The bit of half-stripped grape-bunch he desires,
And who will curse or kick him for his pains,—
Which gentleman processional and fine,

Holding a candle to the Sacrament,
Will wink and let him lift a plate and catch
The droppings of the wax to sell again,
Or holla for the Eight and have him whipped,—
How say I?—nay, which dog bites, which lets drop
His bone from the heap of offal in the street,—
Why, soul and sense of him grow sharp alike,
He learns the look of things, and none the less
For admonition from the hunger-pinch.
I had a store of such remarks, be sure,
Which, after I found leisure, turned to use.
I drew men's faces on my copy-books,
Scrawled them within the antiphonary's marge,
Joined legs and arms to the long music-notes,
Found eyes and nose and chin for A's and B's,
And made a string of pictures of the world
Betwixt the ins and outs of verb and noun,
On the wall, the bench, the door. The monks looked black.
"Nay," quoth the Prior, "turn him out, d'ye say?
In no wise. Lose a crow and catch a lark.
What if at last we get our man of parts,
We Carmelites, like those Camaldolese
And Preaching Friars, to do our church up fine
And put the front on it that ought to be!"
And hereupon he bade me daub away.
Thank you! my head being crammed, the walls a blank,
Never was such prompt disemburdening.
First, every sort of monk, the black and white,
I drew them, fat and lean: then, folk at church,
From good old gossips waiting to confess
Their cribs of barrel-droppings, candle-ends,—
To the breathless fellow at the altar-foot,
Fresh from his murder, safe and sitting there
With the little children round him in a row
Of admiration, half for his beard and half

For that white anger of his victim's son
Shaking a fist at him with one fierce arm,
Signing himself with the other because of Christ
(Whose sad face on the cross sees only this
After the passion of a thousand years)
Till some poor girl, her apron o'er her head,
(Which the intense eyes looked through) came at eve
On tiptoe, said a word, dropped in a loaf,
Her pair of earrings and a bunch of flowers
(The brute took growling), prayed, and so was gone.
I painted all, then cried " 'Tis ask and have;
Choose, for more's ready!"—laid the ladder flat,
And showed my covered bit of cloister-wall.
The monks closed in a circle and praised loud
Till checked, taught what to see and not to see,
Being simple bodies,—"That's the very man!
Look at the boy who stoops to pat the dog!
That woman's like the Prior's niece who comes
To care about his asthma: it's the life!"
But there my triumph's straw-fire flared and funked;
Their betters took their turn to see and say:
The Prior and the learned pulled a face
And stopped all that in no time. "How? what's here?
Quite from the mark of painting, bless us all!
Faces, arms, legs and bodies like the true
As much as pea and pea! it's devil's-game!
Your business is not to catch men with show,
With homage to the perishable clay,
But lift them over it, ignore it all,
Make them forget there's such a thing as flesh.
Your business is to paint the souls of men—
Man's soul, and it's a fire, smoke . . . no, it's not . . .
It's vapour done up like a new-born babe—
(In that shape when you die it leaves your mouth)
It's . . . well, what matters talking, it's the soul!

Give us no more of body than shows soul!
Here's Giotto, with his Saint a-praising God,
That sets us praising,—why not stop with him?
Why put all thoughts of praise out of our head
With wonder at lines, colours, and what not?
Paint the soul, never mind the legs and arms!
Rub all out, try at it a second time.
Oh, that white smallish female with the breasts,
She's just my niece . . . Herodias, I would say,—
Who went and danced and got men's heads cut off!
Have it all out!" Now, is this sense, I ask?
A fine way to paint soul, by painting body
So ill, the eye can't stop there, must go further
And can't fare worse! Thus, yellow does for white
When what you put for yellow's simply black,
And any sort of meaning looks intense
When all beside itself means and looks nought.
Why can't a painter lift each foot in turn,
Left foot and right foot, go a double step,
Make his flesh liker and his soul more like,
Both in their order? Take the prettiest face,
The Prior's niece . . . patron-saint—is it so pretty
You can't discover if it means hope, fear,
Sorrow or joy? won't beauty go with these?
Suppose I've made her eyes all right and blue,
Can't I take breath and try to add life's flash,
And then add soul and heighten them threefold?
Or say there's beauty with no soul at all—
(I never saw it—put the case the same—)
If you get simple beauty and nought else,
You get about the best thing God invents:
That's somewhat: and you'll find the soul you have missed,
Within yourself, when you return him thanks.
"Rub all out!" Well, well, there's my life in short,
And so the thing has gone on ever since.

I'm grown a man no doubt, I've broken bounds:
You should not take a fellow eight years old
And make him swear to never kiss the girls.
I'm my own master, paint now as I please—
Having a friend, you see, in the Corner-house!
Lord, it's fast holding by the rings in front—
Those great rings serve more purposes than just
To plant a flag in, or tie up a horse!
And yet the old schooling sticks, the old grave eyes
Are peeping o'er my shoulder as I work,
The heads shake still—"It's art's decline, my son!
You're not of the true painters, great and old;
Brother Angelico's the man, you'll find;
Brother Lorenzo stands his single peer:
Fag on at flesh, you'll never make the third!"
Flower o' the pine,
You keep your mistr . . . manners, and I'll stick to mine!
I'm not the third, then: bless us, they must know!
Don't you think they're the likeliest to know,
They with their Latin? So, I swallow my rage,
Clench my teeth, suck my lips in tight, and paint
To please them—sometimes do and sometimes don't;
For, doing most, there's pretty sure to come
A turn, some warm eve finds me at my saints—
A laugh, a cry, the business of the world—
(*Flower o' the peach,*
Death for us all, and his own life for each!)
And my whole soul revolves, the cup runs over,
The world and life's too big to pass for a dream,
And I do these wild things in sheer despite,
And play the fooleries you catch me at,
In pure rage! The old mill-horse, out at grass
After hard years, throws up his stiff heels so,
Although the miller does not preach to him
The only good of grass is to make chaff.

What would men have? Do they like grass or no—
May they or mayn't they? all I want's the thing
Settled for ever one way. As it is,
You tell too many lies and hurt yourself:
You don't like what you only like too much,
You do like what, if given you at your word
You find abundantly detestable.
For me, I think I speak as I was taught;
I always see the garden and God there
A-making man's wife: and, my lesson learned,
The value and significance of flesh,
I can't unlearn ten minutes afterwards.

You understand me: I'm a beast, I know.
But see, now—why, I see as certainly
As that the morning-star's about to shine,
What will hap some day. We've a youngster here
Comes to our convent, studies what I do,
Slouches and stares and lets no atom drop:
His name is Guidi—he'll not mind the monks—
They call him Hulking Tom, he lets them talk—
He picks my practice up—he'll paint apace,
I hope so—though I never live so long,
I know what's sure to follow. You be judge!
You speak no Latin more than I, belike;
However, you're my man, you've seen the world
—The beauty and the wonder and the power,
The shapes of things, their colours, lights and shades,
Changes, surprises,—and God made it all!
—For what? Do you feel thankful, ay or no,
For this fair town's face, yonder river's line,
The mountain round it and the sky above,
Much more the figures of man, woman, child,
These are the frame to? What's it all about?
To be passed over, despised? or dwelt upon,

Wondered at? oh, this last course!—you say.
But why not do as well as say,—paint these
Just as they are, careless what comes of it?
God's works—paint anyone, and count it crime
To let a truth slip. Don't object, "His works
Are here already; nature is complete:
Suppose you reproduce her—(which you can't)
There's no advantage! you must beat her, then."
For, don't you mark? we're made so that we love
First when we see them painted, things we have passed
Perhaps a hundred times nor cared to see;
And so they are better, painted—better to us,
Which is the same thing. Art was given for that:
God uses us to help each other so,
Lending our minds out. Have you noticed, now,
Your cullion's hanging face? A bit of chalk,
And trust me but you should, though! How much more,
If I drew higher things with the same truth!
That were to take the Prior's pulpit-place,
Interpret God to all of you! Oh, oh,
It makes me mad to see what men shall do
And we in our graves! This world's no blot for us,
Nor blank; it means intensely, and means good:
To find its meaning is my meat and drink.
"Ay, but you don't so instigate to prayer!"
Strikes in the Prior: "when your meaning's plain
It does not say to folk—remember matins,
Or, mind you fast next Friday!" Why, for this
What need of art at all? A skull and bones,
Two bits of stick nailed crosswise, or what's best,
A bell to chime the hour with, does as well.
I painted a Saint Laurence six months since
At Prato, splashed the fresco in fine style:
"How looks my painting, now the scaffold's down?"
I ask a brother: "Hugely," he returns—

Already not one phiz of your three slaves
Who turn the Deacon off his toasted side,
But's scratched and prodded to our heart's content,
The pious people have so eased their own
With coming to say prayers there in a rage:
We get on fast to see the bricks beneath.
Expect another job this time next year,
For pity and religion grow i' the crowd—
Your painting serves its purpose!" Hang the fools!

—That is—you'll not mistake an idle word
Spoke in a huff by a poor monk, God wot,
Tasting the air this spicy night which turns
The unaccustomed head like Chianti wine!
Oh, the church knows! don't misreport me, now!
It's natural a poor monk out of bounds
Should have his apt word to excuse himself:
And hearken how I plot to make amends.
I have bethought me: I shall paint a piece
. . . There's for you! Give me six months, then go, see
Something in Sant' Ambrogio's! Bless the nuns!
They want a cast o' my office. I shall paint
God in the midst, Madonna and her babe,
Ringed by a bowery flowery angel-brood,
Lilies and vestments and white faces, sweet
As puff on puff of grated orris-root
When ladies crowd to Church at midsummer.
And then i' the front, of course a saint or two—
Saint John, because he saves the Florentines,
Saint Ambrose, who puts down in black and white
The convent's friends and gives them a long day,
And Job, I must have him there past mistake,
The man of Uz (and Us without the z,
Painters who need his patience). Well, all these
Secured at their devotion, up shall come

Out of a corner when you least expect,
As one by a dark stair into a great light,
Music and talking, who but Lippo! I!—
Mazed, motionless and moonstruck—I'm the man!
Back I shrink—what is this I see and hear?
I, caught up with my monk's-things by mistake,
My old serge gown and rope that goes all round,
I, in this presence, this pure company!
Where's a hole, where's a corner for escape?
Then steps a sweet angelic slip of a thing
Forward, puts out a soft palm—"Not so fast!"
—Addresses the celestial presence, "nay—
He made you and devised you, after all,
Though he's none of you! Could Saint John there draw—
His camel-hair make up a painting-brush?
We come to brother Lippo for all that,
Iste perfecit opus!" So, all smile—
I shuffle sideways with my blushing face
Under the cover of a hundred wings
Thrown like a spread of kirtles when you're gay
And play hot cockles, all the doors being shut,
Till, wholly unexpected, in there pops
The hothead husband! Thus I scuttle off
To some safe bench behind, not letting go
The palm of her, the little lily thing
That spoke the good word for me in the nick,
Like the Prior's niece . . . Saint Lucy, I would say.
And so all's saved for me, and for the church
A pretty picture gained. Go, six months hence!
Your hand, sir, and good-bye: no lights, no lights!
The street's hushed and I know my own way back,
Don't fear me! There's the grey beginning. Zooks!

ROBERT BROWNING

An excellent criticism and interpretation of this poem is in Owen Wister's *The Virginian;* only the meeting was not at dusk, but late at night. The man of course is speaking in both pieces; if there is any doubt about this, Browning settled it by saying so, in an explanation of the work published after his death.

As showing his care for details, he corrected the late Mrs. LeMoyne when she read the piece aloud to him
And the little startled waves that leap
which gives a different rhythm from the one he wrote and expresses another motion of the sea.

MEETING AT NIGHT

THE grey sea and the long black land;
And the yellow half-moon large and low;
And the startled little waves that leap
In fiery ringlets from their sleep,
As I gain the cove with pushing prow,
And quench its speed i' the slushy sand.

Then a mile of warm sea-scented beach;
Three fields to cross till a farm appears;
A tap at the pane, the quick sharp scratch
And blue spurt of a lighted match,
And a voice less loud, through its joys and fears,
Than the two hearts beating each to each!

PARTING AT MORNING

ROUND the cape of a sudden came the sea,
And the sun looked over the mountain's rim:
And straight was a path of gold for him,
And the need of a world of men for me.

ROBERT BROWNING

[514]

The best of all Browning's poems on music. The theory of music set forth here, distinguishing music from arts like painting and poetry, is precisely similar to that of Schopenhauer; although Browning's conclusion is optimism. The evanescent nature of the improvisation does not fill one with despair, but rather with joy; for its source is inexhaustible.

ABT VOGLER

(After he has been extemporizing upon the musical instrument of his invention)

WOULD that the structure brave, the manifold music I
  build,
  Bidding my organ obey, calling its keys to their work,
Claiming each slave of the sound, at a touch, as when Solomon willed
  Armies of angels that soar, legions of demons that lurk,
Man, brute, reptile, fly,—alien of end and of aim,
  Adverse, each from the other heaven-high, hell-deep
    removed,—
Should rush into sight at once as he named the ineffable
  Name,
  And pile him a palace straight, to pleasure the princess
    he loved!

Would it might tarry like his, the beautiful building of
  mine,
  This which my keys in a crowd pressed and importuned
    to raise!
Ah, one and all, how they helped, would dispart now and
  now combine,
  Zealous to hasten the work, heighten their master his
    praise!

And one would bury his brow with a blind plunge down to
    hell,
Burrow awhile and build, broad on the roots of things,
Then up again swim into sight, having based me my palace
    well,
Founded it, fearless of flame, flat on the nether springs.

And another would mount and march, like the excellent
    minion he was,
Ay, another and yet another, one crowd but with many a
    crest,
Raising my rampired walls of gold as transparent as
    glass,
Eager to do and die, yield each his place to the rest:
For higher still and higher (as a runner tips with fire,
When a great illumination surprises a festal night—
Outlined round and round Rome's dome from space to
    spire)
Up, the pinnacled glory reached, and the pride of my soul
    was in sight.

In sight? Not half! for it seemed, it was certain, to match
    man's birth,
Nature in turn conceived, obeying an impulse as I;
And the emulous heaven yearned down, made effort to reach
    the earth,
As the earth had done her best, in my passion, to scale the
    sky:
Novel splendours burst forth, grew familiar and dwelt with
    mine,
Not a point nor peak but found and fixed its wandering
    star;
Meteor-moons, balls of blaze: and they did not pale nor
    pine,

For earth had attained to heaven, there was no more near
    nor far.

Nay more; for there wanted not who walked in the glare
    and glow,
    Presences plain in the place; or, fresh from the Proto-
      plast,
Furnished for ages to come, when a kindlier wind should
    blow,
    Lured now to begin and live, in a house to their liking at
      last;
Or else the wonderful Dead who have passed through the
    body and gone,
    But were back once more to breathe in an old world worth
      their new:
What never had been, was now; what was, as it shall be
    anon;
    And what is,—shall I say, matched both? for I was made
      perfect too.

All through my keys that gave their sounds to a wish of my
    soul,
    All through my soul that praised as its wish flowed visibly
    forth,
All through music and me! For think, had I painted the
    whole,
    Why, there it had stood, to see, nor the process so wonder-
    worth:
Had I written the same, made verse—still, effect proceeds
    from cause,
    Ye know why the forms are fair, ye hear how the tale is
    told;
It is all triumphant art, but art in obedience to laws,
    Painter and poet are proud in the artist-list enrolled:—

But here is the finger of God, a flash of the will that can,
   Existent behind all laws, that made them and, lo, they are!
And I know not if, save in this, such gift be allowed to man,
   That out of three sounds he frame, not a fourth sound,
      but a star.
Consider it well: each tone of our scale in itself is naught;
   It is everywhere in the world—loud, soft, and all is said:
Give it to me to use! I mix it with two in my thought:
   And there! Ye have heard and seen: consider and bow the
      head!

Well, it is gone at last, the palace of music I reared;
   Gone! and the good tears start, the praises that come too
      slow;
For one is assured at first, one scarce can say that he feared,
   That he even gave it a thought, the gone thing was to go.
Never to be again! But many more of the kind
   As good, nay, better perchance: is this your comfort to
      me?
To me, who must be saved because I cling with my mind
   To the same, same self, same love, same God: ay, what
      was, shall be.

Therefore to whom turn I but to thee, the ineffable Name?
   Builder and maker, thou, of houses not made with hands!
What, have fear of change from thee who art ever the same?
   Doubt that thy power can fill the heart that thy power
      expands?
There shall never be one lost good! What was, shall live as
      before;
   The evil is null, is naught, is silence implying sound;
What was good shall be good, with, for evil, so much good
      more;
   On the earth the broken arcs; in the heaven a perfect
      round.

All we have willed or hoped or dreamed of good shall exist;
  Not its semblance, but itself; no beauty, nor good, nor
    power
Whose voice has gone forth, but each survives for the
    melodist
  When eternity affirms the conception of an hour.
The high that proved too high, the heroic for earth too
    hard,
  The passion that left the ground to lose itself in the sky,
Are music sent up to God by the lover and the bard;
  Enough that he heard it once: we shall hear it by and by.

And what is our failure here but a triumph's evidence
  For the fulness of the days? Have we withered or agon-
    ized?
Why else was the pause prolonged but that singing might
    issue thence?
  Why rushed the discords in but that harmony should be
    prized?
Sorrow is hard to bear, and doubt is slow to clear,
  Each sufferer says his say, his scheme of the weal and
    woe:
But God has a few of us whom he whispers in the ear;
  The rest may reason and welcome: 't is we musicians know.

Well, it is earth with me; silence resumes her reign:
  I will be patient and proud, and soberly acquiesce.
Give me the keys. I feel for the common chord again,
  Sliding by semitones till I sink to the minor, yes,
And I blunt it into a ninth, and I stand on alien ground,
  Surveying awhile the heights I rolled from into the deep;
Which, hark, I have dared and done, for my resting-place is
    found,
  The C Major of this life: so, now I will try to sleep.

ROBERT BROWNING

She is a young American poet who is steadily advancing.

THE SHADOW

THIS is the time when we have all we need . . .
The hour is quiet, and you are very near.
We can breathe the selfsame air; we can wait and hear
The same late music, measuring time and space
In briefest intervals; or we can read
Our books obliviously, in the usual place.

And there is the bowl of flowers, and meat and bread
Set out, and wine in amber-tinted glasses
Full of the evening light . . . If a shadow passes
There, by the window, on the familiar street,
Why should I feel this moment full of dread?
Why should you stand and watch its slow retreat?

Since we are here, look not so far away . . .
What can you find past any window's rim
More marvellous than this? . . . The day grows dim—
I am afraid the dark will cover me
Too closely . . . You might turn, with a word to say,
And so find no one for your eyes to see. . . .

Turn back to me! What would you have—what more?
This is our long tomorrow—the wave of time
Ready to break, with one high reach to climb
Before it bends and sweeps us wide apart—
The long, long reach—out—upward—towards some
       shore
Remote and far and frightening to the heart.

                                    BERNICE KENYON

Whittier reached his highest altitude in religious aspiration and nothing can ever make this poem obsolete.

THE ETERNAL GOODNESS

O FRIENDS! with whom my feet have trod
    The quiet aisles of prayer,
Glad witness to your zeal for God
    And love of man I bear.

I trace your lines of argument,
    Your logic linked and strong
I weigh as one who dreads dissent,
    And fears a doubt as wrong.

But still my human hands are weak
    To hold your iron creeds:
Against the words you bid me speak
    My heart within me pleads.

Who fathoms the Eternal Thought?
    Who talks of scheme and plan?
The Lord is God! He needeth not
    The poor device of man.

I walk with bare, hushed feet the ground
    Ye tread with boldness shod;
I dare not fix with mete and bound
    The love and power of God.

Ye praise His justice; even such
    His pitying love I deem:
Ye seek a king; I fain would touch
    The robe that hath no seam.

Ye see the curse which overbroods
  A world of pain and loss;
I hear our Lord's beatitudes
  And prayer upon the cross.

More than your schoolmen teach, within
  Myself, alas! I know:
Too dark ye cannot paint the sin,
  Too small the merit show.

I bow my forehead to the dust,
  I veil mine eyes for shame,
And urge, in trembling self-distrust,
  A prayer without a claim.

I see the wrong that round me lies,
  I feel the guilt within;
I hear, with groan and travail-cries,
  The world confess its sin.

Yet, in the maddening maze of things,
  And tossed by storm and flood,
·To one fixed trust my spirit clings;
  I know that God is good!

Not mine to look where cherubim
  And seraphs may not see,
But nothing can be good in Him
  Which evil is in me.

The wrong that pains my soul below
  I dare not throne above,
·I know not of His hate,—I know
  His goodness and His love.

I dimly guess from blessings known
  Of greater out of sight,
And with the chastened Psalmist, own
  His judgments too are right.

I long for household voices gone,
  For vanished smiles I long,
But God hath led my dear ones on,
  And He can do no wrong.

I know not what the future hath
  Of marvel or surprise,
Assured alone that life and death
  His mercy underlies.

And if my heart and flesh are weak
  To bear an untried pain,
The bruisèd reed He will not break,
  But strengthen and sustain.

No offering of my own I have,
  Nor works my faith to prove;
I can but give the gifts He gave,
  And plead His love for love.

And so beside the Silent Sea
  I wait the muffled oar;
No harm from Him can come to me
  On ocean or on shore.

I know not where His islands lift
  Their fronded palms in air;
I only know I cannot drift
  Beyond His love and care.

O brothers! if my faith is vain,
   If hopes like these betray,
Pray for me that my feet may gain
   The sure and safer way.

And Thou, O Lord! by whom are seen
   Thy creatures as they be,
Forgive me if too close I lean
   My human heart on Thee!
JOHN GREENLEAF WHITTIER

━━

Although his belief in himself was not small, even Walt
Whitman would have been astonished if he could have known
of his future fame and influence. No man has ever written
a finer *apologia* in verse than the few lines *Spirit that formed
this scene.*

To the Man-of-War Bird

[*The "frigate-bird," or petrel, is distinguished for its
size, swiftness, and endurance—never alighting to rest on
the water.*]

THOU who hast slept all night upon the storm,
Waking renew'd on thy prodigious pinions
(Burst the wild storm? above it thou ascend'st,
And rested on the sky, thy slave that cradled thee),
Now a blue point, far, far in heaven floating,
As to the light emerging here on deck I watch thee
(Myself a speck, a point on the world's floating vast).

Far, far at sea,
After the night's fierce drifts have strewn the shore with
    wrecks,
With re-appearing day as now so happy and serene,
The rosy and elastic dawn, the flashing sun,
The limpid spread of air cerulean,
Thou also re-appearest.

Thou born to match the gale (thou art all wings),
To cope with heaven and earth and sea and hurricane,
Thou ship of air that never furl'st thy sails,
Days, even weeks untired and onward, through spaces,
    realms gyrating,
At dusk that look'st on Senegal, at morn America,
That sport'st amid the lightning-flash and thunder-cloud,
In them, in thy experience, had'st thou my soul,
What joys! what joys were thine!
                      WALT WHITMAN

When I Heard the Learn'd Astronomer

When I heard the learn'd astronomer;
When the proofs, the figures, were ranged in columns before
    me;
When I was shown the charts and the diagrams, to add,
    divide, and measure them;
When I, sitting, heard the astronomer, where he lectured
    with much applause in the lecture-room,
How soon, unaccountable, I became tired and sick;
Till rising and gliding out, I wander'd off by myself,
In the mystical moist night-air, and from time to time,
Look'd up in perfect silence at the stars.
                      WALT WHITMAN

WHEN LILACS LAST IN THE DOORYARD BLOOM'D

1

WHEN lilacs last in the dooryard bloom'd,
And the great star early droop'd in the western sky in the
    night,
I mourn'd, and yet shall mourn with ever-returning spring.

Ever-returning spring, trinity sure to me you bring,
Lilac blooming perennial and drooping star in the west,
And thought of him I love.

2

O powerful western fallen star!
O shades of night—O moody, tearful night!
O great star disappear'd—O the black murk that hides the
    star!
O cruel hands that hold me powerless—O helpless soul of
    me!
O harsh surrounding cloud that will not free my soul.

3

In the dooryard fronting an old farm-house near the white-
    wash'd palings,
Stands the lilac-bush tall-growing with heart-shaped leaves
    of rich green,
With many a pointed blossom rising delicate, with the
    perfume strong I love,
With every leaf a miracle—and from this bush in the door-
    yard,
With delicate-colour'd blossoms and heart-shaped leaves of
    rich green,
A sprig with its flower I break.

4

In the swamp in secluded recesses,
A shy and hidden bird is warbling a song.

Solitary the thrush,
The hermit withdrawn to himself, avoiding the settlements,
Sings by himself a song.

Song of the bleeding throat,
Death's outlet song of life, (for well dear brother I know,
If thou wast not granted to sing thou would'st surely die.)

5

Over the breast of the spring, the land, amid cities,
Amid lanes and through old woods, where lately the violets
    peep'd from the ground, spotting the grey debris,
Amid the grass in the fields each side of the lanes, passing
    the endless grass,
Passing the yellow-spear'd wheat, every grain from its
    shroud in the dark-brown fields uprisen,
Passing the apple-tree blows of white and pink in the
    orchards,
Carrying a corpse to where it shall rest in the grave,
Night and day journeys a coffin.

6

Coffin that passes through lanes and streets,
Through day and night with the great cloud darkening the
    land,
With the pomp of the inloop'd flags with the cities draped in
    black,
With the show of the States themselves as of crape-veil'd
    women standing,

With processions long and winding and the flambeaus of
    the night,
With the countless torches lit, with the silent sea of faces
    and the unbared heads
With the waiting depot, the arriving coffin, and the sombre
    faces,
With dirges through the night, with the thousand voices
    rising strong and solemn,
With all the mournful voices of the dirges pour'd around
    the coffin,
The dim-lit churches and the shuddering organs—where
    amid these you journey,
With the tolling tolling bells' perpetual clang,
Here, coffin that slowly passes,
I give you my sprig of lilac.

7

(Not for you, for one alone,
Blossoms and branches green to coffins all I bring,
For fresh as the morning, thus would I chant a song for you
    O sane and sacred death.

All over bouquets of roses,
O death, I cover you over with roses and early lilies,
But mostly and now the lilac that blooms the first,
Copious I break, I break the sprigs from the bushes,
With loaded arms I come, pouring for you,
For you and the coffins all of you O death.)

8

O western orb sailing the heaven,
Now I know what you must have meant as a month since I
    walk'd,
As I walk'd in silence the transparent shadowy night,

As I saw you had something to tell as you bent to me night
    after night,
As you droop'd from the sky low down as if to my side,
    (while the other stars all look'd on,)
As we wander'd together the solemn night, (for something I
    know not what kept me from sleep,)
As the night advanced, and I saw on the rim of the west
    how full you were of woe,
As I stood on the rising ground in the breeze in the cool
    transparent night,
As I watch'd where you pass'd and was lost in the nether-
    ward black of the night,
As my soul in its trouble dissatisfied sank, as where you
    sad orb,
Concluded, dropt in the night, and was gone.

9

Sing on there in the swamp,
O singer bashful and tender, I hear your notes, I hear your
    call,
I hear, I come presently, I understand you,
But a moment I linger, for the lustrous star has detain'd me,
The star my departing comrade holds and detains me.

10

O how shall I warble myself for the dead one there I loved?
And how shall I deck my song for the large sweet soul that
    has gone?
And what shall my perfume be for the grave of him I love?

Sea-winds blown from east and west,
Blown from the Eastern sea and blown from the Western
    sea, till there on the prairies meeting,
These and with these and the breath of my chant,
I'll perfume the grave of him I love.

11

O what shall I hang on the chamber walls?
And what shall the pictures be that I hang on the walls,
To adorn the burial-house of him I love?

Pictures of growing spring and farms and homes,
With the Fourth-month eve at sundown, and the grey smoke
    lucid and bright,
With floods of the yellow gold of the gorgeous, indolent,
    sinking sun, burning, expanding the air,
With the fresh sweet herbage under foot, and the pale green
    leaves of the trees prolific,
In the distance the flowing glaze, the breast of the river,
    with a wind-dapple here and there,
With ranging hills on the banks, with many a line against
    the sky, and shadows,
And the city at hand with dwellings so dense, and stacks of
    chimneys,
And all the scenes of life and the workshops, and the work-
    men homeward returning.

12

Lo, body and soul—this land,
My own Manhattan with spires, and the sparkling and
    hurrying tides, and the ships,
The varied and ample land, the South and the North in the
    light, Ohio's shores and flashing Missouri,
And ever the far-spreading prairies cover'd with grass and
    corn.

Lo, the most excellent sun so calm and haughty,
The violet and purple morn with just-felt breezes,
The gentle soft-born measureless light,

The miracle spreading bathing all, the fulfill'd noon,
The coming eve delicious, the welcome night and the stars,
Over my cities shining all, enveloping man and land.

13

Sing on, sing on you grey-brown bird,
Sing from the swamps, the recesses, pour your chant from
    the bushes,
Limitless out of the dusk, out of the cedars and pines.

Sing on, dearest brother, warble your reedy song,
Loud human song, with voice of uttermost woe.

O liquid and free and tender!
O wild and loose to my soul—O wondrous singer!
You only I hear—yet the star holds me, (but will soon
    depart,)
Yet the lilac with mastering odor holds me.

14

Now while I sat in the day and look'd forth,
In the close of the day with its light and the fields of spring,
    and the farmers preparing their crops,
In the large unconscious scenery of my land with its lakes
    and forests,
In the heavenly aerial beauty, (after the perturb'd winds
    and the storms,)
Under the arching heavens of the afternoon swift passing,
    and the voices of children and women,
The many-moving sea-tides, and I saw the ships how they
    sail'd,
And the summer approaching with richness, and the fields
    all busy with labour,

And the infinite separate houses, how they all went on, each
    with its meals and minutia of daily usages,
And the streets how their throbbings throbb'd, and the cities
    pent—lo, then and there,
Falling upon them all and among them all, enveloping me
    with the rest,
Appear'd the cloud, appear'd the long black trail,
And I knew death, its thought, and the sacred knowledge of
    death.

Then with the knowledge of death as walking one side of me,
And the thought of death close-walking the other side of me,
And I in the middle as with companions, and as holding the
    hands of companions,
I fled forth to the hiding receiving night that talks not,
Down to the shores of the water, the path by the swamp in
    the dimness,
To the solemn shadowy cedars and ghostly pines so still.
And the singer so shy to the rest receiv'd me,
The grey-brown bird I know receiv'd us comrades three,
And he sang the carol of death, and a verse for him I love.

From deep secluded recesses,
From the fragrant cedars and the ghostly pines so still,
Came the carol of the bird.

And the charm of the carol rapt me,
As I held as if by their hands my comrades in the night,
And the voice of my spirit tallied the song of the bird.

Come lovely and soothing death,
Undulate round the world, serenely arriving, arriving,
In the day, in the night, to all, to each,
Sooner or later delicate death.

Prais'd be the fathomless universe,
For life and joy, and for objects and knowledge curious,
And for love, sweet love—but praise! praise! praise!
For the sure-enwinding arms of cool-enfolding death.

Dark mother always gliding near with soft feet,
Have none chanted for thee a chant of fullest welcome?
Then I chant it for thee, I glorify thee above all,
I bring thee a song that when thou must indeed come, come
    unfalteringly.

Approach strong deliveress,
When it is so, when thou hast taken them I joyously sing
    the dead,
Lost in the loving floating ocean of thee,
Laved in the flood of thy bliss O death.

From me to thee glad serenades,
Dances for thee I propose saluting thee, adornments and
    feastings for thee,
And the sights of the open landscape and the high-spread
    sky are fitting,
And life and the fields, and the huge and thoughtful night.

The night in silence under many a star,
The ocean shore and the husky whispering wave whose voice
    I know,
And the soul turning to thee O vast and well-veil'd death,
And the body gratefully nestling close to thee.

Over the tree-tops I float thee a song,
Over the rising and sinking waves, over the myriad fields
    and the prairies wide,

Over the dense-pack'd cities all and the teeming wharves
and ways,
I float this carol with joy, with joy to thee O death.

15

To the tally of my soul,
Loud and strong kept up the grey-brown bird,
With pure deliberate notes spreading filling the night.
Loud in the pines and cedars dim,
Clear in the freshness moist and the swamp-perfume,
And I with my comrades there in the night.

While my sight that was bound in my eyes unclosed,
As to long panoramas of visions.

And I saw askant the armies,
I saw as in noiseless dreams hundreds of battle-flags,
Borne through the smoke of the battles and pierc'd with
    missiles I saw them,
And carried hither and yon through the smoke, and torn
    and bloody,
And at last but a few shreds left on the staffs, (and all in
    silence,)
And the staffs all splinter'd and broken.

I saw battle-corpses, myriads of them,
And the white skeletons of young men, I saw them,
I saw the debris and debris of all the slain soldiers of the
    war,
But I saw they were not as was thought,
They themselves were fully at rest, they suffer'd not,
The living remain'd and suffer'd, the mother suffer'd,
And the wife and the child and the musing comrade suffer'd,
And the armies that remain'd suffer'd.

16

Passing the visions, passing the night,
Passing, unloosing the hold of my comrades' hands,
Passing the song of the hermit bird and the tallying song of
    my soul,
Victorious song, death's outlet song, yet varying ever-
    altering song,
As low and wailing, yet clear the notes, rising and falling,
    flooding the night,
Sadly sinking and fainting, as warning and warning, and
    yet again bursting with joy,
Covering the earth and filling the spread of the heaven,
As that powerful psalm in the night I heard from recesses,
Passing, I leave thee lilac with heart-shaped leaves,
I leave thee there in the dooryard, blooming, returning with
    spring.

I cease from my song for thee,
From my gaze on thee in the west, fronting the west, com-
    muning with thee,
O comrade lustrous with silver face in the night.

Yet each to keep and all, retrievements out of the night,
The song, the wondrous chant of the grey-brown bird,
And the tallying chant, the echo arous'd in my soul,
With the lustrous and drooping star with the countenance
    full of woe,
With the holders holding my hand nearing the call of the bird,
Comrades mine and I in the midst, and their memory ever
    to keep, for the dead I loved so well,
For the sweetest, wisest soul of all my days and lands—and
    this for his dear sake,
Lilac and star and bird twined with the chant of my soul,
There in the fragrant pines and the cedars dusk and dim.

WALT WHITMAN

George Wither, who wrote this "devil take her" song, was a lawyer, a captain of cavalry in several bloody battles, a Puritan who wrote many hymns to be sung in churches, and a man of such outspoken opinions that he was repeatedly put in prison. He was once captured by the enemy and was saved from death only by Sir John Denham, who said that so long as Wither lived, he himself would not be regarded as the worst living poet.

SHALL I, WASTING IN DESPAIR

SHALL I, wasting in despair,
Die because a woman's fair?
Or make pale my cheeks with care
'Cause another's rosy are?
Be she fairer than the day,
Or the flowery meads in May,
   If she be not so to me,
    What care I how fair she be?

Should my heart be grieved or pined
'Cause I see a woman kind?
Or a well-disposèd nature
Joinèd with a lovely feature?
Be she meeker, kinder than
Turtle-dove or pelican,
   If she be not so to me,
    What care I how kind she be?

Shall a woman's virtues move
Me to perish for her love?
Or her well-deserving known
Make me quite forget mine own?

Be she with that goodness blest
Which may gain her name of best,
 If she be not such to me,
 What care I how good she be?

'Cause her fortune seems too high
Shall I play the fool and die?
Those that bear a noble mind,
Where they want of riches find,
Think what with them they would do
That without them dare to woo.
 And unless that mind I see
 What care I though great she be?

Great, or good, or kind, or fair,
I will ne'er the more despair;
If she love me, this believe,
I will die ere she shall grieve.
If she slight me when I woo,
I can scorn and let her go;
 For if she be not for me,
 What care I for whom she be?

GEORGE WITHER

Carl Sandburg has in his own fashion harmonised the discordant noises of Chicago and has expressed the tumultuous variety of modern life. Yet I like most of all his poems the quiet ones like these.

NOCTURNE IN A DESERTED BRICKYARD

STUFF of the moon
Runs on the lapping sand
Out to the longest shadows.

Under the curving willows,
And round the creep of the wave line,
Fluxions of yellow and dusk on the waters
Make a wide dreaming pansy of an old pond in the night.

CARL SANDBURG

Fog

THE fog comes
on little cat feet.
It sits looking
over harbour and city
on silent haunches
and then moves on.

CARL SANDBURG

It is fortunate Emily Brontë had so much courage, for she needed it.

Last Lines: No Coward Soul Is Mine

No coward soul is mine,
No trembler in the world's storm-troubled sphere.
I see Heaven's glories shine,
And Faith shines equal, arming me from Fear.

O God within my breast,
Almighty, ever-present Deity!
Life—that in me hast rest,
As I—undying Life—have power in Thee!

Vain are the thousand creeds
That move men's hearts: unutterably vain;
Worthless as withered weeds,
Or idlest froth amid the boundless main,

To waken doubt in one
Holding so fast by Thy infinity,
So surely anchored on
The steadfast rock of immortality.

With wide-embracing love
Thy Spirit animates eternal years,
Pervades and broods above,
Changes, sustains, dissolves, creates, and rears.

Though earth and moon were gone,
And suns and universes ceased to be,
And Thou wert left alone,
Every existence would exist in Thee.

There is not room for Death,
Nor atom that his might could render void:
Since Thou art Being and Breath,
And what THOU art may never be destroyed.

EMILY BRONTË

Henley's *Invictus* was born of suffering.

INVICTUS

OUT of the night that covers me,
    Black as the pit from pole to pole,
I thank whatever gods may be
    For my unconquerable soul.

[539]

In the fell clutch of circumstance
  I have not winced nor cried aloud.
Under the bludgeonings of chance
  My head is bloody, but unbowed.

Beyond this place of wrath and tears
  Looms but the horror of the shade,
And yet the menace of the years
  Finds, and shall find, me unafraid.

It matters not how strait the gate,
  How charged with punishments the scroll,
I am the master of my fate:
  I am the captain of my soul.

WILLIAM ERNEST HENLEY

The best poem celebrating the courage of the Confederates
was written by this Englishman.

ROMANCE

'TALK of pluck!' pursued the sailor,
Set at euchre on his elbow,
'I was on the wharf at Charleston,
Just ashore from off the runner.

'It was grey and dirty weather,
And I heard a drum go rolling,
Rub-a-dubbing in the distance,
Awful, dour-like, and defiant.

'In and out among the cotton,
Mud, and chains, and stores, and anchors,
Tramped a squad of battered scarecrows,—
Poor old Dixie's bottom dollar!

[540]

'Some had toes, but all had rifles.
Them that wasn't bald, was beardless,
And the drum was rolling *Dixie*,
And they stepped to it like men, sir!

'Rags and tatters, belts and bayonets,
On they swung, the drum a-rolling,
Mum and sour. It looked like fighting,
And they meant it too, by thunder!'

WILLIAM ERNEST HENLEY

"A bit of nonsense now and then."

THE ROOF

THE roof it has an easy time,
     A-lying in the sun;
The walls they have to hold it up;
     They do not have much fun.

GELETT BURGESS

There are many cat poems in literature, as nearly all writers love cats. Gray, who cared little for his own work, was rather fond of this mock-heroic poem, and always included it when he collected his verse. The cat belonged to his friend Horace Walpole.

ON THE DEATH OF A FAVOURITE CAT

DROWNED IN A TUB OF GOLD-FISHES

'TWAS on a lofty vase's side,
Where China's gayest art had dy'd
The azure flowers, that blow;

Demurest of the tabby kind,
The pensive Selima reclin'd,
Gazed on the lake below.

Her conscious tail her joy declar'd;
The fair round face, the snowy beard,
The velvet of her paws,
Her coat, that with the tortoise vies,
Her ears of jet, and emerald eyes,
She saw; and purr'd applause.

Still had she gazed; but 'midst the tide
Two angel forms were seen to glide,
Two Genii of the stream:
Their scaly armour's Tyrian hue
Thro' richest purple to the view
Betray'd a golden gleam.

The hapless nymph with wonder saw:
A whisker first, and then a claw,
With many an ardent wish,
She stretch'd in vain to reach the prize:—
What female heart can gold despise?
What Cat's averse to fish?

Presumptuous maid! with looks intent
Again she stretch'd, again she bent,
Nor knew the gulf between.
(Malignant fate sat by, and smiled)
The slippery verge her feet beguiled,
She tumbled headlong in.

Eight times emerging from the flood
She mew'd to every watery God,
Some speedy aid to send.

No Dolphin came, no Nereid stirr'd:
Nor cruel Tom, nor Susan heard.
A favourite has no friend!

From hence, ye beauties undeceived,
Know, one false step is ne'er retrieved,
And be with caution bold.
Not all that tempts your wandering eyes
And heedless hearts, is lawful prize:
Nor all, that glisters, gold.

THOMAS GRAY

Although nothing is easier to understand than Tennyson's ideas as expressed in verse, he himself is to me one of the greatest of mysteries. I cannot discover that he ever said anything in conversation that was memorable; his mind, although richly stored with the best of the world's literature, seemed to lack originality. Once, meeting Browning at an evening party, he asked him "What do you think of Shelley?" just like that, and Browning did not know what to think of Tennyson. When he went to Switzerland, he said he was disappointed in the mountains. Yet he had intimate friends like Carlyle, who admired him immensely. He was perhaps a good listener.

But he had the one gift of magnificent poetic expression. He will forever be one of the great poets of the world. It is language, and not thought, that makes the poet. Sooner or later, we all come back to Tennyson.

BREAK, BREAK, BREAK

BREAK, break, break,
On thy cold grey stones, O Sea!
And I would that my tongue could utter
The thoughts that arise in me.

O well for the fisherman's boy,
   That he shouts with his sister at play!
O well for the sailor lad,
   That he sings in his boat on the bay!

And the stately ships go on
   To their haven under the hill;
But O for the touch of a vanish'd hand,
   And the sound of a voice that is still!

Break, break, break,
   At the foot of thy crags, O Sea!
But the tender grace of a day that is dead
   Will never come back to me.

ALFRED TENNYSON

Tears, Idle Tears

Tears, idle tears, I know not what they mean,
Tears from the depth of some divine despair
Rise in the heart, and gather to the eyes,
In looking on the happy Autumn-fields,
And thinking of the days that are no more.

Fresh as the first beam glittering on a sail,
That brings our friends up from the underworld,
Sad as the last which reddens over one
That sinks with all we love below the verge;
So sad, so fresh, the days that are no more.

Ah, sad and strange as in dark summer dawns
The earliest pipe of half-awaken'd birds
To dying ears, when unto dying eyes
The casement slowly grows a glimmering square;
So sad, so strange, the days that are no more.

Dear as remember'd kisses after death,
And sweet as those by hopeless fancy feign'd
On lips that are for others; deep as love,
Deep as first love, and wild with all regret;
O Death in Life, the days that are no more.

ALFRED TENNYSON

═══

John Stuart Mill, in the most famous passage in his
Autobiography, has expressed for many readers the peculiar
healing power of Wordsworth; and in his poem *Wordsworth's Grave,* Sir William Watson has shown why it is,
that with so many limitations, Wordsworth is one of the
greatest of all English poets. He is the best illustration
of his own definition—*emotion remembered in tranquillity.*
His poetry was never needed more than now.

WE ARE SEVEN

——A SIMPLE Child,
That lightly draws its breath,
And feels its life in every limb,
What should it know of death?

I met a little cottage Girl:
She was eight years old, she said;
Her hair was thick with many a curl
That clustered round her head.

She had a rustic, woodland air,
And she was wildly clad:
Her eyes were fair, and very fair;
—Her beauty made me glad.

"Sisters and brothers, little Maid,
How many may you be?"
"How many? Seven in all," she said,
And wondering looked at me.

"And where are they? I pray you tell."
She answered, "Seven are we;
And two of us at Conway dwell,
And two are gone to sea.

"Two of us in the church-yard lie,
My sister and my brother;
And, in the church-yard cottage, I
Dwell near them with my mother."

"You say that two at Conway dwell,
And two are gone to sea,
Yet ye are seven!—I pray you tell,
Sweet maid, how this may be."

Then did the little Maid reply,
"Seven boys and girls are we;
Two of us in the church-yard lie,
Beneath the church-yard tree."

"You run about, my little Maid,
Your limbs they are alive;
If two are in the church-yard laid,
Then ye are only five."

"Their graves are green, they may be seen,"
The little maid replied,
"Twelve steps or more from my mother's door,
And they are side by side.

"My stockings there I often knit,
My kerchief there I hem;
And there upon the ground I sit,
And sing a song to them.

"And often after sunset, sir,
When it is light and fair,
I take my little porringer,
And eat my supper there.

"The first that died was sister Jane;
In bed she moaning lay,
Till God released her of her pain;
And then she went away.

"So in the church-yard she was laid;
And, when the grass was dry,
Together round her grave we played,
My brother John and I.

"And when the ground was white with snow,
And I could run and slide,
My brother John was forced to go,
And he lies by her side."

"How many are you, then," said I,
"If they two are in heaven?"
Quick was the little maid's reply,
"O master! we are seven."

"But they are dead; those two are dead!
Their spirits are in heaven!"
'T was throwing words away; for still
The little Maid would have her will,
And said, "Nay, we are seven!"

WILLIAM WORDSWORTH

SONNET

THE world is too much with us; late and soon,
Getting and spending, we lay waste our powers:
Little we see in Nature that is ours;
We have given our hearts away, a sordid boon!
The Sea that bares her bosom to the moon;
The winds that will be howling at all hours,
And are up-gathered now like sleeping flowers;
For this, for everything, we are out of tune;
It moves us not.——Great God! I'd rather be
A Pagan suckled in a creed outworn;
So might I, standing on this pleasant lea,
Have glimpses that would make me less forlorn;
Have sight of Proteus rising from the sea;
Or hear old Triton blow his wreathèd horn.

WILLIAM WORDSWORTH

THE SOLITARY REAPER

BEHOLD her, single in the field,
Yon solitary Highland Lass!
Reaping and singing by herself;
Stop here, or gently pass!
Alone she cuts and binds the grain,
And sings a melancholy strain;
O listen! for the Vale profound
Is overflowing with the sound.

No Nightingale did ever chant
More welcome notes to weary bands
Of travellers in some shady haunt,
Among Arabian sands:

A voice so thrilling ne'er was heard
In spring-time from the Cuckoo-bird,
Breaking the silence of the seas
Among the farthest Hebrides.

Will no one tell me what she sings?—
Perhaps the plaintive numbers flow
For old, unhappy, far-off things,
And battles long ago:
Or is it some more humble lay,
Familiar matter of today?
Some natural sorrow, loss, or pain,
That has been, and may be again?

Whate'er the theme, the maiden sang
As if her song could have no ending;
I saw her singing at her work,
And o'er the sickle bending;—
I listened, motionless and still;
And, as I mounted up the hill,
The music in my heart I bore
Long after it was heard no more.

WILLIAM WORDSWORTH

My Heart Leaps Up

My heart leaps up when I behold
    A rainbow in the sky:
So was it when my life began;
So is it now I am a man;
So be it when I shall grow old,
    Or let me die!
The Child is father of the Man;
And I could wish my days to be
Bound each to each by natural piety.

WILLIAM WORDSWORTH

[549]

I WANDERED LONELY AS A CLOUD

I WANDERED lonely as a cloud
That floats on high o'er vales and hills,
When all at once I saw a crowd,
A host, of golden daffodils;
Beside the lake, beneath the trees,
Fluttering and dancing in the breeze.

Continuous as the stars that shine
And twinkle on the milky-way,
They stretched in never-ending line
Along the margin of a bay:
Ten thousand saw I at a glance,
Tossing their heads in sprightly dance.

The waves beside them danced; but they
Out-did the sparkling waves in glee:
A poet could not but be gay,
In such a jocund company:
I gazed—and gazed—but little thought
What wealth the show to me had brought:

For oft, when on my couch I lie
In vacant or in pensive mood,
They flash upon that inward eye
Which is the bliss of solitude;
And then my heart with pleasure fills,
And dances with the daffodils.

WILLIAM WORDSWORTH

LINES

COMPOSED A FEW MILES ABOVE TINTERN ABBEY, ON REVISITING THE BANKS OF THE WYE DURING A TOUR. JULY 13, 1798.

FIVE years have past; five summers, with the length
Of five long winters! and again I hear
These waters, rolling from their mountain-springs
With a soft inland murmur.—Once again
Do I behold these steep and lofty cliffs,
That on a wild secluded scene impress
Thoughts of more deep seclusion; and connect
The landscape with the quiet of the sky.
The day is come when I again repose
Here, under this dark sycamore, and view
These plots of cottage-ground, these orchard-tufts,
Which at this season, with their unripe fruits,
Are clad in one green hue, and lose themselves
'Mid groves and copses. Once again I see
These hedge-rows, hardly hedge-rows, little lines
Of sportive wood run wild: these pastoral farms,
Green to the very door; and wreaths of smoke
Sent up, in silence, from among the trees!
With some uncertain notice, as might seem
Of vagrant dwellers in the houseless woods,
Or of some Hermit's cave, where by his fire
The Hermit sits alone.
     These beauteous forms,
Through a long absence, have not been to me
As is a landscape to a blind man's eye:
But oft, in lonely rooms, and 'mid the din
Of towns and cities, I have owed to them,
In hours of weariness, sensations sweet,
Felt in the blood, and felt along the heart;

And passing even into my purer mind,
With tranquil restoration:—feelings too
Of unremembered pleasure: such, perhaps,
As have no slight or trivial influence
On that best portion of a good man's life,
His little, nameless, unremembered, acts
Of kindness and of love. Nor less, I trust,
To them I may have owed another gift,
Of aspect more sublime; that blessèd mood,
In which the burthen of the mystery,
In which the heavy and the weary weight
Of all this unintelligible world,
Is lightened:—that serene and blessèd mood,
In which the affections gently lead us on,—
Until, the breath of this corporeal frame
And even the motion of our human blood
Almost suspended, we are laid asleep
In body, and become a living soul:
While with an eye made quiet by the power
Of harmony, and the deep power of joy,
We see into the life of things.
                                        If this
Be but a vain belief, yet, oh! how oft—
In darkness and amid the many shapes
Of joyless daylight; when the fretful stir
Unprofitable, and the fever of the world,
Have hung upon the beatings of my heart—
How oft, in spirit, have I turned to thee,
O sylvan Wye! thou wanderer through the woods,
How often has my spirit turned to thee!

  And now, with gleams of half-extinguished thought,
With many recognitions dim and faint,
And somewhat of a sad perplexity,
The picture of the mind revives again:
While here I stand, not only with the sense

Of present pleasure, but with pleasing thoughts
That in this moment there is life and food
For future years. And so I dare to hope,
Though changed, no doubt, from what I was when first
I came among these hills; when like a roe
I bounded o'er the mountains, by the sides
Of the deep rivers, and the lonely streams,
Wherever nature led: more like a man
Flying from something that he dreads than one
Who sought the thing he loved. For nature then
(The coarser pleasures of my boyish days,
And their glad animal movements all gone by)
To me was all in all.—I cannot paint
What then I was. The sounding cataract
Haunted me like a passion: the tall rock,
The mountain, and the deep and gloomy wood,
Their colours and their forms, were then to me
An appetite; a feeling and a love,
That had no need of a remoter charm,
By thought supplied, nor any interest
Unborrowed from the eye.—That time is past,
And all its aching joys are now no more,
And all its dizzy raptures. Not for this
Faint I, nor mourn nor murmur; other gifts
Have followed; for such loss, I would believe,
Abundant recompense. For I have learned
To look on nature, not as in the hour
Of thoughtless youth; but hearing oftentimes
The still, sad music of humanity,
Nor harsh nor grating, though of ample power
To chasten and subdue. And I have felt
A presence that disturbs me with the joy
Of elevated thoughts; a sense sublime
Of something far more deeply interfused,
Whose dwelling is the light of setting suns,

And the round ocean and the living air,
And the blue sky, and in the mind of man:
A motion and a spirit, that impels
All thinking things, all objects of all thought,
And rolls through all things. Therefore am I still
A lover of the meadows and the woods,
And mountains; and of all that we behold
From this green earth; of all the mighty world
Of eye, and ear,—both what they half create,
And what perceive; well pleased to recognise
In nature and the language of the sense
The anchor of my purest thoughts, the nurse,
The guide, the guardian of my heart, and soul
Of all my moral being.
                Nor perchance,
If I were not thus taught, should I the more
Suffer my genial spirits to decay:
For thou art with me here upon the banks
Of this fair river; thou my dearest Friend,
My dear, dear Friend; and in thy voice I catch
The language of my former heart, and read
My former pleasures in the shooting lights
Of thy wild eyes. Oh! yet a little while
May I behold in thee what I was once,
My dear, dear Sister! and this prayer I make,
Knowing that Nature never did betray
The heart that loved her; 't is her privilege,
Through all the years of this our life, to lead
From joy to joy: for she can so inform
The mind that is within us, so impress
With quietness and beauty, and so feed
With lofty thoughts, that neither evil tongues,
Rash judgments, nor the sneers of selfish men,
Nor greetings where no kindness is, nor all
The dreary intercourse of daily life,

Shall e'er prevail against us, or disturb
Our cheerful faith, that all which we behold
Is full of blessings. Therefore let the moon
Shine on thee in thy solitary walk;
And let the misty mountain-winds be free
To blow against thee; and, in after years,
When these wild ecstasies shall be matured
Into a sober pleasure; when thy mind
Shall be a mansion for all lovely forms,
Thy memory be as a dwelling-place
For all sweet sounds and harmonies; oh! then,
If solitude, or fear, or pain, or grief,
Should be thy portion, with what healing thoughts
Of tender joy wilt thou remember me,
And these my exhortations! Nor, perchance—
If I should be where I no more can hear
Thy voice, nor catch from thy wild eyes these gleams
Of past existence—wilt thou then forget
That on the banks of this delightful stream
We stood together; and that I, so long
A worshipper of Nature, hither came
Unwearied in that service: rather say
With warmer love—oh! with far deeper zeal
Of holier love. Nor wilt thou then forget
That after many wanderings, many years
Of absence, these steep woods and lofty cliffs,
And this green pastoral landscape, were to me
More dear, both for themselves and for thy sake!

WILLIAM WORDSWORTH

Mr. Sargent began to write poetry when a boy in Groton school.

THE LAST DAY

Now, skulls, rise from the hills, your hour is come.
Clavicles, digits, shin-bones, vertebrae.
And as a drummer-boy resumes his drum
Take up again your hearts familiarly.

Stand up like men, you rib-cases, you thighs,
Leap to your sockets, hip and humerus.
Put on your strength of tendons. In the skies
A light is coming. You must be valorous.

Put on that armour white you knew so well
Which though as soft as leather stood you by
In life's brief tournament until you fell.
It now will take reflection from the sky.

Rise out of hills, rise out of fields, rise from
Marshes and garden plots where no one knew
Any one could be crouching in a tomb.
Rise from the graveyards green, from oceans blue.

The world you find will never strike you strange.
You know it from its roof down to its rut.
But all of it has suffered a sea-change.
Somehow a charm is lost. You can't say what.

That mighty bulk, the huge department store
Shines with its lights still brilliant, like a ship
Ready to sink beneath the ocean floor
And drown its myriad eyes on its last trip.

Ten thousand miles of trains and trolley-cars
Stand in their tracks as if an armistice—
An armistice that really ends all wars—
Had just arrived. What victory is this?

Our bones stand now like an army on review.
Mankind at last is marshalled to discipline.
I wonder where this army is marching to!
They have no banners. What are they going to win?

In usual war those who are cowards flee—
Unless machine-guns whip them from behind—
Those who are brave go on courageously
And win the war and then fall out of mind.

This battle-front is solid. No one stirs.
No ankle-bone is moved. They all are chained.
Here is the last fight of all warriors.
Here is the battle lost, or the battle gained.

Some weep; their tears are joy. Some weep a tear
That turns the cheeks to chalk. No battle-dread
To their most terrible terror ere came near.
Stand up, ye bones. Your heaven is overhead.

DANIEL SARGENT

Shelley is the only first-class poet who ever studied at Oxford, and he was expelled. Browning, in his first poem, *Pauline*, written nine years after Shelley's death, called him the Sun-treader, and expressed the radiance of Shelley's poetry in the line

The air seems bright with thy past presence yet.

Matthew Arnold's famous tribute to Shelley is marred by two phrases extraordinary for their ineptitude—"ineffectual" and "in vain."

STANZAS

WRITTEN IN DEJECTION, NEAR NAPLES

The sun is warm, the sky is clear,
  The waves are dancing fast and bright,
Blue isles and snowy mountains wear

The purple noon's transparent might;
The breath of the moist earth is light
Around its unexpanded buds;
Like many a voice of one delight,
The winds, the birds, the ocean floods,
The City's voice itself, is soft like Solitude's.

I see the Deep's untrampled floor
With green and purple seaweeds strown;
I see the waves upon the shore,
Like light dissolved in star-showers, thrown:
I sit upon the sands alone,—
The lightning of the noontide ocean
Is flashing round me, and a tone
Arises from its measured motion,
How sweet! did any heart now share in my emotion.

Alas! I have nor hope nor health,
Nor peace within nor calm around,
Nor that content surpassing wealth
The sage in meditation found,
And walked with inward glory crowned—
Nor fame, nor power, nor love, nor leisure.
Others I see whom these surround—
Smiling they live, and call life pleasure;—
To me that cup has been dealt in another measure.

Yet now despair itself is mild,
Even as the winds and waters are;
I could lie down like a tired child,
And weep away the life of care
Which I have borne and yet must bear,
Till death like sleep might steal on me,
And I might feel in the warm air
My cheek grow cold, and hear the sea
Breathe o'er my dying brain its last monotony.

Some might lament that I were cold,
  As I, when this sweet day is gone,
Which my lost heart, too soon grown old,
  Insults with this untimely moan;
  They might lament—for I am one
Whom men love not,—and yet regret,
  Unlike this day, which, when the sun
Shall on its stainless glory set,
Will linger, though enjoyed, like joy in memory yet.

PERCY BYSSHE SHELLEY

To ——

Music, when soft voices die,
Vibrates in the memory;
Odours, when sweet violets sicken,
Live within the sense they quicken.

Rose leaves, when the rose is dead,
Are heaped for the belovèd's bed;
And so thy thoughts, when thou art gone,
Love itself shall slumber on.

PERCY BYSSHE SHELLEY

To a Skylark

Hail to thee, blithe Spirit!
  Bird thou never wert,
That from Heaven, or near it,
  Pourest thy full heart
In profuse strains of unpremeditated art.

Higher still and higher
From the earth thou springest
Like a cloud of fire;
The blue deep thou wingest,
And singing still dost soar, and soaring ever singest.

In the golden lightning
Of the sunken sun,
O'er which clouds are bright'ning,
Thou dost float and run;
Like an unbodied joy whose race is just begun.

The pale purple even
Melts around thy flight;
Like a star of Heaven,
In the broad daylight
Thou art unseen, but yet I hear thy shrill delight,

Keen as are the arrows
Of that silver sphere,
Whose intense lamp narrows
In the white dawn clear
Until we hardly see—we feel that it is there.

All the earth and air
With thy voice is loud,
As, when night is bare,
From one lonely cloud
The moon rains out her beams, and Heaven is overflowed.

What thou art we know not;
What is most like thee?
From rainbow clouds there flow not
Drops so bright to see
As from thy presence showers a rain of melody.

Like a Poet hidden
  In the light of thought,
Singing hymns unbidden,
  Till the world is wrought
To sympathy with hopes and fears it heeded not:

Like a high-born maiden
  In a palace-tower
Soothing her love-laden
  Soul in secret hour
With music sweet as love, which overflows her bower:

Like a glow-worm golden
  In a dell of dew,
Scattering unbeholden
  Its aëreal hue
Among the flowers and grass, which screen it from the view!

Like a rose embowered
  In its own green leaves,
By warm winds deflowered,
  Till the scent it gives
Makes faint with too much sweet those heavy-wingèd thieves:

Sound of vernal showers
  On the twinkling grass,
Rain-awakened flowers,
  All that ever was
Joyous, and clear, and fresh, thy music doth surpass:

Teach us, Sprite or Bird,
  What sweet thoughts are thine:
I have never heard
  Praise of love or wine
That panted forth a flood of rapture so divine.

Chorus Hymeneal,
    Or triumphal chant,
Matched with thine would be all
    But an empty vaunt,
A thing wherein we feel there is some hidden want.

What objects are the fountains
    Of thy happy strain?
What fields, or waves, or mountains?
    What shapes of sky or plain?
What love of thine own kind? what ignorance of pain?

With thy clear keen joyance
    Languor cannot be:
Shadow of annoyance
    Never came near thee:
Thou lovest—but ne'er knew love's sad satiety.

Waking or asleep,
    Thou of death must deem
Things more true and deep
    Than we mortals dream,
Or how could thy notes flow in such a crystal stream?

We look before and after,
    And pine for what is not:
Our sincerest laughter
    With some pain is fraught;
Our sweetest songs are those that tell of saddest thought.

Yet if we could scorn
    Hate, and pride, and fear;
If we were things born
    Not to shed a tear,
I know not how thy joy we ever should come near.

Better than all measures
  Of delightful sound,
Better than all treasures
  That in books are found,
Thy skill to poet were, thou scorner of the ground!

Teach me half the gladness
  That thy brain must know,
Such harmonious madness
  From my lips would flow
The world should listen then—as I am listening now.

PERCY BYSSHE SHELLEY

To ——

I

One word is too often profaned
  For me to profane it,
One feeling too falsely disdained
  For thee to disdain it;
One hope is too like despair
  For prudence to smother,
And pity from thee more dear
  Than that from another.

II

I can give not what men call love,
  But wilt thou accept not
The worship the heart lifts above
  And the Heavens reject not:
The desire of the moth for the star,
  Of the night for the morrow,
The devotion to something afar
  From the sphere of our sorrow?

PERCY BYSSHE SHELLEY

ODE TO THE WEST WIND

This poem was conceived and chiefly written in a wood that
skirts the Arno, near Florence, and on a day when that tempestuous wind, whose temperature is at once mild and animating,
was collecting the vapours which pour down the autumnal
rains. They began, as I foresaw, at sunset with a violent
tempest of hail and rain, attended by that magnificent thunder
and lightning peculiar to the Cisalpine regions.

The phenomenon alluded to at the conclusion of the third
stanza is well known to naturalists. The vegetation at the
bottom of the sea, of rivers, and of lakes, sympathizes with that
of the land in the change of seasons, and is consequently
influenced by the winds which announce it.—[SHELLEY's NOTE.]

I

O WILD West Wind, thou breath of Autumn's being,
Thou, from whose unseen presence the leaves dead
Are driven, like ghosts from an enchanter fleeing,

Yellow, and black, and pale, and hectic red,
Pestilence-stricken multitudes: O thou,
Who chariotest to their dark wintry bed

The wingèd seeds, where they lie cold and low,
Each like a corpse within its grave, until
Thine azure sister of the Spring shall blow

Her clarion o'er the dreaming earth, and fill
(Driving sweet buds like flocks to feed in air)
With living hues and odours plain and hill:

Wild Spirit, which art moving everywhere;
Destroyer and preserver; hear, oh, hear!

II

Thou on whose stream, mid the steep sky's commotion
Loose clouds like earth's decaying leaves are shed,
Shook from the tangled boughs of Heaven and Ocean,

Angels of rain and lightning: there are spread
On the blue surface of thine aëry surge,
Like the bright hair uplifted from the head

Of some fierce Maenad, even from the dim verge
Of the horizon to the zenith's height,
The locks of the approaching storm. Thou dirge

Of the dying year, to which this closing night
Will be the dome of a vast sepulchre,
Vaulted with all thy congregated might

Of vapours, from whose solid atmosphere
Black rain, and fire, and hail will burst: oh, hear!

III

Thou who didst waken from his summer dreams
The blue Mediterranean, where he lay,
Lulled by the coil of his crystàlline streams,

Beside a pumice isle on Baiæ's bay,
And saw in sleep old palaces and towers
Quivering within the wave's intenser day,

All overgrown with azure moss and flowers
So sweet, the sense faints picturing them! Thou
For whose path the Atlantic's level powers

Cleave themselves into chasms, while far below
The sea-blooms and the oozy woods which wear
The sapless foliage of the ocean, know

Thy voice, and suddenly grow gray with fear,
And tremble and despoil themselves: oh, hear!

IV

If I were a dead leaf thou mightest bear;
If I were a swift cloud to fly with thee;
A wave to pant beneath thy power, and share

The impulse of thy strength, only less free
Than thou, O uncontrollable! If even
I were as in my boyhood, and could be

The comrade of thy wanderings over Heaven,
As then, when to outstrip thy skiey speed
Scarce seemed a vision; I would ne'er have striven

As thus with thee in prayer in my sore need.
Oh, lift me as a wave, a leaf, a cloud!
I fall upon the thorns of life! I bleed!

A heavy weight of hours has chained and bowed
One too like thee: tameless, and swift, and proud.

V

Make me thy lyre, even as the forest is:
What if my leaves are falling like its own!
The tumult of thy mighty harmonies

Will take from both a deep, autumnal tone,
Sweet though in sadness. Be thou, Spirit fierce,
My spirit! Be thou me, impetuous one!

[566]

Drive my dead thoughts over the universe
Like withered leaves to quicken a new birth!
And, by the incantation of this verse,

Scatter, as from an unextinguished hearth
Ashes and sparks, my words among mankind!
Be through my lips to unawakened earth

The trumpet of a prophecy! O, Wind,
If Winter comes, can Spring be far behind?

PERCY BYSSHE SHELLEY

This is a perfect illustration of the poetry of transfiguration.

OVERTONES

I HEARD a bird at break of day
    Sing from the autumn trees
A song so mystical and calm,
    So full of certainties,
No man, I think, could listen long
    Except upon his knees.
Yet this was but a simple bird,
    Alone, among dead trees.

WILLIAM ALEXANDER PERCY

INDEX OF POETS

INDEX OF POETS

INDEX OF POETS

INDEX OF TITLES

[582]

INDEX OF TITLES

INDEX OF TITLES

INDEX OF TITLES

INDEX OF TITLES

INDEX OF TITLES

INDEX OF TITLES

INDEX OF FIRST LINES

INDEX OF FIRST LINES

INDEX OF FIRST LINES

INDEX OF FIRST LINES